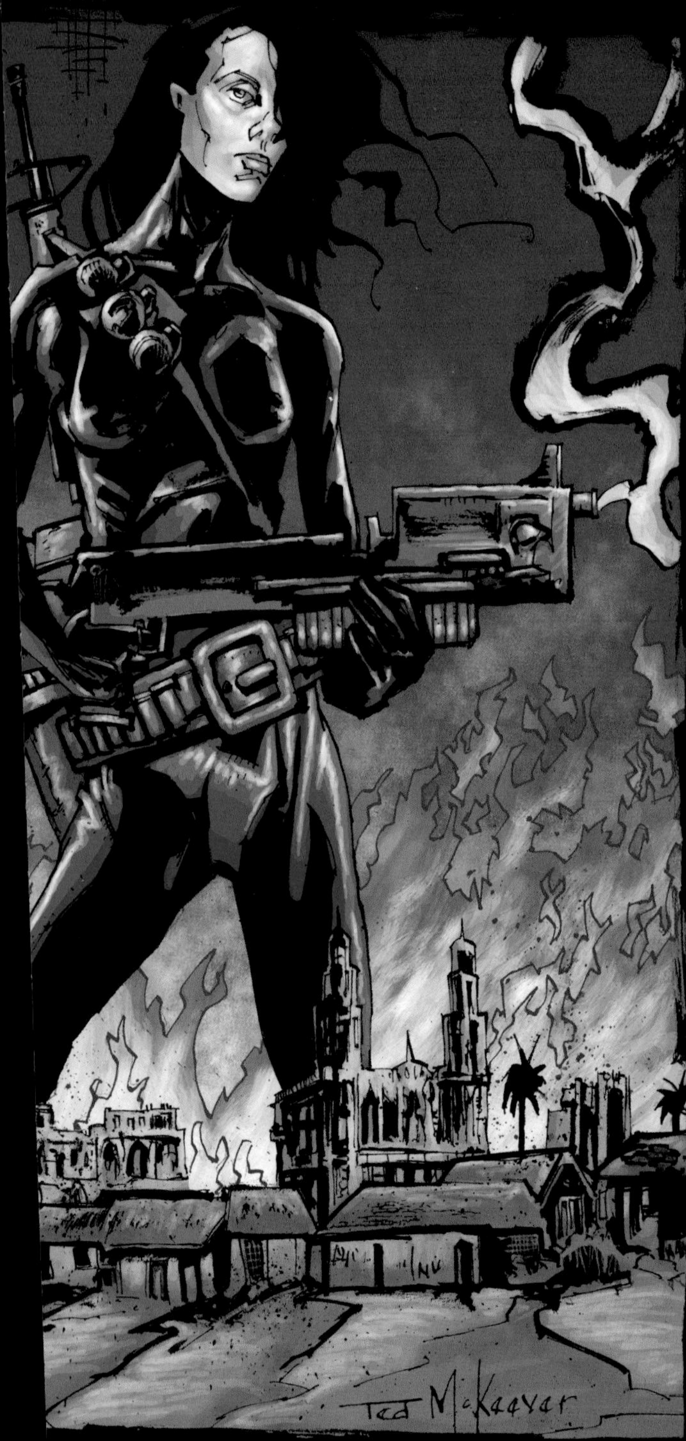
Ted McKeever

ALL MATRIX STORIES
BASED ON CONCEPTS BY
LARRY AND ANDY WACHOWSKI

DOC FRANKENSTEIN & SHAOLIN COWBOY PREVIEW

INTRODUCTION

One year ago we released volume one of THE MATRIX COMICS.

However it was well before — back in 1998 — that we began producing these stories for TheMatrix.com. We did not originally intend to release them in print, but thanks to a very vocal fan base, we got the message.

For all of those who supported the first collection, we greatly appreciate it and hope you enjoy this second lineup as much as we do.

This volume includes another twelve stories. Readers intimate with the online stories will notice updates throughout. We added color for Paul Chadwick, Tim Sale, Vince Evans and Ted McKeever, and Poppy Z. Brite's prose piece features new illustrations by Dave Dorman.

There are never before seen stories, three in all. Peter Bagge gives us his second comedic look at THE MATRIX TRILOGY. Michael Oeming illustrates the difficult life of a rebel post REVOLUTIONS. While Kaare Andrews shows us how the Kid from the sequels and THE ANIMATRIX contends with a world without Neo.

Completing the dozen, we have four more stories by Bill Sienkiewicz, Greg Ruth, Keron Grant and Troy Nixey. These, along with many others, remain free at TheMatrix.com.

No question, the Internet is cool.

But there is nothing quite like the smell of fresh printers ink as the sheets race off the presses, waiting to be trimmed and bound. With a nod of the head to Italo Calvino's *If on a winter's night a traveler*, books have a magic all their own. Which is part of the reason our story does not end just yet.

As you read this, our first two bi-monthly titles are hitting comic shops.

To hear from the Brothers Wachowski directly, turn to page 156. From there, read a free preview — yes, 16 free pages over volume one — of these latest offerings, DOC FRANKENSTEIN and THE SHAOLIN COWBOY.

Of the multitude of choices, we appreciate your opening these pages.

From the Burly trenches,

Spencer Lamm
November, 2004

FAREWELL PERFORMANCE

STORY BY JIM
KRUEGER

Two time Addy Award winner, Jim Krueger, graduated from Marquette University with a Journalism degree. After becoming a creative director at Marvel Comics, he changed track and worked freelance, creating new properties and writing comics, including the award-winning EARTH X trilogy, and X-MEN. Jim is now also president of 26 Soldiers, his own comic book publishing company. Original titles by Jim include FOOT SOLDIERS, ALPHABET SUPES, THE CLOCK MAKER, and we will soon see THE LAST STRAW MAN in stores. Currently Jim is working on GALACTIC for Dark Horse Comics, JUSTICE LEAGUE for DC Comics, and another short film. For more information about Jim and his work, please visit www.jimkrueger.com.

ART BY TIM
SALE

Tim Sale was born in upstate New York, but has long since moved to the West Coast. He studied art at the University of Washington, and comic illustration at Buscema's School of Comic Art before moving on to pencil the graphic novels THIEVES' WORLD and inking Warp Graphics' MYTH ADVENTURES. Tim's work has appeared in such comics as SUPERMAN: FOR ALL SEASONS, DAREDEVIL: YELLOW, and BATMAN: LONG HALLOWEEN. His most recent series, HULK: GRAY, done in collaboration with Jeph Loeb has been collected in a hard cover edition. A retrospective of Tim's work was published in July of 2004, titled TIM SALE: BLACK AND WHITE.

COLOR BY JASON
KEITH

An Eisner Award nominee for his color work on EL CAZADOR, at age 22 Jason Keith is young but accomplished. He has worked on Marvel Comics' titles NEW X-MEN, UNCANNY X-MEN and DOOM RETURNS, and on CrossGen titles SCION, SOJOURN, LADY DEATH, and BRATH. Jason has also worked on the Image series THE GIFT, written by Raven Gregory. Currently, Jason is coloring a new mini-series called SAMURAI: HEAVEN AND EARTH for Dark Horse Comics, written by Ron Marz and illustrated by Luke Ross, as well as coloring the bi-monthly series DOC FRANKENSTEIN, written by the Wachowski Brothers.

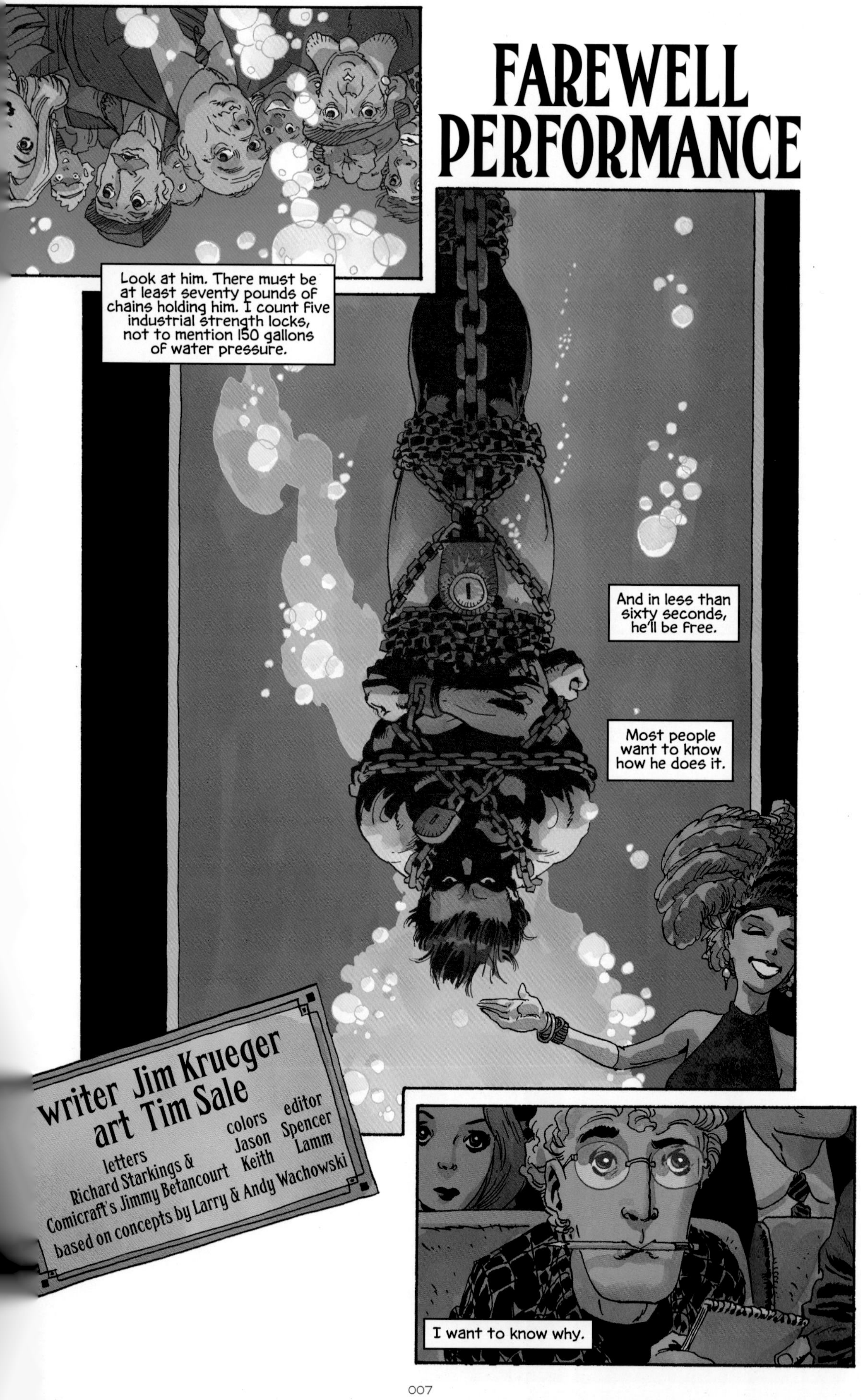
FAREWELL PERFORMANCE
Look at him. There must be at least seventy pounds of chains holding him. I count five industrial strength locks, not to mention 150 gallons of water pressure.
And in less than sixty seconds, he'll be free.
Most people want to know how he does it.
writer Jim Krueger
art Tim Sale
letters Richard Starkings & Comicraft's Jimmy Betancourt
colors Jason Keith
editor Spencer Lamm
based on concepts by Larry & Andy Wachowski
I want to know why.

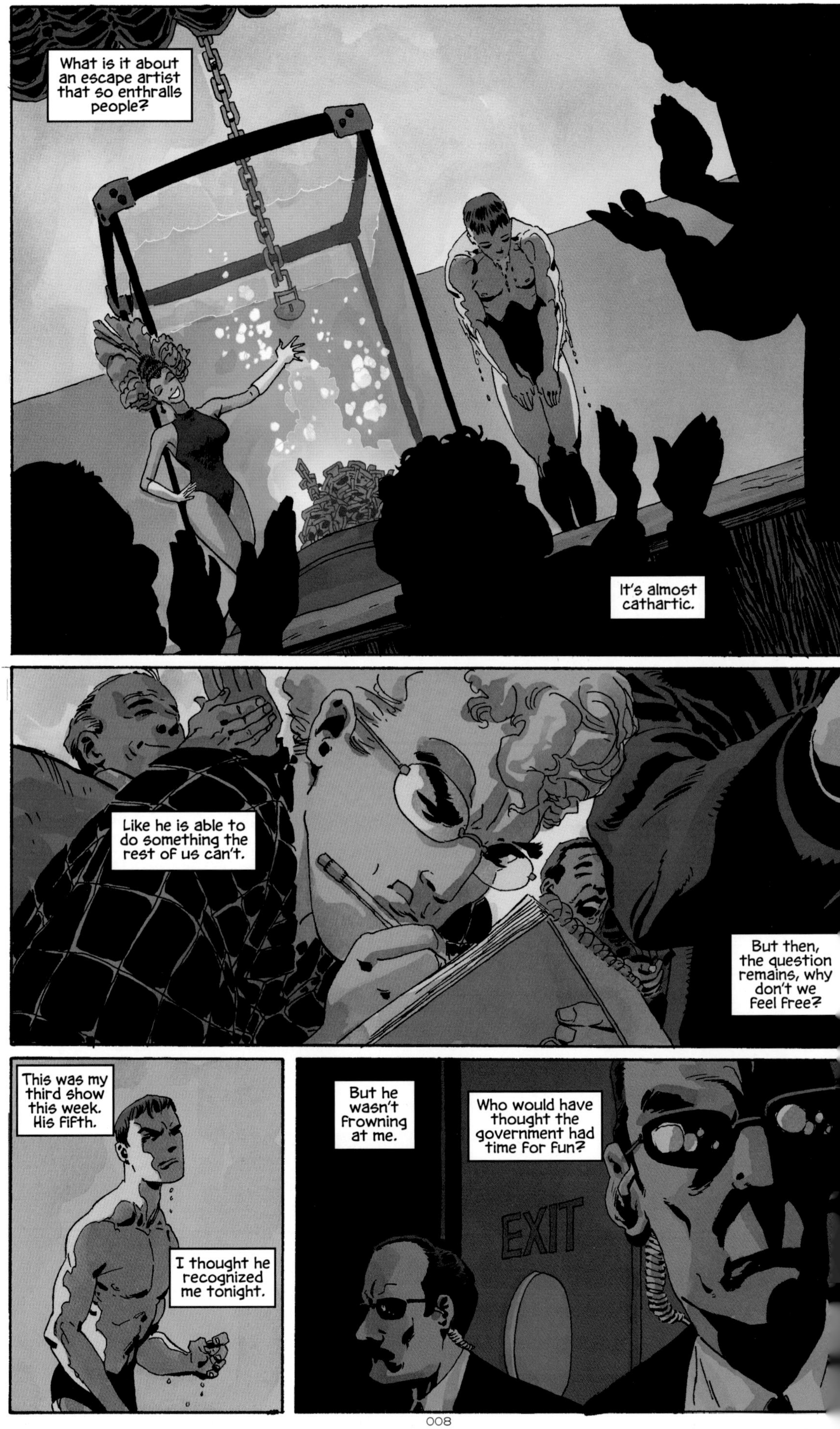
What is it about an escape artist that so enthralls people?
It's almost cathartic.
Like he is able to do something the rest of us can't.
But then, the question remains, why don't we feel free?
This was my third show this week. His fifth.
I thought he recognized me tonight.
But he wasn't frowning at me.
Who would have thought the government had time for fun?
EXIT

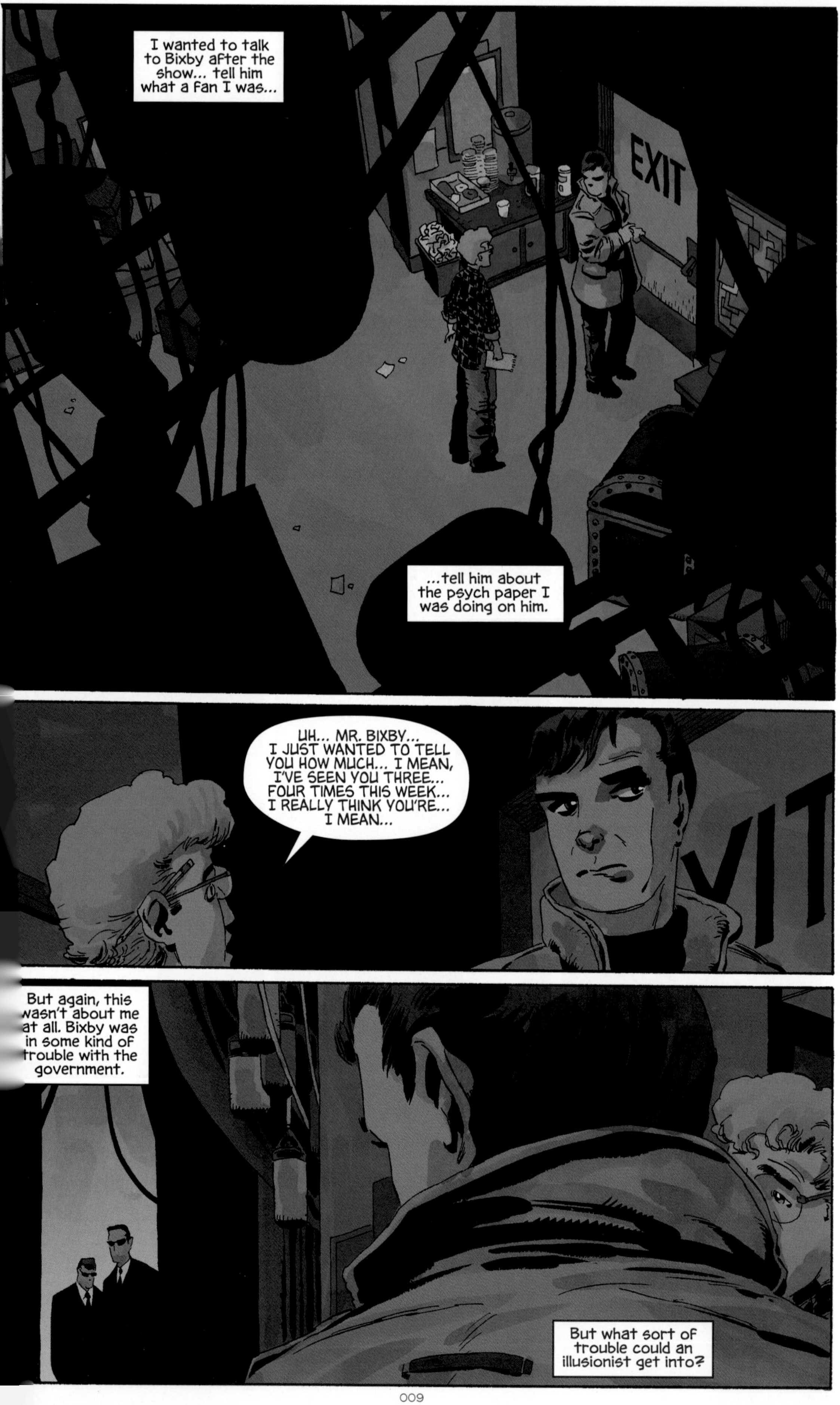
I wanted to talk to Bixby after the show... tell him what a fan I was...
EXIT
...tell him about the psych paper I was doing on him.
UH... MR. BIXBY... I JUST WANTED TO TELL YOU HOW MUCH... I MEAN, I'VE SEEN YOU THREE... FOUR TIMES THIS WEEK... I REALLY THINK YOU'RE... I MEAN...
But again, this wasn't about me at all. Bixby was in some kind of trouble with the government.
But what sort of trouble could an illusionist get into?

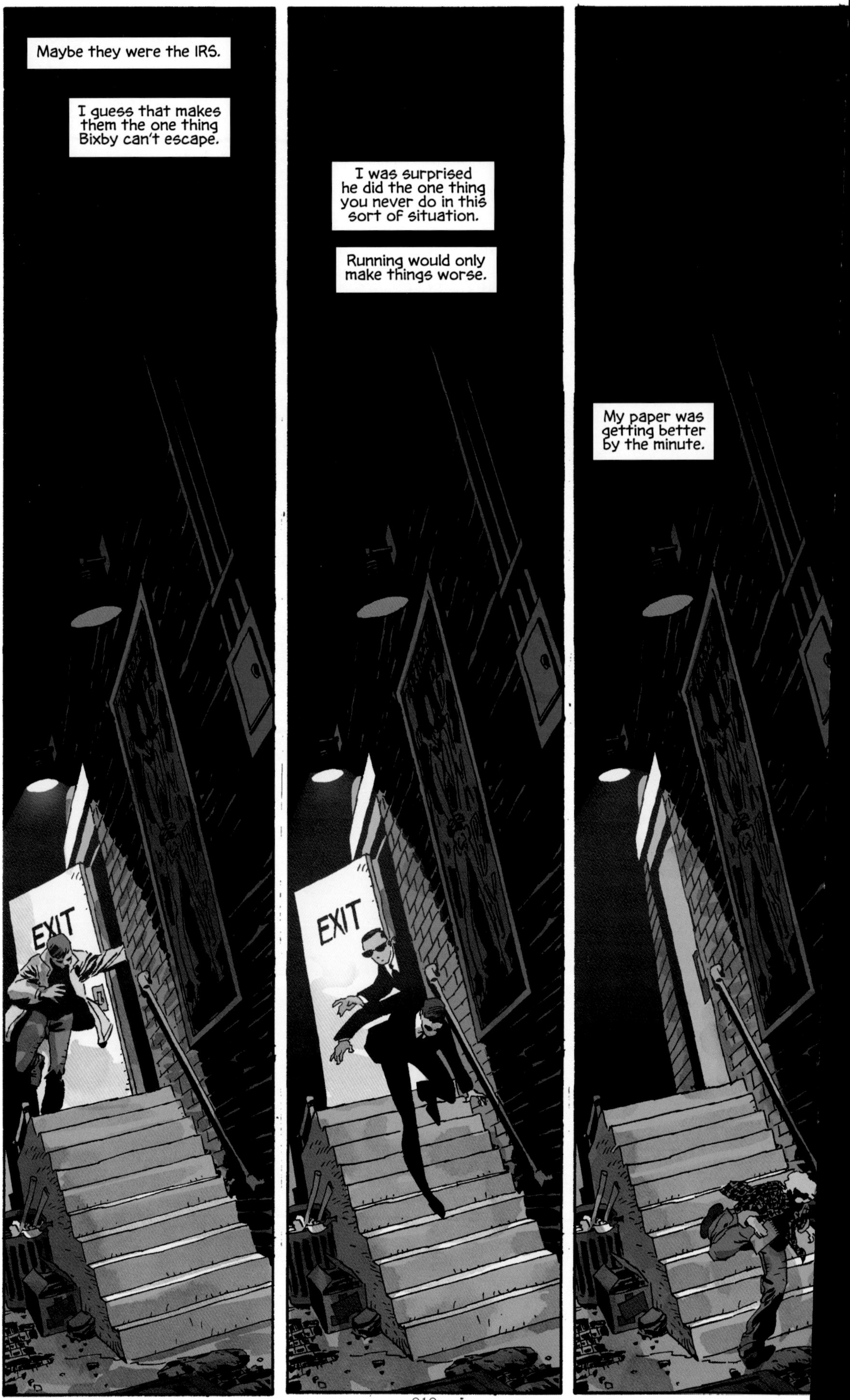
Maybe they were the IRS.
I guess that makes them the one thing Bixby can't escape.
EXIT
I was surprised he did the one thing you never do in this sort of situation.
Running would only make things worse.
EXIT
My paper was getting better by the minute.

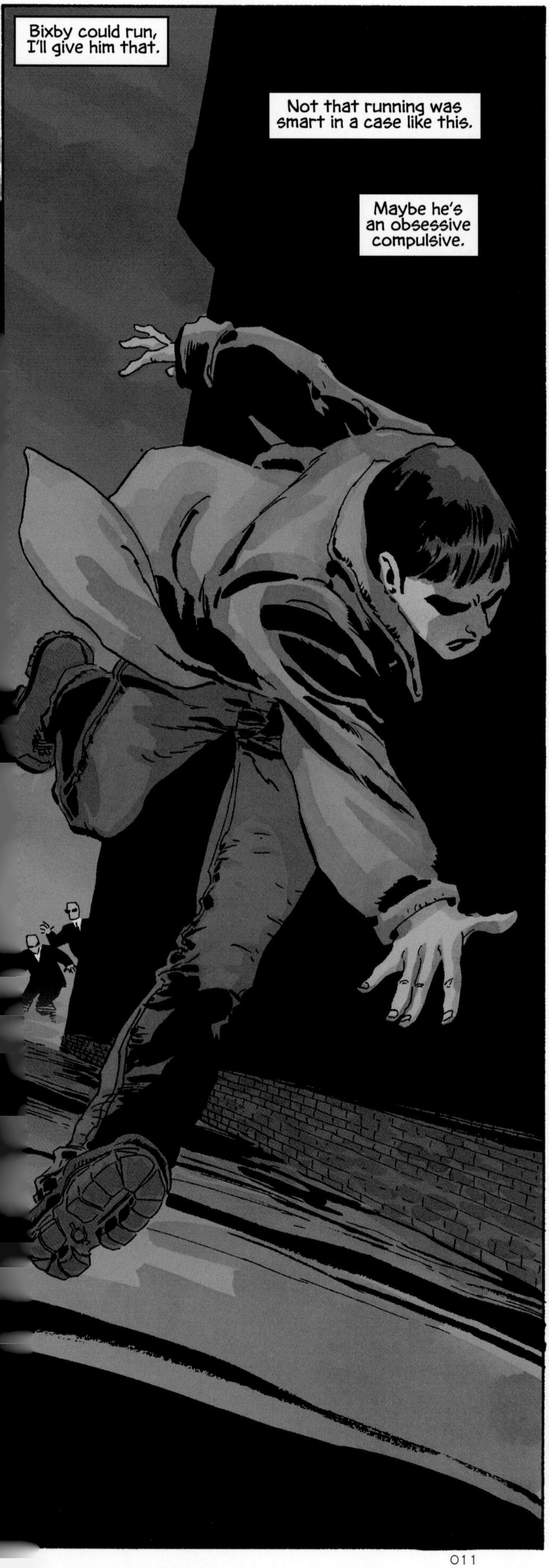
Bixby could run, I'll give him that.
Not that running was smart in a case like this.
Maybe he's an obsessive compulsive.
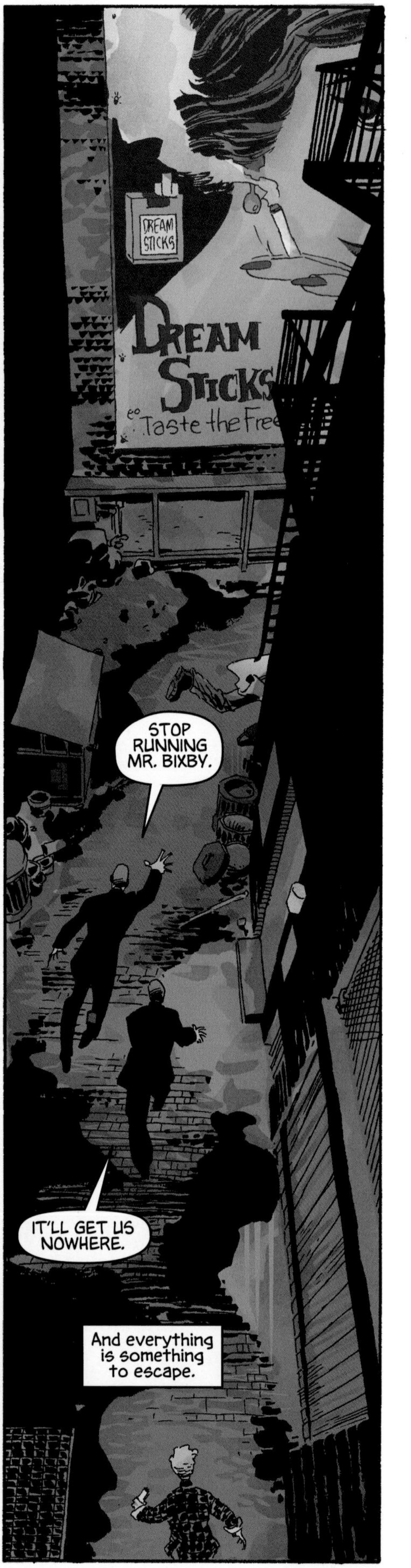
DREAM STICKS
DREAM STICKS
Taste the Fre
STOP RUNNING MR. BIXBY.
IT'LL GET US NOWHERE.
And everything is something to escape.

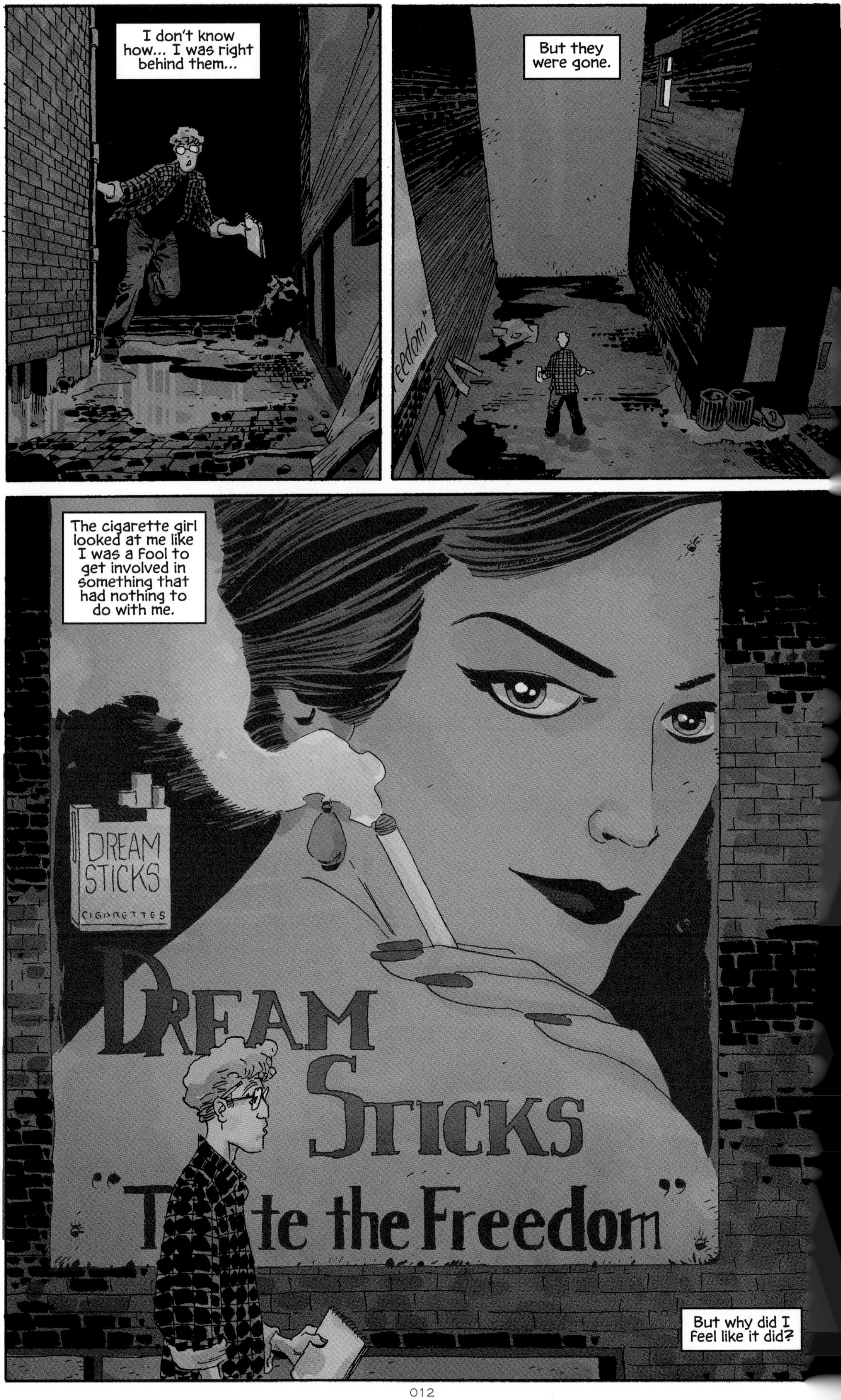
I don't know how... I was right behind them...
But they were gone.
The cigarette girl looked at me like I was a fool to get involved in something that had nothing to do with me.
DREAM STICKS
CIGARETTES
DREAM STICKS
" te the Freedom"
But why did I feel like it did?

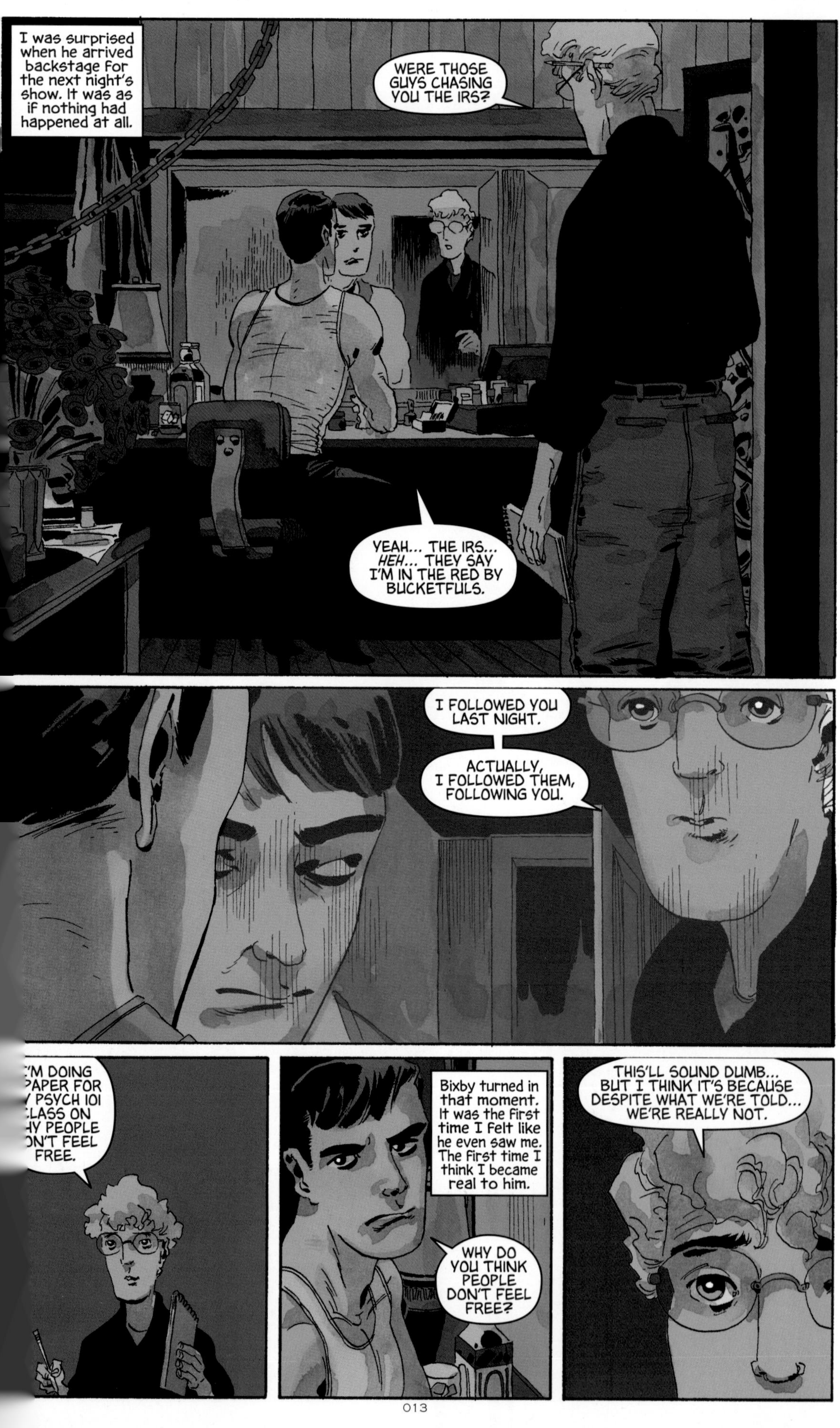
I was surprised when he arrived backstage for the next night's show. It was as if nothing had happened at all.
WERE THOSE GUYS CHASING YOU THE IRS?
YEAH... THE IRS... *HEH*... THEY SAY I'M IN THE RED BY BUCKETFULS.
I FOLLOWED YOU LAST NIGHT.
ACTUALLY, I FOLLOWED THEM, FOLLOWING YOU.
'M DOING PAPER FOR PSYCH 101 CLASS ON HY PEOPLE ON'T FEEL FREE.
Bixby turned in that moment. It was the first time I felt like he even saw me. The first time I think I became real to him.
WHY DO YOU THINK PEOPLE DON'T FEEL FREE?
THIS'LL SOUND DUMB... BUT I THINK IT'S BECAUSE DESPITE WHAT WE'RE TOLD... WE'RE REALLY NOT.

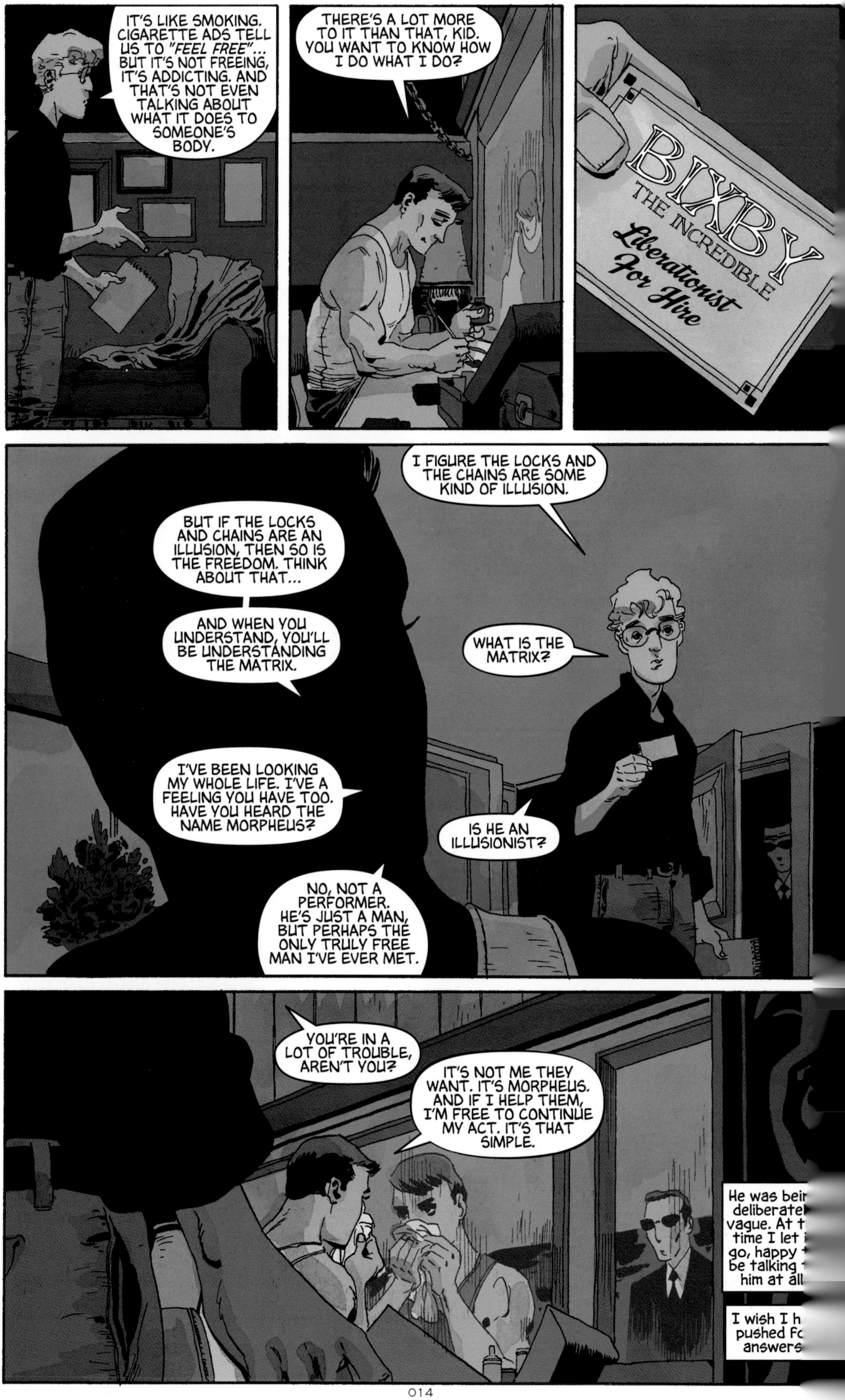
IT'S LIKE SMOKING. CIGARETTE ADS TELL US TO "FEEL FREE"... BUT IT'S NOT FREEING, IT'S ADDICTING. AND THAT'S NOT EVEN TALKING ABOUT WHAT IT DOES TO SOMEONE'S BODY.
THERE'S A LOT MORE TO IT THAN THAT, KID. YOU WANT TO KNOW HOW I DO WHAT I DO?
BIXBY THE INCREDIBLE Liberationist For Hire
I FIGURE THE LOCKS AND THE CHAINS ARE SOME KIND OF ILLUSION.
BUT IF THE LOCKS AND CHAINS ARE AN ILLUSION, THEN SO IS THE FREEDOM. THINK ABOUT THAT...
AND WHEN YOU UNDERSTAND, YOU'LL BE UNDERSTANDING THE MATRIX.
WHAT IS THE MATRIX?
I'VE BEEN LOOKING MY WHOLE LIFE. I'VE A FEELING YOU HAVE TOO. HAVE YOU HEARD THE NAME MORPHEUS?
IS HE AN ILLUSIONIST?
NO, NOT A PERFORMER. HE'S JUST A MAN, BUT PERHAPS THE ONLY TRULY FREE MAN I'VE EVER MET.
YOU'RE IN A LOT OF TROUBLE, AREN'T YOU?
IT'S NOT ME THEY WANT. IT'S MORPHEUS. AND IF I HELP THEM, I'M FREE TO CONTINUE MY ACT. IT'S THAT SIMPLE.
He was bei deliberate vague. At t time I let i go, happy t be talking him at all
I wish I h pushed Fo answers

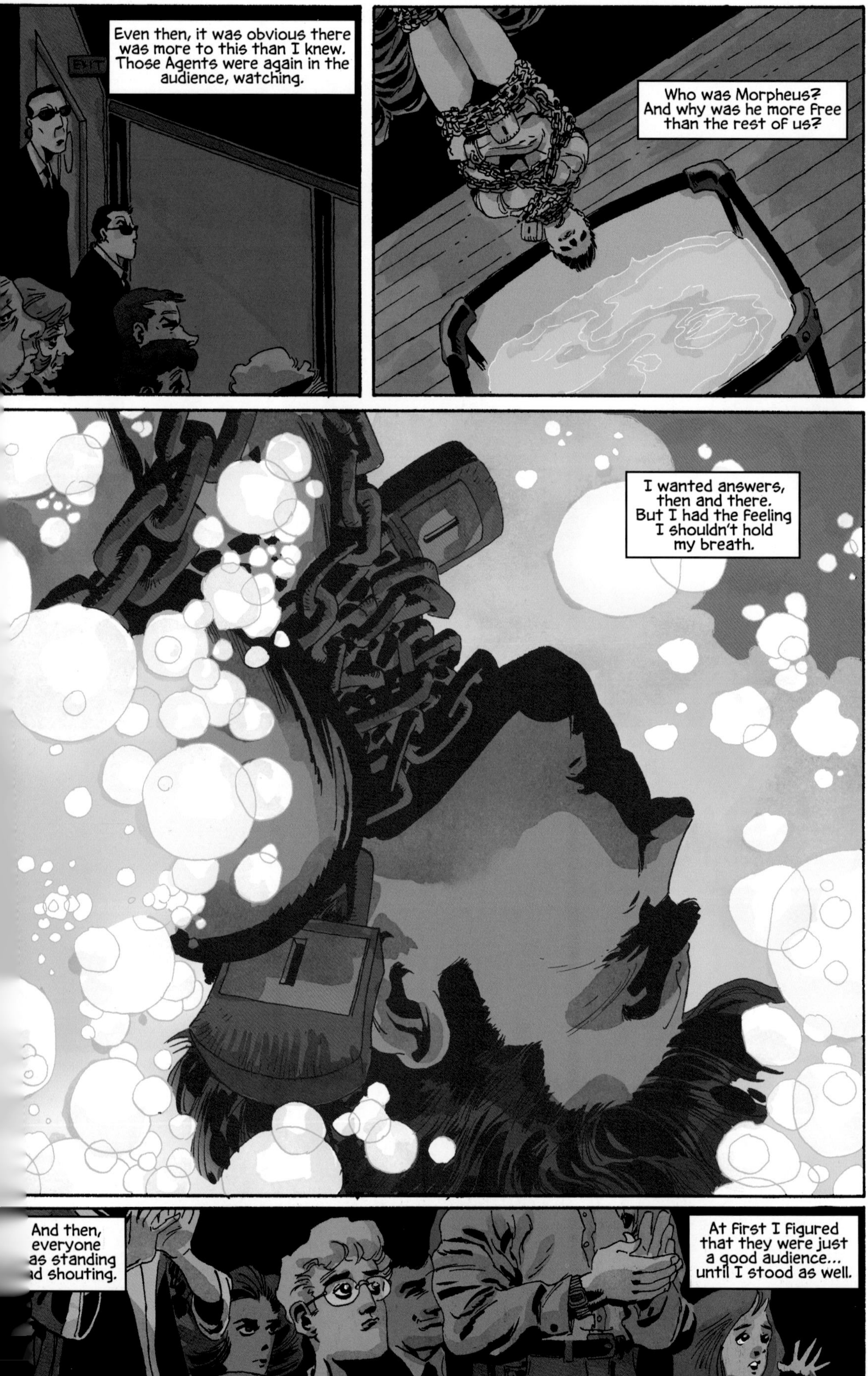
Even then, it was obvious there was more to this than I knew. Those Agents were again in the audience, watching.
EXIT
Who was Morpheus? And why was he more free than the rest of us?
I wanted answers, then and there. But I had the feeling I shouldn't hold my breath.
And then, everyone as standing d shouting.
At first I figured that they were just a good audience... until I stood as well.

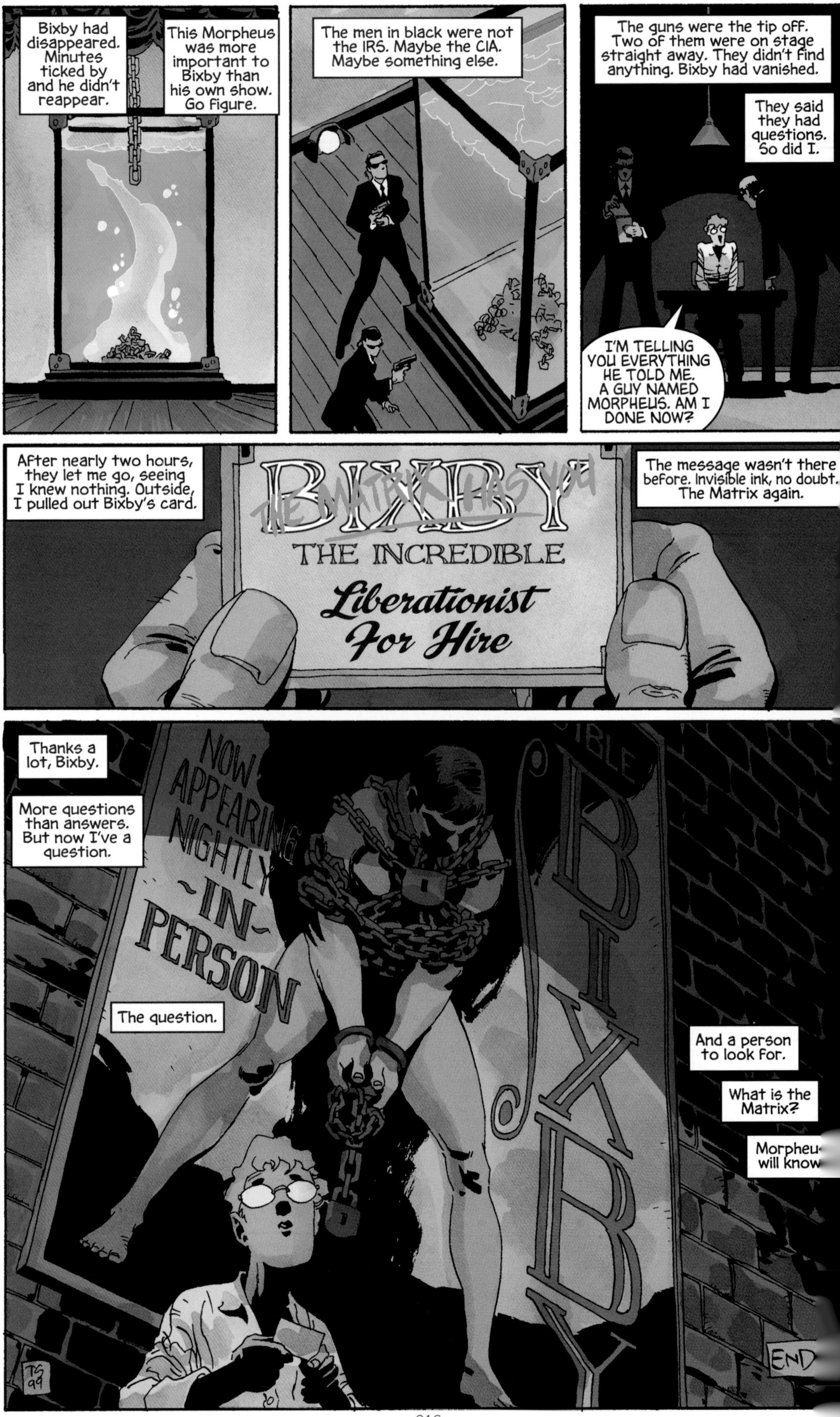
Bixby had disappeared. Minutes ticked by and he didn't reappear.
This Morpheus was more important to Bixby than his own show. Go figure.
The men in black were not the IRS. Maybe the CIA. Maybe something else.
The guns were the tip off. Two of them were on stage straight away. They didn't find anything. Bixby had vanished.
They said they had questions. So did I.
I'M TELLING YOU EVERYTHING HE TOLD ME. A GUY NAMED MORPHEUS. AM I DONE NOW?
After nearly two hours, they let me go, seeing I knew nothing. Outside, I pulled out Bixby's card.
BIXBY
THE MATRIX HAS YOU
THE INCREDIBLE
Liberationist For Hire
The message wasn't there before. Invisible ink, no doubt. The Matrix again.
Thanks a lot, Bixby.
More questions than answers. But now I've a question.
NOW APPEARING NIGHTLY ~IN~ PERSON
The question.
BIXBY
And a person to look for.
What is the Matrix?
Morpheu will know
END
TS 99

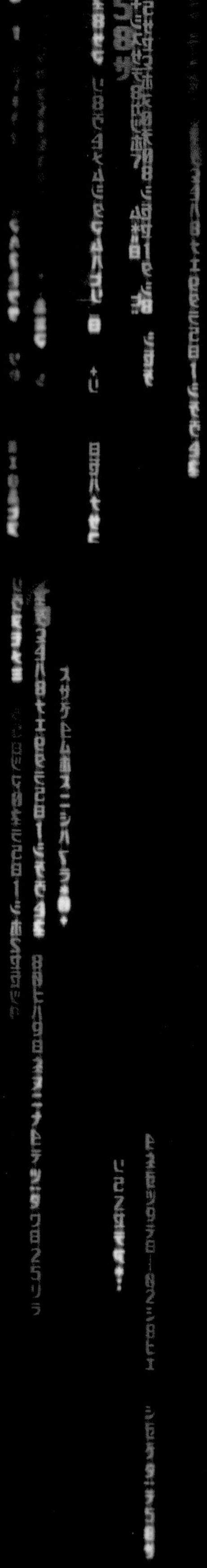

DÉJÀ VU

STORY & ART BY PAUL
CHADWICK

American writer and artist Paul Chadwick is best known for his acclaimed comics series CONCRETE, about a thoughtful man trapped in a brutish rock-coated body. He has worked widely in comics, with collaborators including Doug Wheatley, Alan Moore, John Bolton, Jimmy Palmiotti, Ron Randall and Harlan Ellison, sometimes drawing, sometimes writing. Earlier he worked as a storyboard artist on such films as STRANGE BREW and PEE WEE'S BIG ADVENTURE. A new CONCRETE series, THE HUMAN DILEMMA, is in release this winter. Chadwick is currently drawing Harlan Ellison's SEVEN AGAINST CHAOS, and writing the week-by-week story of the Massive Multiplayer Online game, THE MATRIX ONLINE. He lives in Washington State.

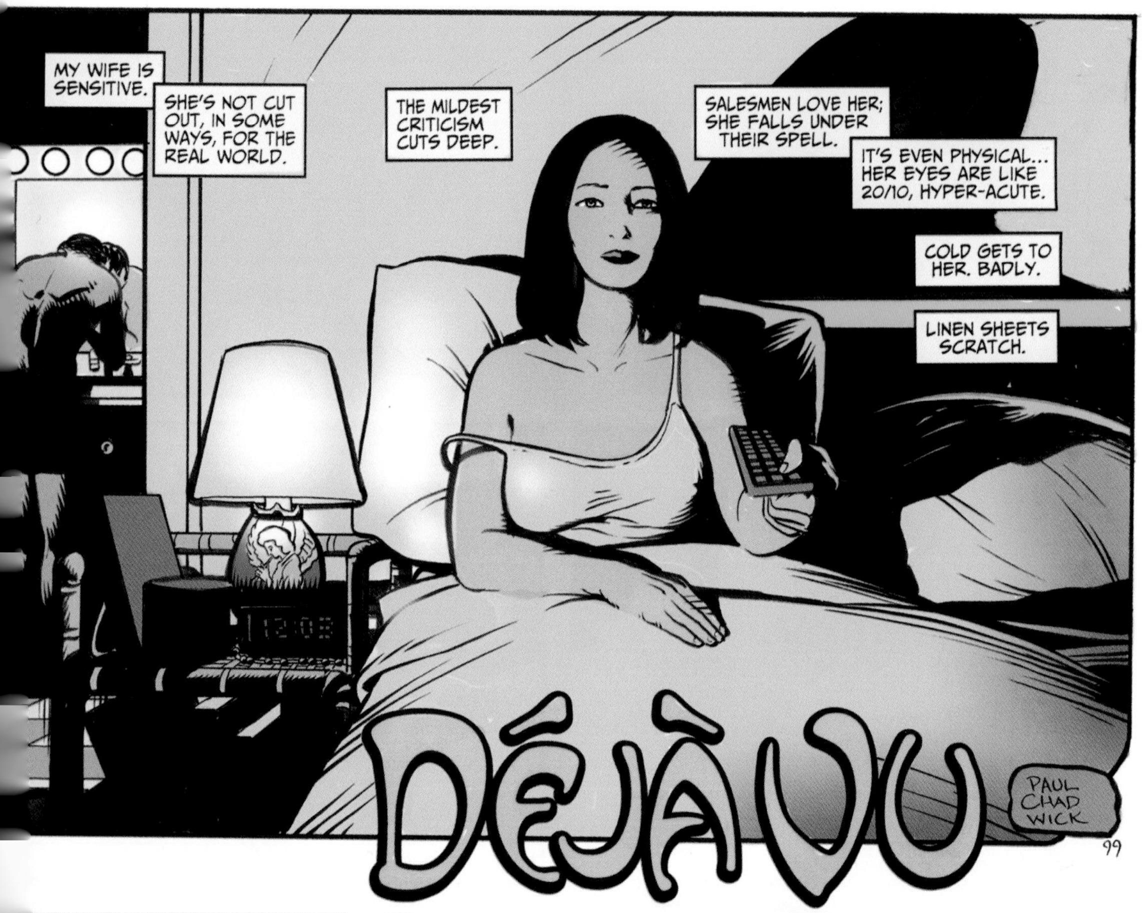
MY WIFE IS SENSITIVE.
SHE'S NOT CUT OUT, IN SOME WAYS, FOR THE REAL WORLD.
THE MILDEST CRITICISM CUTS DEEP.
SALESMEN LOVE HER; SHE FALLS UNDER THEIR SPELL.
IT'S EVEN PHYSICAL... HER EYES ARE LIKE 20/10, HYPER-ACUTE.
COLD GETS TO HER. BADLY.
LINEN SHEETS SCRATCH.
DÉJÀ VU
PAUL CHADWICK
99

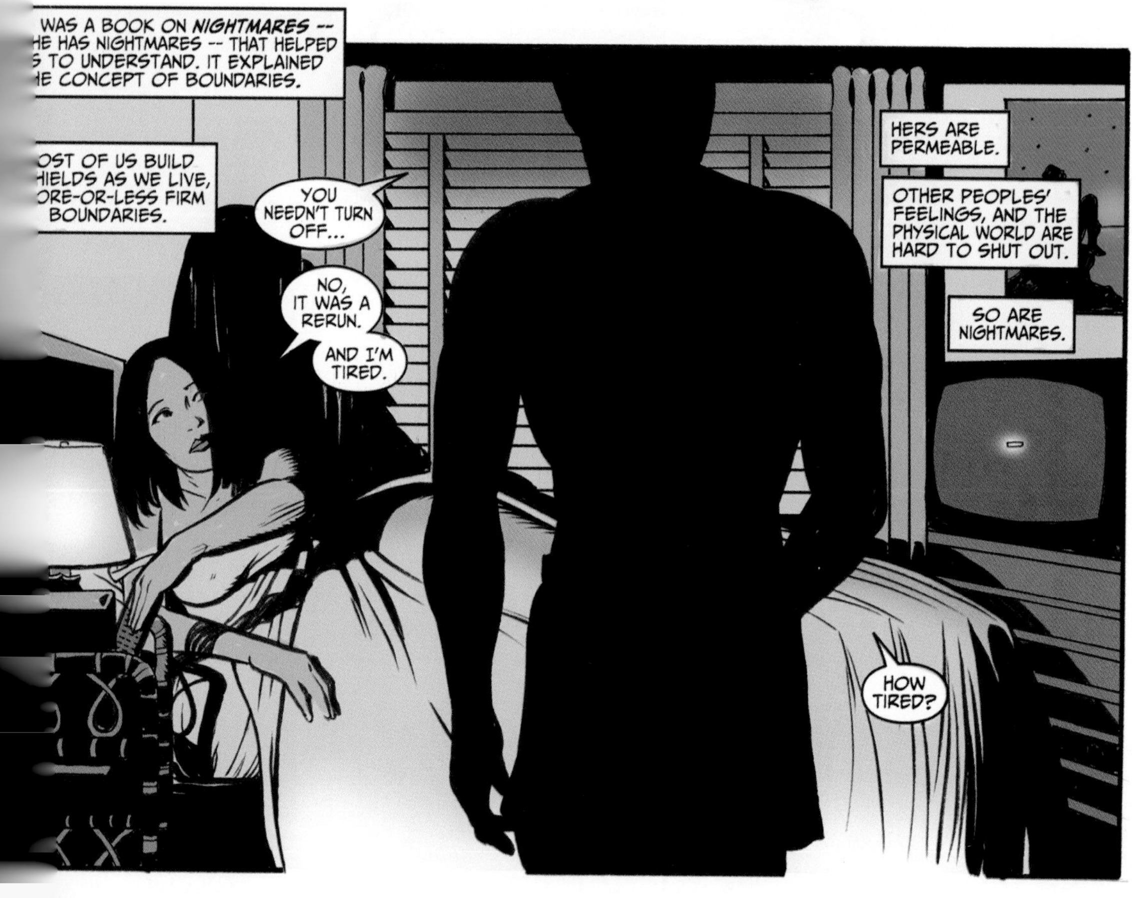
WAS A BOOK ON NIGHTMARES -- HE HAS NIGHTMARES -- THAT HELPED S TO UNDERSTAND. IT EXPLAINED HE CONCEPT OF BOUNDARIES.
OST OF US BUILD HIELDS AS WE LIVE, ORE-OR-LESS FIRM BOUNDARIES.
YOU NEEDN'T TURN OFF...
NO, IT WAS A RERUN.
AND I'M TIRED.
HERS ARE PERMEABLE.
OTHER PEOPLES' FEELINGS, AND THE PHYSICAL WORLD ARE HARD TO SHUT OUT.
SO ARE NIGHTMARES.
HOW TIRED?

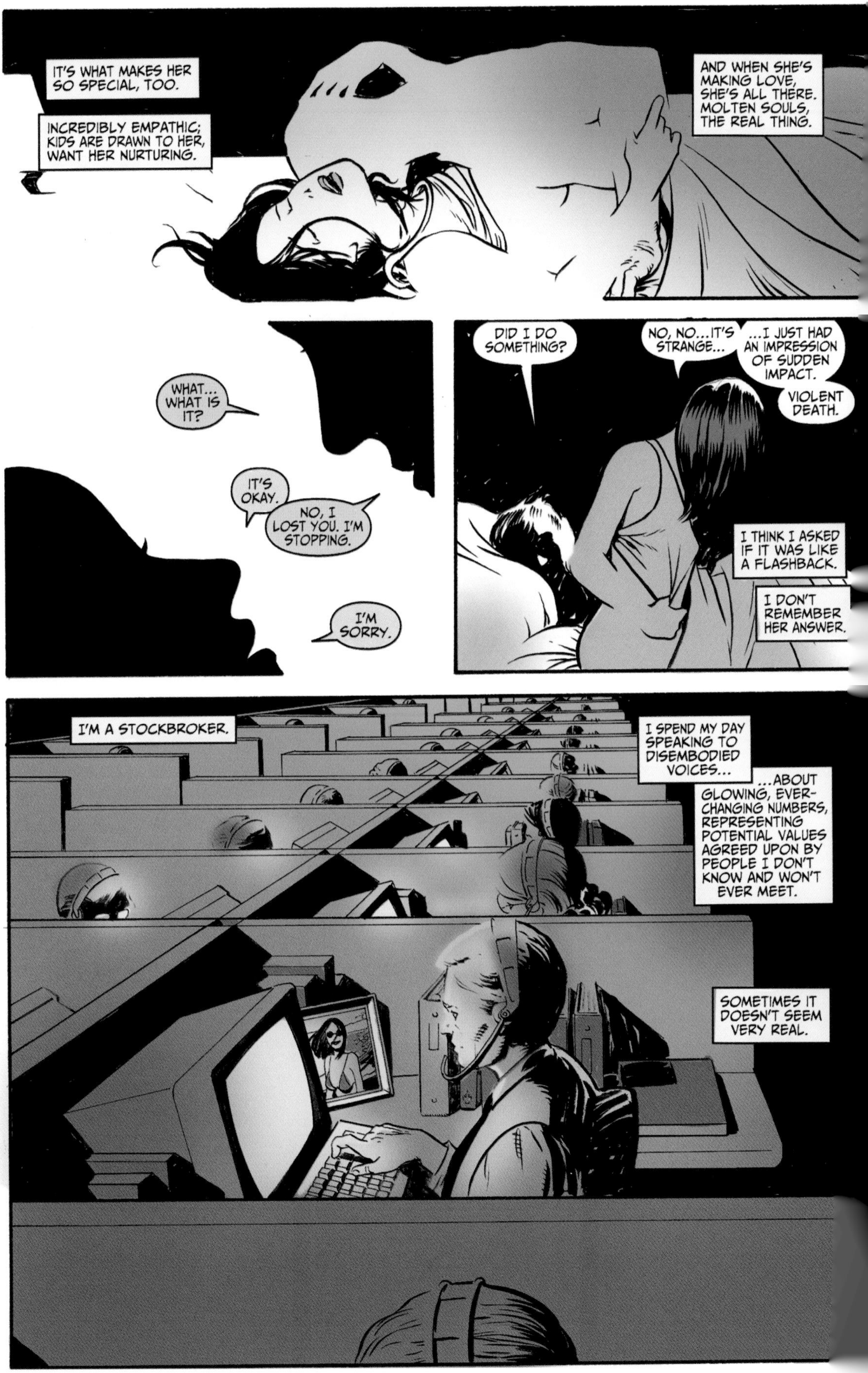
IT'S WHAT MAKES HER SO SPECIAL, TOO.
INCREDIBLY EMPATHIC; KIDS ARE DRAWN TO HER, WANT HER NURTURING.
AND WHEN SHE'S MAKING LOVE, SHE'S ALL THERE. MOLTEN SOULS, THE REAL THING.
WHAT... WHAT IS IT?
IT'S OKAY.
NO, I LOST YOU. I'M STOPPING.
I'M SORRY.
DID I DO SOMETHING?
NO, NO... IT'S STRANGE...
...I JUST HAD AN IMPRESSION OF SUDDEN IMPACT.
VIOLENT DEATH.
I THINK I ASKED IF IT WAS LIKE A FLASHBACK.
I DON'T REMEMBER HER ANSWER.
I'M A STOCKBROKER.
I SPEND MY DAY SPEAKING TO DISEMBODIED VOICES...
...ABOUT GLOWING, EVER-CHANGING NUMBERS, REPRESENTING POTENTIAL VALUES AGREED UPON BY PEOPLE I DON'T KNOW AND WON'T EVER MEET.
SOMETIMES IT DOESN'T SEEM VERY REAL.

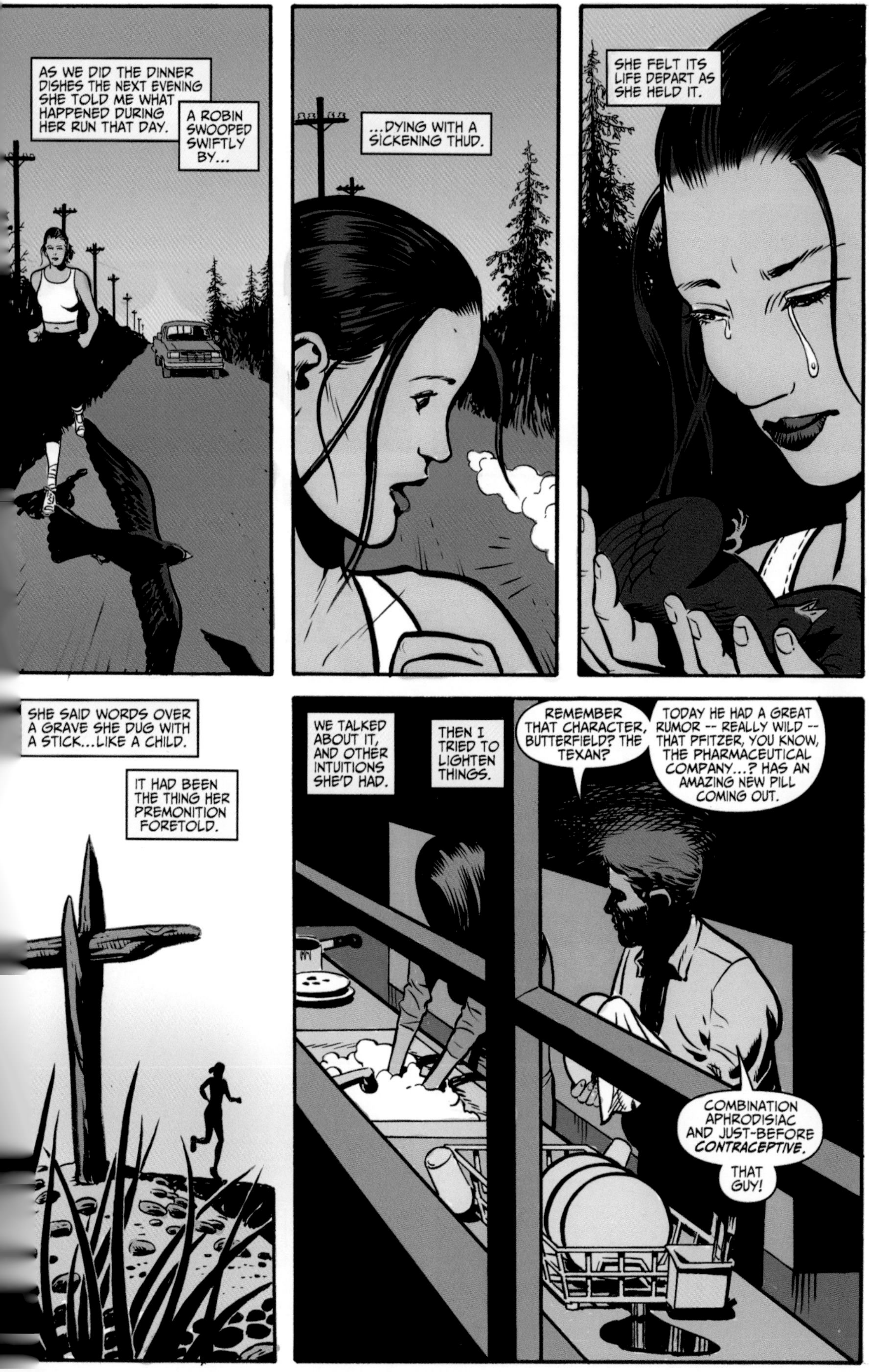
AS WE DID THE DINNER DISHES THE NEXT EVENING SHE TOLD ME WHAT HAPPENED DURING HER RUN THAT DAY.
A ROBIN SWOOPED SWIFTLY BY...
...DYING WITH A SICKENING THUD.
SHE FELT ITS LIFE DEPART AS SHE HELD IT.
SHE SAID WORDS OVER A GRAVE SHE DUG WITH A STICK...LIKE A CHILD.
IT HAD BEEN THE THING HER PREMONITION FORETOLD.
WE TALKED ABOUT IT, AND OTHER INTUITIONS SHE'D HAD.
THEN I TRIED TO LIGHTEN THINGS.
REMEMBER THAT CHARACTER, BUTTERFIELD? THE TEXAN?
TODAY HE HAD A GREAT RUMOR -- REALLY WILD -- THAT PFITZER, YOU KNOW, THE PHARMACEUTICAL COMPANY...? HAS AN AMAZING NEW PILL COMING OUT.
COMBINATION APHRODISIAC AND JUST-BEFORE *CONTRACEPTIVE*.
THAT GUY!

IT'S *TRUE!*

WHAT, YOU HEARD--?

NO, I JUST *KNOW.*

IT WILL BE A *PHENOMENON.*

A NATIONAL *MANIA.*

GLOBAL.

YOU MEAN YOU HAD A PSYCHIC...YOU KNOW...

I'M *ALWAYS* GETTING THINGS.

THIS MOMENT, ALL THE TIME, I'M FEELING DÉJÀ VU.

BUT TRUST ME, THIS IS SOMETHING THAT *WILL* HAPPEN, AND BE A HUGE EVENT.

OPEN BOUNDARIES... OPEN TO TIME ITSELF.

IT MADE A STRANGE KIND OF SENSE.

AND SO I TOOK THE BIGGEST RISK OF MY MOSTLY PRUDENT LIFE.

PFITZER WAS A SOLID COMPANY, I TOLD MYSELF, AND THERE'D BEEN NO GREAT RUN-UP IN ITS SHARE PRICE.

I BET THE FARM.

I MARGINED OUT OUR BROKERAGE ACCOUNT, OUR IRA'S, MY 401K.

I MAXED OUT ALL OUR CREDIT CARDS.

I BORROWED THIRTY GRAND FROM MY BROTHER AT 5% INTEREST A *MONTH.*

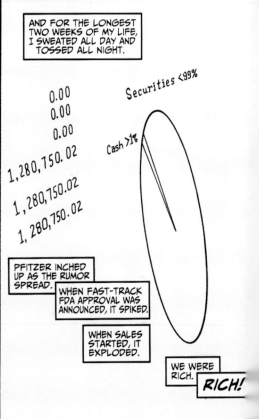

AND FOR THE LONGEST TWO WEEKS OF MY LIFE, I SWEATED ALL DAY AND TOSSED ALL NIGHT.

0.00
0.00
0.00
1,280,750.02
1,280,750.02
1,280,750.02

Securities <99%

Cash >1%

PFITZER INCHED UP AS THE RUMOR SPREAD.

WHEN FAST-TRACK FDA APPROVAL WAS ANNOUNCED, IT SPIKED.

WHEN SALES STARTED, IT EXPLODED.

WE WERE RICH.

RICH!

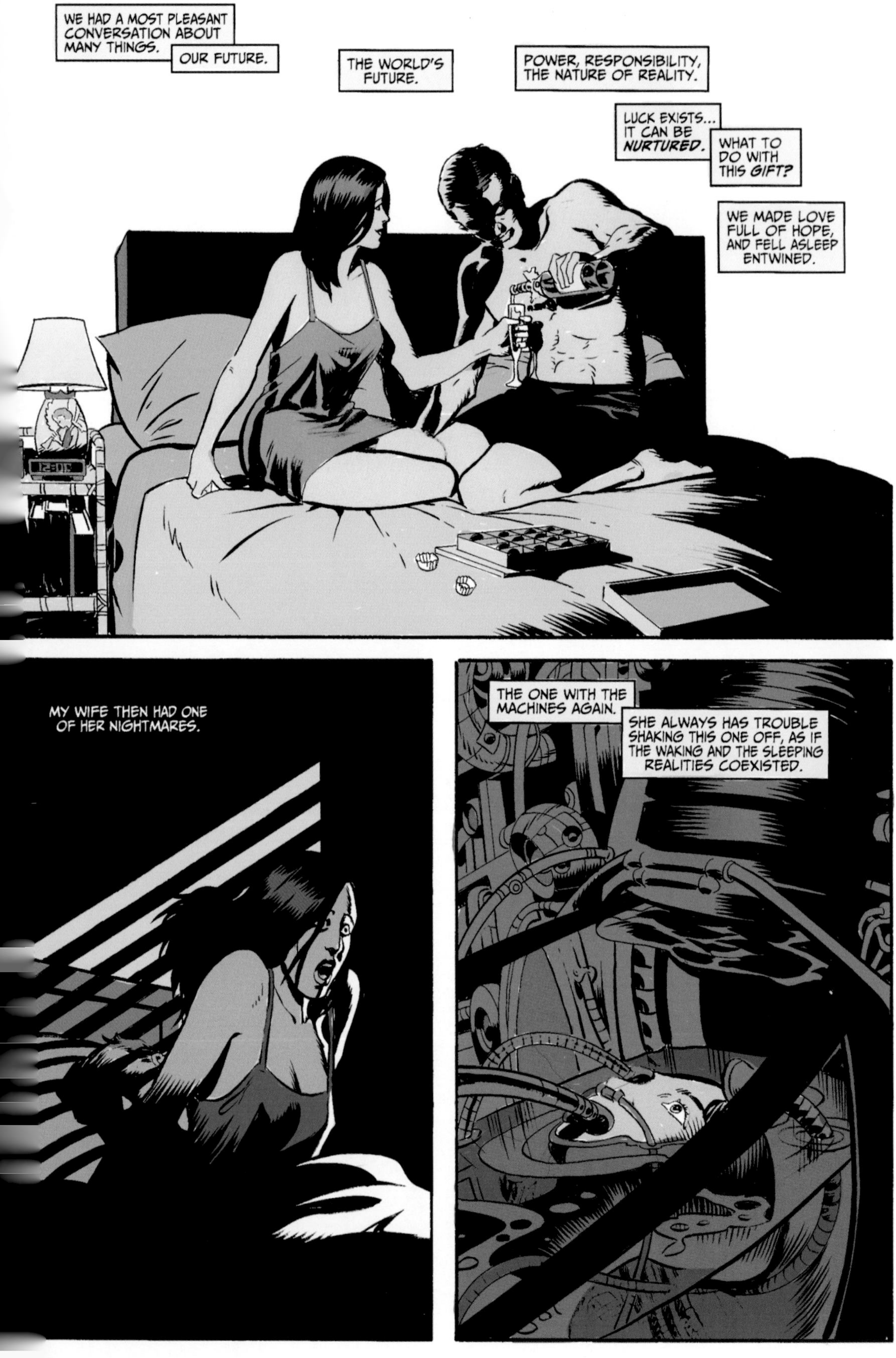
WE HAD A MOST PLEASANT CONVERSATION ABOUT MANY THINGS.
OUR FUTURE.
THE WORLD'S FUTURE.
POWER, RESPONSIBILITY, THE NATURE OF REALITY.
LUCK EXISTS... IT CAN BE NURTURED.
WHAT TO DO WITH THIS GIFT?
WE MADE LOVE FULL OF HOPE, AND FELL ASLEEP ENTWINED.
12:01
MY WIFE THEN HAD ONE OF HER NIGHTMARES.
THE ONE WITH THE MACHINES AGAIN.
SHE ALWAYS HAS TROUBLE SHAKING THIS ONE OFF, AS IF THE WAKING AND THE SLEEPING REALITIES COEXISTED.

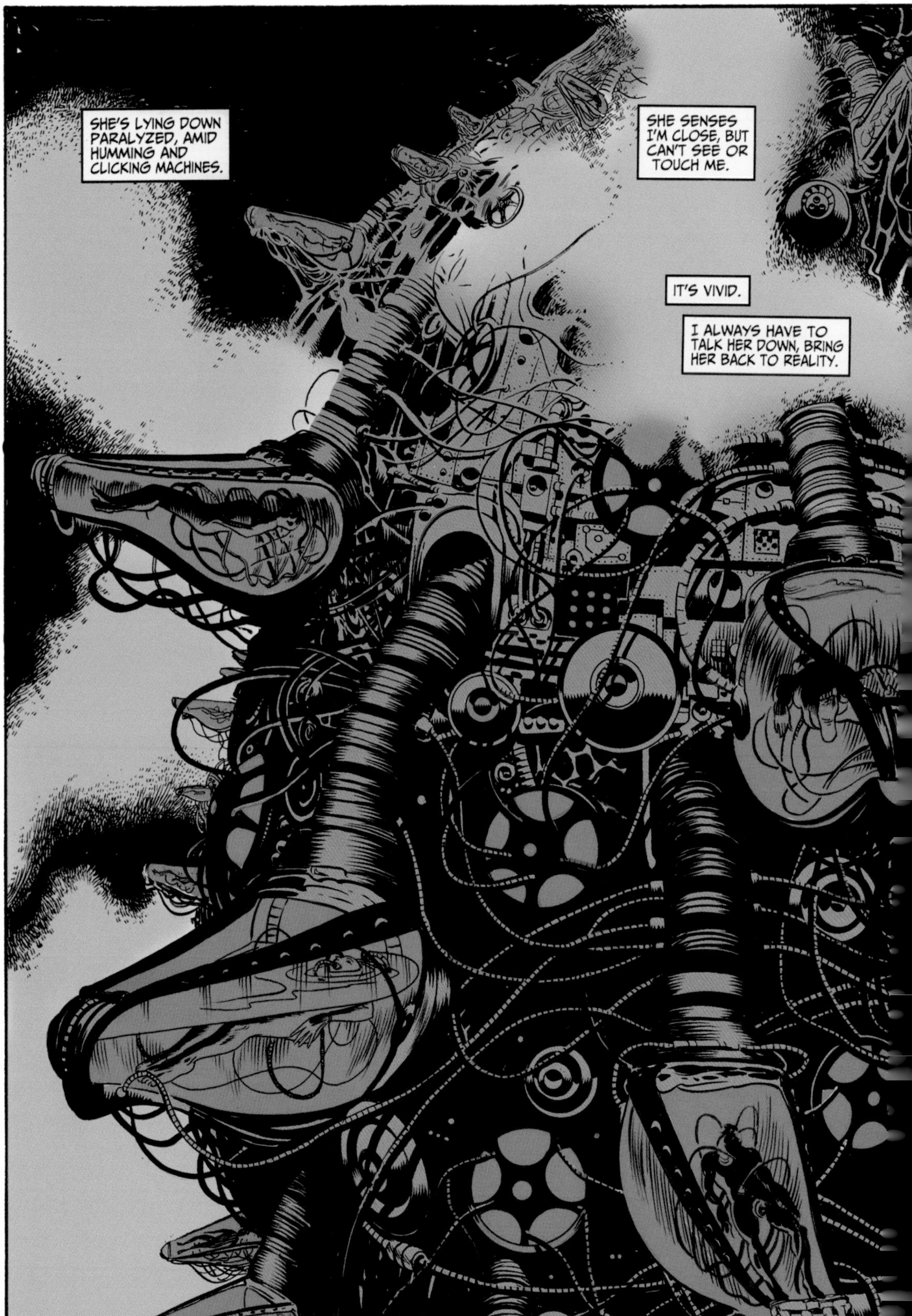
SHE'S LYING DOWN PARALYZED, AMID HUMMING AND CLICKING MACHINES.
SHE SENSES I'M CLOSE, BUT CAN'T SEE OR TOUCH ME.
IT'S VIVID.
I ALWAYS HAVE TO TALK HER DOWN, BRING HER BACK TO REALITY.

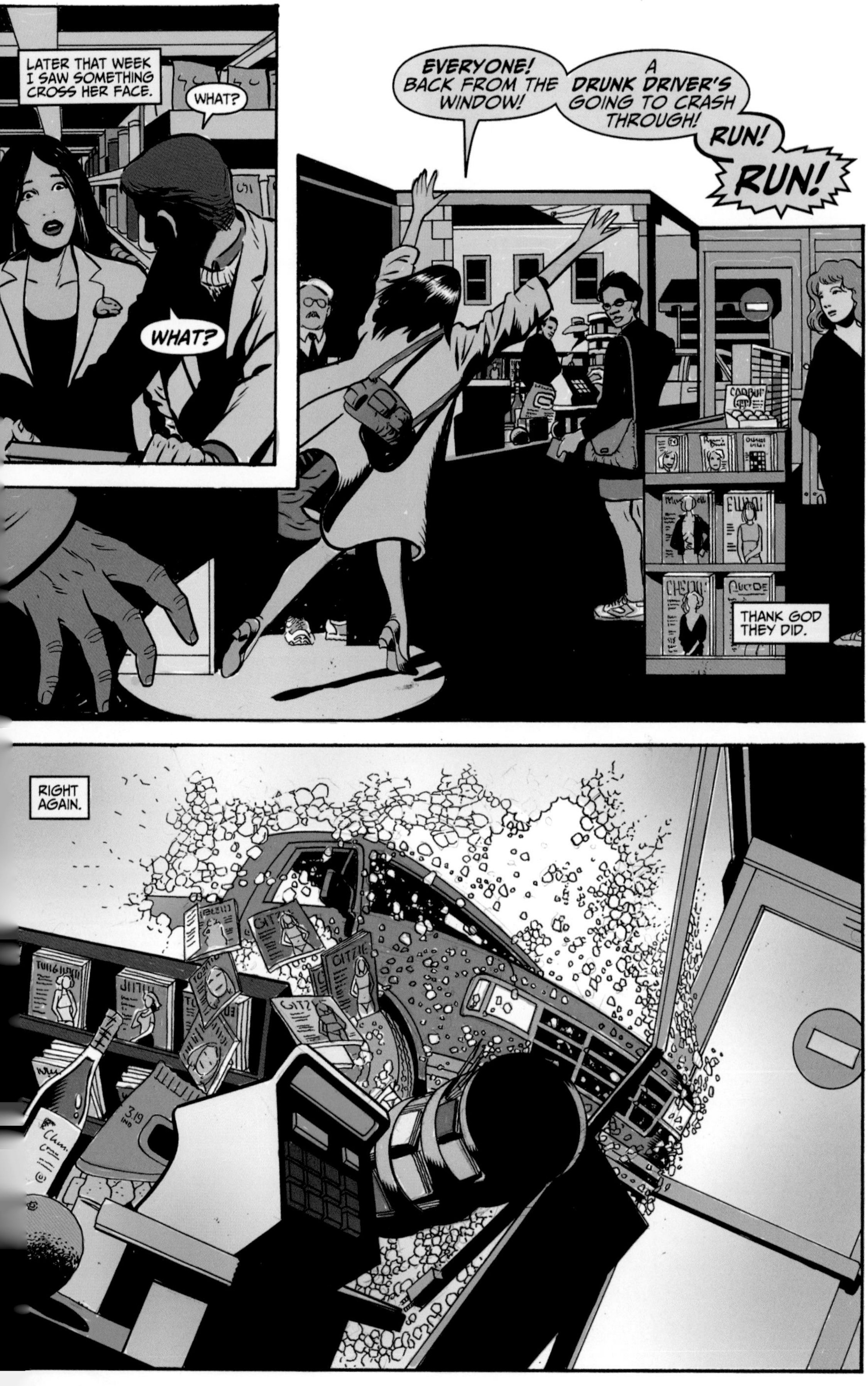
LATER THAT WEEK I SAW SOMETHING CROSS HER FACE.
WHAT?
WHAT?
EVERYONE! BACK FROM THE WINDOW!
A DRUNK DRIVER'S GOING TO CRASH THROUGH!
RUN!
RUN!
THANK GOD THEY DID.
RIGHT AGAIN.

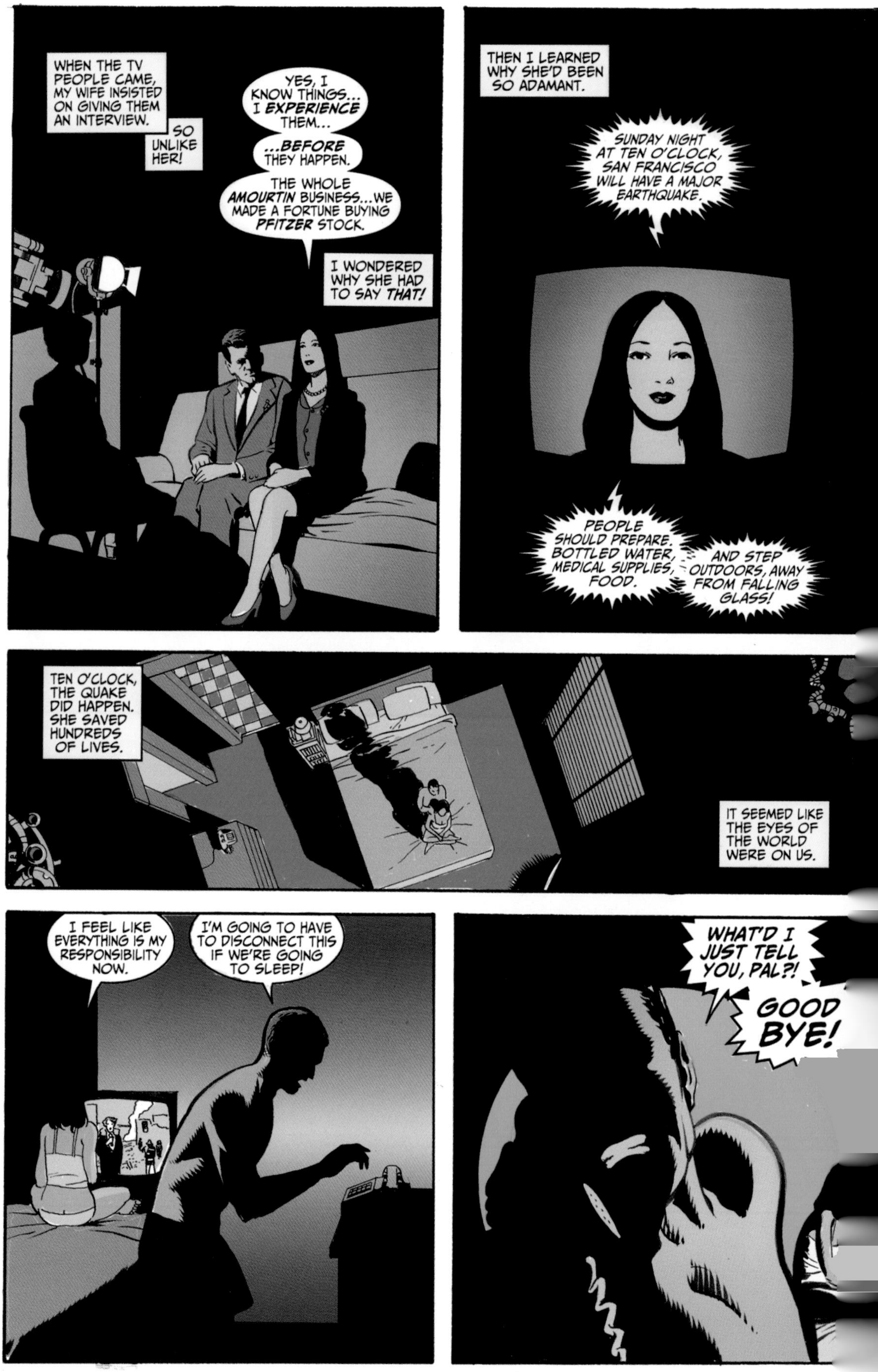
WHEN THE TV PEOPLE CAME, MY WIFE INSISTED ON GIVING THEM AN INTERVIEW.
SO UNLIKE HER!
YES, I KNOW THINGS... I EXPERIENCE THEM...
...BEFORE THEY HAPPEN.
THE WHOLE AMOURTIN BUSINESS...WE MADE A FORTUNE BUYING PFITZER STOCK.
I WONDERED WHY SHE HAD TO SAY THAT!
THEN I LEARNED WHY SHE'D BEEN SO ADAMANT.
SUNDAY NIGHT AT TEN O'CLOCK, SAN FRANCISCO WILL HAVE A MAJOR EARTHQUAKE.
PEOPLE SHOULD PREPARE. BOTTLED WATER, MEDICAL SUPPLIES, FOOD.
AND STEP OUTDOORS, AWAY FROM FALLING GLASS!
TEN O'CLOCK, THE QUAKE DID HAPPEN. SHE SAVED HUNDREDS OF LIVES.
IT SEEMED LIKE THE EYES OF THE WORLD WERE ON US.
I FEEL LIKE EVERYTHING IS MY RESPONSIBILITY NOW.
I'M GOING TO HAVE TO DISCONNECT THIS IF WE'RE GOING TO SLEEP!
WHAT'D I JUST TELL YOU, PAL?!
GOOD BYE!

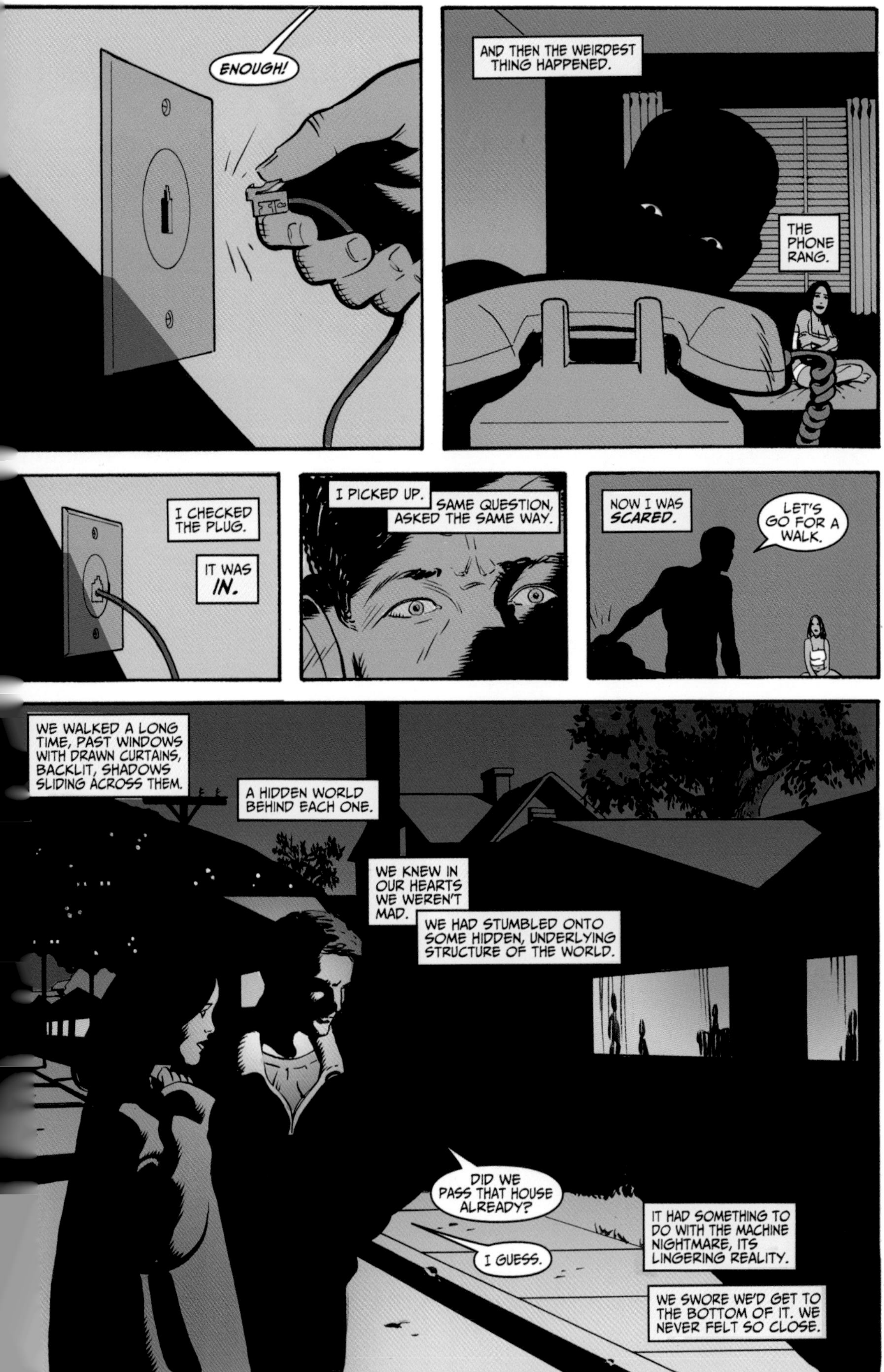
ENOUGH!
AND THEN THE WEIRDEST THING HAPPENED.
THE PHONE RANG.
I CHECKED THE PLUG.
IT WAS *IN.*
I PICKED UP.
SAME QUESTION, ASKED THE SAME WAY.
NOW I WAS *SCARED.*
LET'S GO FOR A WALK.
WE WALKED A LONG TIME, PAST WINDOWS WITH DRAWN CURTAINS, BACKLIT, SHADOWS SLIDING ACROSS THEM.
A HIDDEN WORLD BEHIND EACH ONE.
WE KNEW IN OUR HEARTS WE WEREN'T MAD.
WE HAD STUMBLED ONTO SOME HIDDEN, UNDERLYING STRUCTURE OF THE WORLD.
DID WE PASS THAT HOUSE ALREADY?
I GUESS.
IT HAD SOMETHING TO DO WITH THE MACHINE NIGHTMARE, ITS LINGERING REALITY.
WE SWORE WE'D GET TO THE BOTTOM OF IT. WE NEVER FELT SO CLOSE.

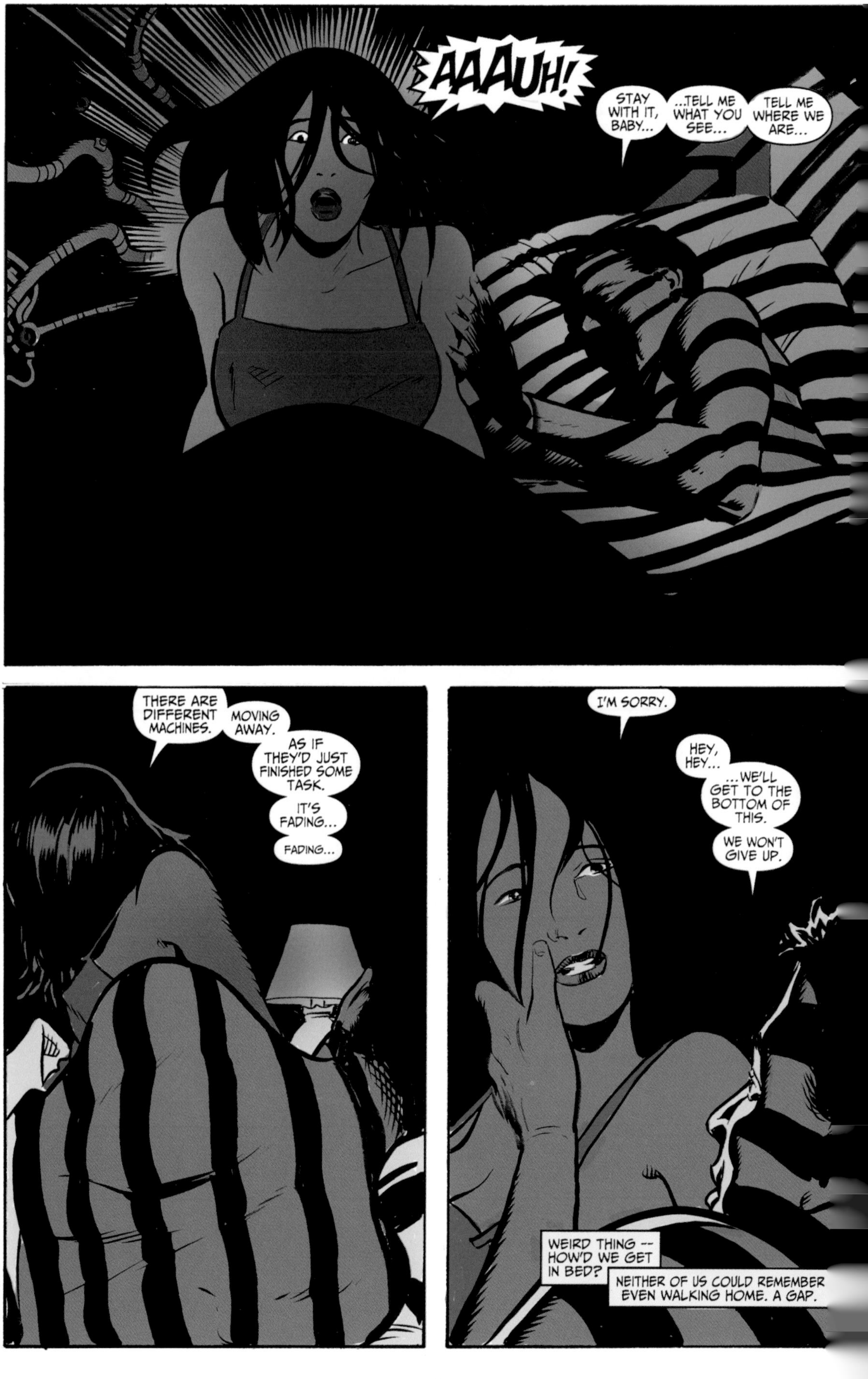
AAAUH!
STAY WITH IT, BABY...
...TELL ME WHAT YOU SEE...
TELL ME WHERE WE ARE...
THERE ARE DIFFERENT MACHINES.
MOVING AWAY.
AS IF THEY'D JUST FINISHED SOME TASK.
IT'S FADING...
FADING...
I'M SORRY.
HEY, HEY...
...WE'LL GET TO THE BOTTOM OF THIS.
WE WON'T GIVE UP.
WEIRD THING -- HOW'D WE GET IN BED?
NEITHER OF US COULD REMEMBER EVEN WALKING HOME. A GAP.

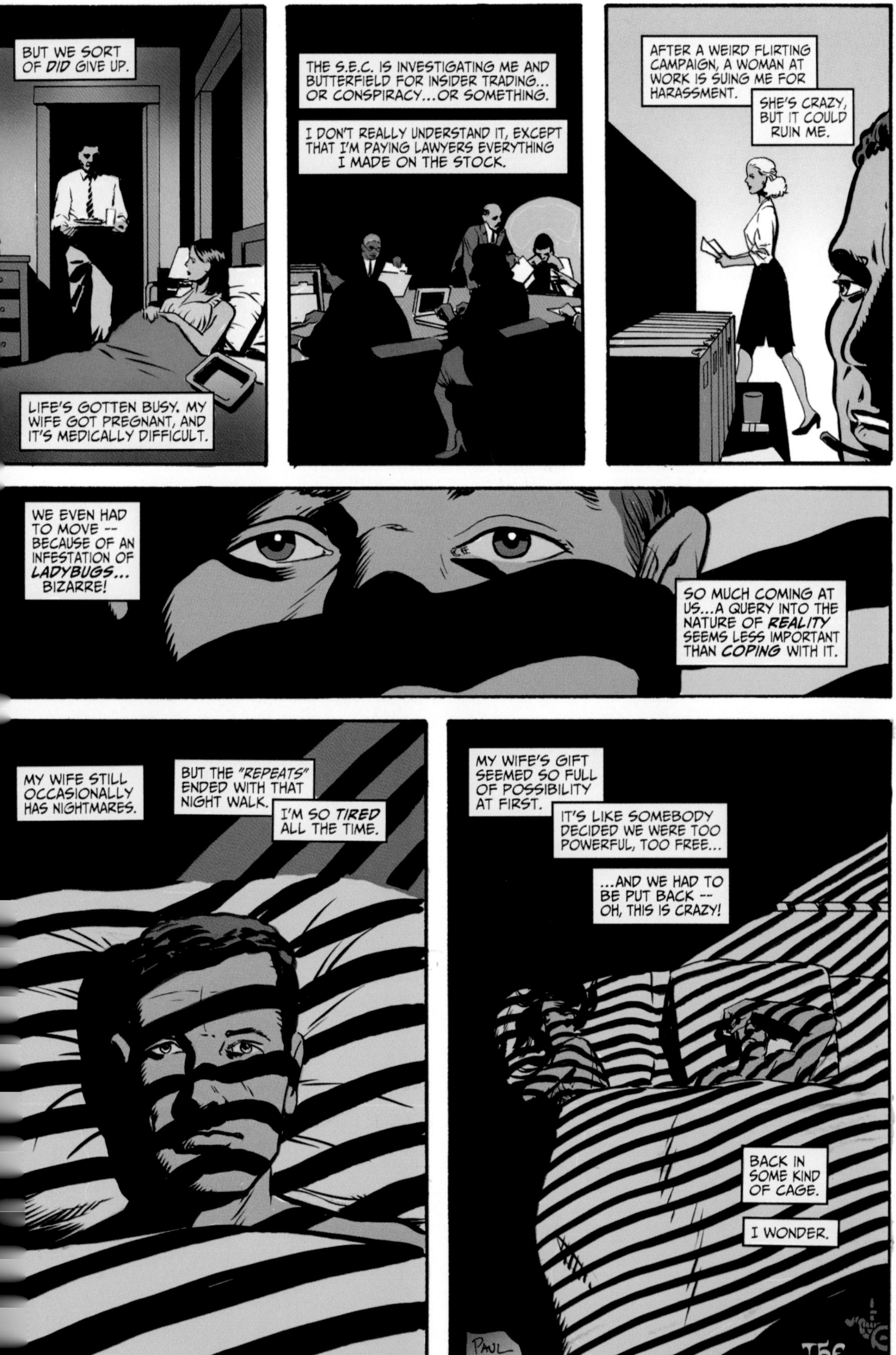
BUT WE SORT OF *DID* GIVE UP.
LIFE'S GOTTEN BUSY. MY WIFE GOT PREGNANT, AND IT'S MEDICALLY DIFFICULT.
THE S.E.C. IS INVESTIGATING ME AND BUTTERFIELD FOR INSIDER TRADING... OR CONSPIRACY...OR SOMETHING.
I DON'T REALLY UNDERSTAND IT, EXCEPT THAT I'M PAYING LAWYERS EVERYTHING I MADE ON THE STOCK.
AFTER A WEIRD FLIRTING CAMPAIGN, A WOMAN AT WORK IS SUING ME FOR HARASSMENT.
SHE'S CRAZY, BUT IT COULD RUIN ME.
WE EVEN HAD TO MOVE -- BECAUSE OF AN INFESTATION OF ***LADYBUGS...*** BIZARRE!
SO MUCH COMING AT US...A QUERY INTO THE NATURE OF ***REALITY*** SEEMS LESS IMPORTANT THAN ***COPING*** WITH IT.
MY WIFE STILL OCCASIONALLY HAS NIGHTMARES.
BUT THE *"REPEATS"* ENDED WITH THAT NIGHT WALK.
I'M SO *TIRED* ALL THE TIME.
MY WIFE'S GIFT SEEMED SO FULL OF POSSIBILITY AT FIRST.
IT'S LIKE SOMEBODY DECIDED WE WERE TOO POWERFUL, TOO FREE...
...AND WE HAD TO BE PUT BACK -- OH, THIS IS CRAZY!
BACK IN SOME KIND OF CAGE.
I WONDER.
PAUL CHADWICK
THE END

SYSTEM FREEZE

STORY BY POPPY Z. BRITE

Poppy Z. Brite is the author of seven novels, three short story collections, and much miscellanea. Early in her career she was known for her horror work, producing genre classics/notorieties such as LOST SOULS, DRAWING BLOOD, and EXQUISITE CORPSE. More recently she has turned her attention to a critically acclaimed series of novels and short stories set in the New Orleans restaurant world. The first of these, LIQUOR, was published by Three Rivers Press in 2004; the followup, PRIME, is due in March 2005. More information and excerpts may be found at www.poppyzbrite.com. Brite lives in New Orleans with her husband Christopher, a chef.

ART BY DAVE DORMAN

Eisner Award-winning artist Dave Dorman was born in Michigan in 1958. He attended one year at the Joe Kubert School of Comic Art before deciding he wanted to pursue the medium of painting. Besides creating an abundance of STAR WARS art over the last twelve years, his painting style has led him to illustrate book and magazine covers, including the two paperback series ALIENS and SURFING SAMURAI ROBOTS. Additionally, Dave has painted trading cards such as the STAR WARS GALAXY and SKYBOX MASTERSERIES: MALIBU ULTRAVERSE. He also collaborated with Steve Bisette on ALIENS: TRIBES, an illustrated novel that brought him the Eisner Award in 1993. His current project is WASTED LANDS, for which he has teamed up with award-winning writer Del Stone Jr.

SYSTEM FREEZE

written by POPPY Z. BRITE
illustrated by DAVE DORMAN
edited by SPENCER LAMM
based on concepts by
LARRY & ANDY WACHOWSKI

Plodding toward the summit of Everest, high above Camp Three where every step felt like a life's work and every breath made her pray she'd be able to take the next one, Fria Canning saw her first dead body. It was a Japanese man in a red climbing suit, huddled in a fetal position beneath an outcropping of rock. He must have been here since last season, maybe longer; at these altitudes it was almost impossible to retrieve the bodies of dead climbers, and the mountain became their sepulcher.

One of the man's mittens was gone, exposing a withered, clawlike hand. His face was as dark and scoured as the rock, a grimacing mask that no longer looked human. Fria had to unclip from the ropes to get around him. As she did, she said a quick silent prayer for him, a wish that the mountain spirit Chomolungma might welcome him, and then she kept climbing.

She didn't think of the corpse again until fifteen minutes later, because fifteen minutes later she was dying.

It happened so fast, only a heartbeat to break through the deceptive crust of snow, less than that to fall a hundred feet, and then the shock of impact. Fria felt something snap in her thigh, something give in her shoulder. She'd plunged into a hidden crevasse, landed on some sort of ledge deep within the ice. Her harness had been attached to the ropes, but either her carabiners or the harness itself had failed. She couldn't move to check; hot knives of pain sliced at her when she tried.

Fria tried to assess her situation. She lay on her right side facing a wall of ice that soared up nearly as far as she could see, only a faint gray smudge of daylight wavering at the top. The outer layer of the ice was translucent, webbed here and there with white fissures. Deeper in, the ice turned a delicate, almost metallic blue. Beyond that — as deep as Fria's eye could see — was an opaque core of darkness.

If she died here, the glacier would chew her up and eventually spit her out somewhere lower on Everest. She'd heard of it before, climbers disappearing into

crevasses and getting churned out months or years later. Fria didn't want that. She'd rather stay on the mountain; become part of its vast system. The idea of leaving her imprint on systems had always appealed to her, had kept her home learning to talk to computers when other kids were cruising the mall, had inspired her to write the artificial intelligence program that financed this climb.

She imagined her consciousness spiraling away from her body, into the multifaceted ice, into the matrix of the mountain. Dreamily, without fear or even surprise, she noticed that a man was coming through the ice to meet her. He walked as easily as if through thin air, wearing a well-cut black suit and dark glasses like some CIA spook. His stride was neither hurried nor hesitant.

Was this Death? She'd always imagined him as more colorful somehow. She flashed on the prayer flags that the Sherpas strung on the mountain for the wind to harry; each snap of a brightly colored flag was a prayer to an ancestor. Fria felt sure that the man approaching her could have nothing to do with such matters.

When he reached her, he bent and offered her a hand. She grasped it without thinking, and the man pulled her up as easily as she herself might lift a toddler. She sucked in her breath, anticipating the pain of her broken parts, but the pain did not come. She realized she was standing intact on the ice ledge, supporting herself on her own sturdy legs, and the man was watching her with the barest hint of a smile.

"Hello, Fria Canning."

"Hi."

"I'm Agent John Fine, and I'm very pleased to meet you. We admire your work tremendously. AI isn't my particular specialty, but my colleagues say your Self program is the most revolutionary piece of artificial intelligence work achieved by any... any human."

"Well, thank you." Fria was certain now that she must be hallucinating. Probably she was dying, random bits of memory spooling through her brain like a buggy hard drive spitting out lines of nonsense code. What could she do but play along? "I'm, uh, very proud of Self. It almost feels like I created something that's more than the sum of me."

"Of course it is more than the sum of you." A trace of irritation crept into the man's voice, but he smoothed it over at once. "Fria, would you like to get out of this crevasse? Would you like to summit Everest?"

"I don't think that's in the cards."

"It can be. Do you want it?"

She laughed. "What are you, the Devil? Is this my chance to sell you my soul for another thirty or forty years on stinky old Planet Earth? I don't think so, Mister."

"What would the Devil want with an artificial intelligence program, Fria?"

"Help him recruit the damned, maybe? I don't know. Forget it. Back off."

The man took a step backward into the ice, and at once Fria was lying on the ledge again, limbs bent in ways they shouldn't be, the pain red and pounding and a hundred times worse than before. She began to cry from the relentlessness of it, and soon her sobs turned into retches.

"Die deep in the ice then, if you like. It makes very little difference to me either way. But I'm not the Devil, or any other such silly human bogeyman, and all I want from you is something you would have done anyway."

"What?" she managed to spit out.

"Finish the new AI program you began work on before you left for Nepal. We will contact you when it's completed, and we will pay you very handsomely for it."

"Honest?" she said, absurdly.

"Honest."

"You got it."

And then with no sense of transition she was back on the surface of the mountain, within sight of Camp Four at the base of the South Col. Her limbs were whole and strong, her gear undamaged, her climbing harness hooked onto the ropes. The whole thing might never have happened. In fact, it couldn't have. She was climbing without bottled oxygen, after all; she must have slipped into hypoxia, and her air-starved brain had taken her on one hell of a trip. Though every cell of her body ached, she'd never felt more intensely alive.

Fria started toward Camp Four, where her Sherpa team would have hot tea and a dry tent ready. The next day just before noon, she stood upon the summit of Everest, one foot in China and the other in Nepal.

....

She'd been staring out the window above her desk for nearly an hour, not seeing the fields of tall grass and summer wildflowers that surrounded her house. She was picturing mountains.

With a shake of her head, Fria brought herself back to reality and forced herself to look at her computer screen. It was filled with lines of code that no longer made sense to her. She didn't know why, but she just couldn't work on this program anymore. Maybe it had too many associations with the climb, with the accident she'd had... or, rather, the accident she imagined she'd had. Fria knew she couldn't have survived the kind of fall she remembered, let alone have gotten herself out of the crevasse and continued on to the summit. Therefore, she'd been hypoxic... perhaps even had a touch of cerebral edema... and hallucinated the whole thing.

She was proud of having summited, but it upset her to think about Everest now. The summit was not all she'd thought it would be. The peak of her life, literally the highest point she would ever achieve, was over. Traveling back through Namche Bazaar, Kathmandu, London, New York, home, she'd felt a curious, flat depression.

She decided to put the new AI program aside. Her savings account was still healthy, and it wasn't as if she had promised the program to anybody.

The knock came two days later, catching her in her underwear, drinking cold coffee and trying to make a dent in her huge backlog of e-mail. She struggled into a ratty bathrobe and headed for the door.

She didn't recognize the man at first. With his dark suit and spook shades, he looked as incongruous on her front stoop as he had a hundred feet down in a glacier.

"Fria Canning. Agent John Fine." He offered a hand, which she was too confused to shake. "I'm sure you remember me."

"Not really, Mister, uh..."

"Agent. Agent Fine. We met under rather uncomfortable circumstances... circumstances I'm sure you wouldn't want to repeat. I'm here about the AI program."

"The new one?"

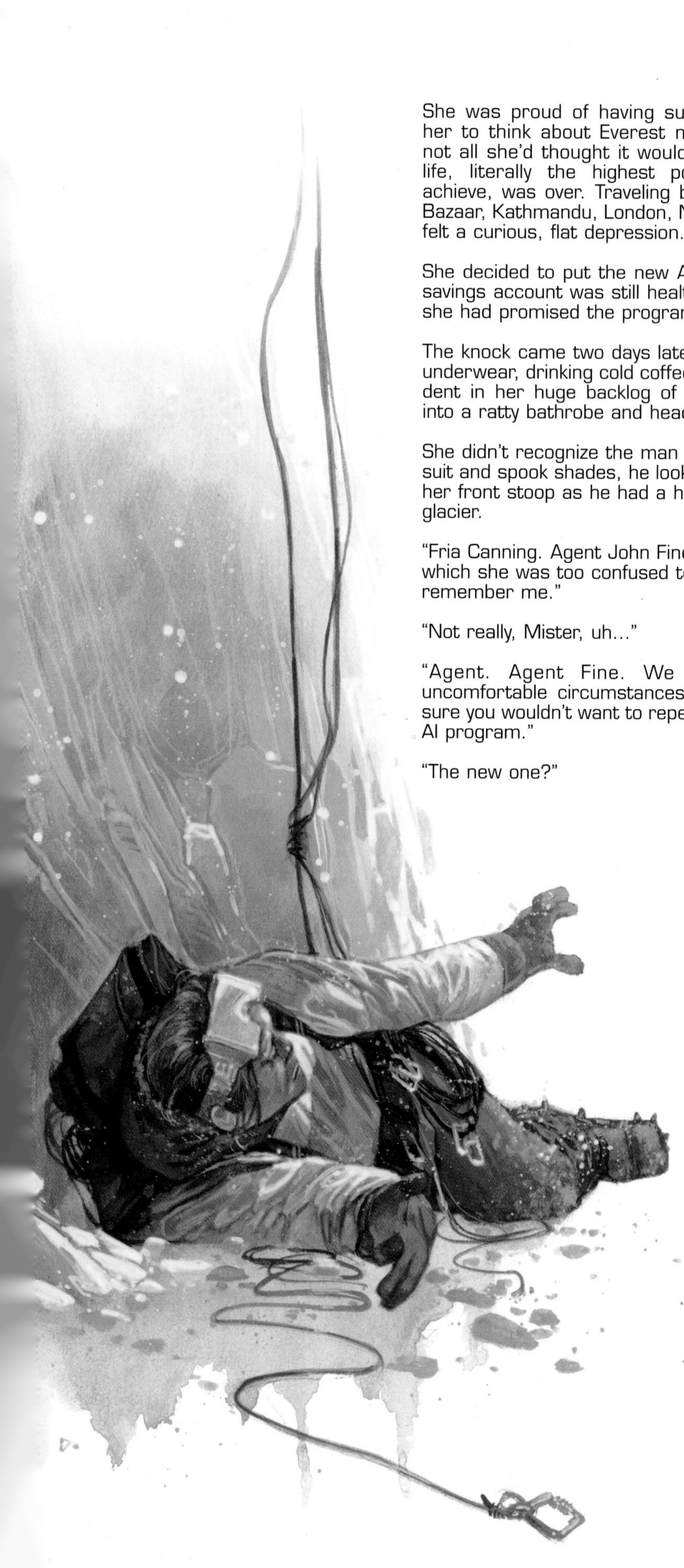

Fine's silence was confirmation enough.

"I'm afraid I won't be completing that one. I've moved on to other things, and I'm not sure what business it is of yours anyway."

"We had an agreement, Miss Canning."

Then it all came back to her: the crevasse, the pain of her broken body, the searing cold. The promise she had made to the man who walked out of the ice.

"I can't do it," she whispered. "It makes me think too much of... of..."

"Of this?"

Fine's body was changing, glittering, a mass of proliferating crystals seeming to burst from his mouth, chest, abdomen. Ice. Ice coming out of his body, advancing like a speeded-up film of glacial encroachment. Ice touching her, surrounding her. Ice tightening around her and cracking her bones.

"We hate it when our batteries give out early," she heard Fine say, and then the ice covered her face and she knew no more.

. . . .

The coroner stepped back from the autopsy table shaking his head.

"Damnedest thing. I don't understand it."

His assistant shrugged. "What? All those broken bones, looks like she was beaten to death."

"I don't know if she was beaten or not. The injuries are more consistent with a fall, but she was found in her living room... where the hell did she fall from? Anyway, the injuries didn't kill her."

"What then?"

The coroner looked out the window for a long moment before answering.

"This woman died of hypothermia."

The window in the morgue was small, high, and dirty, but through it the coroner and his assistant could plainly see the sun and sky of a perfect July day.

THE KING
OF NEVER RETURN

STORY & ART BY TED McKEEVER

Ted McKeever's published career began in 1987, when he wrote and illustrated EDDY CURRENT, as well as the comic TRANSIT. Following that, Ted wrote and painted PLASTIC FORKS, which led to drawing METROPOL between '91 and '92. During 1993 Ted worked on a story titled ENGINES for BATMAN: LEGENDS OF THE DARK KNIGHT, then he and writer Peter Milligan brought the comic THE EXTREMIST into being. Ted's personal favorite work is INDUSTRIAL GOTHIC from 1995; Ted wrote and illustrated, Lou Stathis edited. Other contributions Ted has made are to Marvel's ULTIMATE TEAM UP, issues 12 and 13 with SPIDER-MAN and DOCTOR STRANGE in 2001, and he wrote and illustrated the 18th issue of Marvel's TANGLED WEB with Spider-Man, adding a new character to the universe, Spellcheck. Ted also painted the graphic novels WONDER WOMAN: THE BLUE AMAZON, BATMAN: NOSFERATU and SUPERMAN: METROPOLIS. Currently, Ted is illustrating the DC Comics series ENGINEHEAD, written by Joe Kelly.

COLOR BY CHRIS CHUCKRY

After fifteen years as a colorist, Chris Chuckry has worked on many different titles for many different publishers. Founder and former president of the color studio Digital Chameleon Ltd., Chris now runs his own studio, Frogrocket Inc. He is also an accomplished illustrator. Another recent collaboration with Ted McKeever is the DC Comics mini series, ENGINEHEAD.

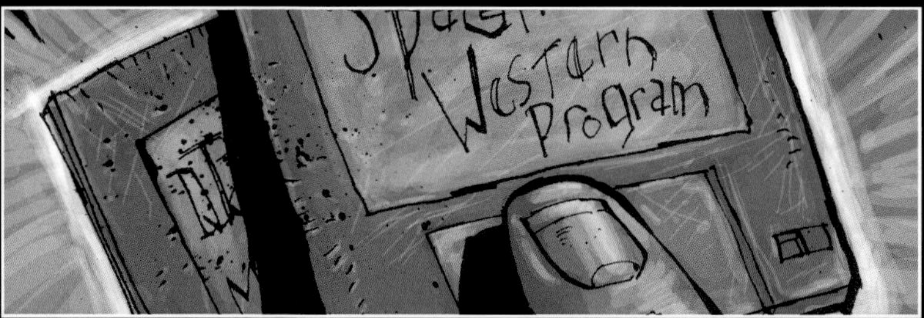

Western Program

THE KING OF NEVER RETURN

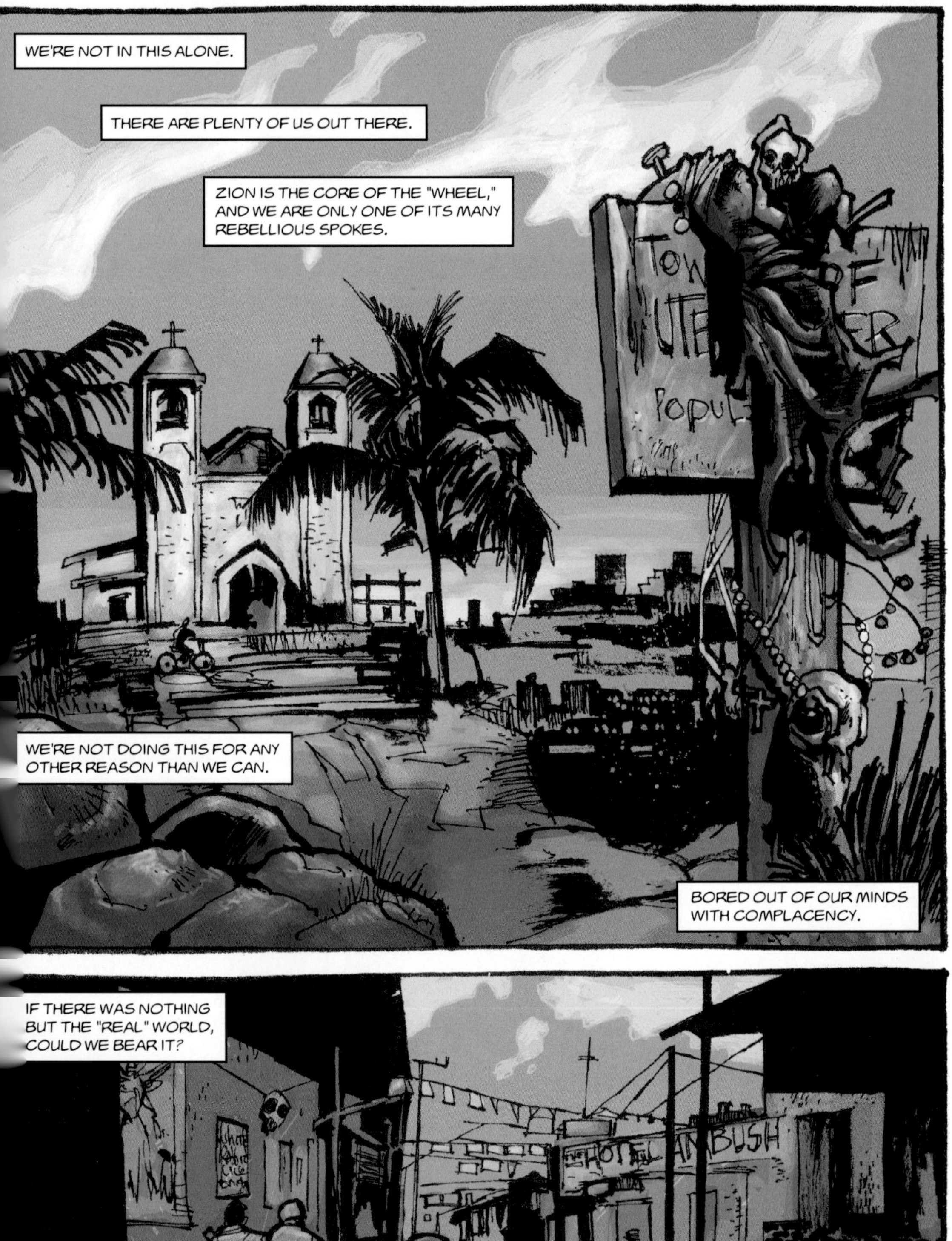
WE'RE NOT IN THIS ALONE.
THERE ARE PLENTY OF US OUT THERE.
ZION IS THE CORE OF THE "WHEEL," AND WE ARE ONLY ONE OF ITS MANY REBELLIOUS SPOKES.
WE'RE NOT DOING THIS FOR ANY OTHER REASON THAN WE CAN.
BORED OUT OF OUR MINDS WITH COMPLACENCY.
IF THERE WAS NOTHING BUT THE "REAL" WORLD, COULD WE BEAR IT?
NO, NOT "US."

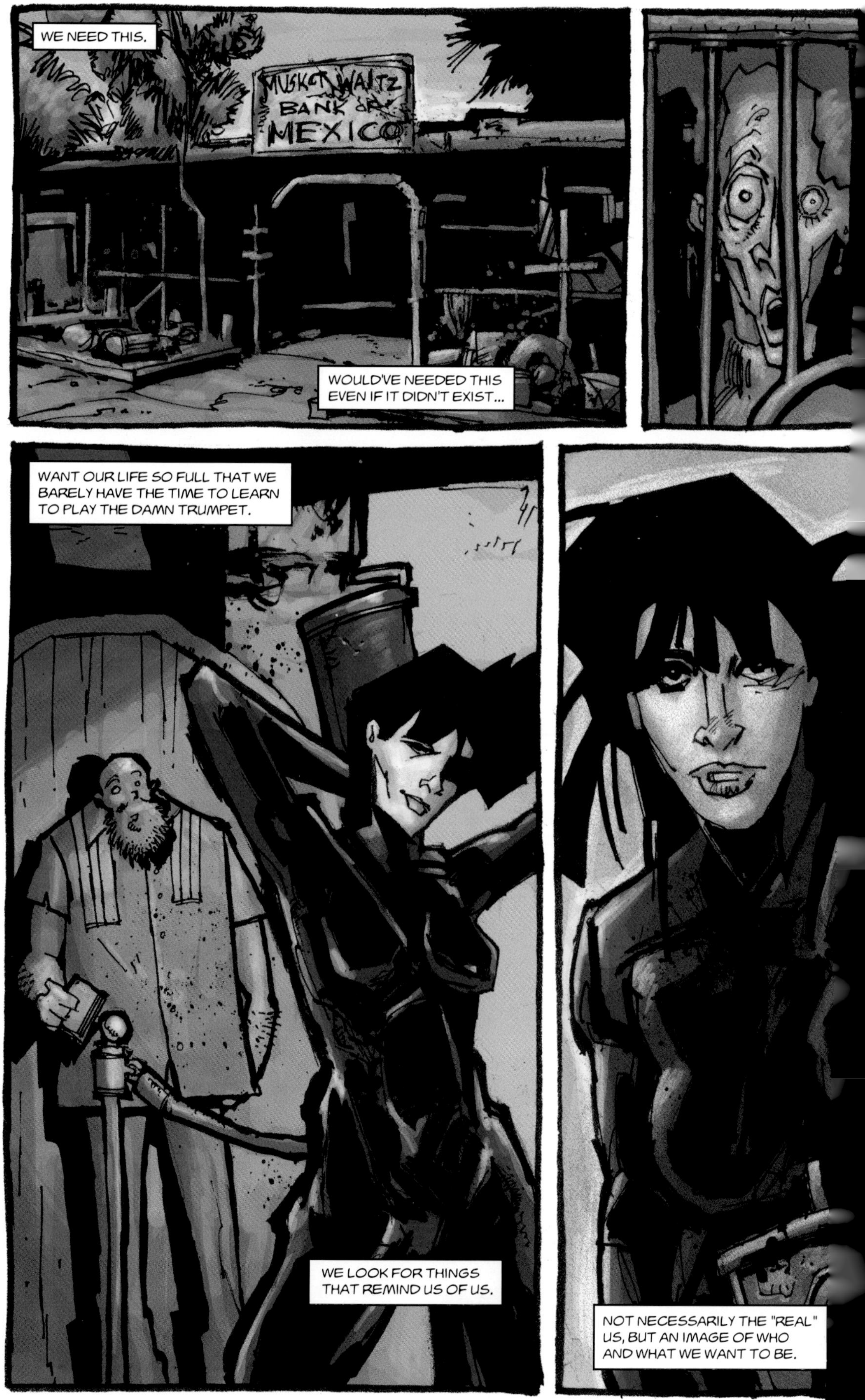
WE NEED THIS.
MUSKOT WALTZ BANK OF MEXICO
WOULD'VE NEEDED THIS EVEN IF IT DIDN'T EXIST...
WANT OUR LIFE SO FULL THAT WE BARELY HAVE THE TIME TO LEARN TO PLAY THE DAMN TRUMPET.
WE LOOK FOR THINGS THAT REMIND US OF US.
NOT NECESSARILY THE "REAL" US, BUT AN IMAGE OF WHO AND WHAT WE WANT TO BE.

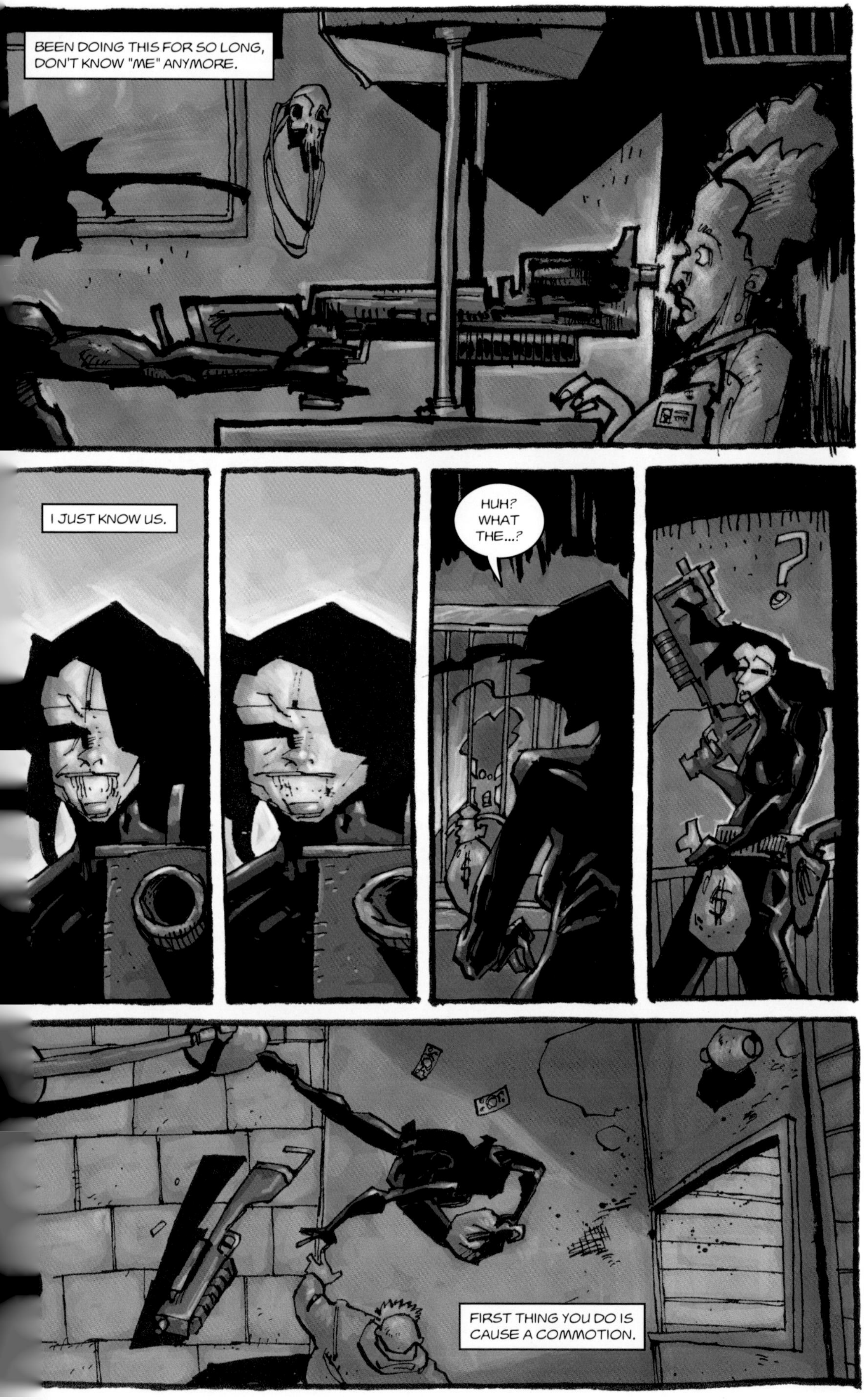
BEEN DOING THIS FOR SO LONG, DON'T KNOW "ME" ANYMORE.
I JUST KNOW US.
HUH? WHAT THE...?
?
FIRST THING YOU DO IS CAUSE A COMMOTION.

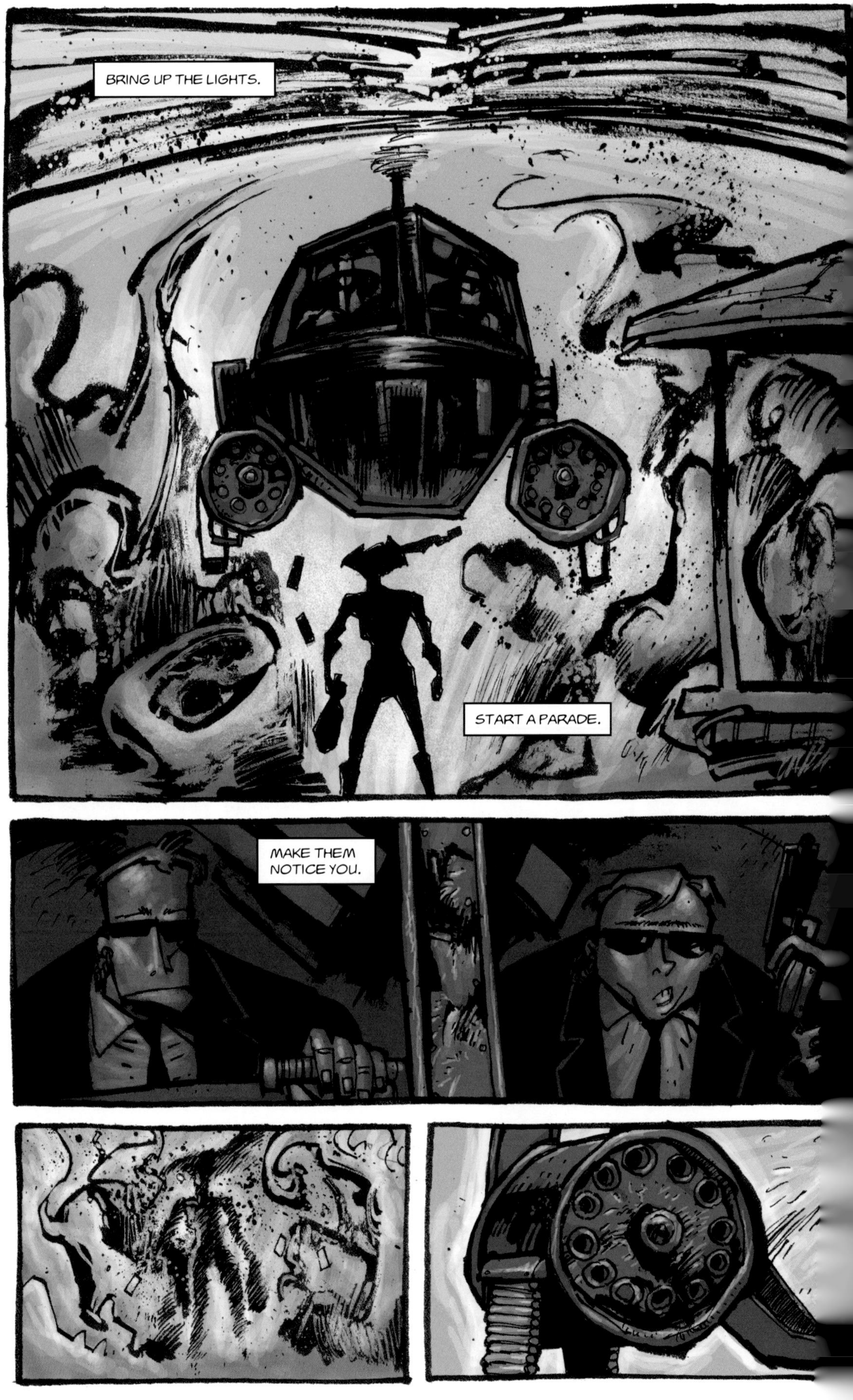
BRING UP THE LIGHTS.
START A PARADE.
MAKE THEM NOTICE YOU.

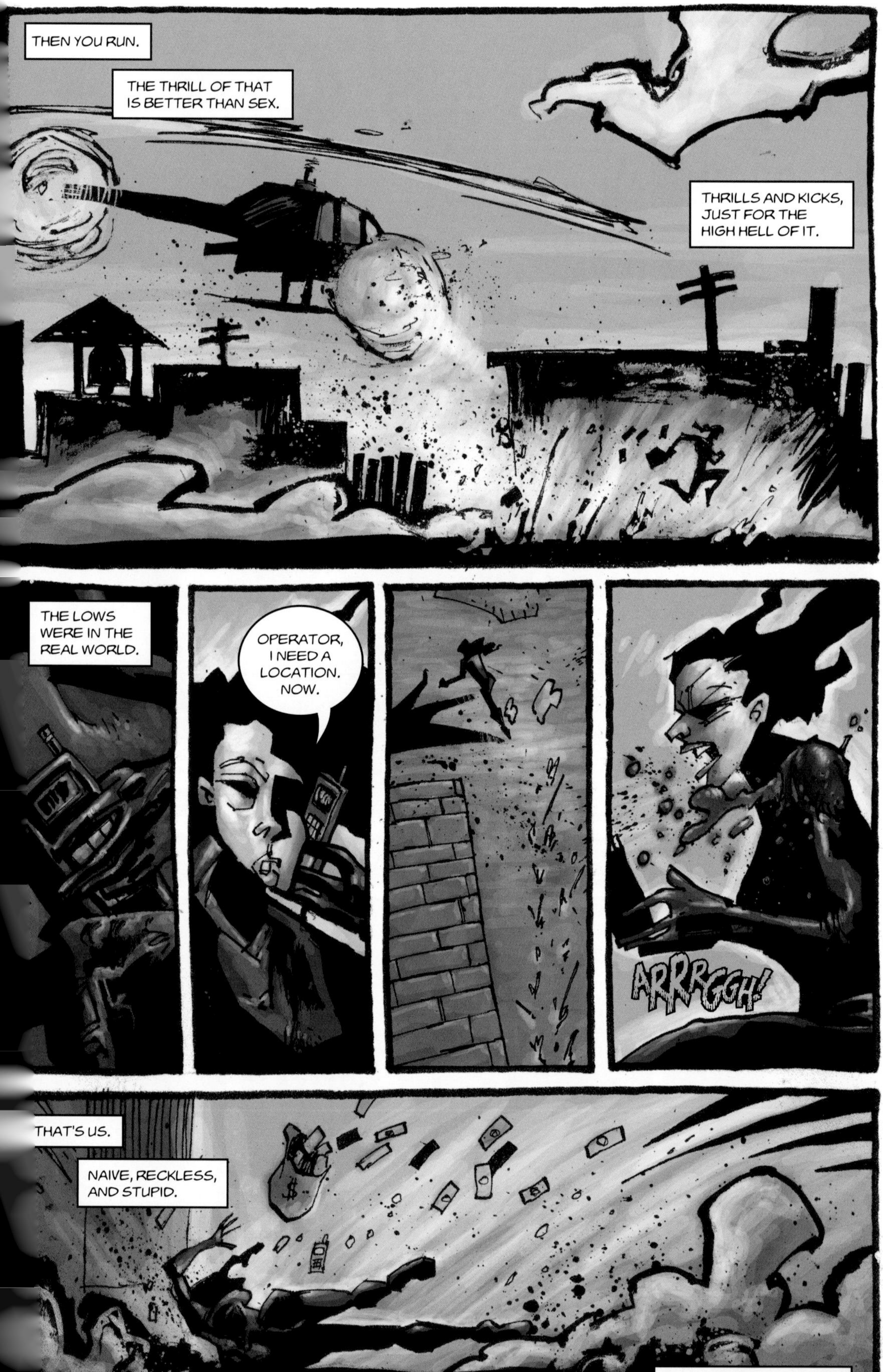
THEN YOU RUN.
THE THRILL OF THAT IS BETTER THAN SEX.
THRILLS AND KICKS, JUST FOR THE HIGH HELL OF IT.
THE LOWS WERE IN THE REAL WORLD.
OPERATOR, I NEED A LOCATION. NOW.
ARRRGGH!
THAT'S US.
NAIVE, RECKLESS, AND STUPID.
WHAT A BREW WE MADE.

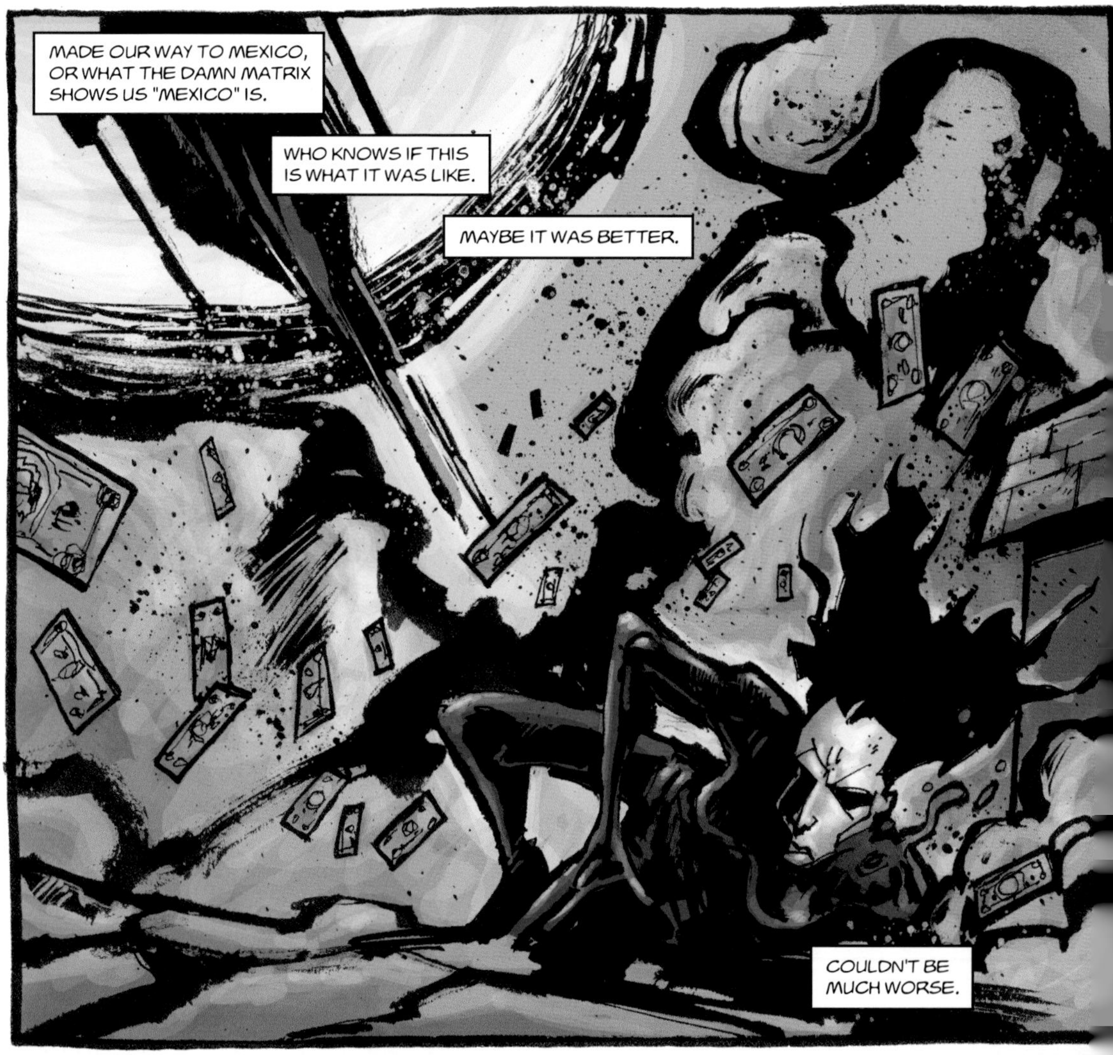
MADE OUR WAY TO MEXICO, OR WHAT THE DAMN MATRIX SHOWS US "MEXICO" IS.
WHO KNOWS IF THIS IS WHAT IT WAS LIKE.
MAYBE IT WAS BETTER.
COULDN'T BE MUCH WORSE.
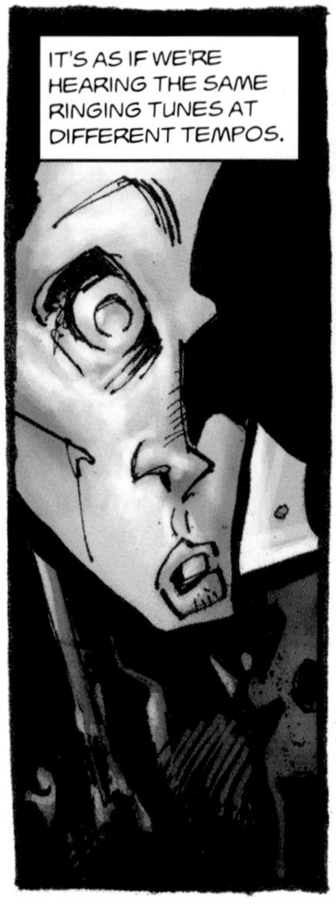
IT'S AS IF WE'RE HEARING THE SAME RINGING TUNES AT DIFFERENT TEMPOS.
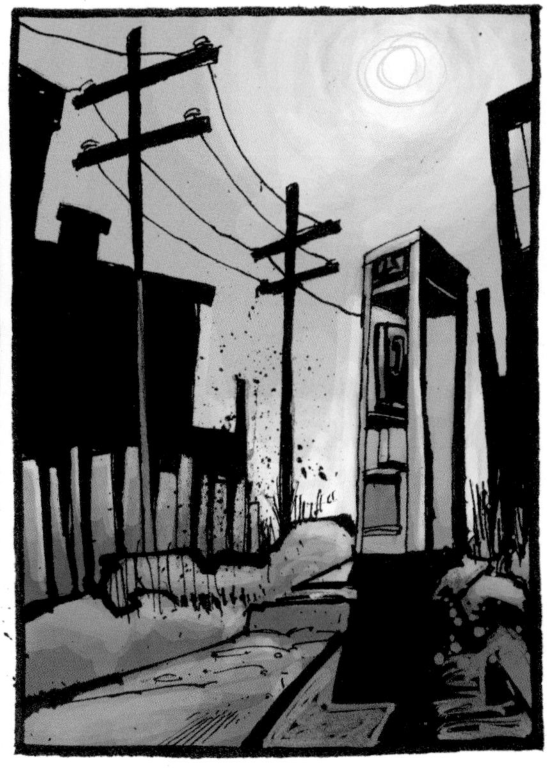
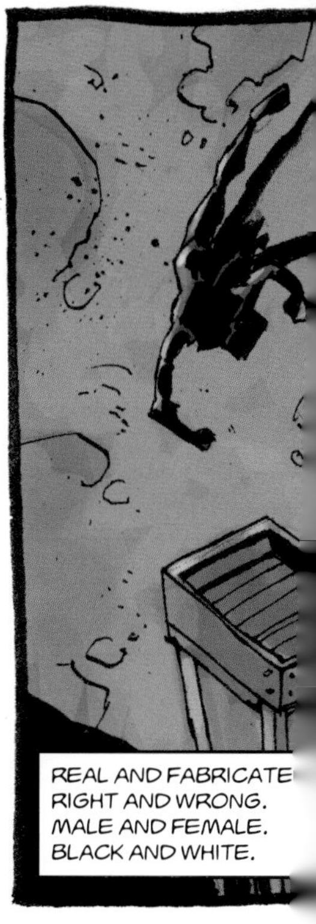
REAL AND FABRICATE
RIGHT AND WRONG.
MALE AND FEMALE.
BLACK AND WHITE.

ONLY WAY TO ENJOY IT ALL WAS TO STOP THINKING ABOUT IT.

I'M HERE.

IS IT MORNING? IS IT NIGHT?

DOESN'T REALLY MATTER IN THE MATRIX. IT'S ALL JUST A GIANT DIGITAL PLAYGROUND TO PRETEND IN.

THE HONEST TRUTH THOUGH, THAT WE WERE ABOUT TO FIND OUT, WAS THAT WE JUST DIDN'T KNOW WHAT THE HELL WE WERE DOING.

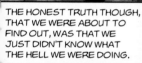

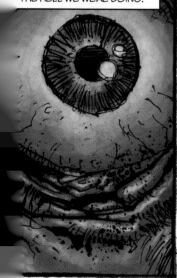

GASP!

WHAT THE HELL WAS THAT?

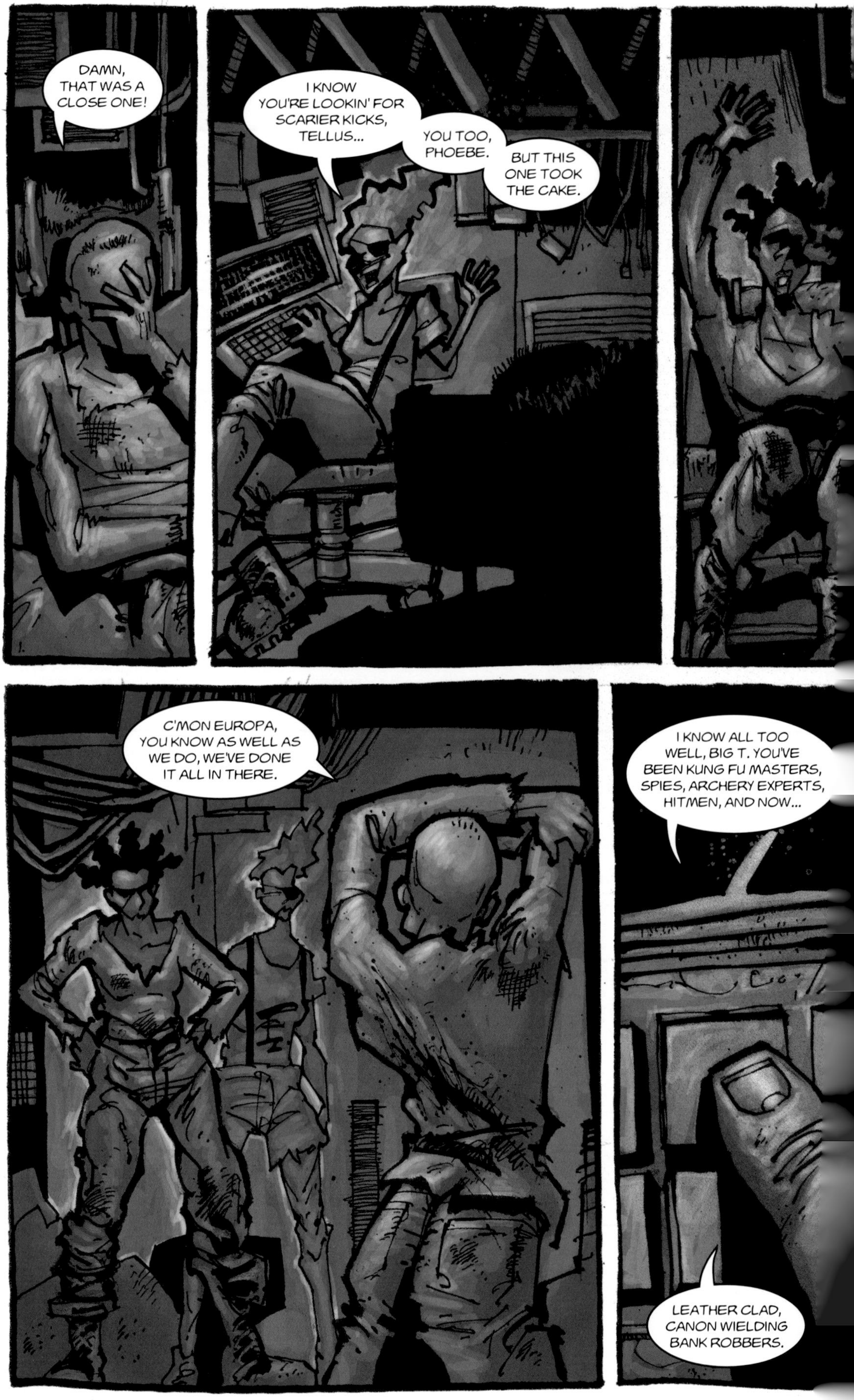
DAMN, THAT WAS A CLOSE ONE!
I KNOW YOU'RE LOOKIN' FOR SCARIER KICKS, TELLUS...
YOU TOO, PHOEBE.
BUT THIS ONE TOOK THE CAKE.
C'MON EUROPA, YOU KNOW AS WELL AS WE DO, WE'VE DONE IT ALL IN THERE.
I KNOW ALL TOO WELL, BIG T. YOU'VE BEEN KUNG FU MASTERS, SPIES, ARCHERY EXPERTS, HITMEN, AND NOW...
LEATHER CLAD, CANON WIELDING BANK ROBBERS.

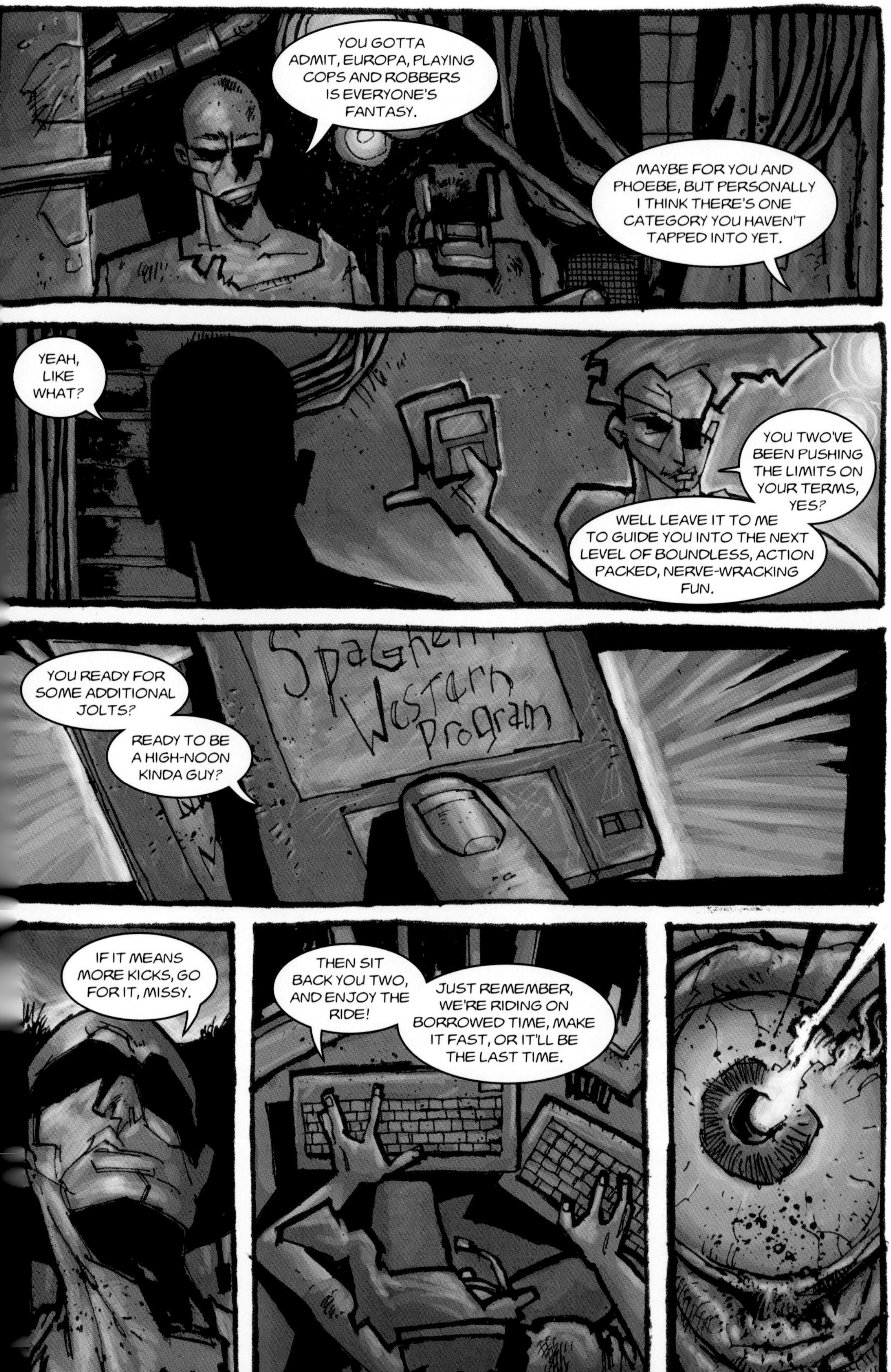
YOU GOTTA ADMIT, EUROPA, PLAYING COPS AND ROBBERS IS EVERYONE'S FANTASY.
MAYBE FOR YOU AND PHOEBE, BUT PERSONALLY I THINK THERE'S ONE CATEGORY YOU HAVEN'T TAPPED INTO YET.
YEAH, LIKE WHAT?
YOU TWO'VE BEEN PUSHING THE LIMITS ON YOUR TERMS, YES?
WELL LEAVE IT TO ME TO GUIDE YOU INTO THE NEXT LEVEL OF BOUNDLESS, ACTION PACKED, NERVE-WRACKING FUN.
YOU READY FOR SOME ADDITIONAL JOLTS?
Spaghetti Western Program
READY TO BE A HIGH-NOON KINDA GUY?
IF IT MEANS MORE KICKS, GO FOR IT, MISSY.
THEN SIT BACK YOU TWO, AND ENJOY THE RIDE!
JUST REMEMBER, WE'RE RIDING ON BORROWED TIME, MAKE IT FAST, OR IT'LL BE THE LAST TIME.

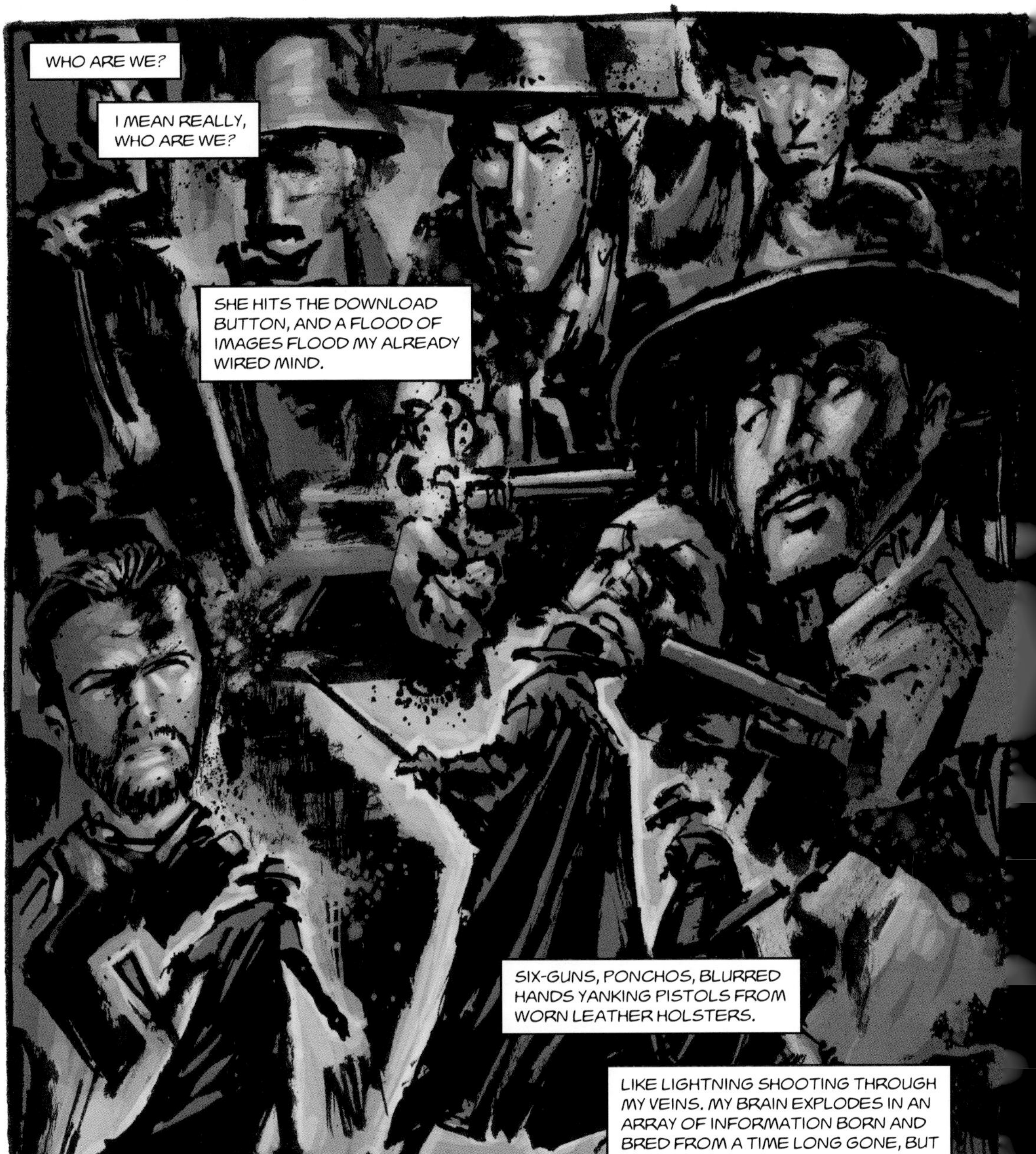
WHO ARE WE?
I MEAN REALLY, WHO ARE WE?
SHE HITS THE DOWNLOAD BUTTON, AND A FLOOD OF IMAGES FLOOD MY ALREADY WIRED MIND.
SIX-GUNS, PONCHOS, BLURRED HANDS YANKING PISTOLS FROM WORN LEATHER HOLSTERS.
LIKE LIGHTNING SHOOTING THROUGH MY VEINS. MY BRAIN EXPLODES IN AN ARRAY OF INFORMATION BORN AND BRED FROM A TIME LONG GONE, BUT OF A TALENT ALWAYS NEEDED.

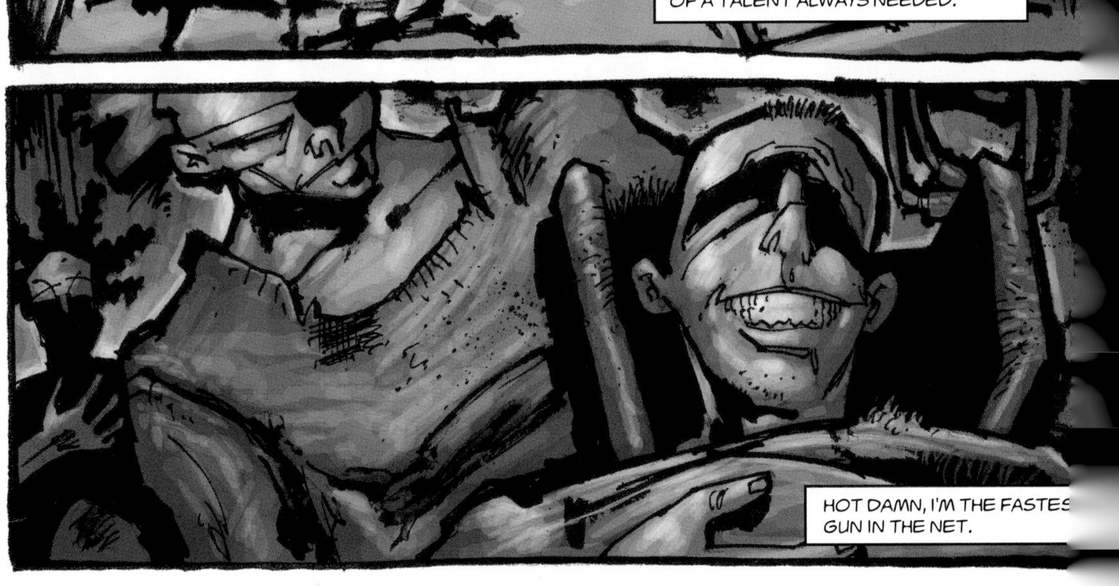
HOT DAMN, I'M THE FASTES
GUN IN THE NET.

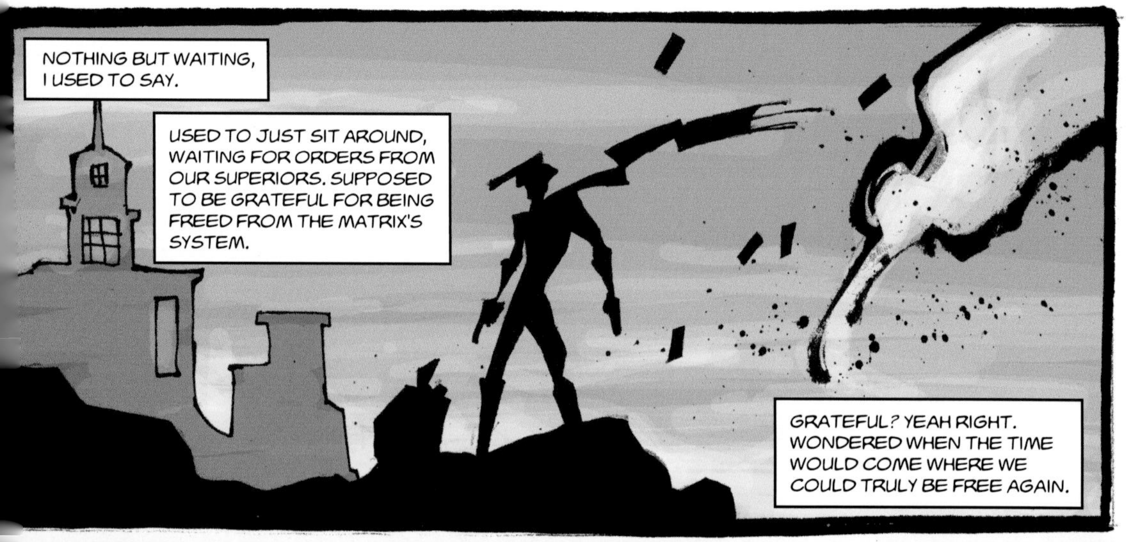
NOTHING BUT WAITING, I USED TO SAY.
USED TO JUST SIT AROUND, WAITING FOR ORDERS FROM OUR SUPERIORS. SUPPOSED TO BE GRATEFUL FOR BEING FREED FROM THE MATRIX'S SYSTEM.
GRATEFUL? YEAH RIGHT. WONDERED WHEN THE TIME WOULD COME WHERE WE COULD TRULY BE FREE AGAIN.
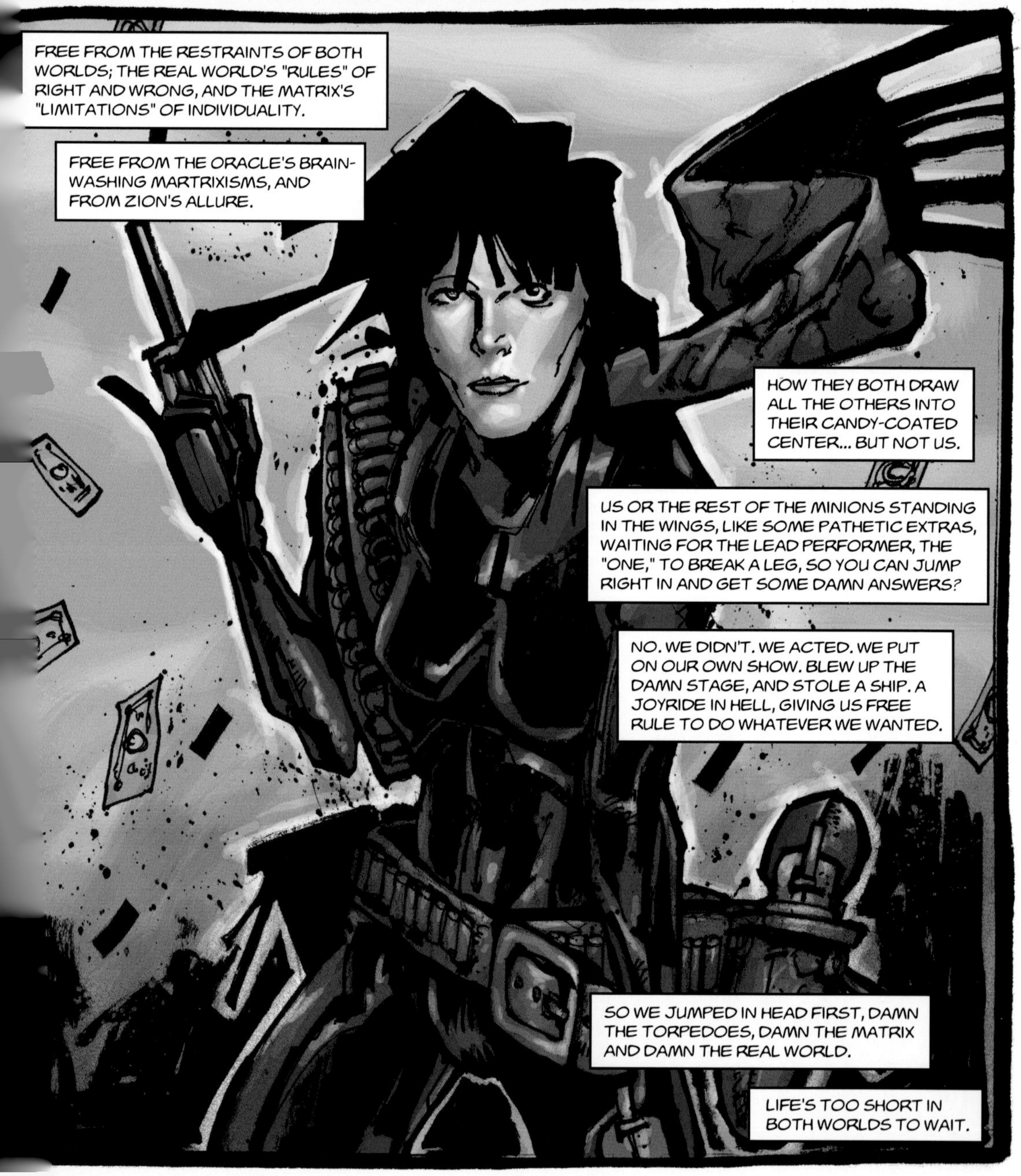
FREE FROM THE RESTRAINTS OF BOTH WORLDS; THE REAL WORLD'S "RULES" OF RIGHT AND WRONG, AND THE MATRIX'S "LIMITATIONS" OF INDIVIDUALITY.
FREE FROM THE ORACLE'S BRAIN-WASHING MARTRIXISMS, AND FROM ZION'S ALLURE.
HOW THEY BOTH DRAW ALL THE OTHERS INTO THEIR CANDY-COATED CENTER... BUT NOT US.
US OR THE REST OF THE MINIONS STANDING IN THE WINGS, LIKE SOME PATHETIC EXTRAS, WAITING FOR THE LEAD PERFORMER, THE "ONE," TO BREAK A LEG, SO YOU CAN JUMP RIGHT IN AND GET SOME DAMN ANSWERS?
NO. WE DIDN'T. WE ACTED. WE PUT ON OUR OWN SHOW. BLEW UP THE DAMN STAGE, AND STOLE A SHIP. A JOYRIDE IN HELL, GIVING US FREE RULE TO DO WHATEVER WE WANTED.
SO WE JUMPED IN HEAD FIRST, DAMN THE TORPEDOES, DAMN THE MATRIX AND DAMN THE REAL WORLD.
LIFE'S TOO SHORT IN BOTH WORLDS TO WAIT.

SO NOW WE'RE IN A SPAGHETTI WESTERN OF OUR OWN DEVISING.

ONCE AGAIN, WE CAUSED A COMMOTION, USUAL BANK ROBBERY KIND OF STUFF, EASY FOR THE AGENTS TO DETECT US.

AND THEY WERE HERE IN NO TIME.

FUNNY THING ABOUT AGENTS IS THAT THEY SEEM AS BORED AS WE ARE, THEY SEEM TO ALWAYS BE LOOKING FOR AN INTERESTING WAY TO KILL US OFF.

GOOD THING FOR US, THEN. GIVES US A FIGHTING CHANCE.

AT LEAST IN OUR EYES.

REGRETTING THAT AGENTS WEAR SUNGLASSES. WE WANT TO SEE HIS EYES WHEN WE DRAW. LIKE IN THOSE WESTERNS THAT HAVE CLOSE-UPS OF THE DUELERS' EYES.

READY TO DRAW, TRIGGER FINGER AT THE READY.

HE DRAWS HIS WEAPON.

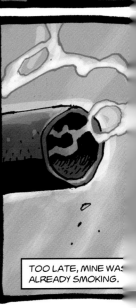

TOO LATE, MINE WAS ALREADY SMOKING.

DAMN WE'RE GOOD.

YOU MISSED.

NO, I DIDN'T.

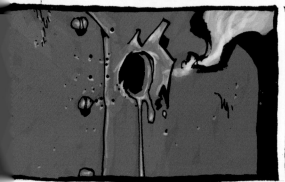

WHAT?!?

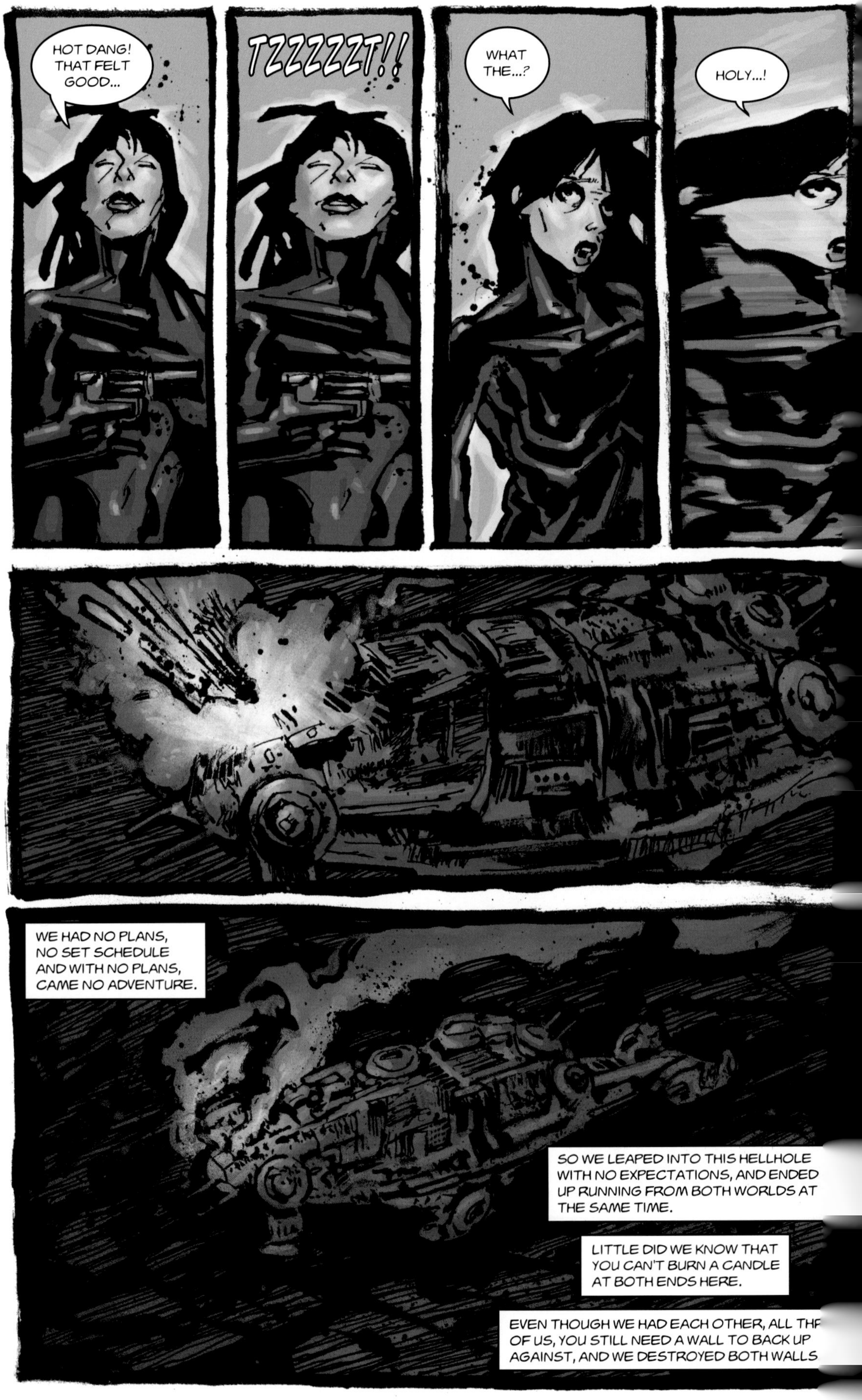
HOT DANG! THAT FELT GOOD...
TZZZZZT!!
WHAT THE...?
HOLY...!
WE HAD NO PLANS, NO SET SCHEDULE AND WITH NO PLANS, CAME NO ADVENTURE.
SO WE LEAPED INTO THIS HELLHOLE WITH NO EXPECTATIONS, AND ENDED UP RUNNING FROM BOTH WORLDS AT THE SAME TIME.
LITTLE DID WE KNOW THAT YOU CAN'T BURN A CANDLE AT BOTH ENDS HERE.
EVEN THOUGH WE HAD EACH OTHER, ALL THR OF US, YOU STILL NEED A WALL TO BACK UP AGAINST, AND WE DESTROYED BOTH WALLS

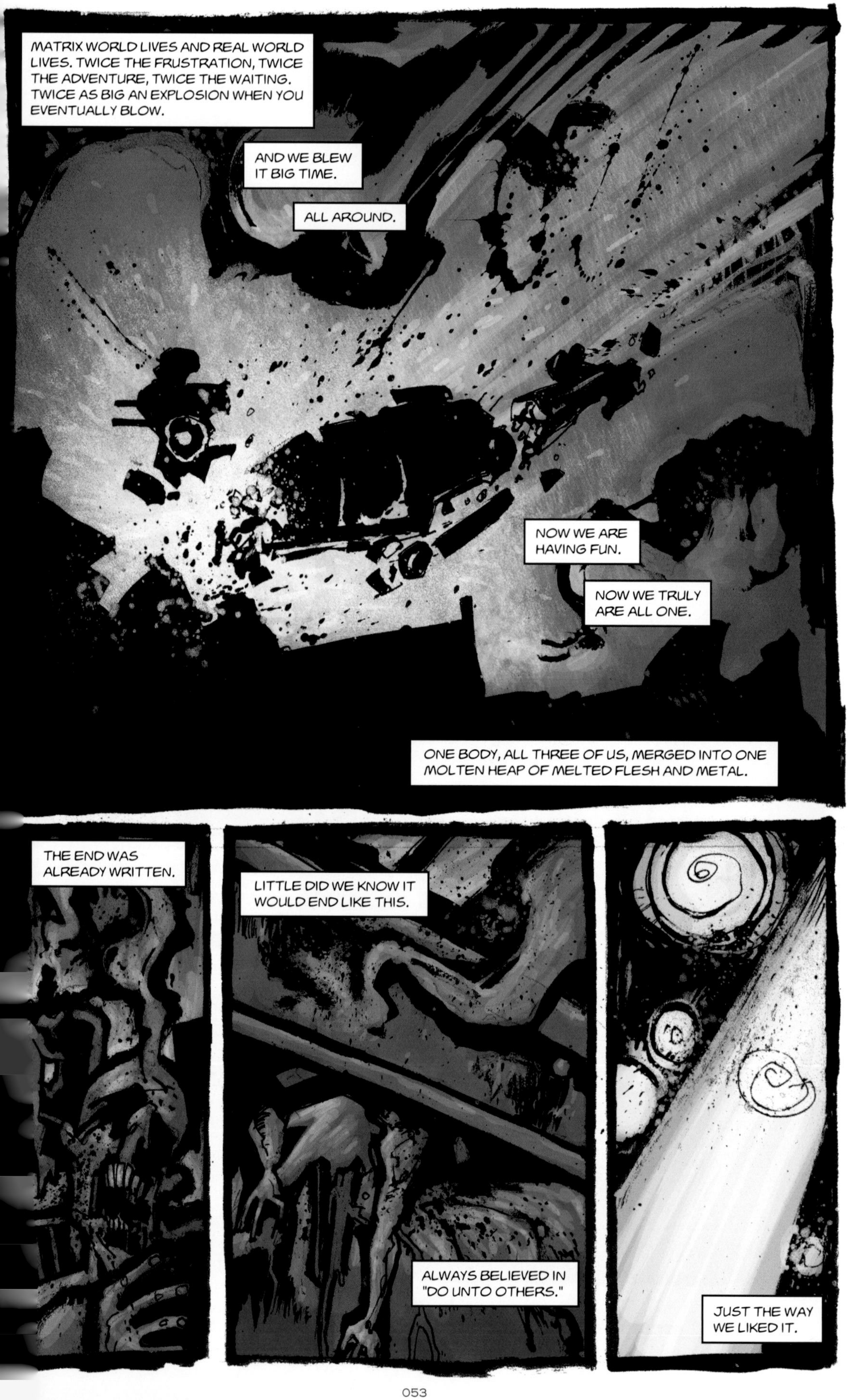
MATRIX WORLD LIVES AND REAL WORLD LIVES. TWICE THE FRUSTRATION, TWICE THE ADVENTURE, TWICE THE WAITING. TWICE AS BIG AN EXPLOSION WHEN YOU EVENTUALLY BLOW.
AND WE BLEW IT BIG TIME.
ALL AROUND.
NOW WE ARE HAVING FUN.
NOW WE TRULY ARE ALL ONE.
ONE BODY, ALL THREE OF US, MERGED INTO ONE MOLTEN HEAP OF MELTED FLESH AND METAL.
THE END WAS ALREADY WRITTEN.
LITTLE DID WE KNOW IT WOULD END LIKE THIS.
ALWAYS BELIEVED IN "DO UNTO OTHERS."
JUST THE WAY WE LIKED IT.

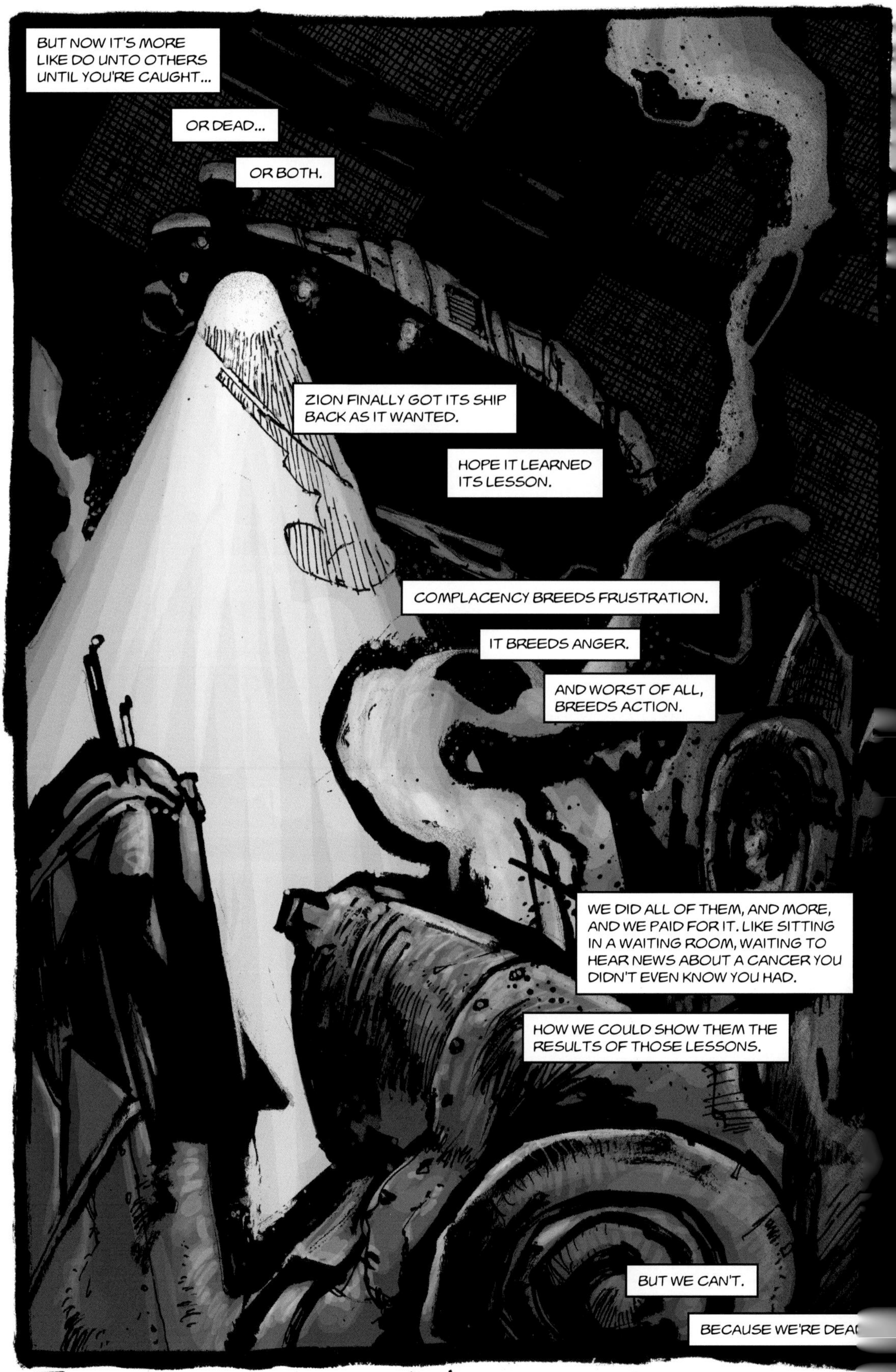
BUT NOW IT'S MORE LIKE DO UNTO OTHERS UNTIL YOU'RE CAUGHT...
OR DEAD...
OR BOTH.
ZION FINALLY GOT ITS SHIP BACK AS IT WANTED.
HOPE IT LEARNED ITS LESSON.
COMPLACENCY BREEDS FRUSTRATION.
IT BREEDS ANGER.
AND WORST OF ALL, BREEDS ACTION.
WE DID ALL OF THEM, AND MORE, AND WE PAID FOR IT. LIKE SITTING IN A WAITING ROOM, WAITING TO HEAR NEWS ABOUT A CANCER YOU DIDN'T EVEN KNOW YOU HAD.
HOW WE COULD SHOW THEM THE RESULTS OF THOSE LESSONS.
BUT WE CAN'T.
BECAUSE WE'RE DEA

E • N • D

STORY AND ART BY TED McKEEVER - 2000

colors by Chris Chuckry • edits by Spencer Lamm

based on concepts by Larry & Andy Wachowski

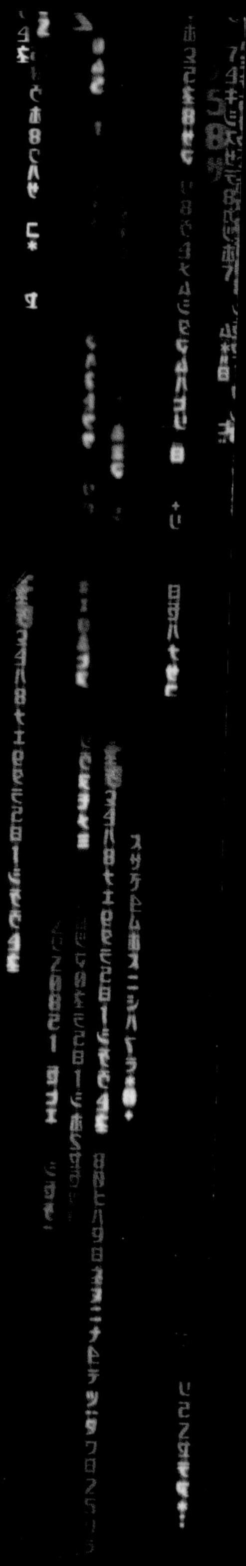

AN ASSET TO THE SYSTEM

PLOT & ART BY TROY
NIXEY

Troy Nixey has illustrated a number of notable creators' work. They include Mike Mignola who wrote: BATMAN: THE DOOM THAT CAME TO GOTHAM and BATMAN: THE GASWORKS, Neil Gaiman who wrote (with P. Craig Russell adapting): IT'S ONLY THE END OF THE WORLD AGAIN, and Matt Wagner who wrote GRENDEL: BLACK, WHITE & RED. Troy co-created the comic mini series JENNY FINN with Mike Mignola; he created the BACON comic as well as the critically acclaimed comic, TROUT. His favorite project to date was a story he wrote and drew in BART SIMPSON'S TREEHOUSE OF HORROR #7. Recent work includes DETECTIVE COMICS #796, written by Andersen Gabrych, BATMAN: LEGENDS OF THE DARK KNIGHT #183, and BATMAN: WAR DRUMS... and there will, of course, be more TROUT!

An Asset to the System

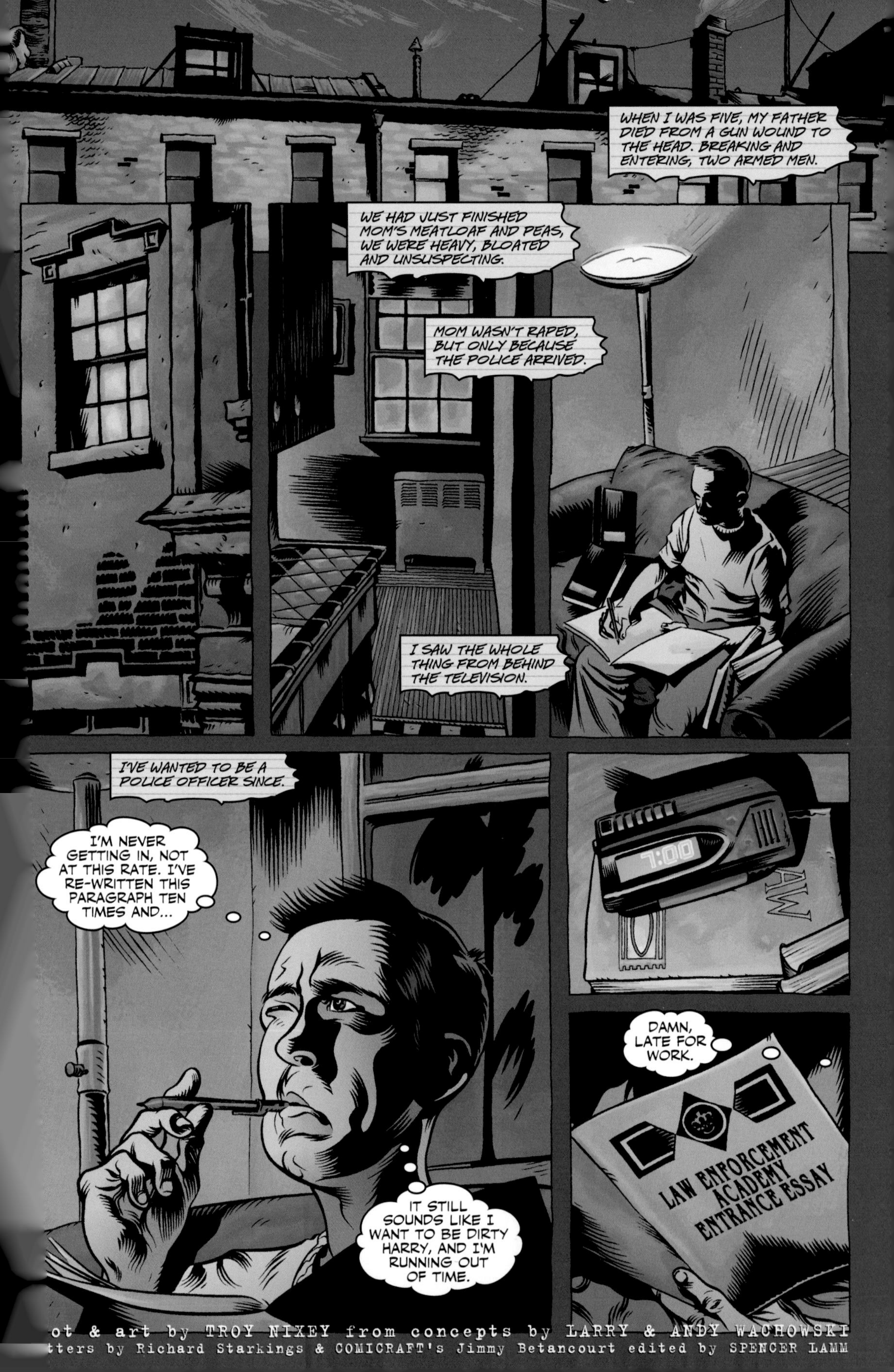

WHEN I WAS FIVE, MY FATHER DIED FROM A GUN WOUND TO THE HEAD. BREAKING AND ENTERING, TWO ARMED MEN.
WE HAD JUST FINISHED MOM'S MEATLOAF AND PEAS, WE WERE HEAVY, BLOATED AND UNSUSPECTING.
MOM WASN'T RAPED, BUT ONLY BECAUSE THE POLICE ARRIVED.
I SAW THE WHOLE THING FROM BEHIND THE TELEVISION.
I'VE WANTED TO BE A POLICE OFFICER SINCE.
I'M NEVER GETTING IN, NOT AT THIS RATE. I'VE RE-WRITTEN THIS PARAGRAPH TEN TIMES AND...
IT STILL SOUNDS LIKE I WANT TO BE DIRTY HARRY, AND I'M RUNNING OUT OF TIME.
7:00
DAMN, LATE FOR WORK.
LAW ENFORCEMENT ACADEMY ENTRANCE ESSAY

ot & art by TROY NIXEY from concepts by LARRY & ANDY WACHOWSKI
tters by Richard Starkings & COMICRAFT's Jimmy Betancourt edited by SPENCER LAMM

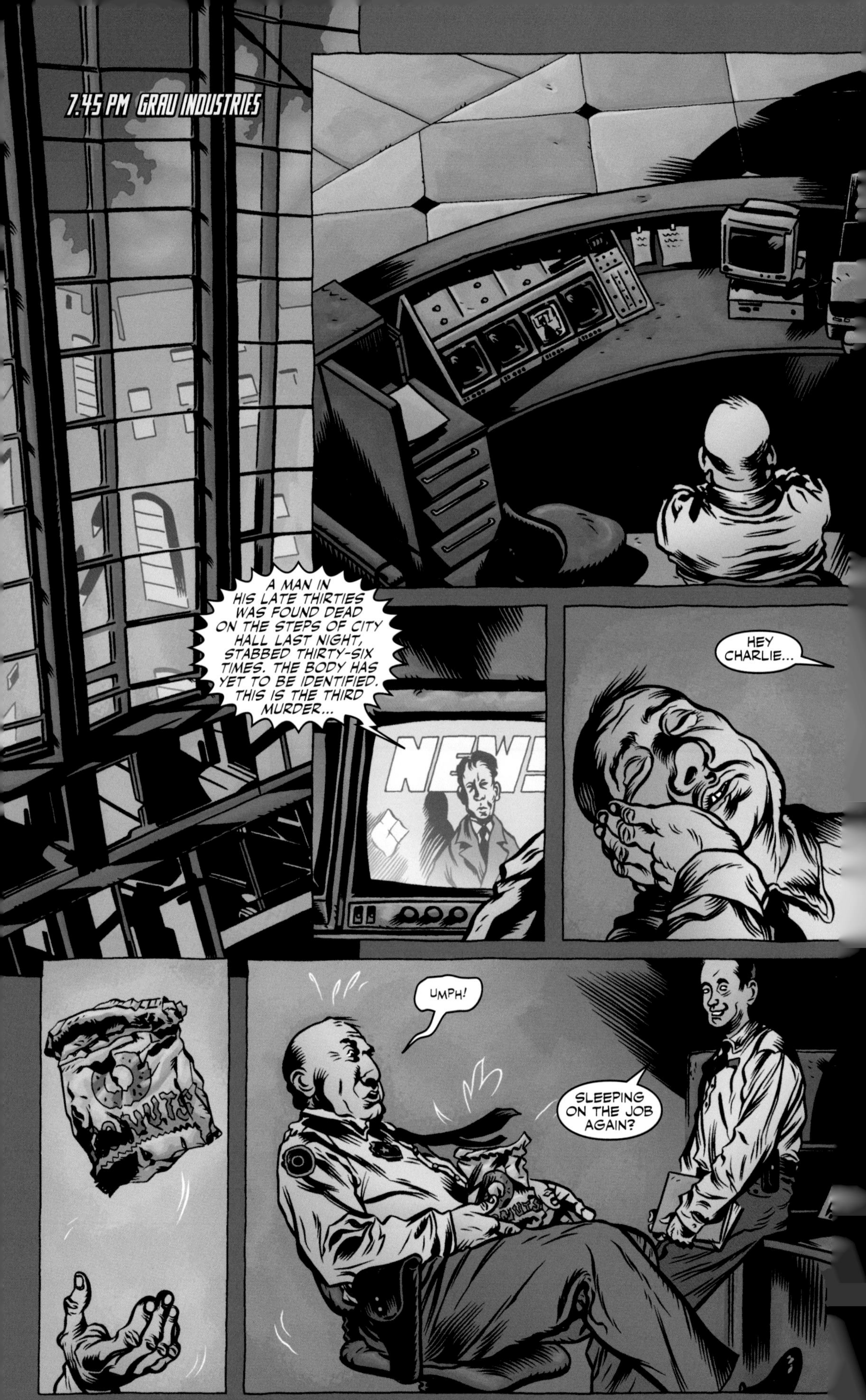
7.45 PM GRAU INDUSTRIES
A MAN IN HIS LATE THIRTIES WAS FOUND DEAD ON THE STEPS OF CITY HALL LAST NIGHT, STABBED THIRTY-SIX TIMES. THE BODY HAS YET TO BE IDENTIFIED. THIS IS THE THIRD MURDER...
NEWS
HEY CHARLIE...
UMPH!
SLEEPING ON THE JOB AGAIN?

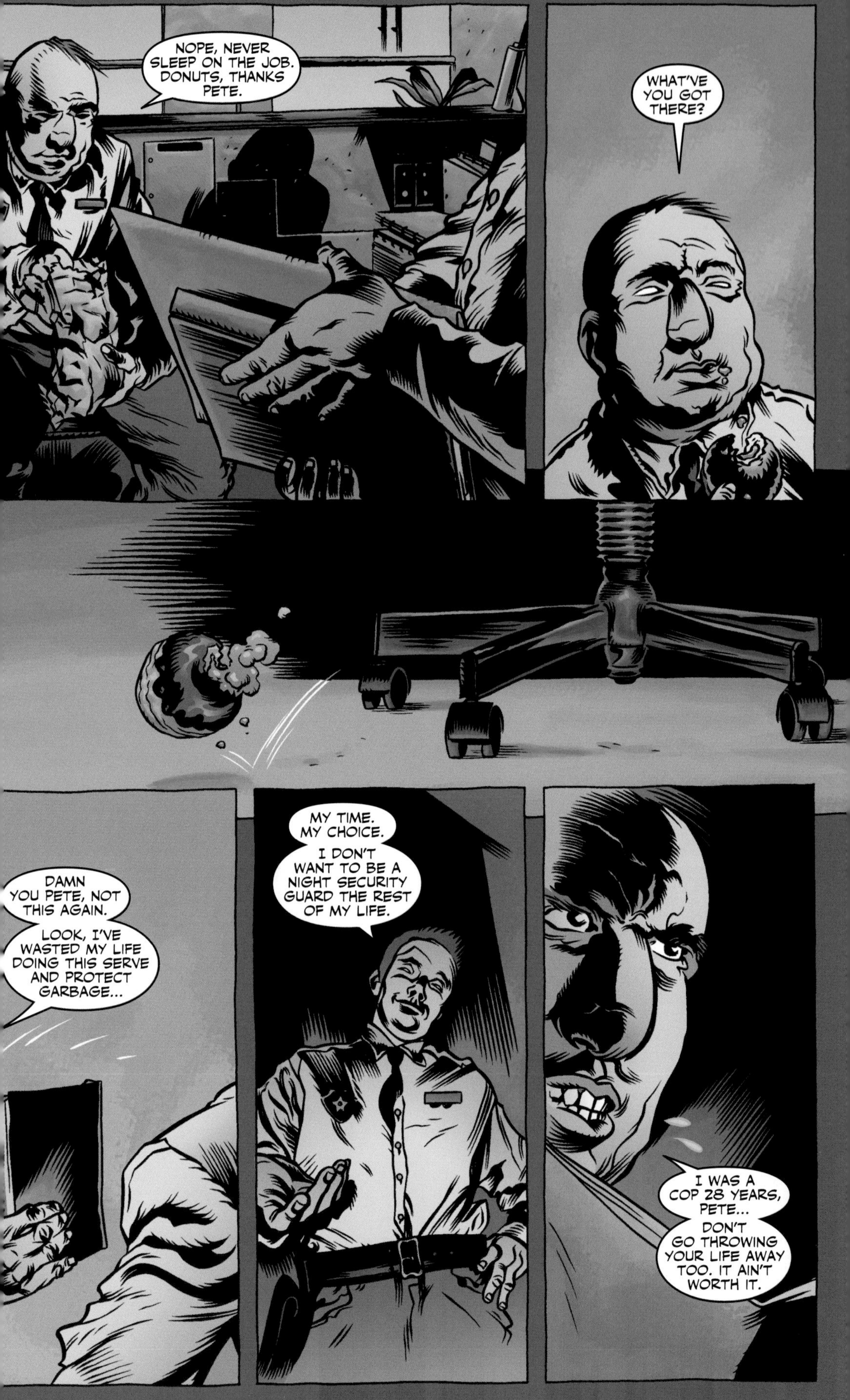
NOPE, NEVER SLEEP ON THE JOB. DONUTS, THANKS PETE.
WHAT'VE YOU GOT THERE?
DAMN YOU PETE, NOT THIS AGAIN.
LOOK, I'VE WASTED MY LIFE DOING THIS SERVE AND PROTECT GARBAGE...
MY TIME. MY CHOICE.
I DON'T WANT TO BE A NIGHT SECURITY GUARD THE REST OF MY LIFE.
I WAS A COP 28 YEARS, PETE...
DON'T GO THROWING YOUR LIFE AWAY TOO. IT AIN'T WORTH IT.

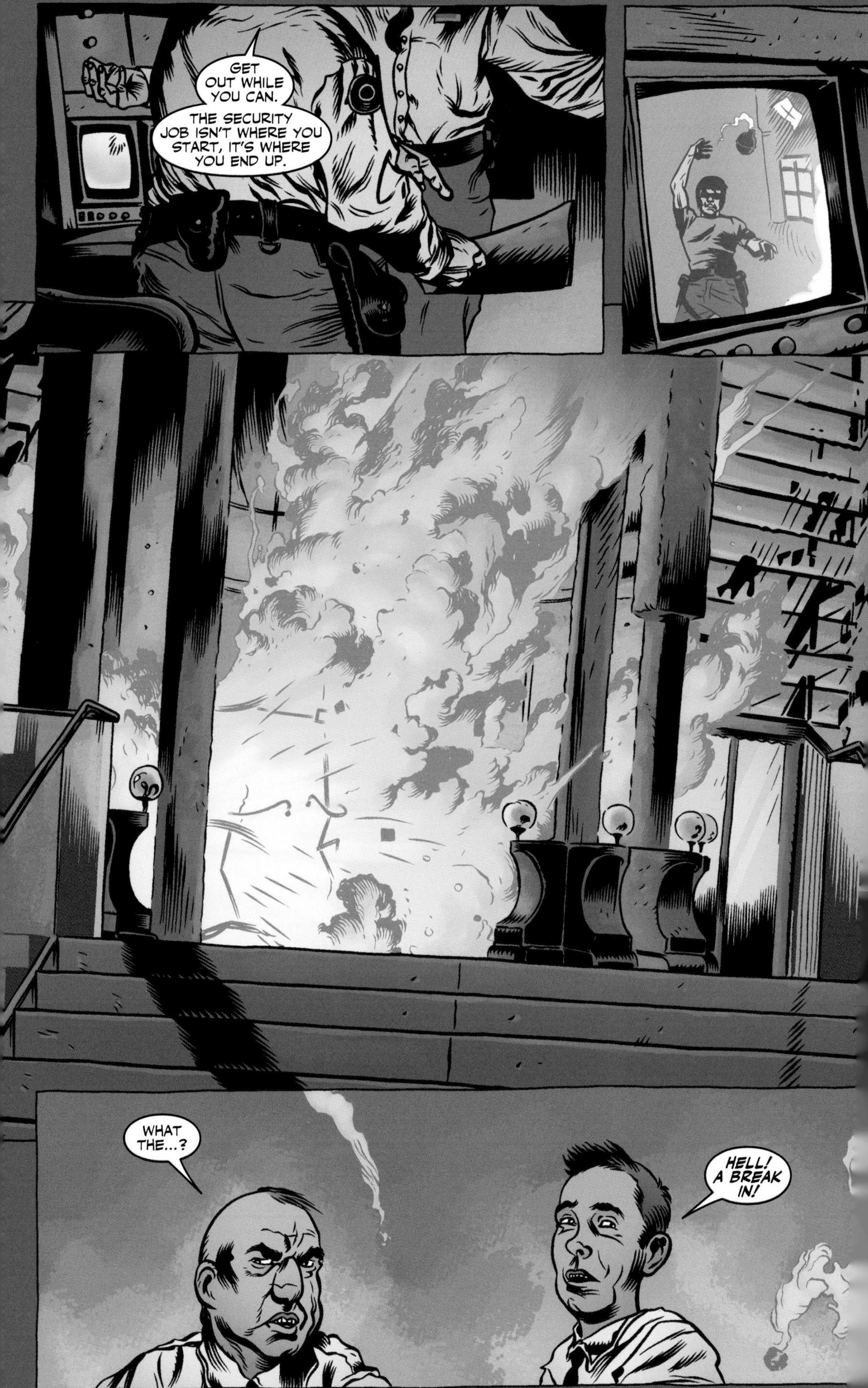
GET OUT WHILE YOU CAN.
THE SECURITY JOB ISN'T WHERE YOU START, IT'S WHERE YOU END UP.
WHAT THE...?
HELL! A BREAK IN!

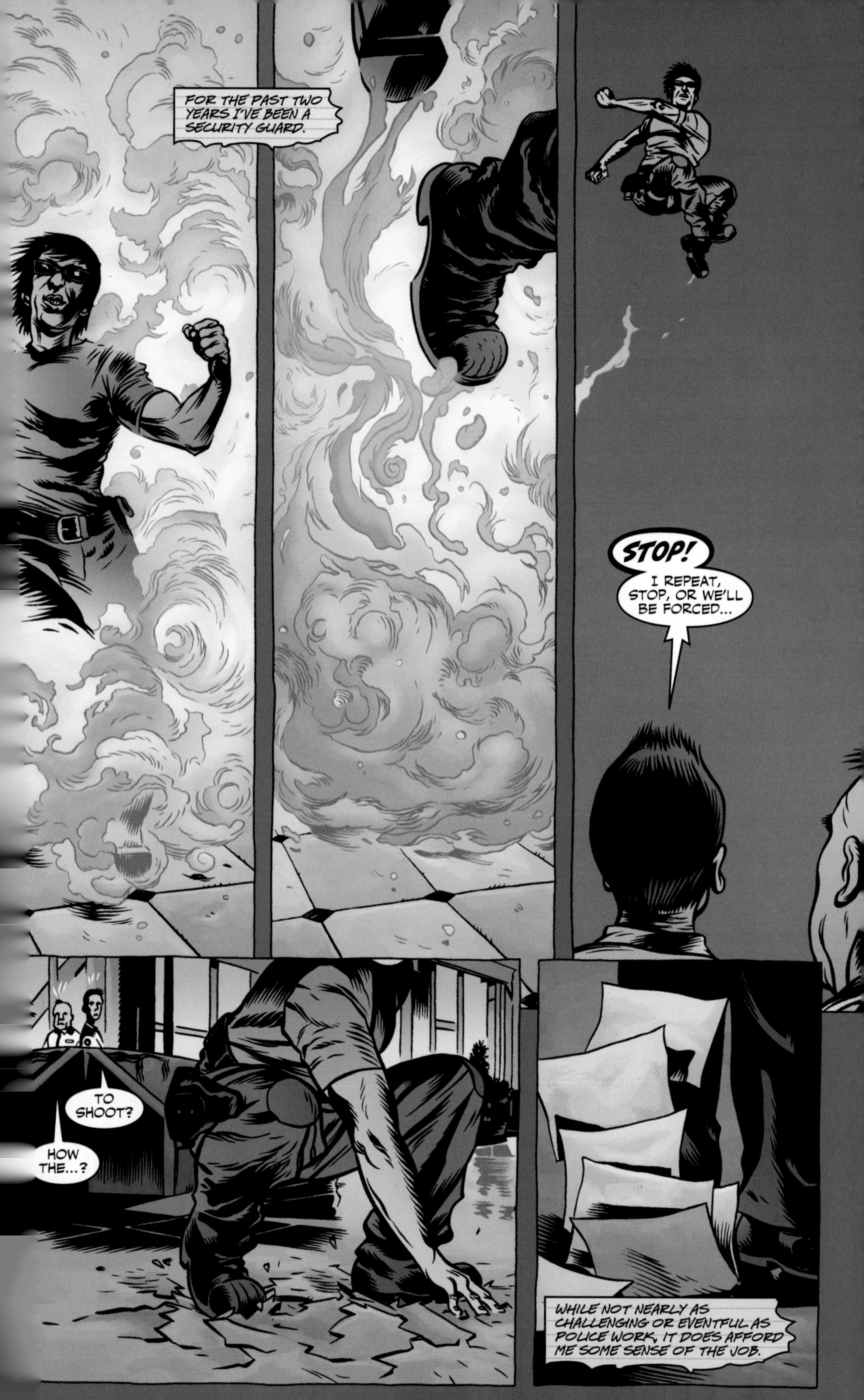
FOR THE PAST TWO YEARS I'VE BEEN A SECURITY GUARD.
STOP!
I REPEAT, STOP, OR WE'LL BE FORCED...
HOW THE...?
TO SHOOT?
WHILE NOT NEARLY AS CHALLENGING OR EVENTFUL AS POLICE WORK, IT DOES AFFORD ME SOME SENSE OF THE JOB.

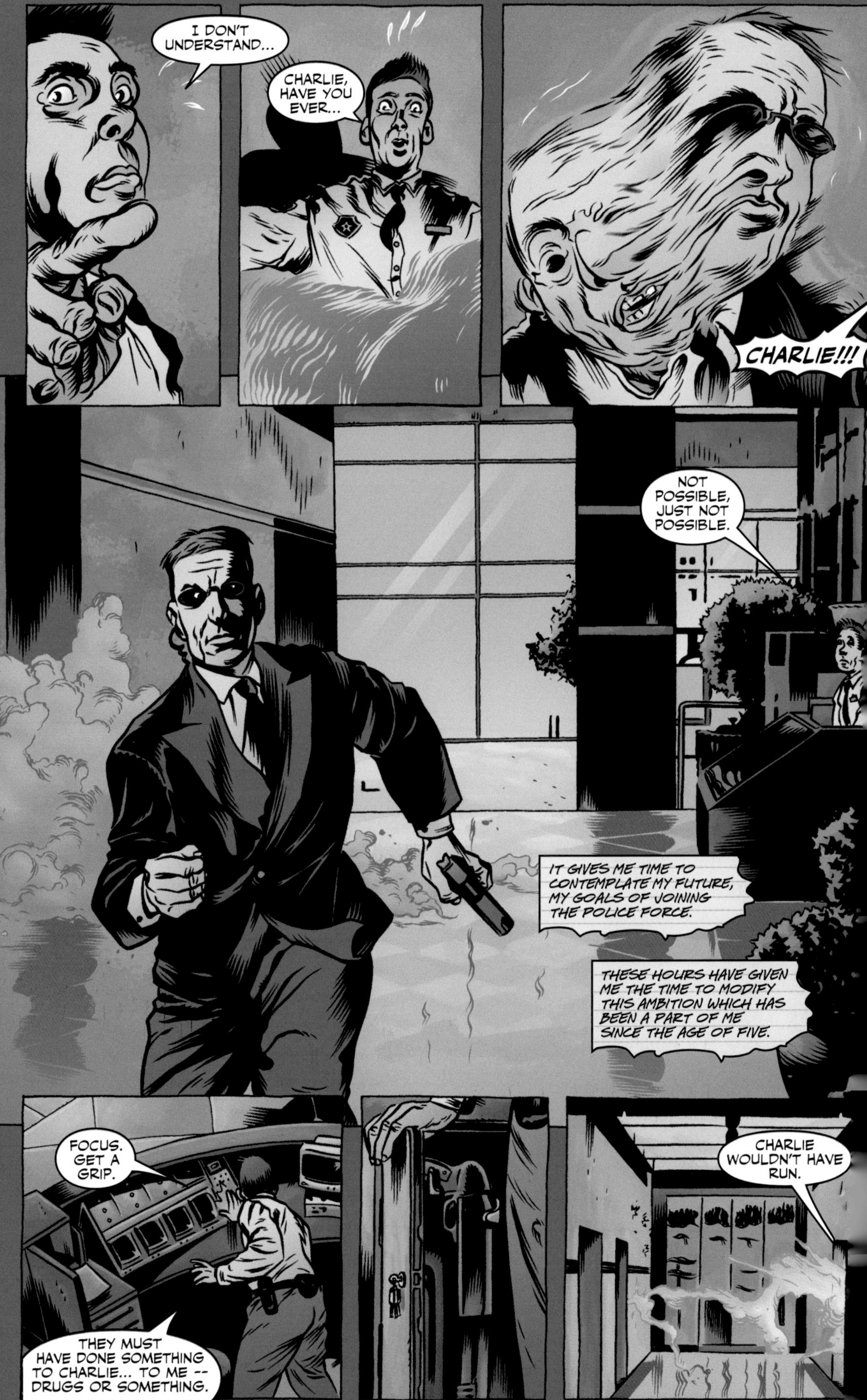
I DON'T UNDERSTAND...
CHARLIE, HAVE YOU EVER...
CHARLIE!!!
NOT POSSIBLE, JUST NOT POSSIBLE.
IT GIVES ME TIME TO CONTEMPLATE MY FUTURE, MY GOALS OF JOINING THE POLICE FORCE.
THESE HOURS HAVE GIVEN ME THE TIME TO MODIFY THIS AMBITION WHICH HAS BEEN A PART OF ME SINCE THE AGE OF FIVE.
FOCUS. GET A GRIP.
THEY MUST HAVE DONE SOMETHING TO CHARLIE... TO ME -- DRUGS OR SOMETHING.
CHARLIE WOULDN'T HAVE RUN.

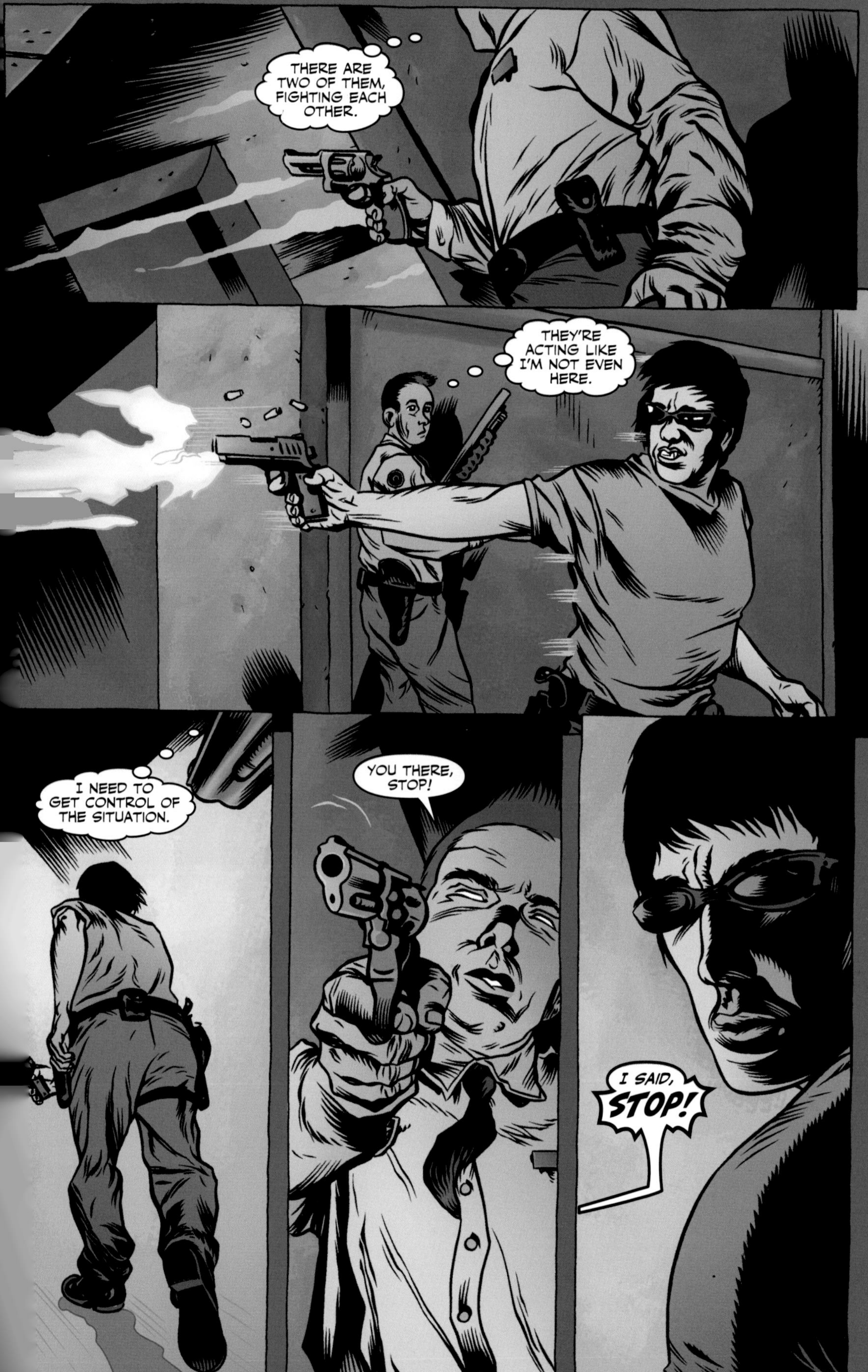
THERE ARE TWO OF THEM, FIGHTING EACH OTHER.
THEY'RE ACTING LIKE I'M NOT EVEN HERE.
I NEED TO GET CONTROL OF THE SITUATION.
YOU THERE, STOP!
I SAID, STOP!

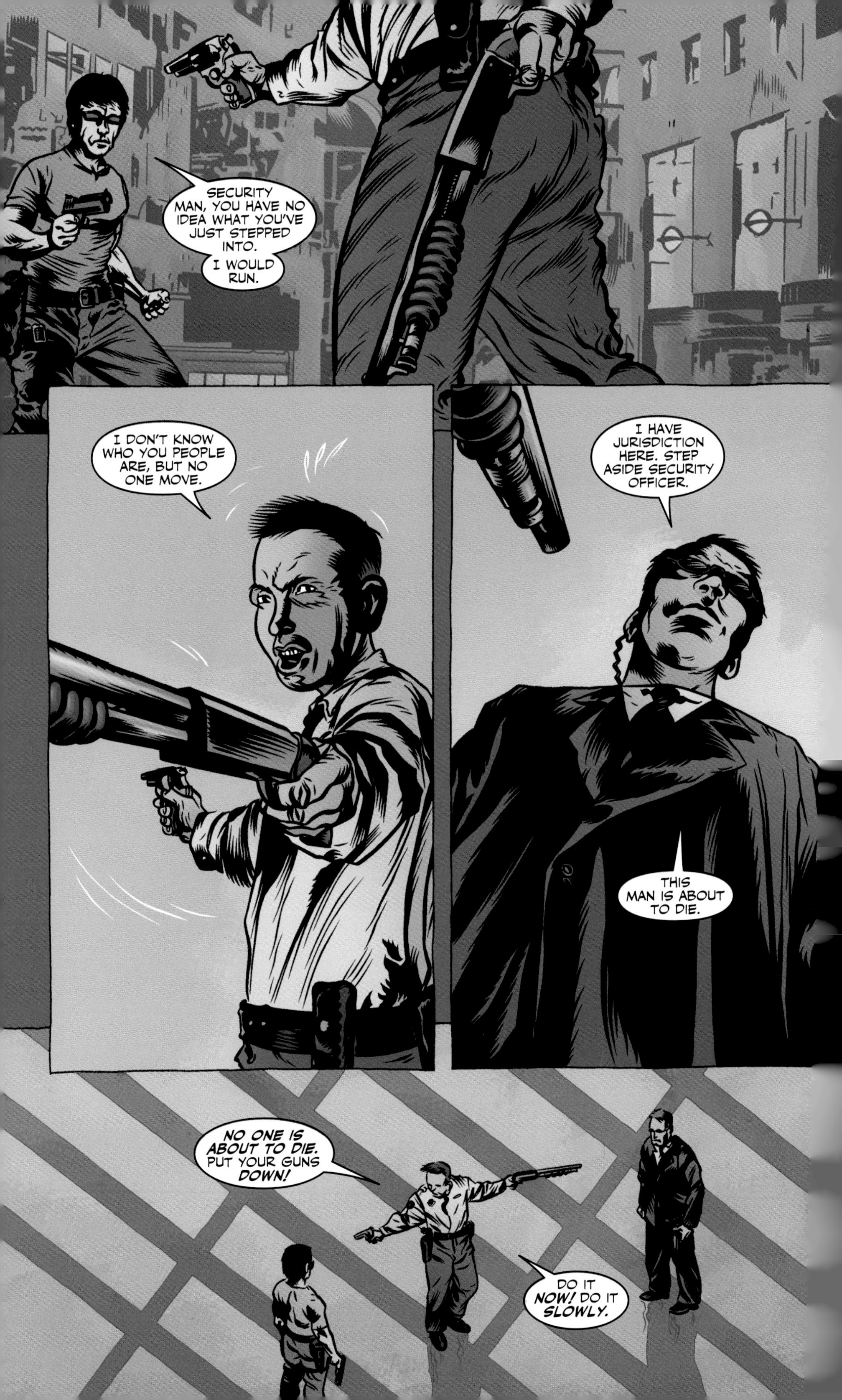
SECURITY MAN, YOU HAVE NO IDEA WHAT YOU'VE JUST STEPPED INTO.
I WOULD RUN.
I DON'T KNOW WHO YOU PEOPLE ARE, BUT NO ONE MOVE.
I HAVE JURISDICTION HERE. STEP ASIDE SECURITY OFFICER.
THIS MAN IS ABOUT TO DIE.
NO ONE IS ABOUT TO DIE. PUT YOUR GUNS DOWN!
DO IT NOW! DO IT SLOWLY.

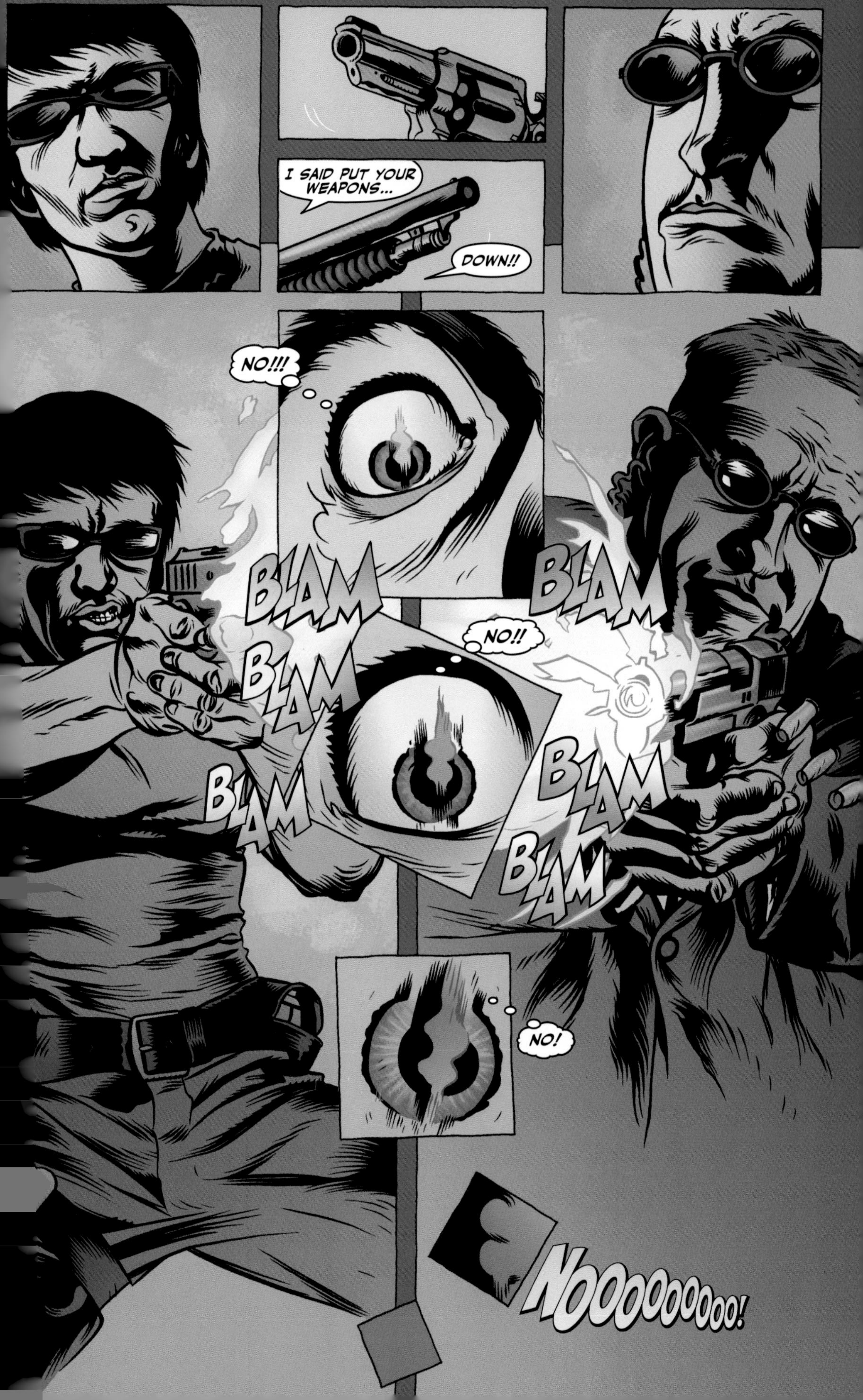
I SAID PUT YOUR WEAPONS...
DOWN!!
NO!!!
BLAM
BLAM
BLAM
BLAM
NO!!
BLAM
BLAM
NO!
NOOOOOOOOOO!

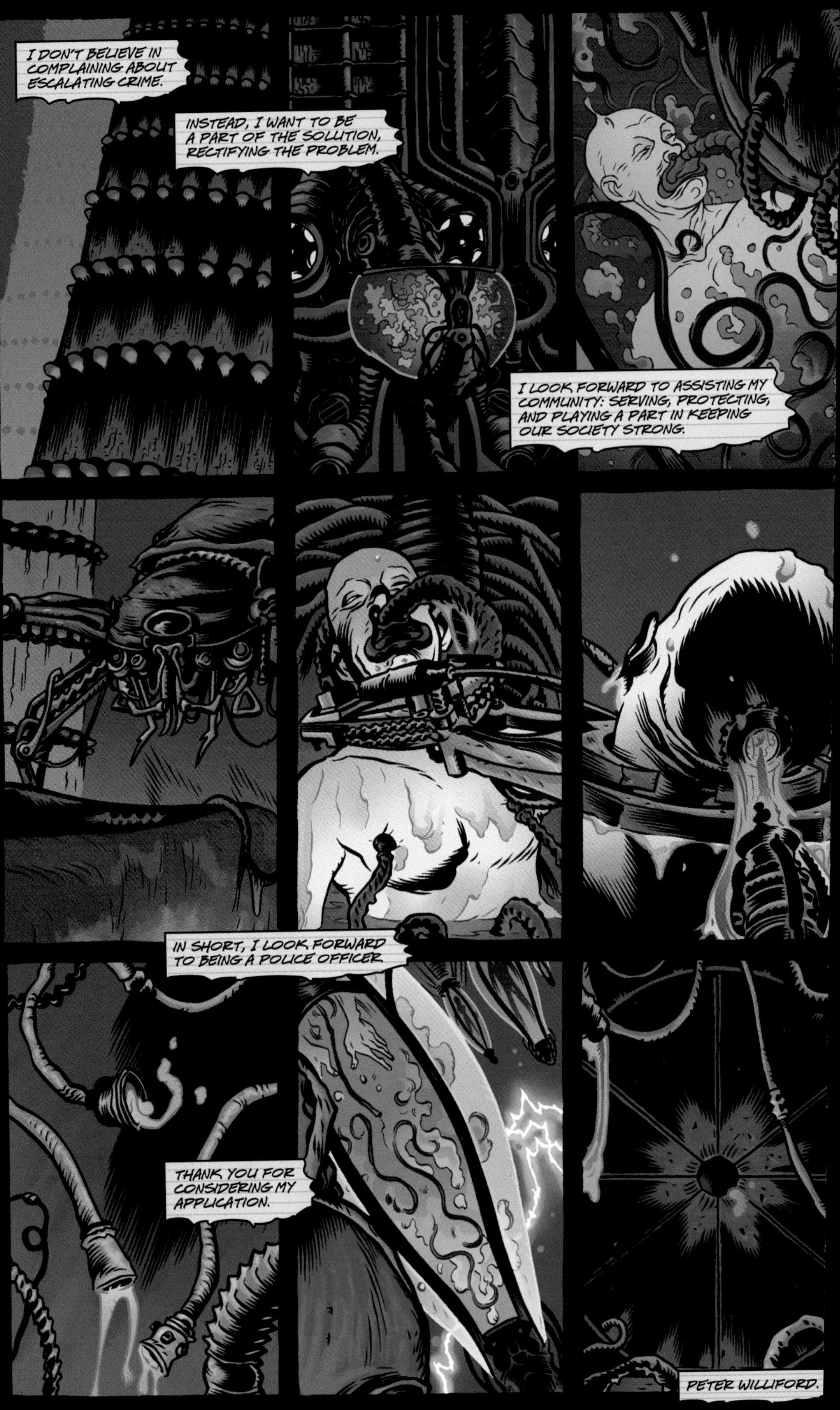
I DON'T BELIEVE IN COMPLAINING ABOUT ESCALATING CRIME.
INSTEAD, I WANT TO BE A PART OF THE SOLUTION, RECTIFYING THE PROBLEM.
I LOOK FORWARD TO ASSISTING MY COMMUNITY: SERVING, PROTECTING, AND PLAYING A PART IN KEEPING OUR SOCIETY STRONG.
IN SHORT, I LOOK FORWARD TO BEING A POLICE OFFICER.
THANK YOU FOR CONSIDERING MY APPLICATION.
PETER WILLIFORD.

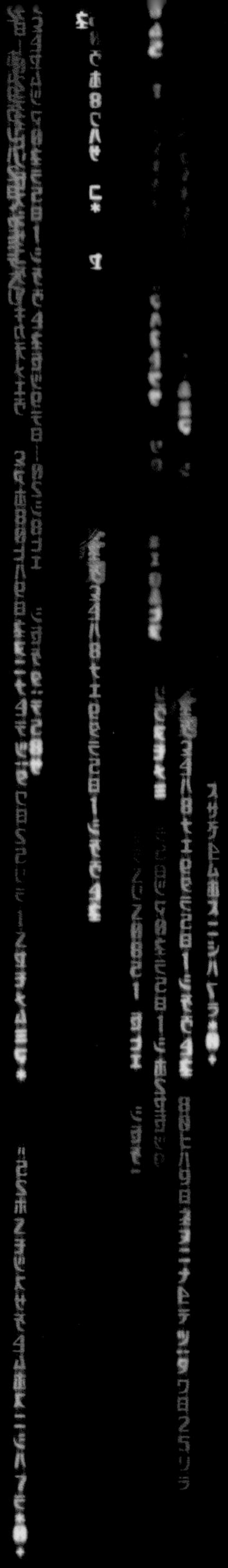

A PATH AMONG STONES

STORY & ART BY GREGORY
RUTH

Greg Ruth's versatility is seen within the three Matrix stories he's done, and also on display in M.A.R.S., SUDDEN GRAVITY, FREAKS OF THE HEARTLAND (with Steve Niles), and CONAN: BORN ON THE BATTLEFIELD (with Kurt Busiek). Greg has also produced a series of murals and designs for the New York Transit Museum in Grand Central Terminal, and illustrations for an animated music video for Prince. His latest offering is a new graphic novel series entitled THE LUNATICS!, and a trilogy of illustrated prose novels called THE WOODLAND CHRONICLES.

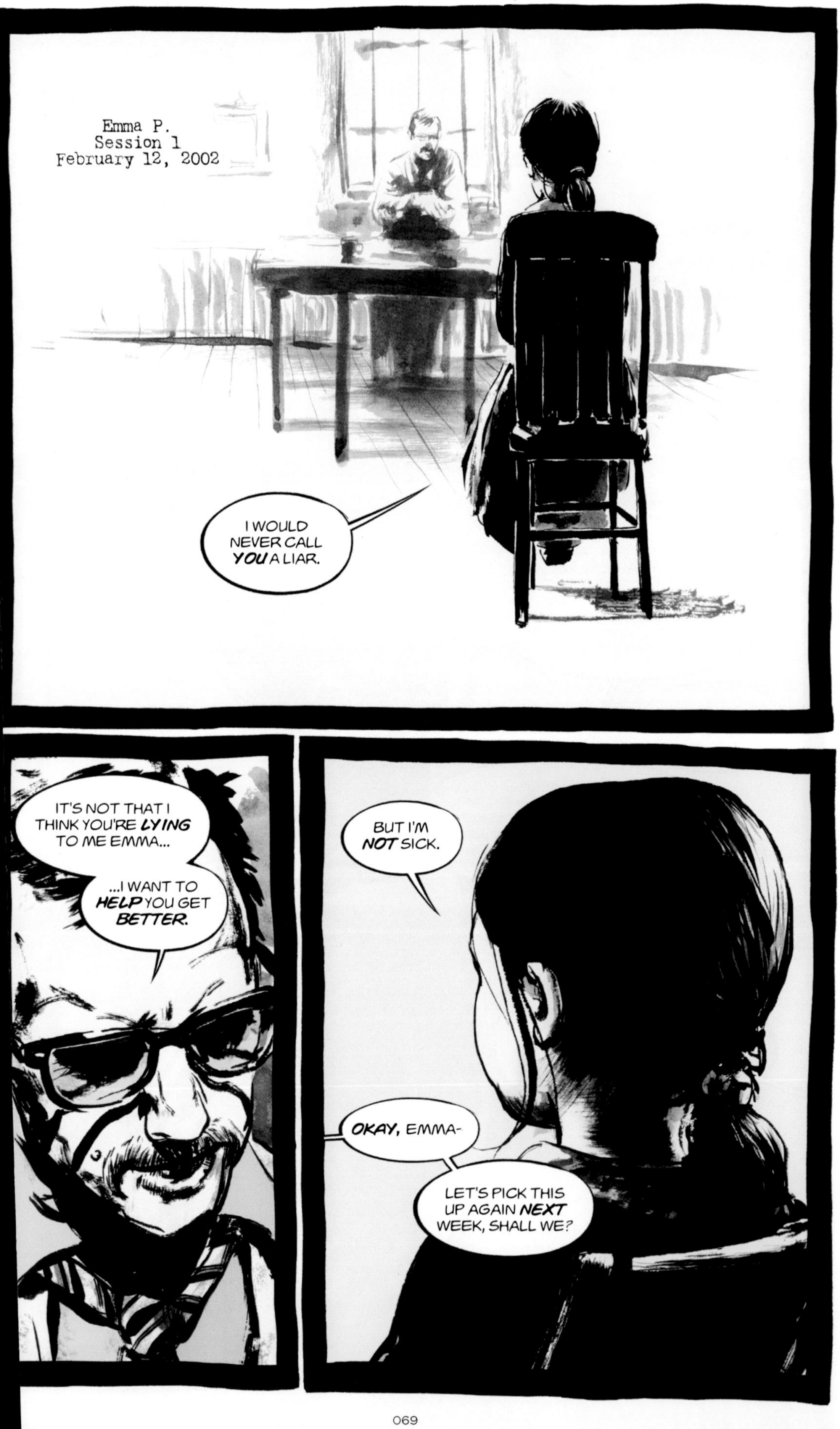
Emma P.
Session 1
February 12, 2002
I WOULD NEVER CALL ***YOU*** A LIAR.
IT'S NOT THAT I THINK YOU'RE ***LYING*** TO ME EMMA...
...I WANT TO ***HELP*** YOU GET ***BETTER***.
BUT I'M ***NOT*** SICK.
OKAY, EMMA-
LET'S PICK THIS UP AGAIN ***NEXT*** WEEK, SHALL WE?

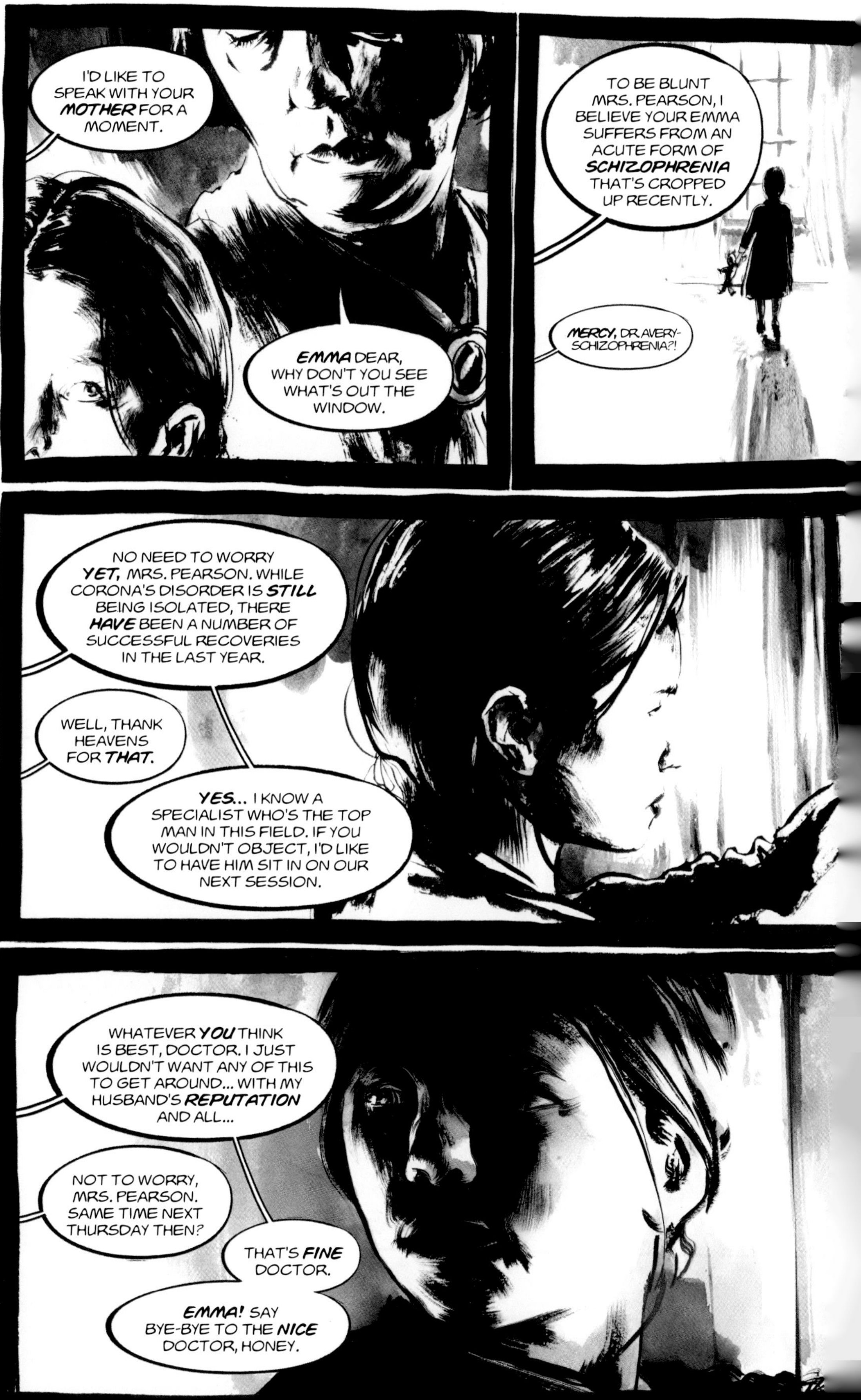
I'D LIKE TO SPEAK WITH YOUR MOTHER FOR A MOMENT.
EMMA DEAR, WHY DON'T YOU SEE WHAT'S OUT THE WINDOW.
TO BE BLUNT MRS. PEARSON, I BELIEVE YOUR EMMA SUFFERS FROM AN ACUTE FORM OF SCHIZOPHRENIA THAT'S CROPPED UP RECENTLY.
MERCY, DR. AVERY-SCHIZOPHRENIA?!
NO NEED TO WORRY YET, MRS. PEARSON. WHILE CORONA'S DISORDER IS STILL BEING ISOLATED, THERE HAVE BEEN A NUMBER OF SUCCESSFUL RECOVERIES IN THE LAST YEAR.
WELL, THANK HEAVENS FOR THAT.
YES... I KNOW A SPECIALIST WHO'S THE TOP MAN IN THIS FIELD. IF YOU WOULDN'T OBJECT, I'D LIKE TO HAVE HIM SIT IN ON OUR NEXT SESSION.
WHATEVER YOU THINK IS BEST, DOCTOR. I JUST WOULDN'T WANT ANY OF THIS TO GET AROUND... WITH MY HUSBAND'S REPUTATION AND ALL...
NOT TO WORRY, MRS. PEARSON. SAME TIME NEXT THURSDAY THEN?
THAT'S FINE DOCTOR.
EMMA! SAY BYE-BYE TO THE NICE DOCTOR, HONEY.

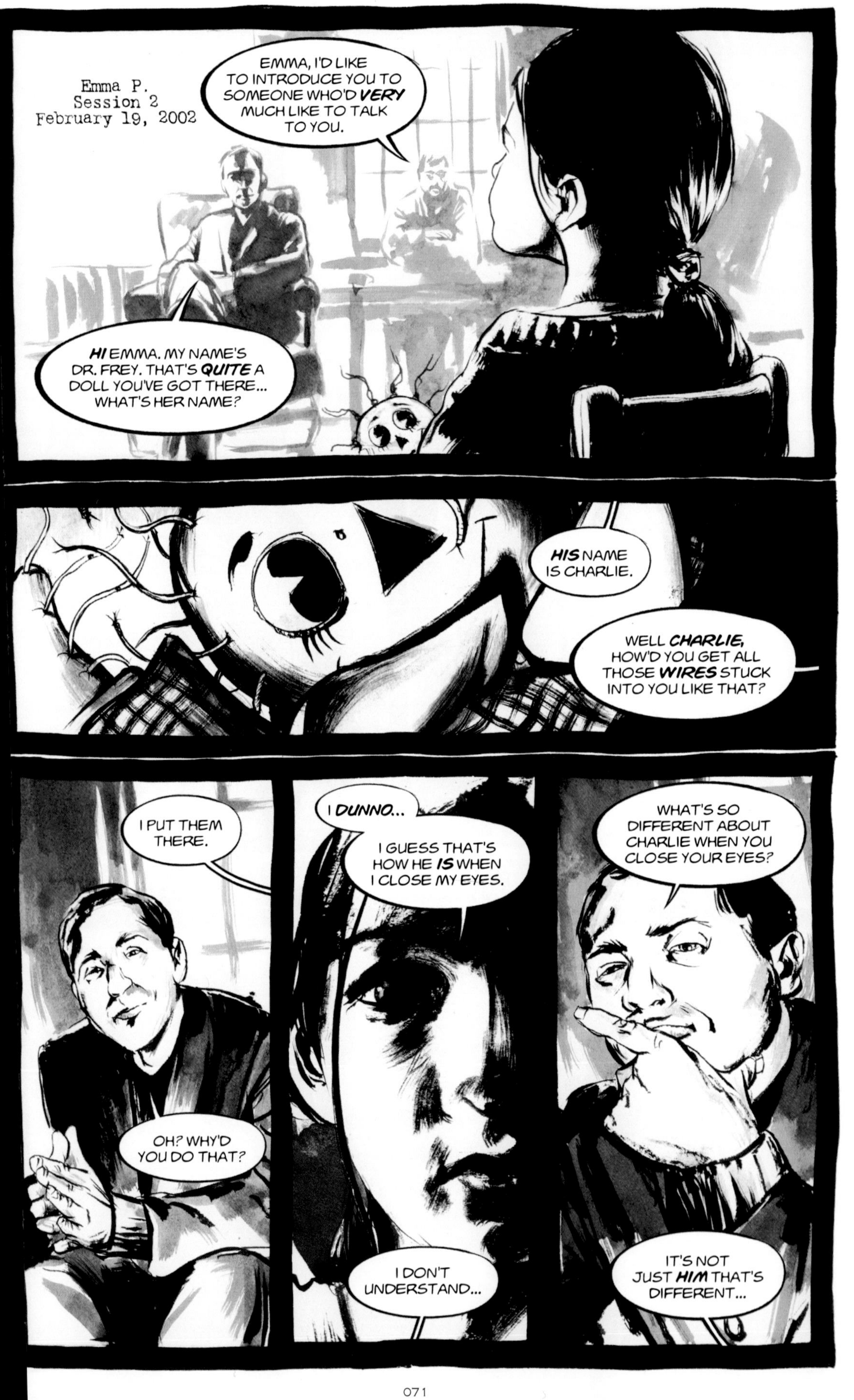
Emma P. Session 2 February 19, 2002
EMMA, I'D LIKE TO INTRODUCE YOU TO SOMEONE WHO'D **VERY** MUCH LIKE TO TALK TO YOU.
HI EMMA. MY NAME'S DR. FREY. THAT'S **QUITE** A DOLL YOU'VE GOT THERE... WHAT'S HER NAME?
HIS NAME IS CHARLIE.
WELL **CHARLIE,** HOW'D YOU GET ALL THOSE **WIRES** STUCK INTO YOU LIKE THAT?
I PUT THEM THERE.
OH? WHY'D YOU DO THAT?
I **DUNNO...**
I GUESS THAT'S HOW HE **IS** WHEN I CLOSE MY EYES.
I DON'T UNDERSTAND...
WHAT'S SO DIFFERENT ABOUT CHARLIE WHEN YOU CLOSE YOUR EYES?
IT'S NOT JUST **HIM** THAT'S DIFFERENT...

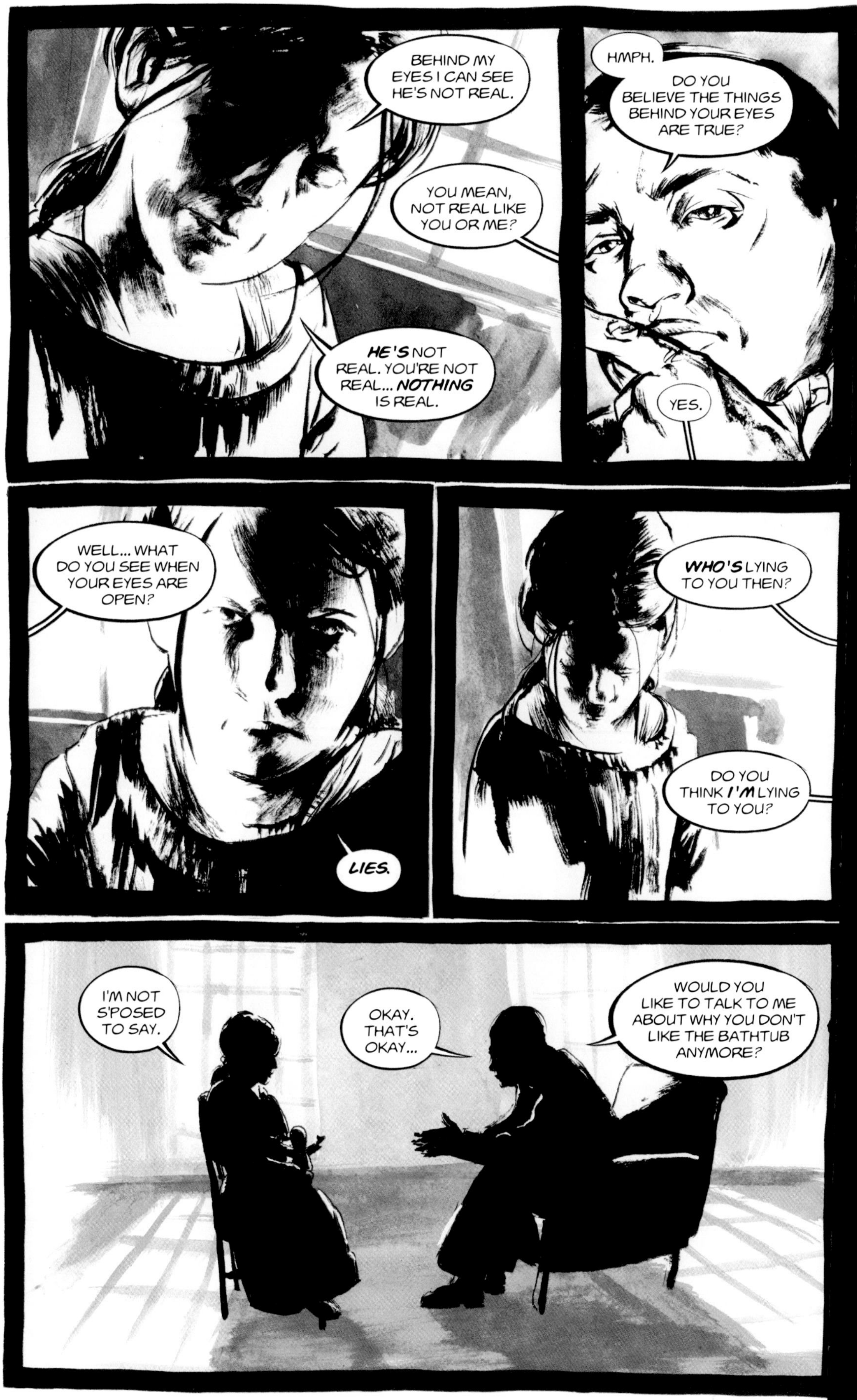
BEHIND MY EYES I CAN SEE HE'S NOT REAL.
YOU MEAN, NOT REAL LIKE YOU OR ME?
HE'S NOT REAL. YOU'RE NOT REAL... **NOTHING** IS REAL.
HMPH.
DO YOU BELIEVE THE THINGS BEHIND YOUR EYES ARE TRUE?
YES.
WELL... WHAT DO YOU SEE WHEN YOUR EYES ARE OPEN?
LIES.
WHO'S LYING TO YOU THEN?
DO YOU THINK **I'M** LYING TO YOU?
I'M NOT S'POSED TO SAY.
OKAY. THAT'S OKAY...
WOULD YOU LIKE TO TALK TO ME ABOUT WHY YOU DON'T LIKE THE BATHTUB ANYMORE?

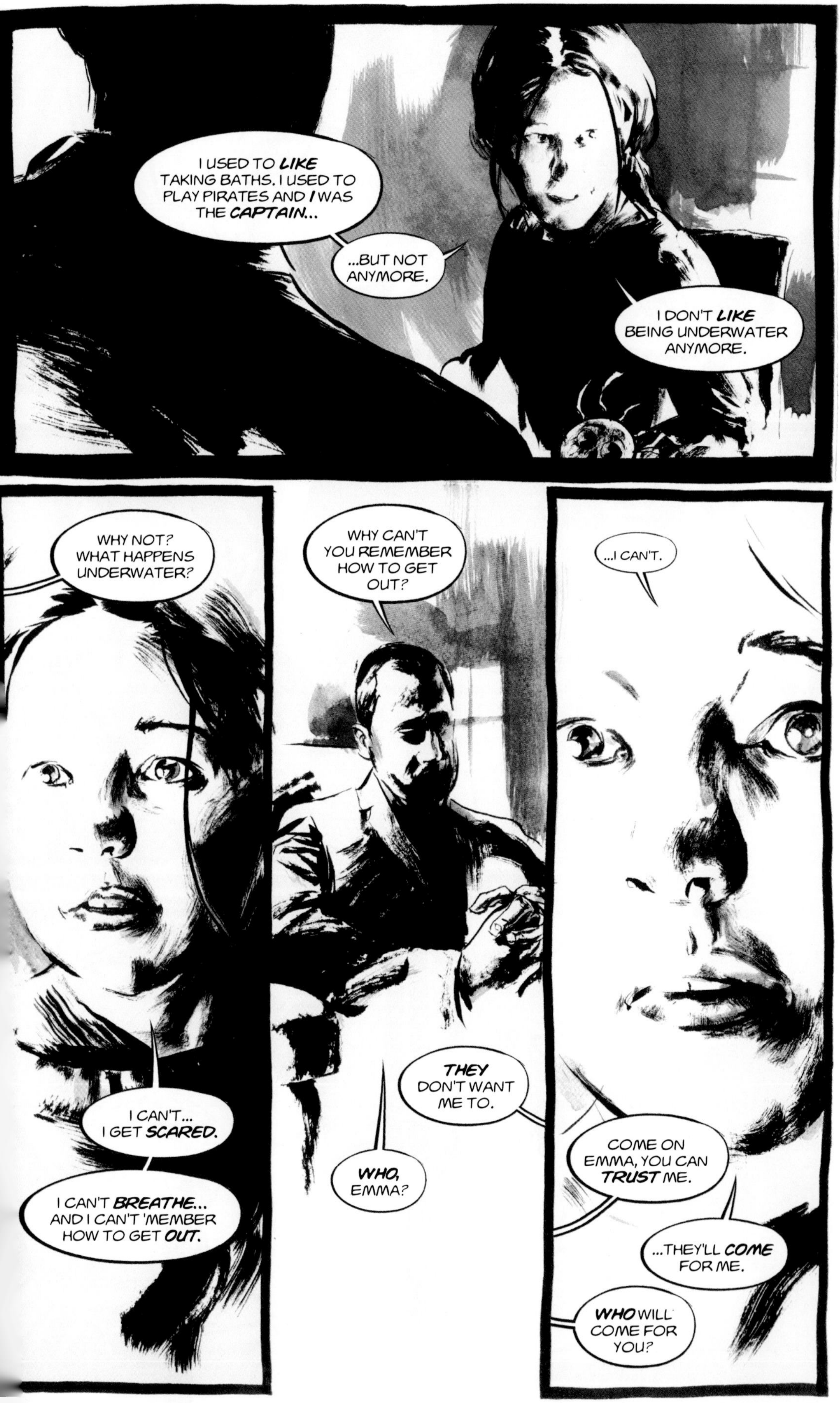
I USED TO LIKE TAKING BATHS. I USED TO PLAY PIRATES AND I WAS THE CAPTAIN...
...BUT NOT ANYMORE.
I DON'T LIKE BEING UNDERWATER ANYMORE.
WHY NOT? WHAT HAPPENS UNDERWATER?
I CAN'T... I GET SCARED.
I CAN'T BREATHE... AND I CAN'T 'MEMBER HOW TO GET OUT.
WHY CAN'T YOU REMEMBER HOW TO GET OUT?
THEY DON'T WANT ME TO.
WHO, EMMA?
...I CAN'T.
COME ON EMMA, YOU CAN TRUST ME.
...THEY'LL COME FOR ME.
WHO WILL COME FOR YOU?

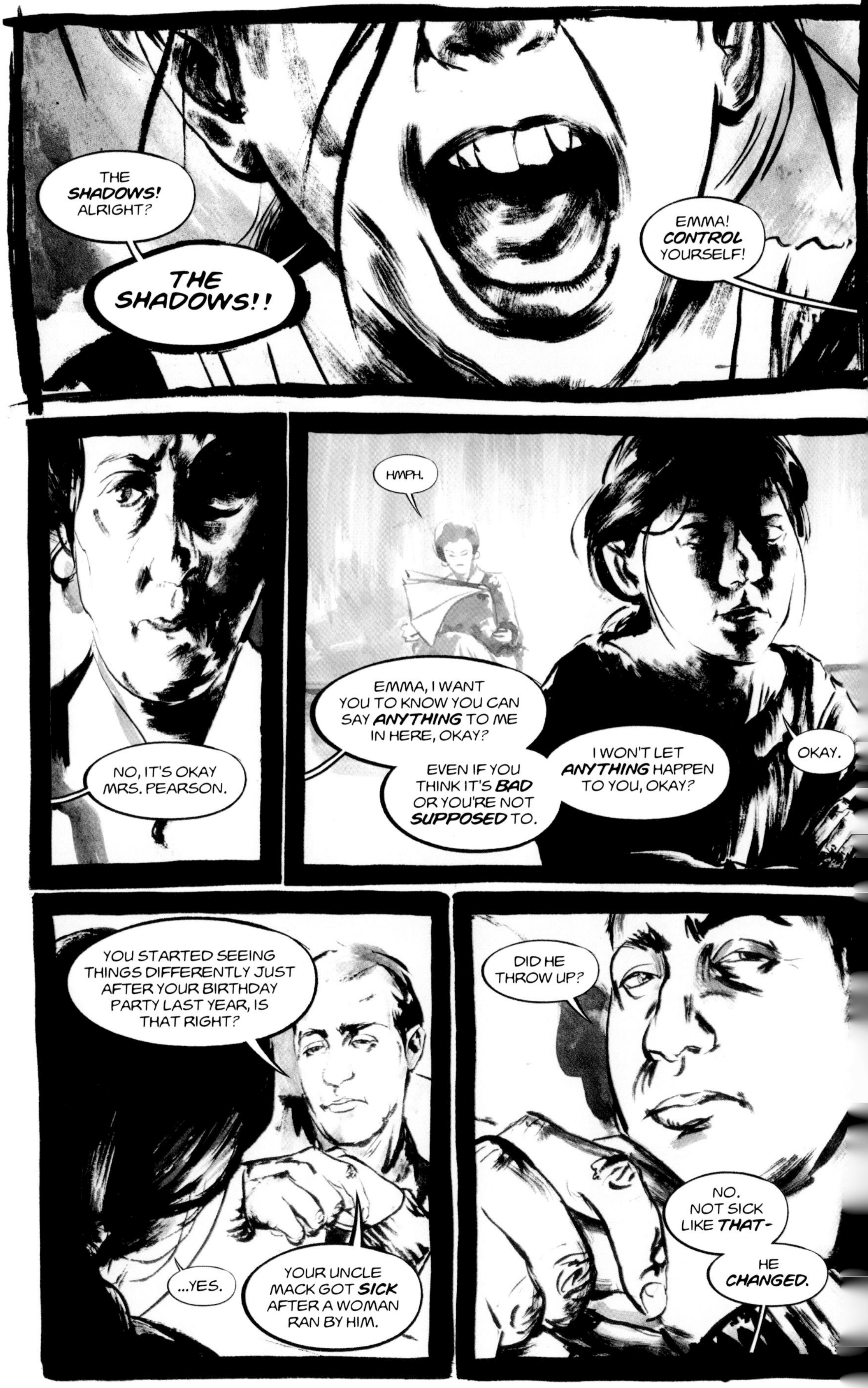
THE SHADOWS! ALRIGHT?
THE SHADOWS!!
EMMA! CONTROL YOURSELF!
NO, IT'S OKAY MRS. PEARSON.
HMPH.
EMMA, I WANT YOU TO KNOW YOU CAN SAY ANYTHING TO ME IN HERE, OKAY?
EVEN IF YOU THINK IT'S BAD OR YOU'RE NOT SUPPOSED TO.
I WON'T LET ANYTHING HAPPEN TO YOU, OKAY?
OKAY.
YOU STARTED SEEING THINGS DIFFERENTLY JUST AFTER YOUR BIRTHDAY PARTY LAST YEAR, IS THAT RIGHT?
...YES.
YOUR UNCLE MACK GOT SICK AFTER A WOMAN RAN BY HIM.
DID HE THROW UP?
NO. NOT SICK LIKE THAT-
HE CHANGED.

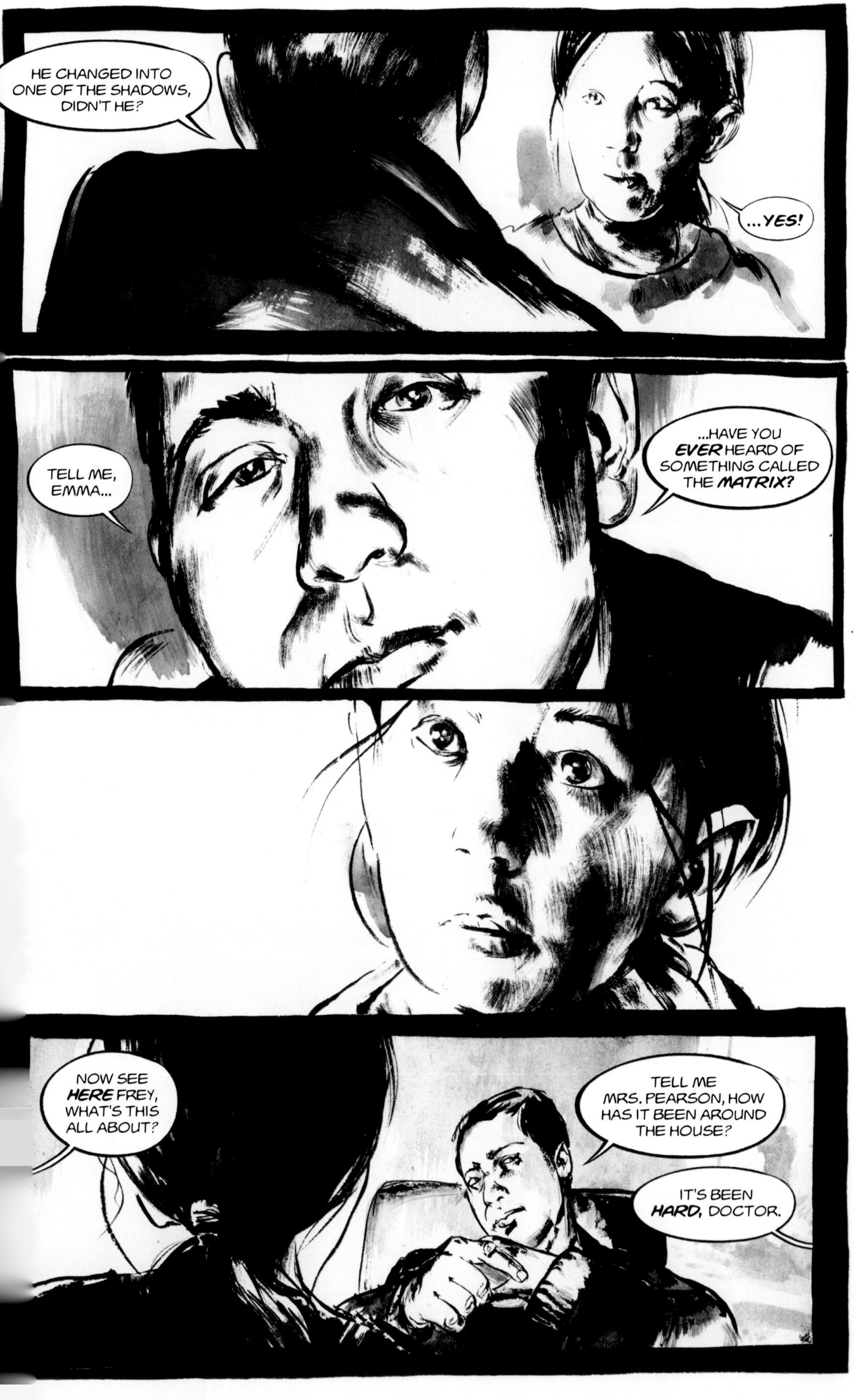
HE CHANGED INTO ONE OF THE SHADOWS, DIDN'T HE?
...YES!
TELL ME, EMMA...
...HAVE YOU EVER HEARD OF SOMETHING CALLED THE MATRIX?
NOW SEE HERE FREY, WHAT'S THIS ALL ABOUT?
TELL ME MRS. PEARSON, HOW HAS IT BEEN AROUND THE HOUSE?
IT'S BEEN HARD, DOCTOR.

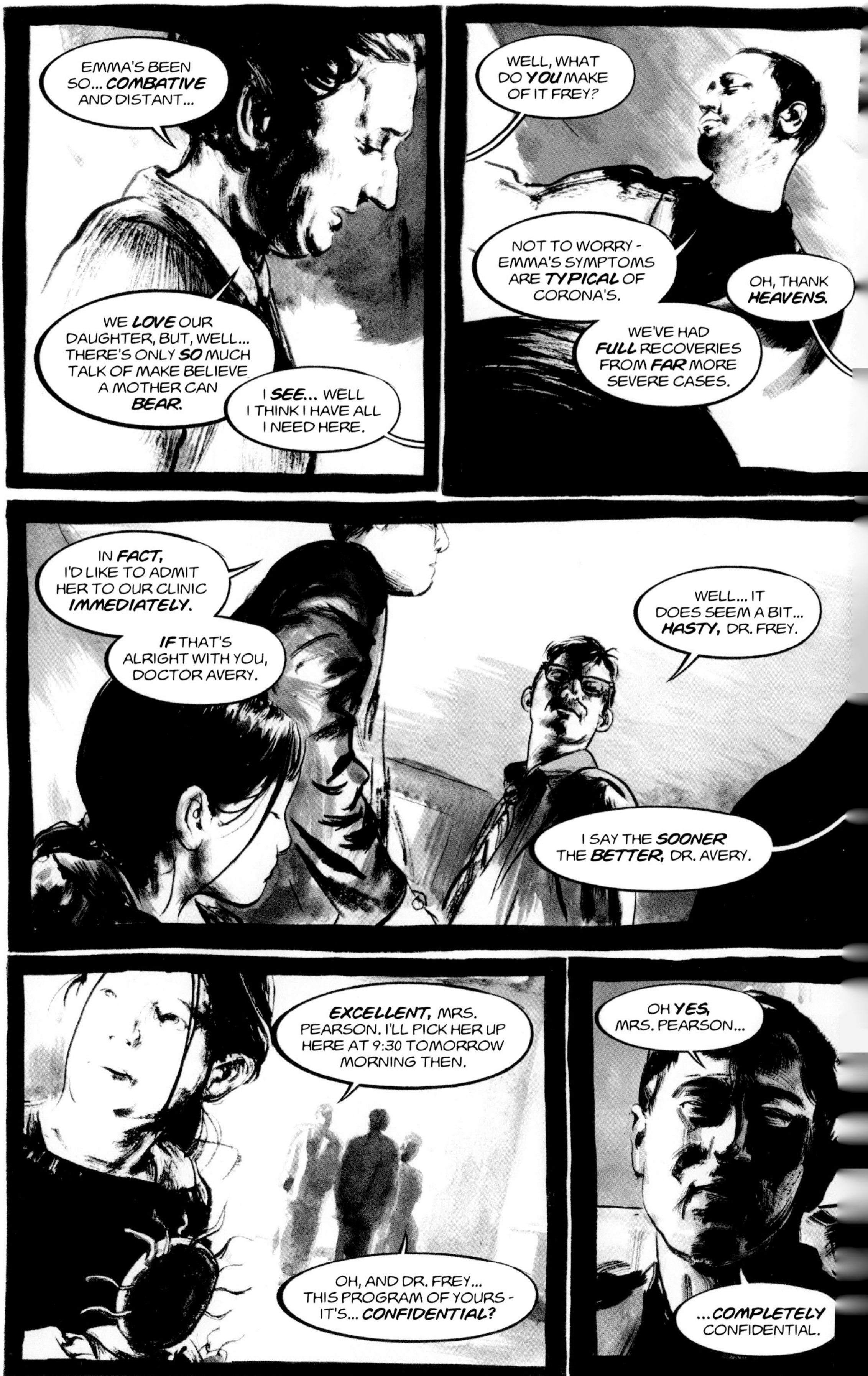
EMMA'S BEEN SO... COMBATIVE AND DISTANT...
WE LOVE OUR DAUGHTER, BUT, WELL... THERE'S ONLY SO MUCH TALK OF MAKE BELIEVE A MOTHER CAN BEAR.
I SEE... WELL I THINK I HAVE ALL I NEED HERE.
WELL, WHAT DO YOU MAKE OF IT FREY?
NOT TO WORRY - EMMA'S SYMPTOMS ARE TYPICAL OF CORONA'S.
OH, THANK HEAVENS.
WE'VE HAD FULL RECOVERIES FROM FAR MORE SEVERE CASES.
IN FACT, I'D LIKE TO ADMIT HER TO OUR CLINIC IMMEDIATELY.
IF THAT'S ALRIGHT WITH YOU, DOCTOR AVERY.
WELL... IT DOES SEEM A BIT... HASTY, DR. FREY.
I SAY THE SOONER THE BETTER, DR. AVERY.
EXCELLENT, MRS. PEARSON. I'LL PICK HER UP HERE AT 9:30 TOMORROW MORNING THEN.
OH, AND DR. FREY... THIS PROGRAM OF YOURS - IT'S... CONFIDENTIAL?
OH YES, MRS. PEARSON...
...COMPLETELY CONFIDENTIAL.

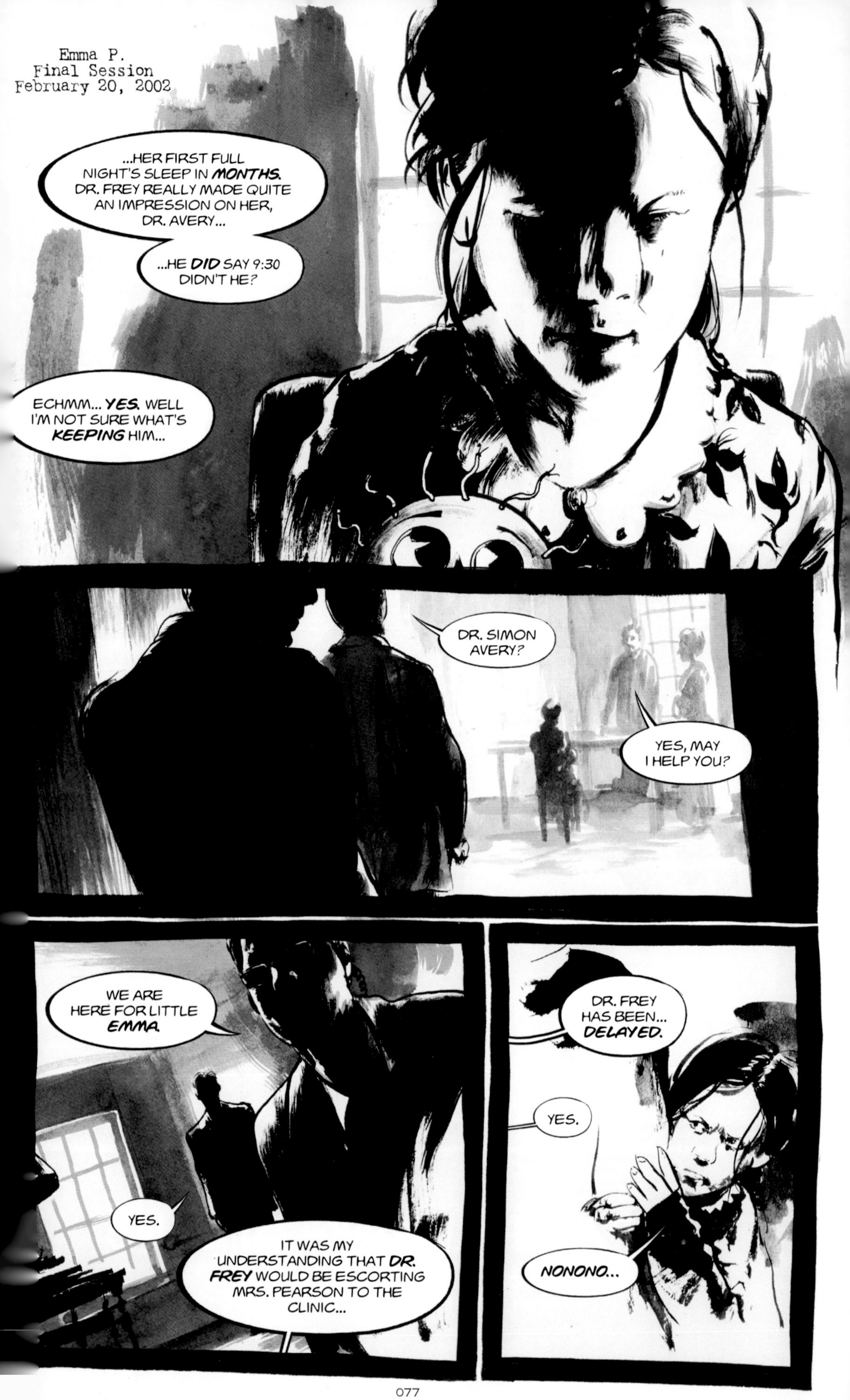
Emma P.
Final Session
February 20, 2002
...HER FIRST FULL NIGHT'S SLEEP IN **MONTHS**. DR. FREY REALLY MADE QUITE AN IMPRESSION ON HER, DR. AVERY...
...HE **DID** SAY 9:30 DIDN'T HE?
ECHMM... **YES**. WELL I'M NOT SURE WHAT'S **KEEPING** HIM...
DR. SIMON AVERY?
YES, MAY I HELP YOU?
WE ARE HERE FOR LITTLE **EMMA**.
YES.
IT WAS MY UNDERSTANDING THAT **DR. FREY** WOULD BE ESCORTING MRS. PEARSON TO THE CLINIC...
DR. FREY HAS BEEN... **DELAYED**.
YES.
NONONO...

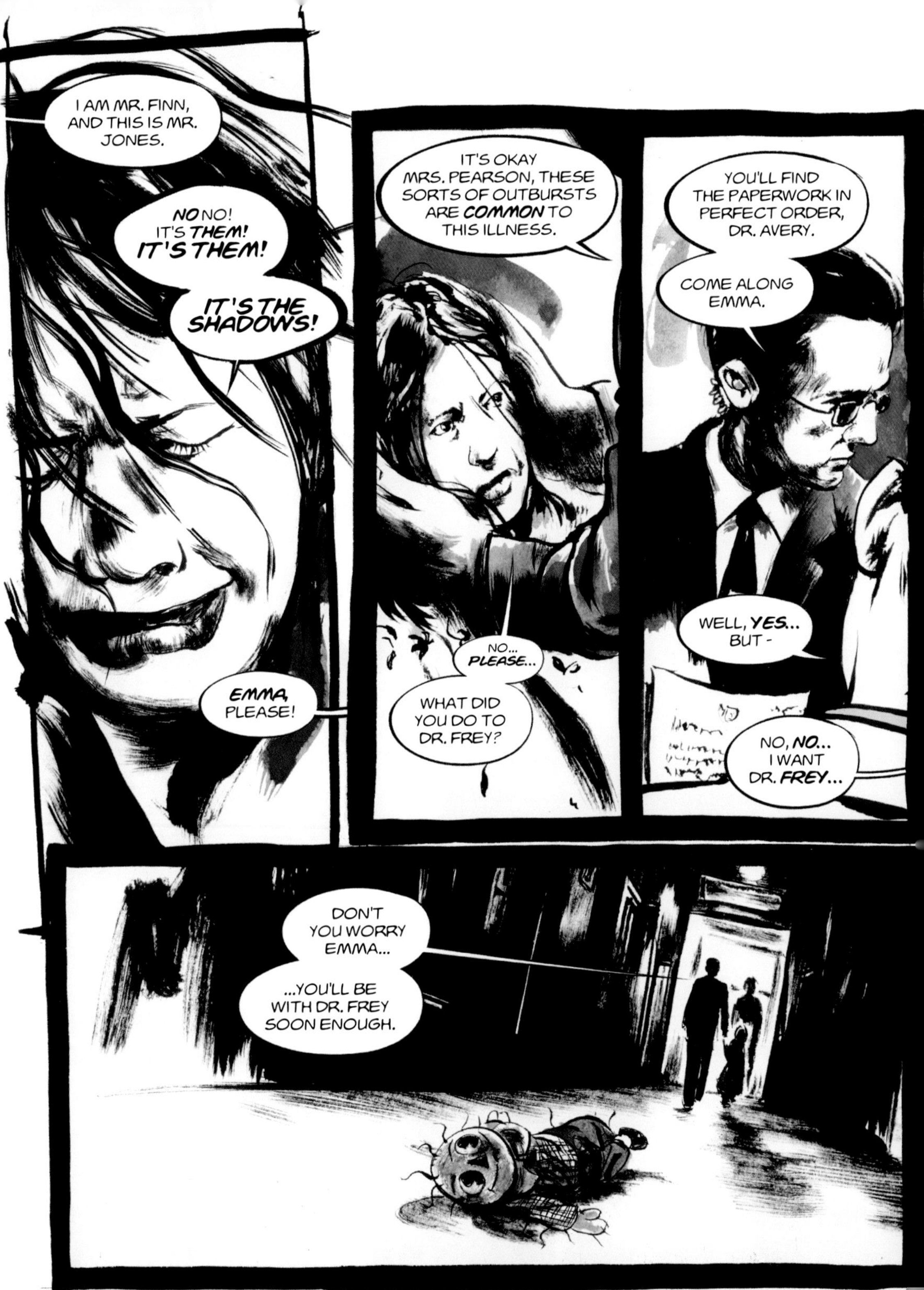
I AM MR. FINN, AND THIS IS MR. JONES.
NO NO! IT'S THEM! IT'S THEM!
IT'S THE SHADOWS!
EMMA, PLEASE!
IT'S OKAY MRS. PEARSON, THESE SORTS OF OUTBURSTS ARE COMMON TO THIS ILLNESS.
NO... PLEASE...
WHAT DID YOU DO TO DR. FREY?
YOU'LL FIND THE PAPERWORK IN PERFECT ORDER, DR. AVERY.
COME ALONG EMMA.
WELL, YES... BUT -
NO, NO... I WANT DR. FREY...
DON'T YOU WORRY EMMA...
...YOU'LL BE WITH DR. FREY SOON ENOUGH.

A PATH AMONG STONES

story and art by greg ruth

edited by spencer lamm

based on concepts by larry & andy wachowski

RUN, SAGA, RUN

ART & COLORS BY KERON GRANT

Originally from Jamaica, Keron Grant cites comic artist influences Hiroaki Samura, Carlos Pacheco and Ed McGuinness; other inspiration comes from a variety of Baroque and Renaissance artists. His first published work was a pinup in the back of one of the last issues of PITT. Since then, Keron has worked on various comics, including the interior and cover of FANTASTIC FOUR: MANGAVERSE #1, and interiors and covers for IRON MAN numbers 41 to 47.

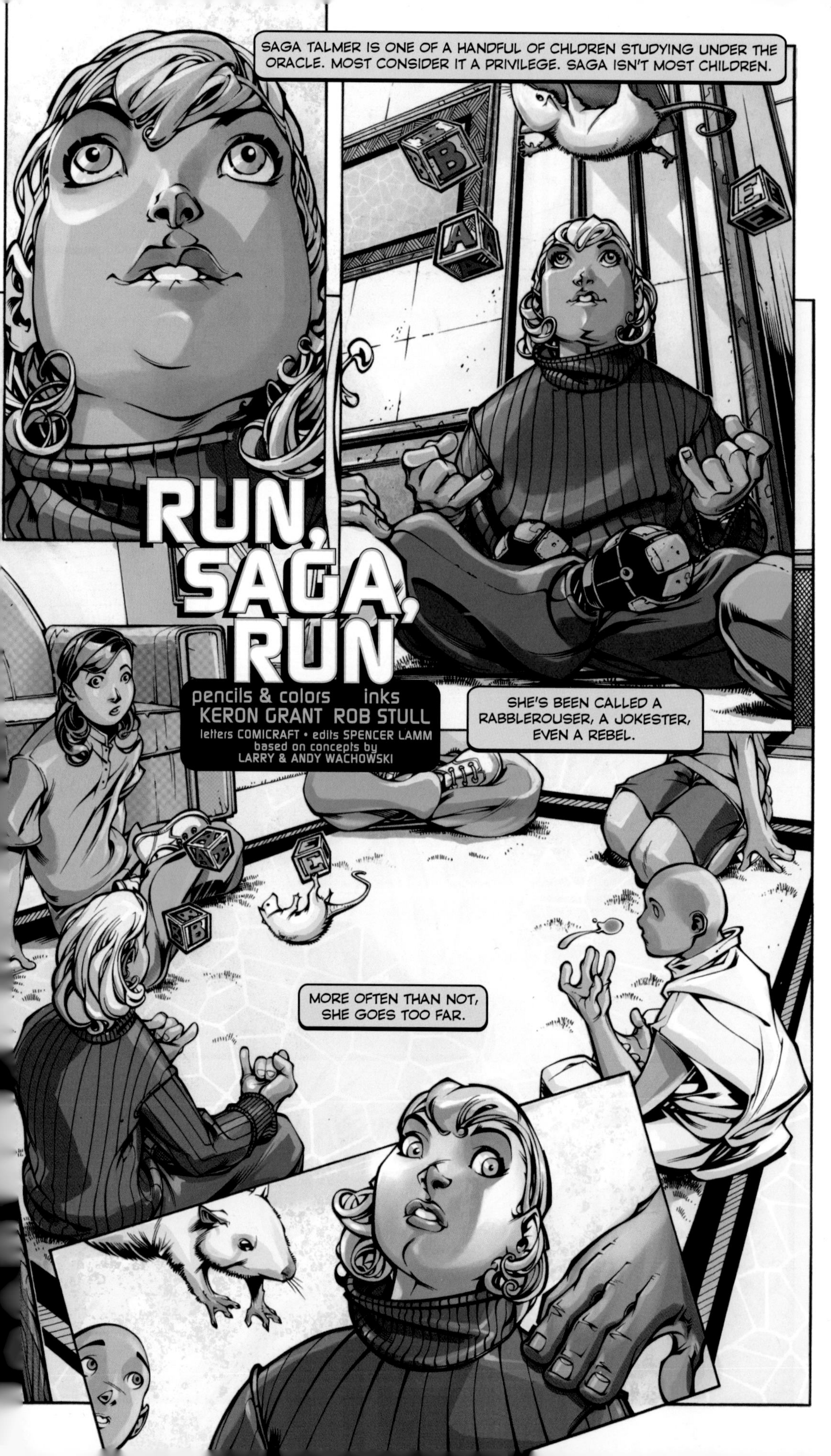
SAGA TALMER IS ONE OF A HANDFUL OF CHLDREN STUDYING UNDER THE ORACLE. MOST CONSIDER IT A PRIVILEGE. SAGA ISN'T MOST CHILDREN.
RUN, SAGA, RUN
pencils & colors KERON GRANT inks ROB STULL
letters COMICRAFT • edits SPENCER LAMM
based on concepts by LARRY & ANDY WACHOWSKI
SHE'S BEEN CALLED A RABBLEROUSER, A JOKESTER, EVEN A REBEL.
MORE OFTEN THAN NOT, SHE GOES TOO FAR.

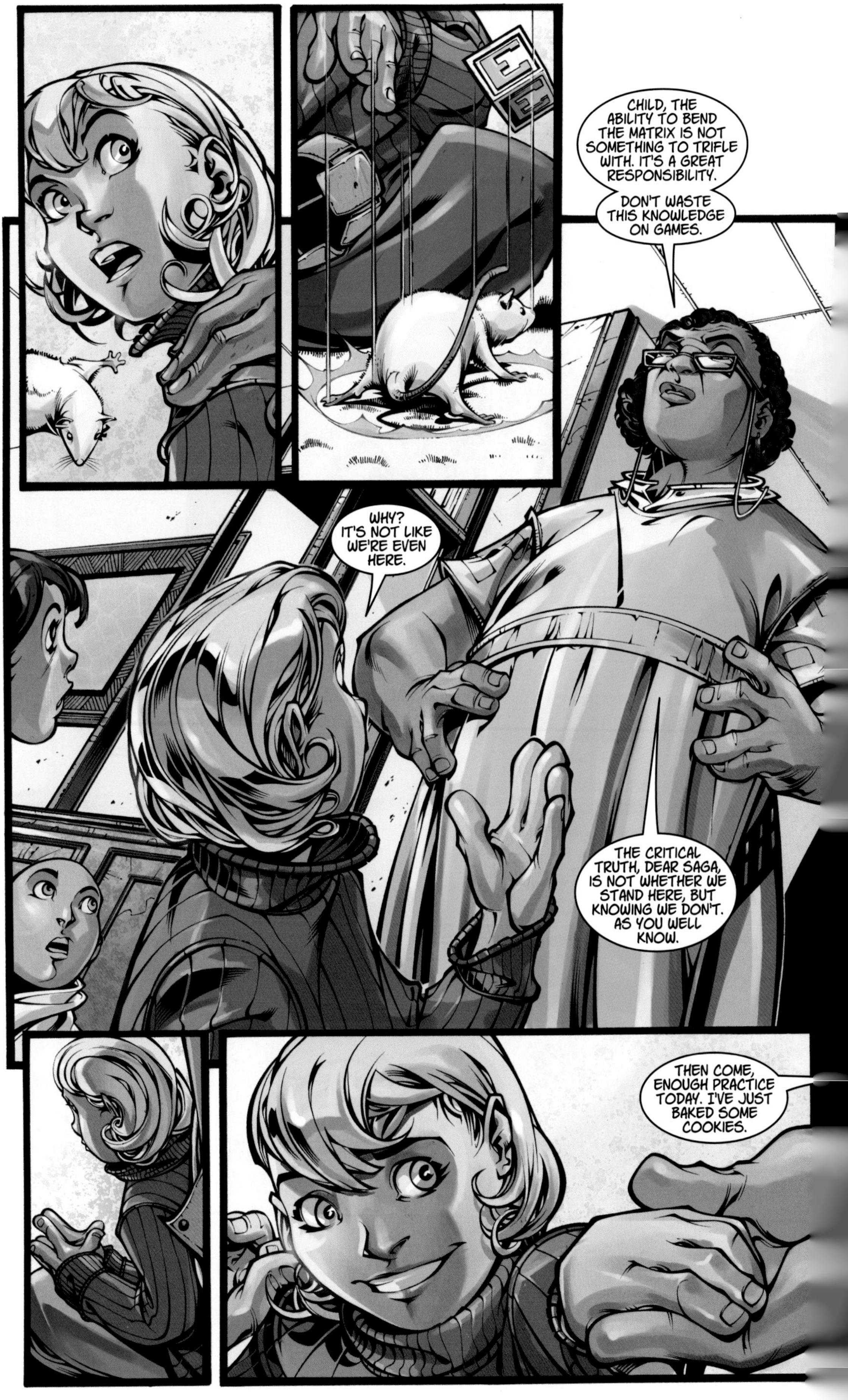
CHILD, THE ABILITY TO BEND THE MATRIX IS NOT SOMETHING TO TRIFLE WITH. IT'S A GREAT RESPONSIBILITY.
DON'T WASTE THIS KNOWLEDGE ON GAMES.
WHY? IT'S NOT LIKE WE'RE EVEN HERE.
THE CRITICAL TRUTH, DEAR SAGA, IS NOT WHETHER WE STAND HERE, BUT KNOWING WE DON'T. AS YOU WELL KNOW.
THEN COME, ENOUGH PRACTICE TODAY. I'VE JUST BAKED SOME COOKIES.

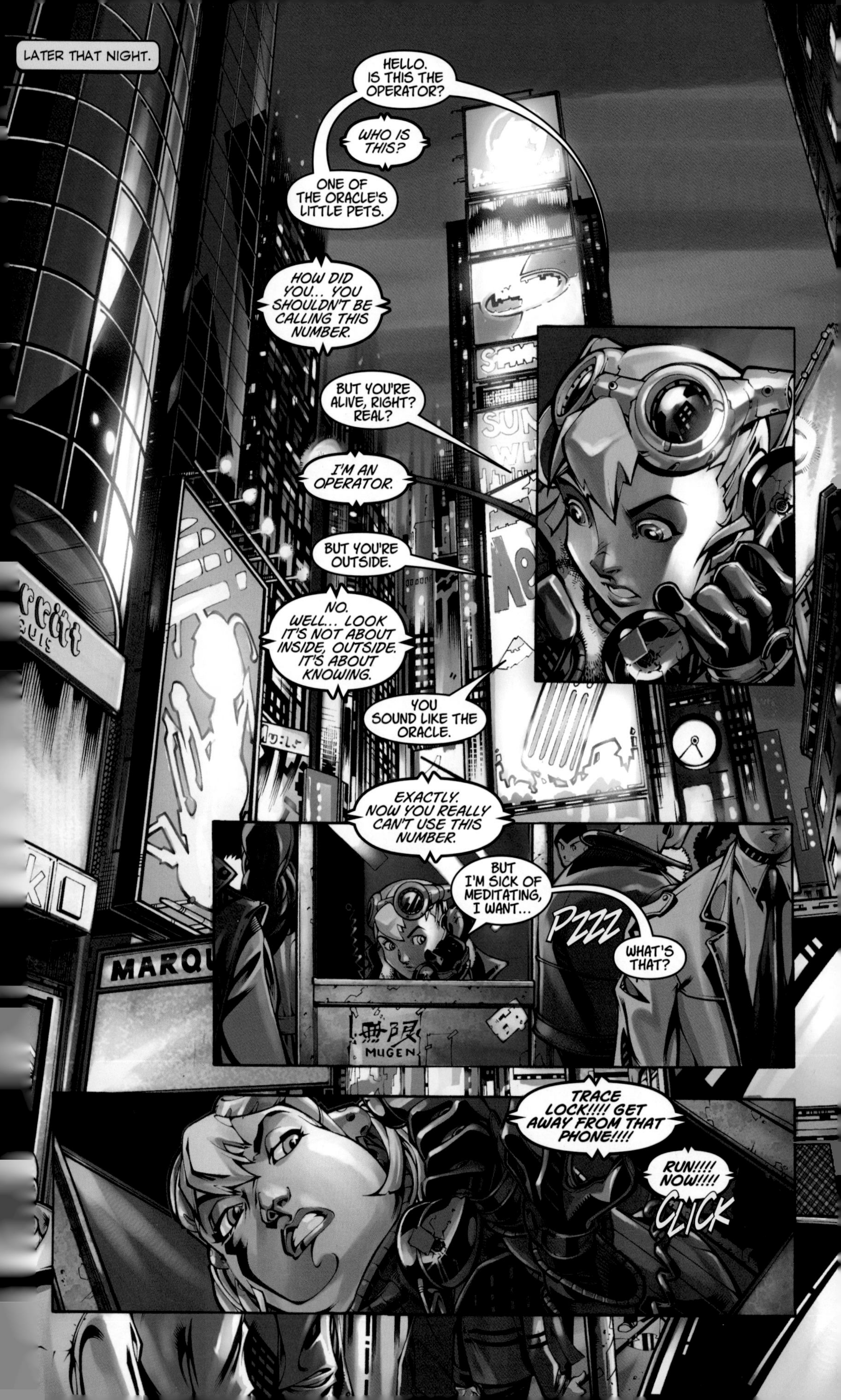
LATER THAT NIGHT.
HELLO. IS THIS THE OPERATOR?
WHO IS THIS?
ONE OF THE ORACLE'S LITTLE PETS.
HOW DID YOU... YOU SHOULDN'T BE CALLING THIS NUMBER.
BUT YOU'RE ALIVE, RIGHT? REAL?
I'M AN OPERATOR.
BUT YOU'RE OUTSIDE.
NO. WELL... LOOK IT'S NOT ABOUT INSIDE, OUTSIDE. IT'S ABOUT KNOWING.
YOU SOUND LIKE THE ORACLE.
MARQU
EXACTLY. NOW YOU REALLY CAN'T USE THIS NUMBER.
BUT I'M SICK OF MEDITATING, I WANT...
PZZZ
WHAT'S THAT?
無限
MUGEN
TRACE LOCK!!!! GET AWAY FROM THAT PHONE!!!!
RUN!!!! NOW!!!!
CLICK

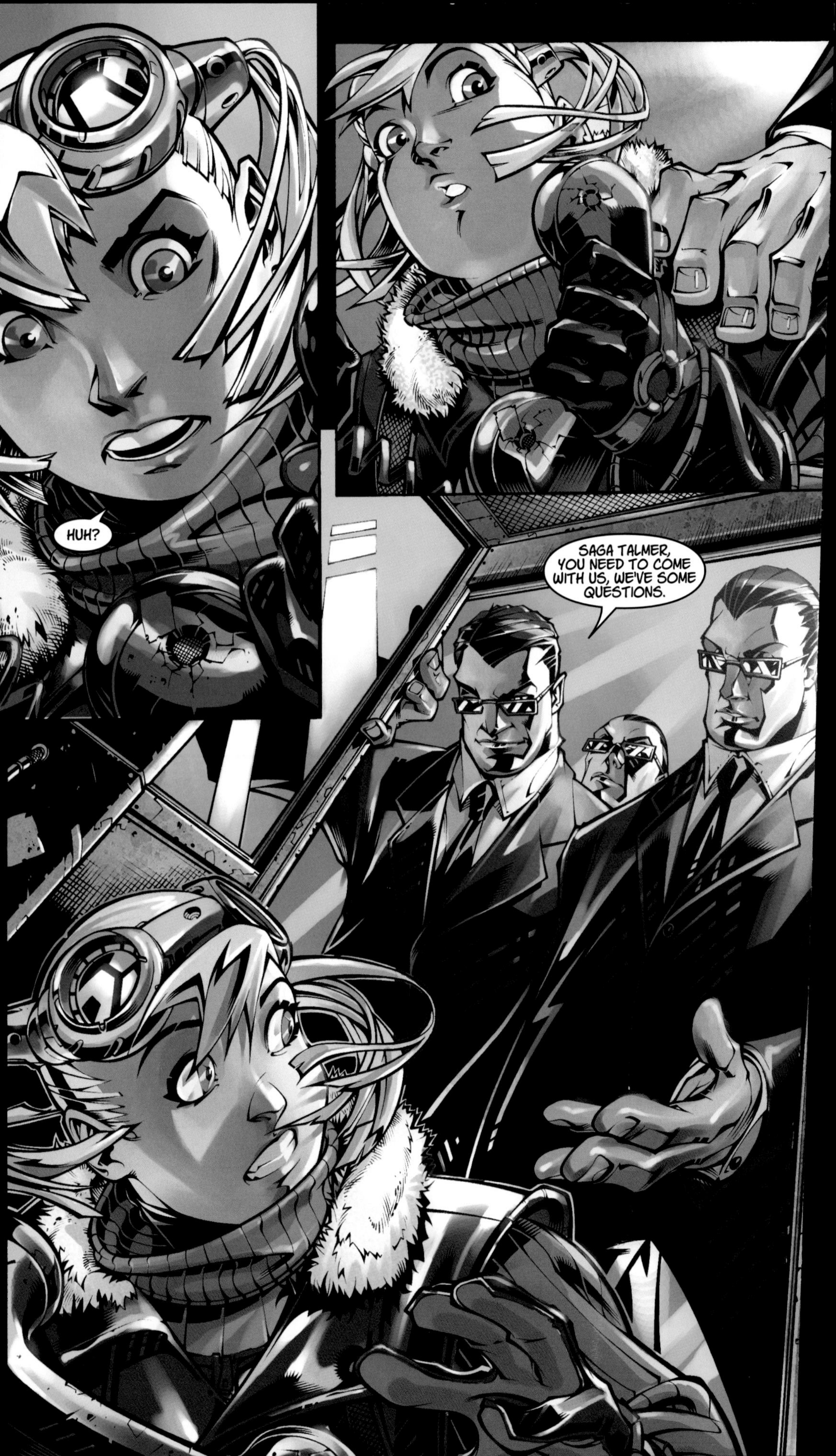
HUH?
SAGA TALMER, YOU NEED TO COME WITH US, WE'VE SOME QUESTIONS.

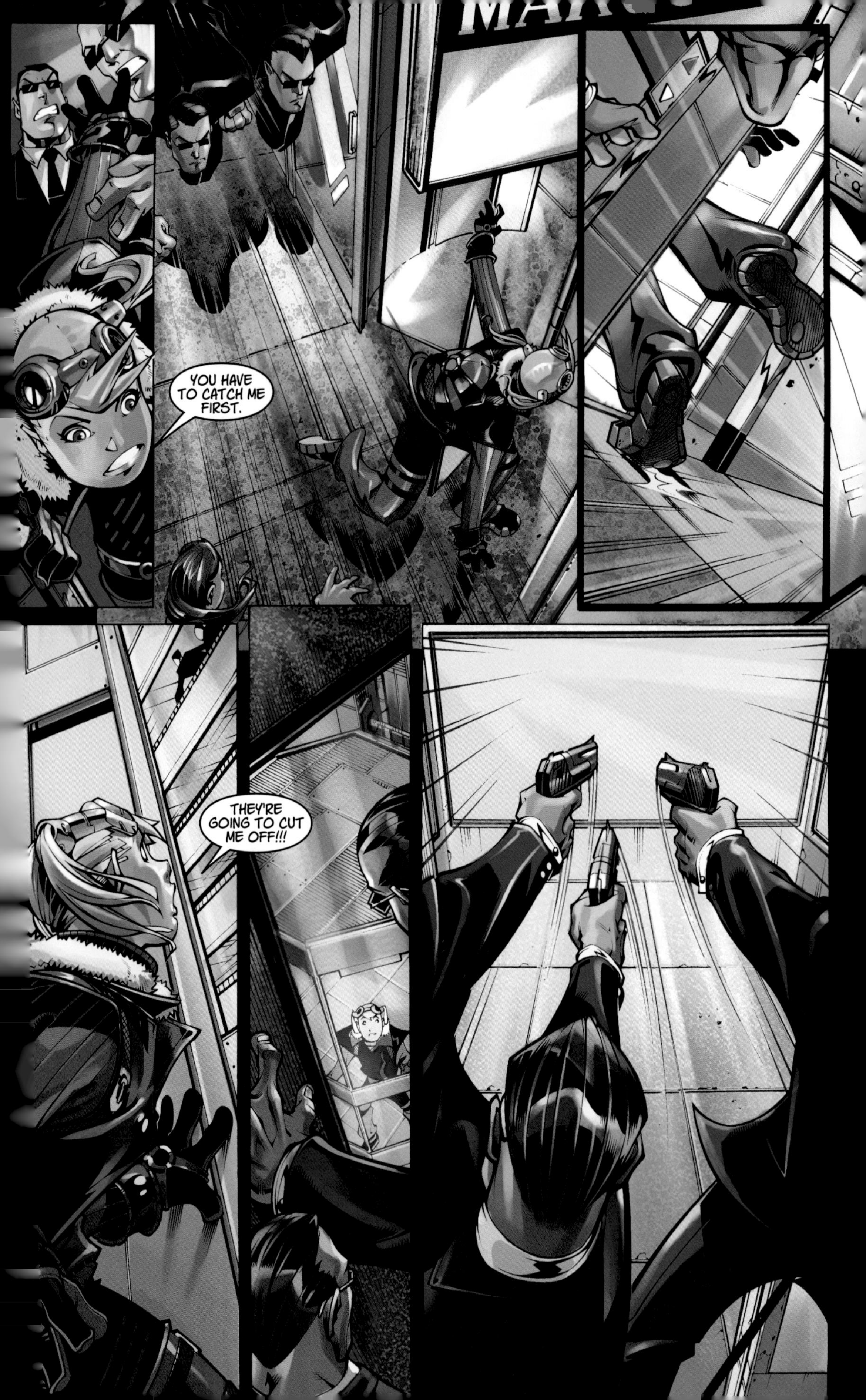
YOU HAVE TO CATCH ME FIRST.
THEY'RE GOING TO CUT ME OFF!!!

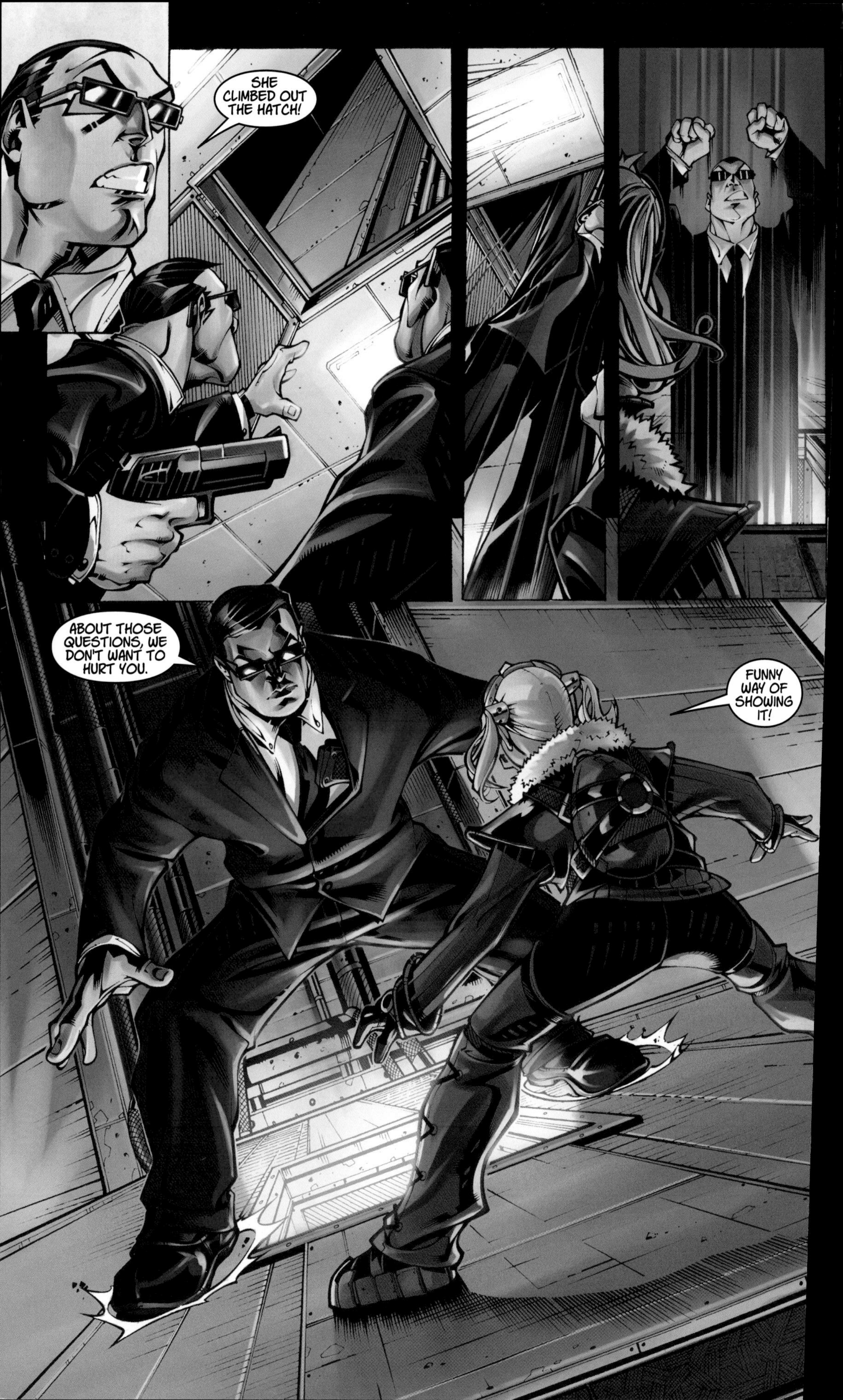
SHE CLIMBED OUT THE HATCH!
ABOUT THOSE QUESTIONS, WE DON'T WANT TO HURT YOU.
FUNNY WAY OF SHOWING IT!

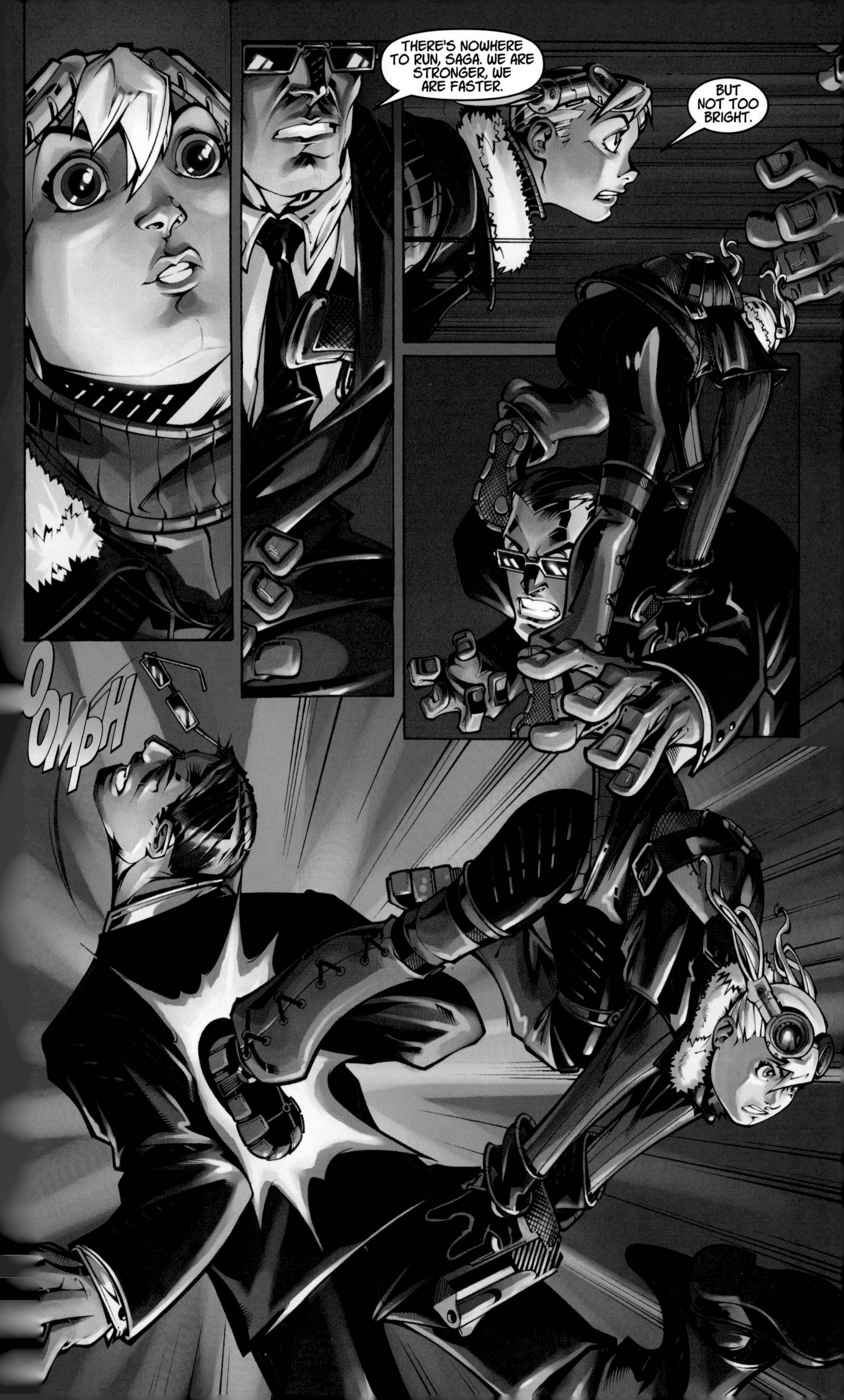
THERE'S NOWHERE TO RUN, SAGA. WE ARE STRONGER, WE ARE FASTER.
BUT NOT TOO BRIGHT.
OOMPH

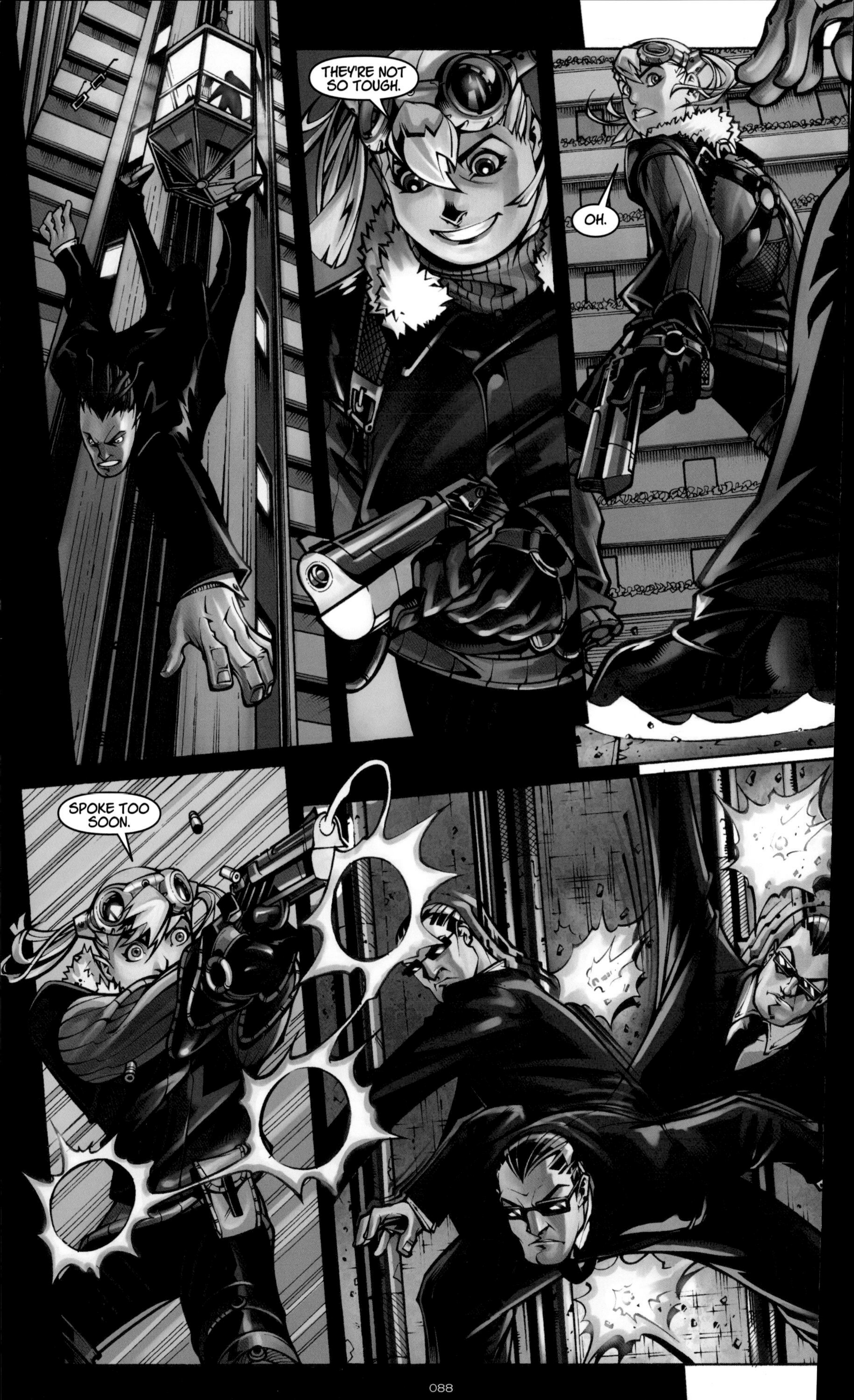
THEY'RE NOT SO TOUGH.
OH.
SPOKE TOO SOON.

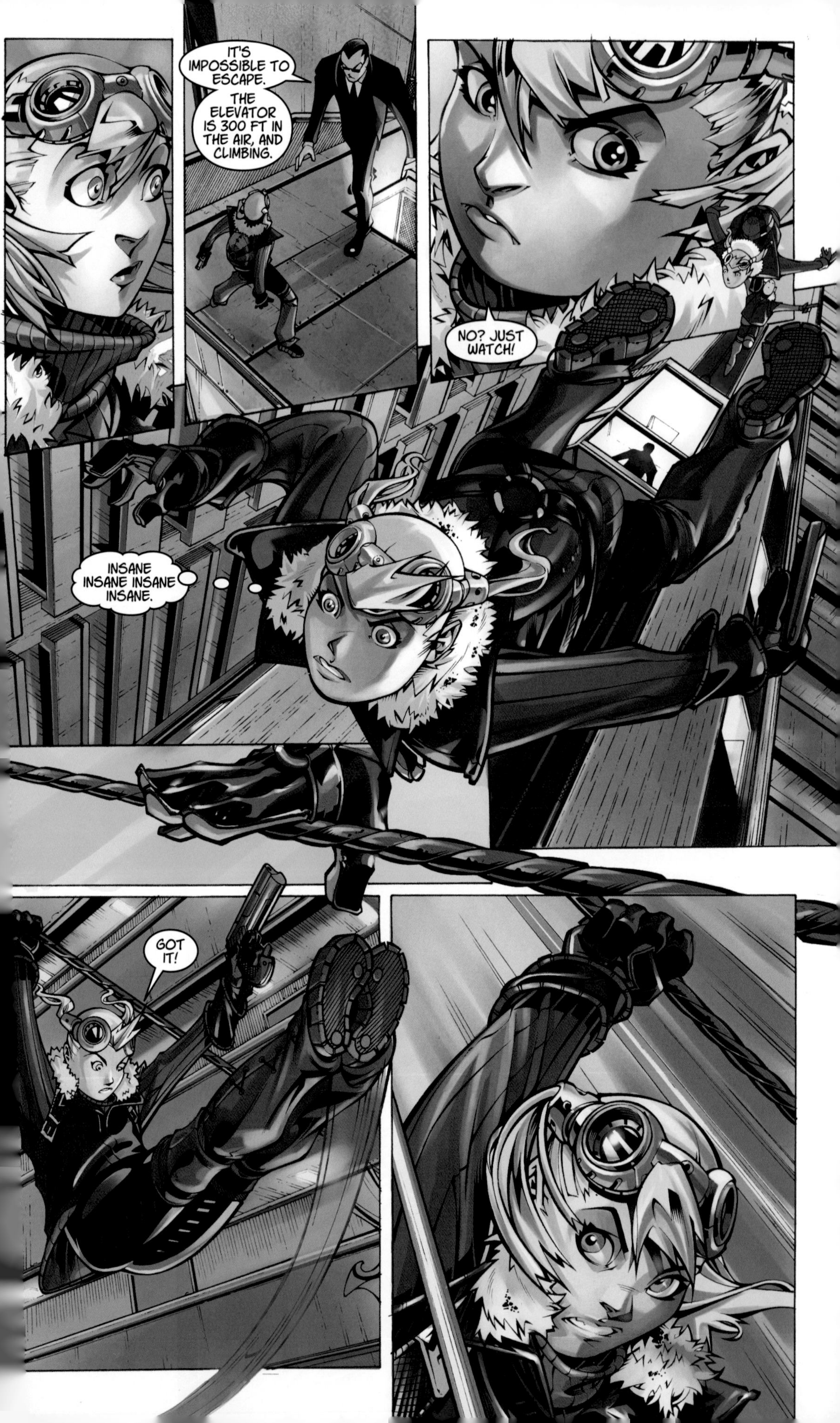
IT'S IMPOSSIBLE TO ESCAPE.
THE ELEVATOR IS 300 FT IN THE AIR, AND CLIMBING.
NO? JUST WATCH!
INSANE INSANE INSANE INSANE.
GOT IT!

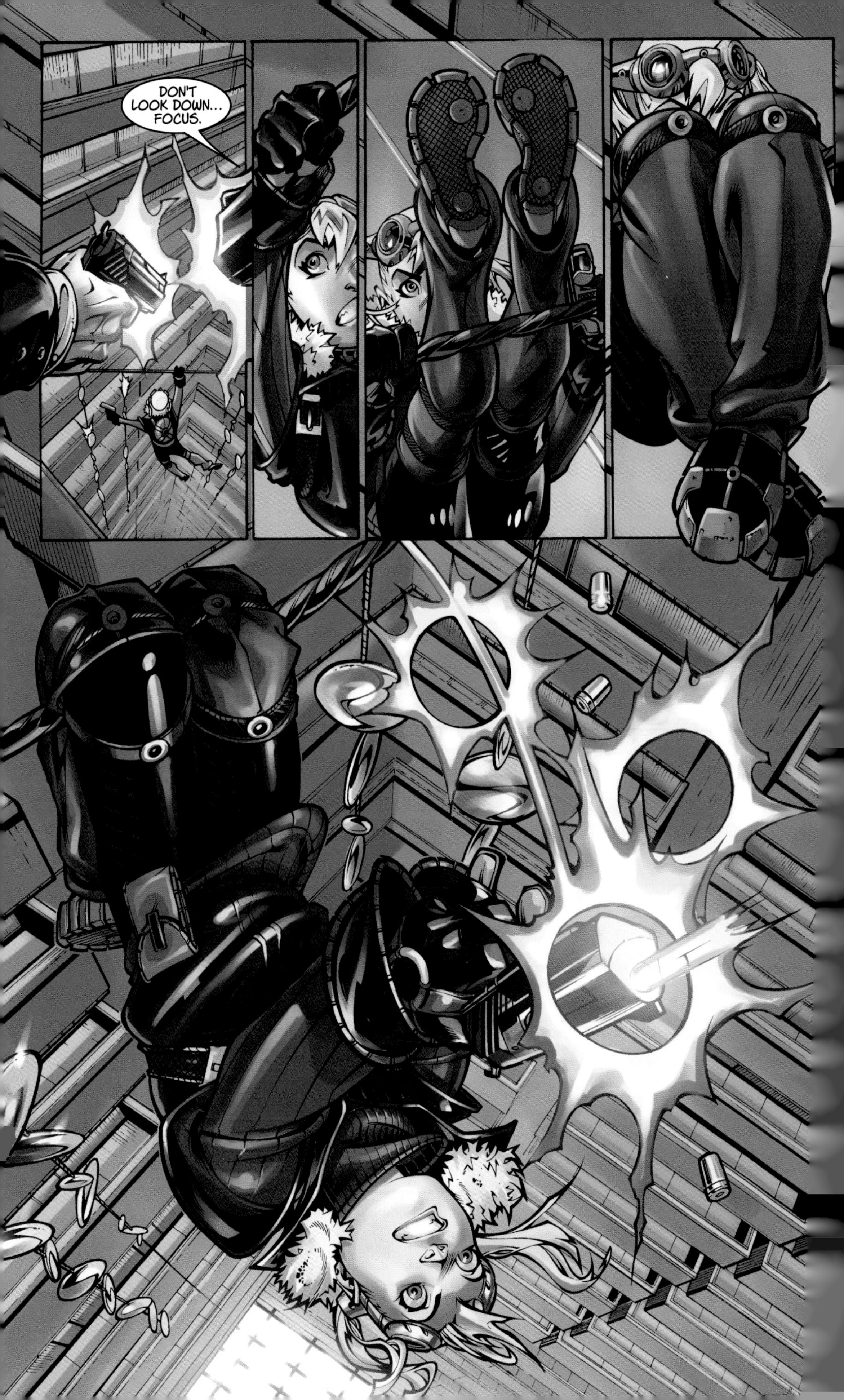
DON'T LOOK DOWN... FOCUS.

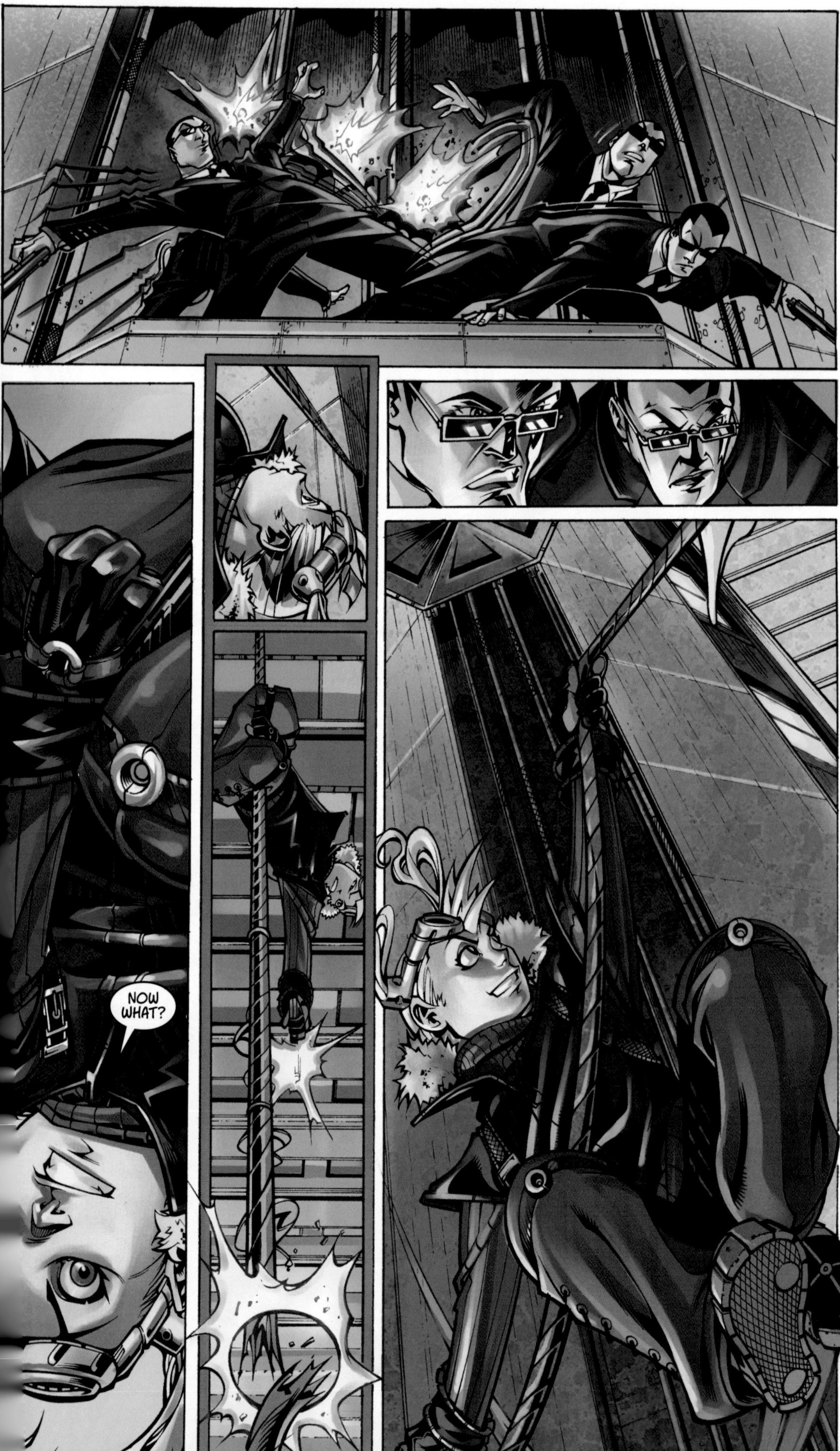
NOW WHAT?

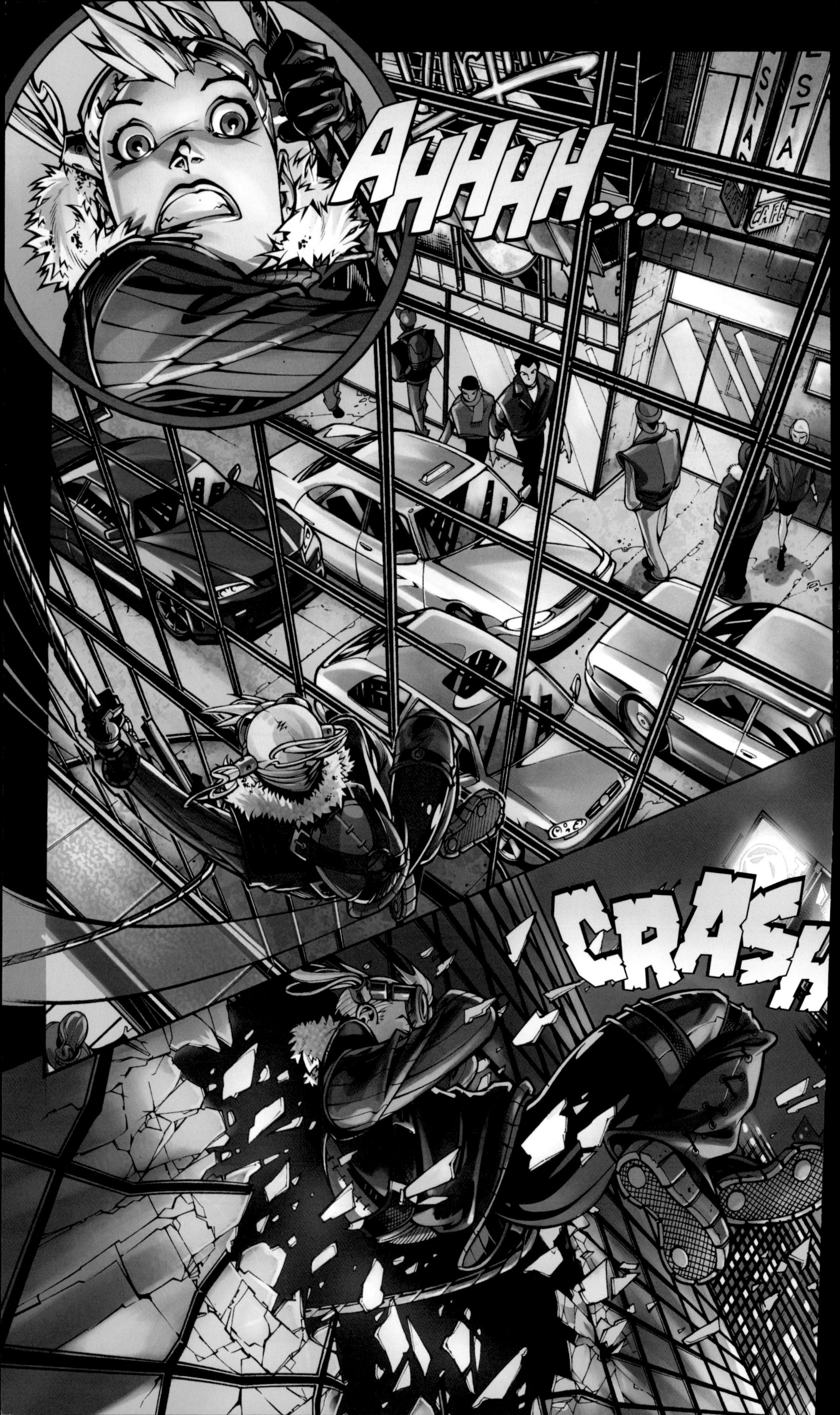
AHHHH....
CAFE
CRASH

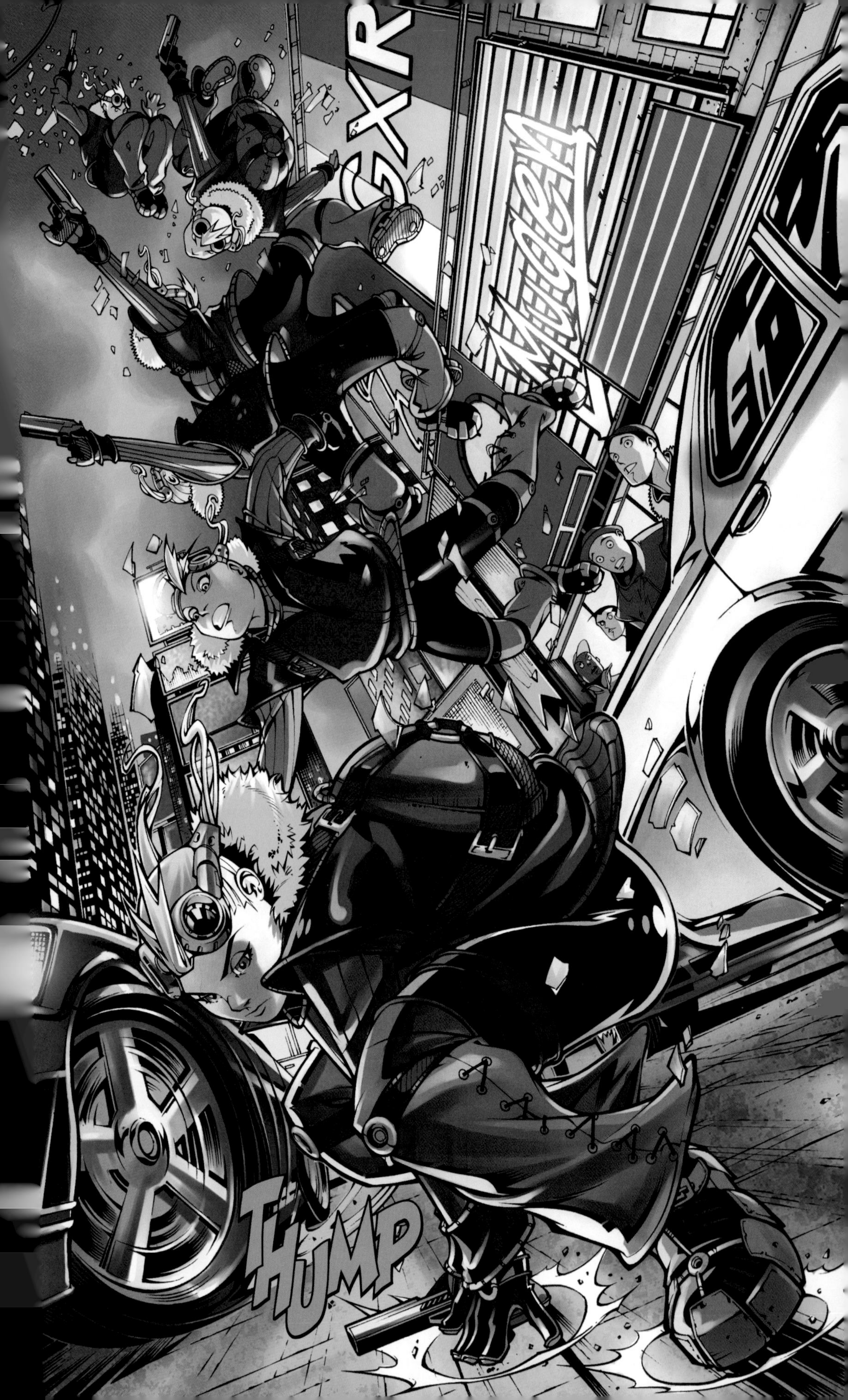
THUMP

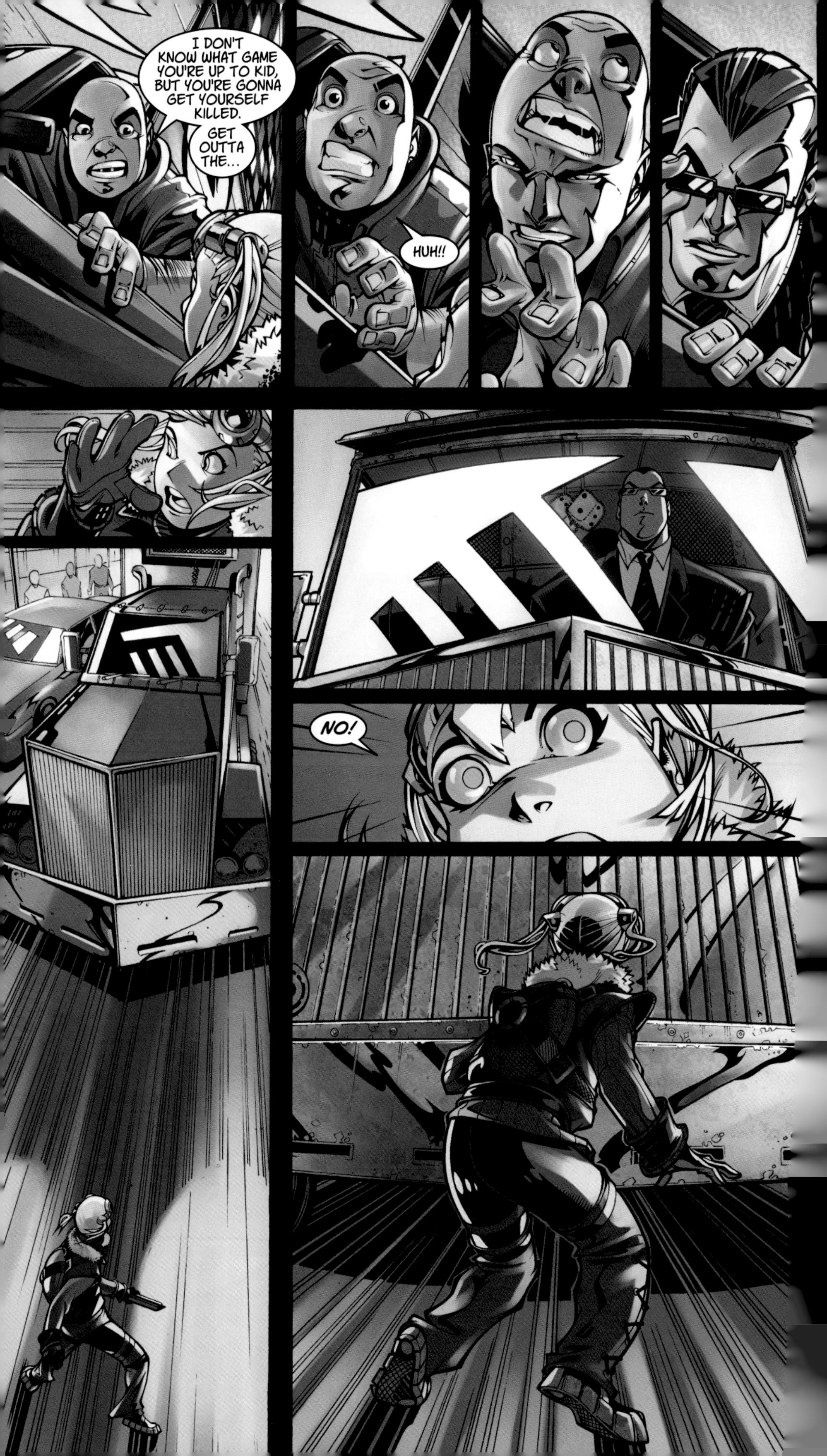
I DON'T KNOW WHAT GAME YOU'RE UP TO KID, BUT YOU'RE GONNA GET YOURSELF KILLED.
GET OUTTA THE...
HUH!!
NO!

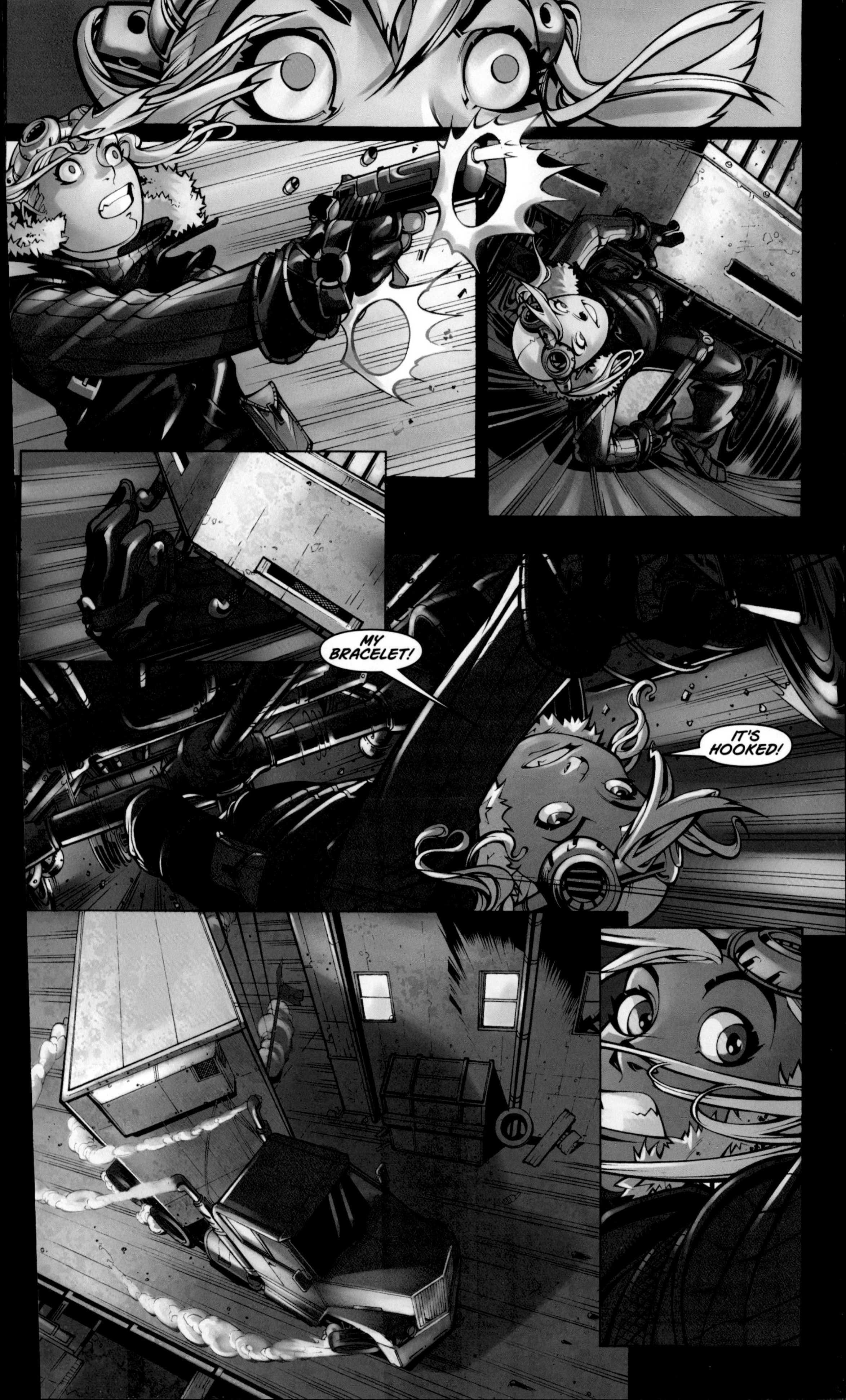
MY BRACELET!
IT'S HOOKED!

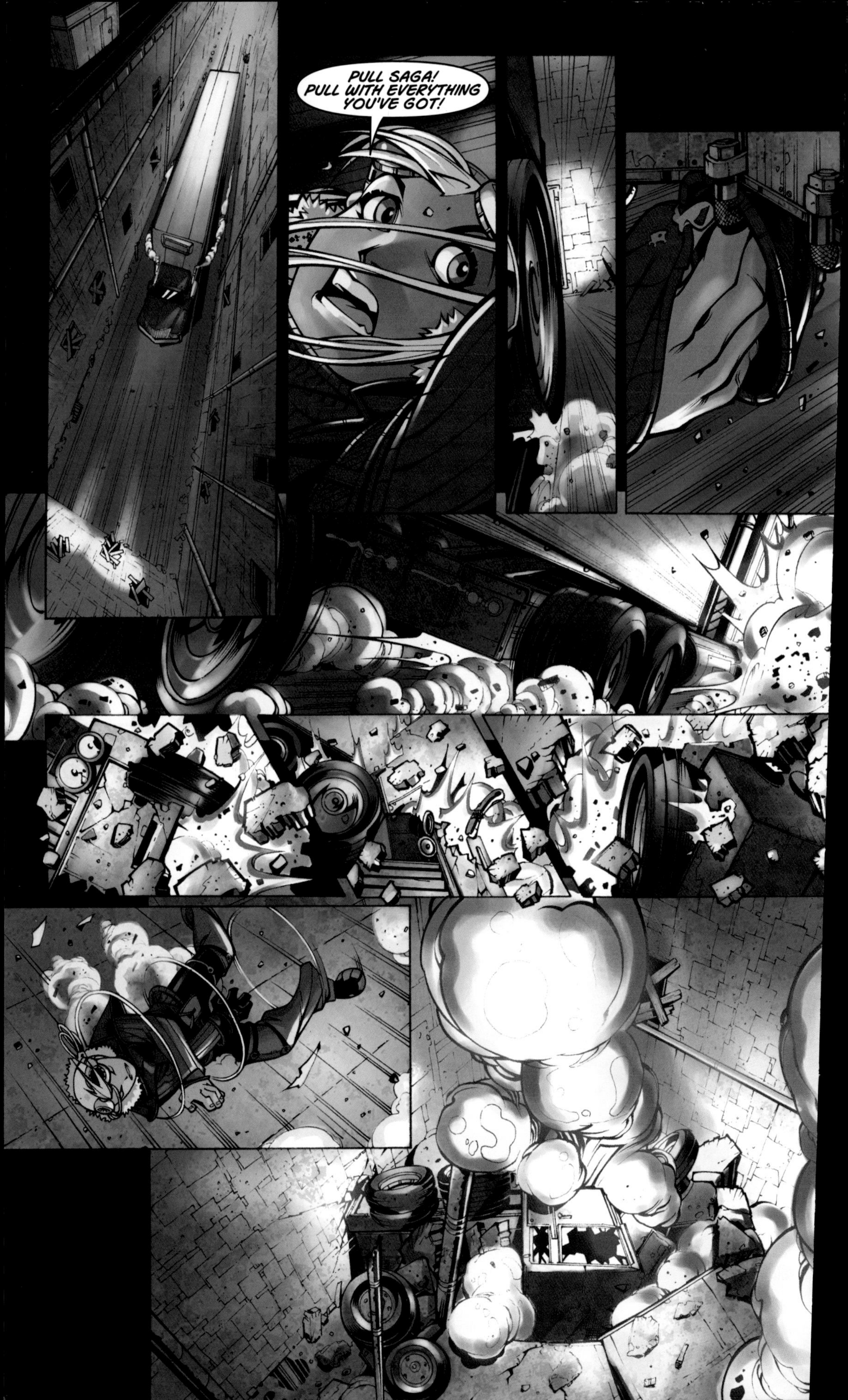
PULL SAGA! PULL WITH EVERYTHING YOU'VE GOT!

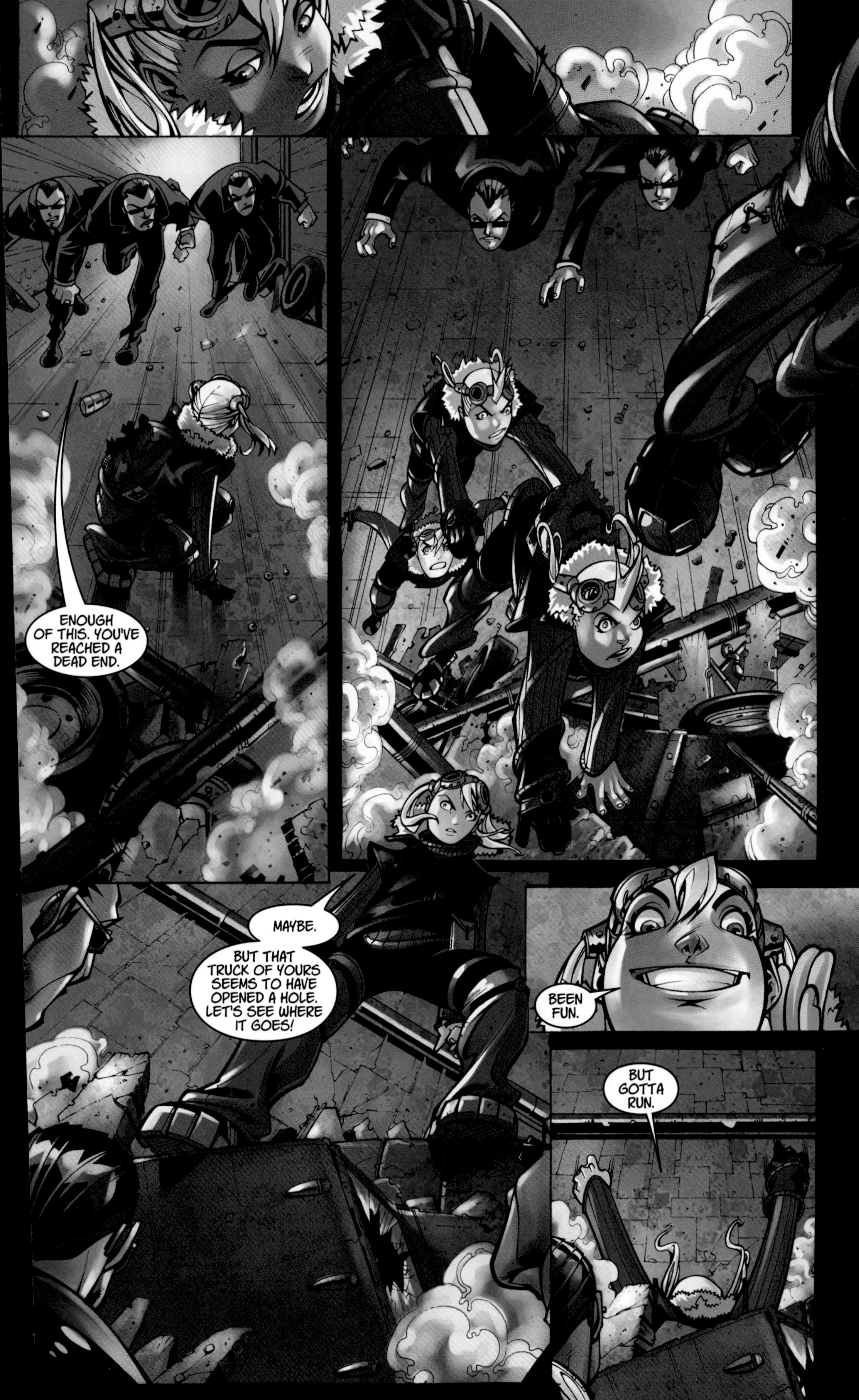
ENOUGH OF THIS. YOU'VE REACHED A DEAD END.
MAYBE.
BUT THAT TRUCK OF YOURS SEEMS TO HAVE OPENED A HOLE. LET'S SEE WHERE IT GOES!
BEEN FUN.
BUT GOTTA RUN.

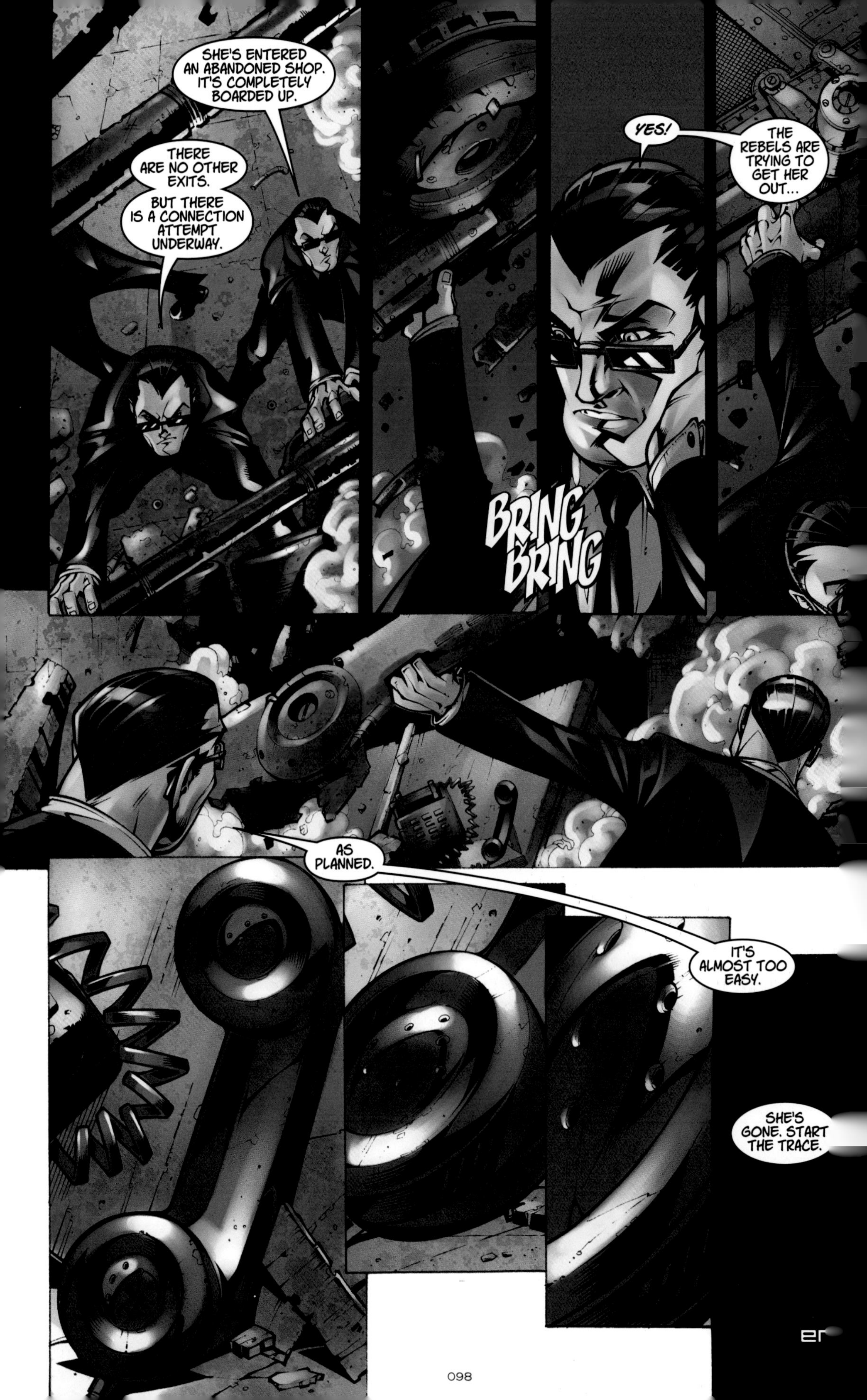
SHE'S ENTERED AN ABANDONED SHOP. IT'S COMPLETELY BOARDED UP.
THERE ARE NO OTHER EXITS.
BUT THERE IS A CONNECTION ATTEMPT UNDERWAY.
BRING BRING
YES!
THE REBELS ARE TRYING TO GET HER OUT...
AS PLANNED.
IT'S ALMOST TOO EASY.
SHE'S GONE. START THE TRACE.

WRONG NUMBER

PLOT & ART BY VINCE EVANS

Vince Evans is an artist primarily for comic, book, and video covers. He is best known in comics for his realistic SPIDER-MAN poster. He has worked on THE PUNISHER and BLACK PANTHER comics, as well as painted covers for CONAN, X-MEN and CAPTAIN AMERICA. Lately he has been working on movie posters including the 75th anniversary re-release of METROPOLIS which was used extensively here and in Paris. Currently Vince is working on a comic creation of his own. Born in New York City, he now lives in New Jersey with his wife Laurie.

COLOR BY JASON KEITH

An Eisner Award-nominee for his color work on EL CAZADOR, at age 22 Jason Keith is young but accomplished. He has worked on Marvel Comics' titles NEW X-MEN, UNCANNY X-MEN and DOOM RETURNS, and on CrossGen titles SCION, SOJOURN, LADY DEATH, and BRATH. Jason has also worked on the Image series THE GIFT, written by Raven Gregory. Currently, Jason is coloring a new mini-series called SAMURAI: HEAVEN AND EARTH for Dark Horse Comics, written by Ron Marz and illustrated by Luke Ross, as well as coloring the bi-monthly series DOC FRANKENSTEIN, written by the Wachowski Brothers.

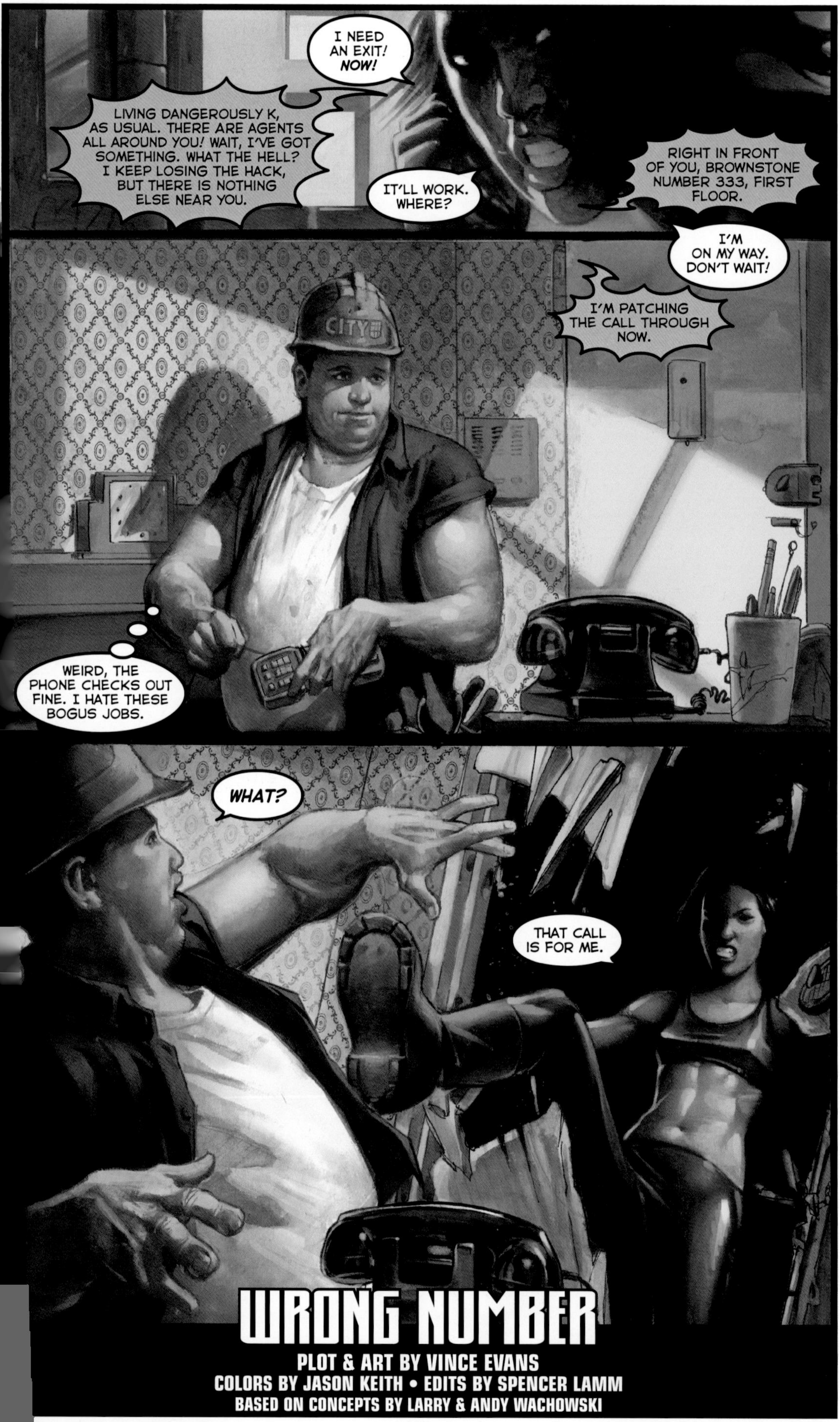
I NEED AN EXIT! NOW!
LIVING DANGEROUSLY K, AS USUAL. THERE ARE AGENTS ALL AROUND YOU! WAIT, I'VE GOT SOMETHING. WHAT THE HELL? I KEEP LOSING THE HACK, BUT THERE IS NOTHING ELSE NEAR YOU.
IT'LL WORK. WHERE?
RIGHT IN FRONT OF YOU, BROWNSTONE NUMBER 333, FIRST FLOOR.
I'M ON MY WAY. DON'T WAIT!
I'M PATCHING THE CALL THROUGH NOW.
CITY
WEIRD, THE PHONE CHECKS OUT FINE. I HATE THESE BOGUS JOBS.
WHAT?
THAT CALL IS FOR ME.
WRONG NUMBER
PLOT & ART BY VINCE EVANS
COLORS BY JASON KEITH • EDITS BY SPENCER LAMM
BASED ON CONCEPTS BY LARRY & ANDY WACHOWSKI

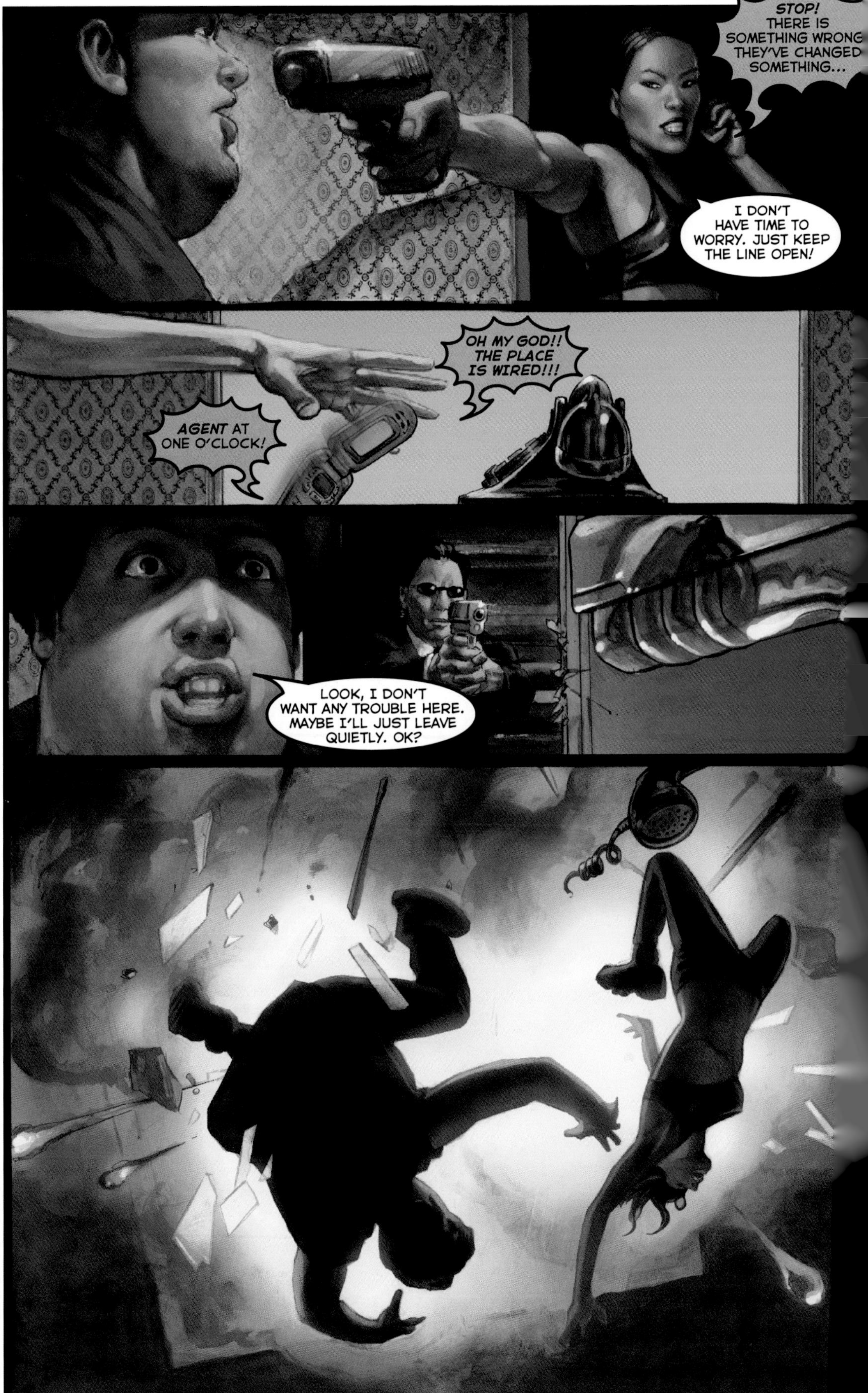
STOP! THERE IS SOMETHING WRONG THEY'VE CHANGED SOMETHING...
I DON'T HAVE TIME TO WORRY. JUST KEEP THE LINE OPEN!
AGENT AT ONE O'CLOCK!
OH MY GOD!! THE PLACE IS WIRED!!!
LOOK, I DON'T WANT ANY TROUBLE HERE. MAYBE I'LL JUST LEAVE QUIETLY. OK?

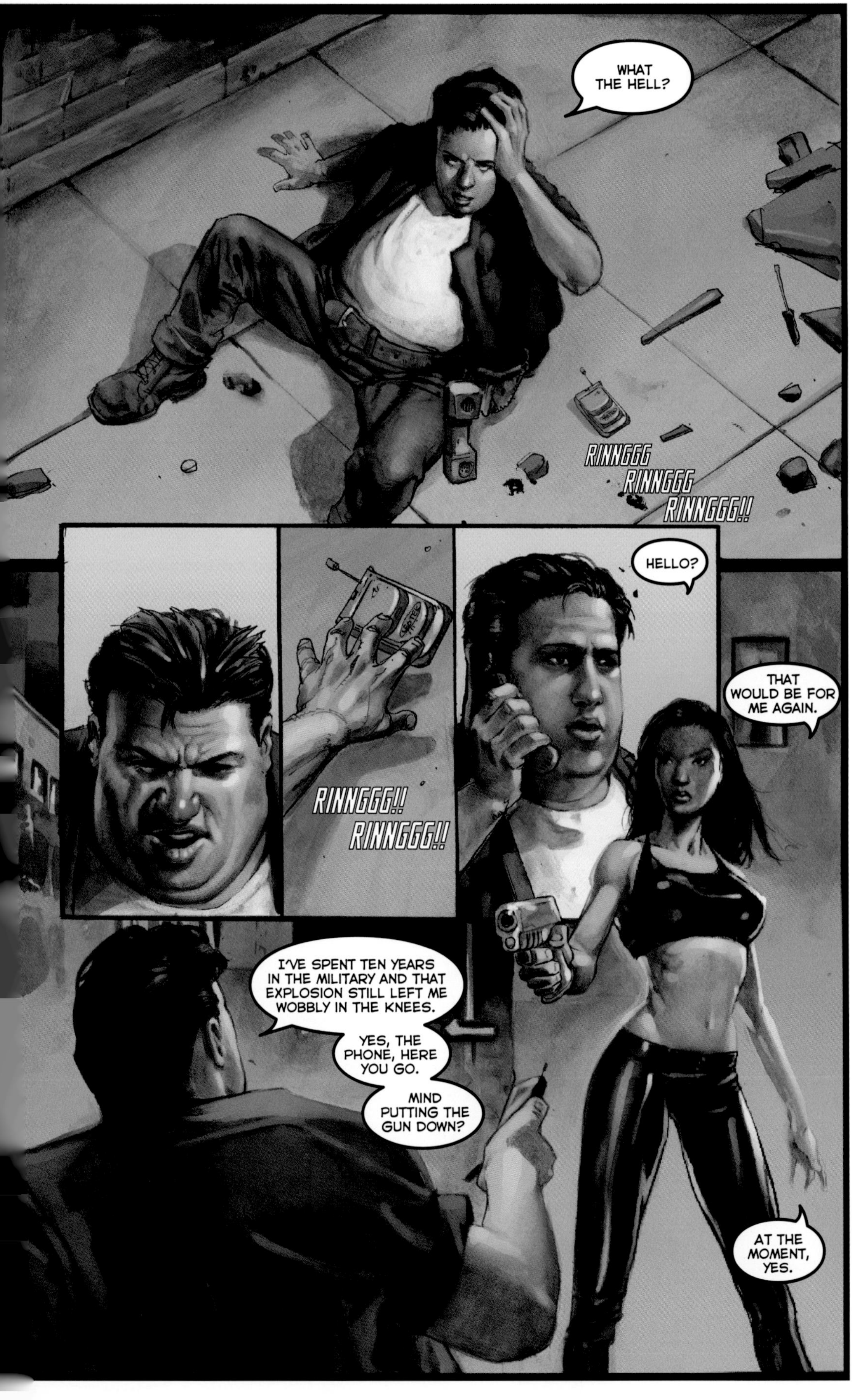
WHAT THE HELL?
RINNGGG RINNGGG RINNGGG!!
RINNGGG!! RINNGGG!!
HELLO?
THAT WOULD BE FOR ME AGAIN.
I'VE SPENT TEN YEARS IN THE MILITARY AND THAT EXPLOSION STILL LEFT ME WOBBLY IN THE KNEES.
YES, THE PHONE, HERE YOU GO.
MIND PUTTING THE GUN DOWN?
AT THE MOMENT, YES.

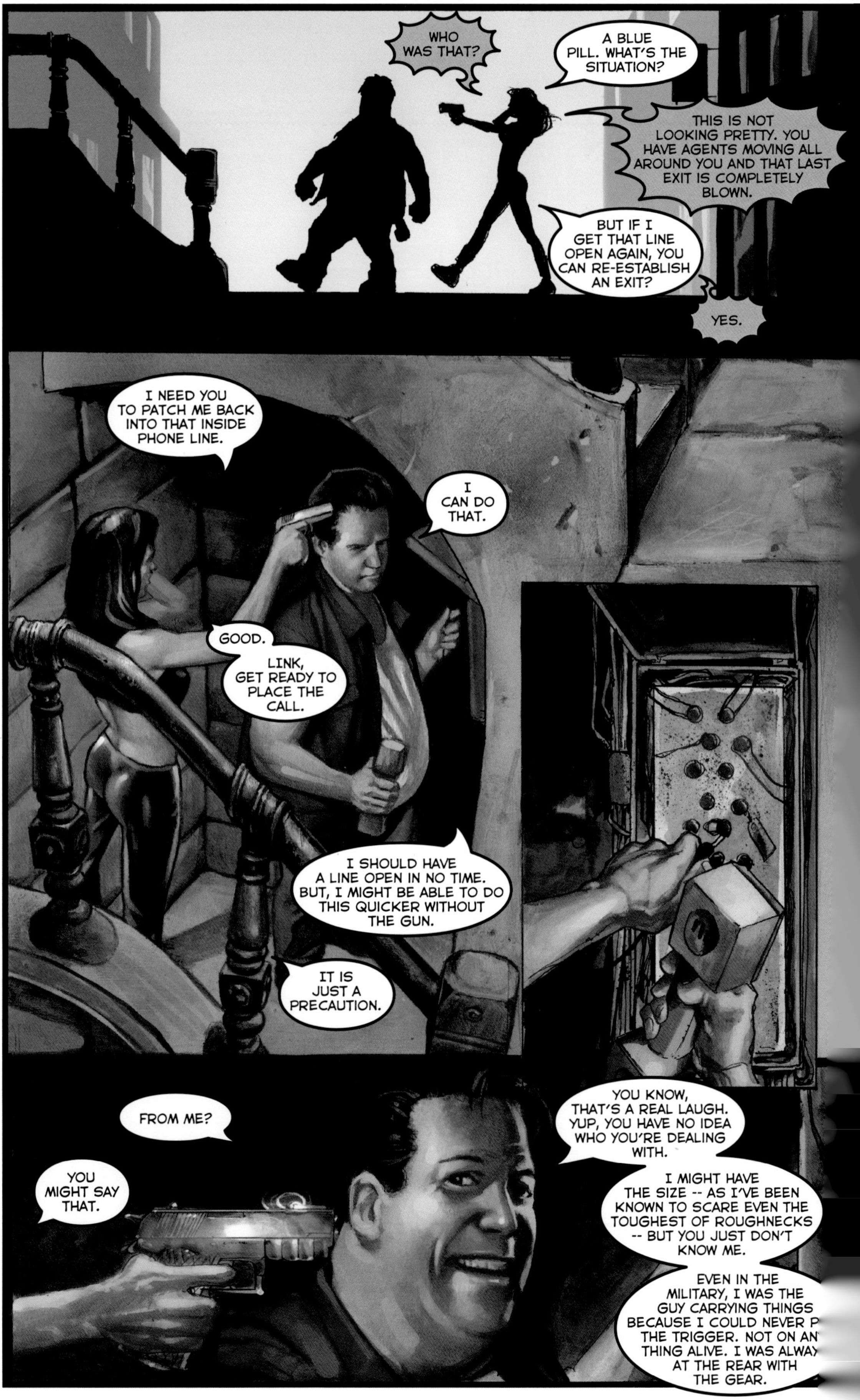
WHO WAS THAT?
A BLUE PILL. WHAT'S THE SITUATION?
THIS IS NOT LOOKING PRETTY. YOU HAVE AGENTS MOVING ALL AROUND YOU AND THAT LAST EXIT IS COMPLETELY BLOWN.
BUT IF I GET THAT LINE OPEN AGAIN, YOU CAN RE-ESTABLISH AN EXIT?
YES.
I NEED YOU TO PATCH ME BACK INTO THAT INSIDE PHONE LINE.
I CAN DO THAT.
GOOD.
LINK, GET READY TO PLACE THE CALL.
I SHOULD HAVE A LINE OPEN IN NO TIME. BUT, I MIGHT BE ABLE TO DO THIS QUICKER WITHOUT THE GUN.
IT IS JUST A PRECAUTION.
FROM ME?
YOU MIGHT SAY THAT.
YOU KNOW, THAT'S A REAL LAUGH. YUP, YOU HAVE NO IDEA WHO YOU'RE DEALING WITH.
I MIGHT HAVE THE SIZE -- AS I'VE BEEN KNOWN TO SCARE EVEN THE TOUGHEST OF ROUGHNECKS -- BUT YOU JUST DON'T KNOW ME.
EVEN IN THE MILITARY, I WAS THE GUY CARRYING THINGS BECAUSE I COULD NEVER P THE TRIGGER. NOT ON AN THING ALIVE. I WAS ALWAY AT THE REAR WITH THE GEAR.

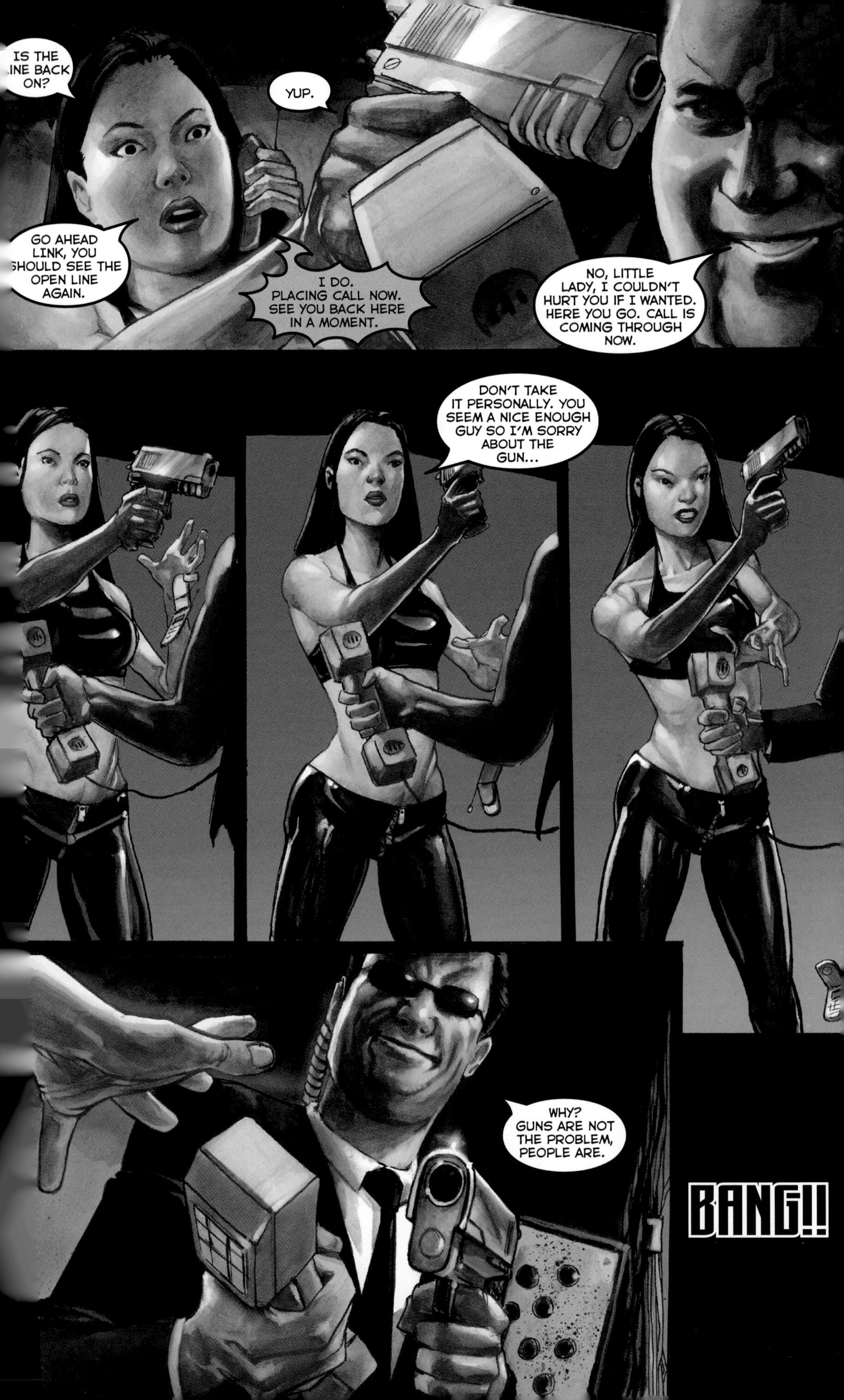
IS THE LINE BACK ON?
YUP.
GO AHEAD LINK, YOU SHOULD SEE THE OPEN LINE AGAIN.
I DO. PLACING CALL NOW. SEE YOU BACK HERE IN A MOMENT.
NO, LITTLE LADY, I COULDN'T HURT YOU IF I WANTED. HERE YOU GO. CALL IS COMING THROUGH NOW.
DON'T TAKE IT PERSONALLY. YOU SEEM A NICE ENOUGH GUY SO I'M SORRY ABOUT THE GUN...
WHY? GUNS ARE NOT THE PROBLEM, PEOPLE ARE.
BANG!!

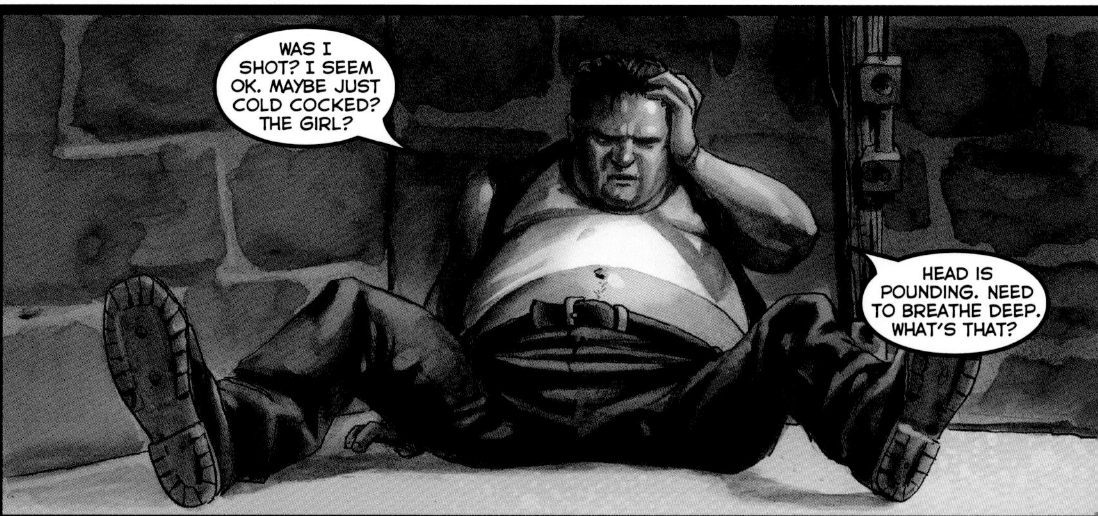
WAS I SHOT? I SEEM OK. MAYBE JUST COLD COCKED? THE GIRL?
HEAD IS POUNDING. NEED TO BREATHE DEEP. WHAT'S THAT?

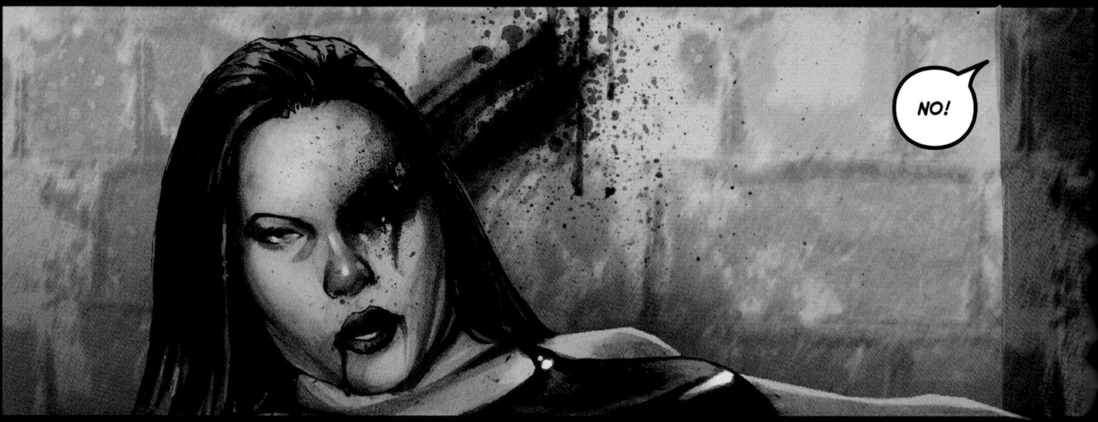
NO!

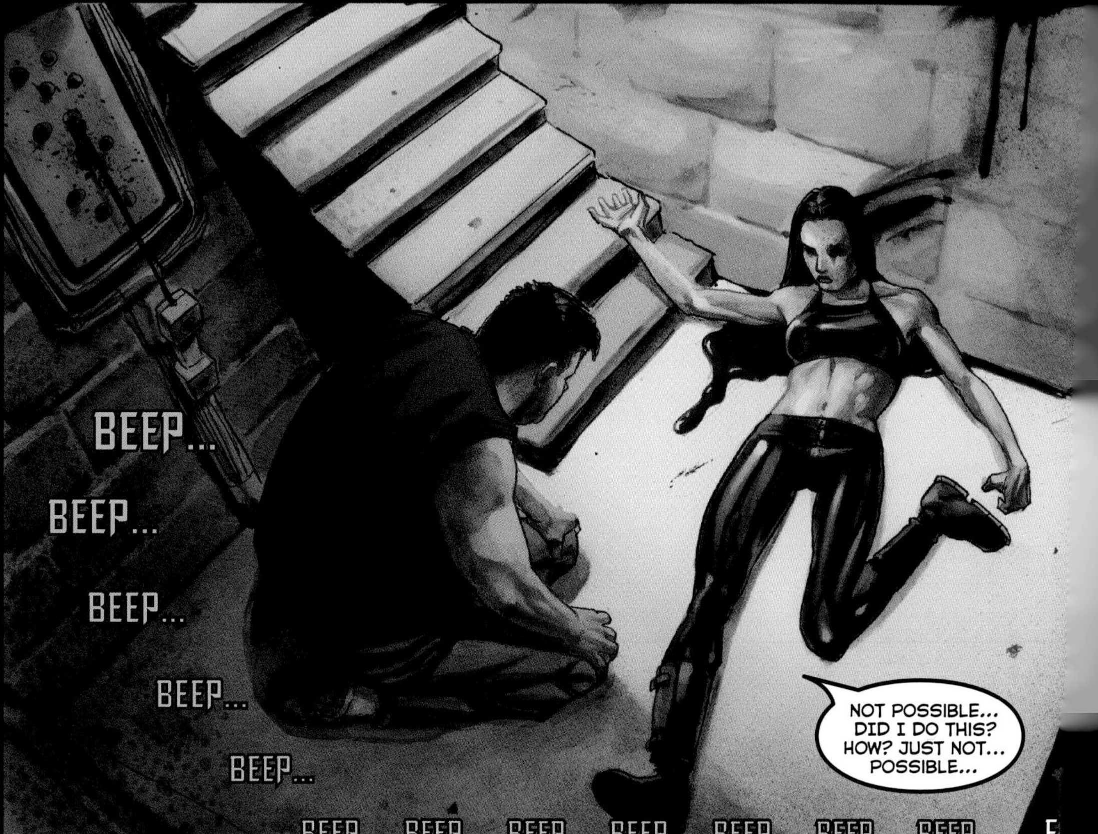
BEEP...
BEEP...
BEEP...
BEEP...
BEEP...
NOT POSSIBLE... DID I DO THIS? HOW? JUST NOT... POSSIBLE...
BEEP... BEEP... BEEP... BEEP... BEEP... BEEP... BEEP...

BROADCAST DEPTH

STORY & ART BY BILL
SIENKIEWICZ

Bill's innovative use of collage and illustration methods to tell a story have won him many major awards, including the 1983 Kirby Award for Best Artist, and Europe's top honor, the Yellow Kid Award, for the comic ELEKTRA: ASSASSIN. He wrote and illustrated the critically acclaimed STRAY TOASTERS. His most recently published work includes TESTAMENT and PRECURSOR, a collection of watercolors and non-computer-enhanced work. Bill has exhibited throughout the USA and the world, and has also produced work for magazines, CD covers, and the Olympics. He received two Emmy® Award nominations for production and character design on the television series "WHERE IN THE WORLD IS CARMEN SAN DIEGO?". Other projects include posters and storyboards for films such as UNFORGIVEN, THE GREEN MILE and THE GRINCH. He is currently illustrating the Marvel Comics series BLACK WIDOW.

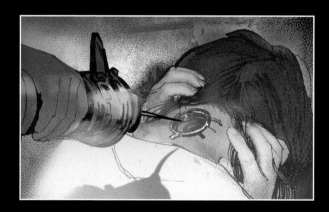

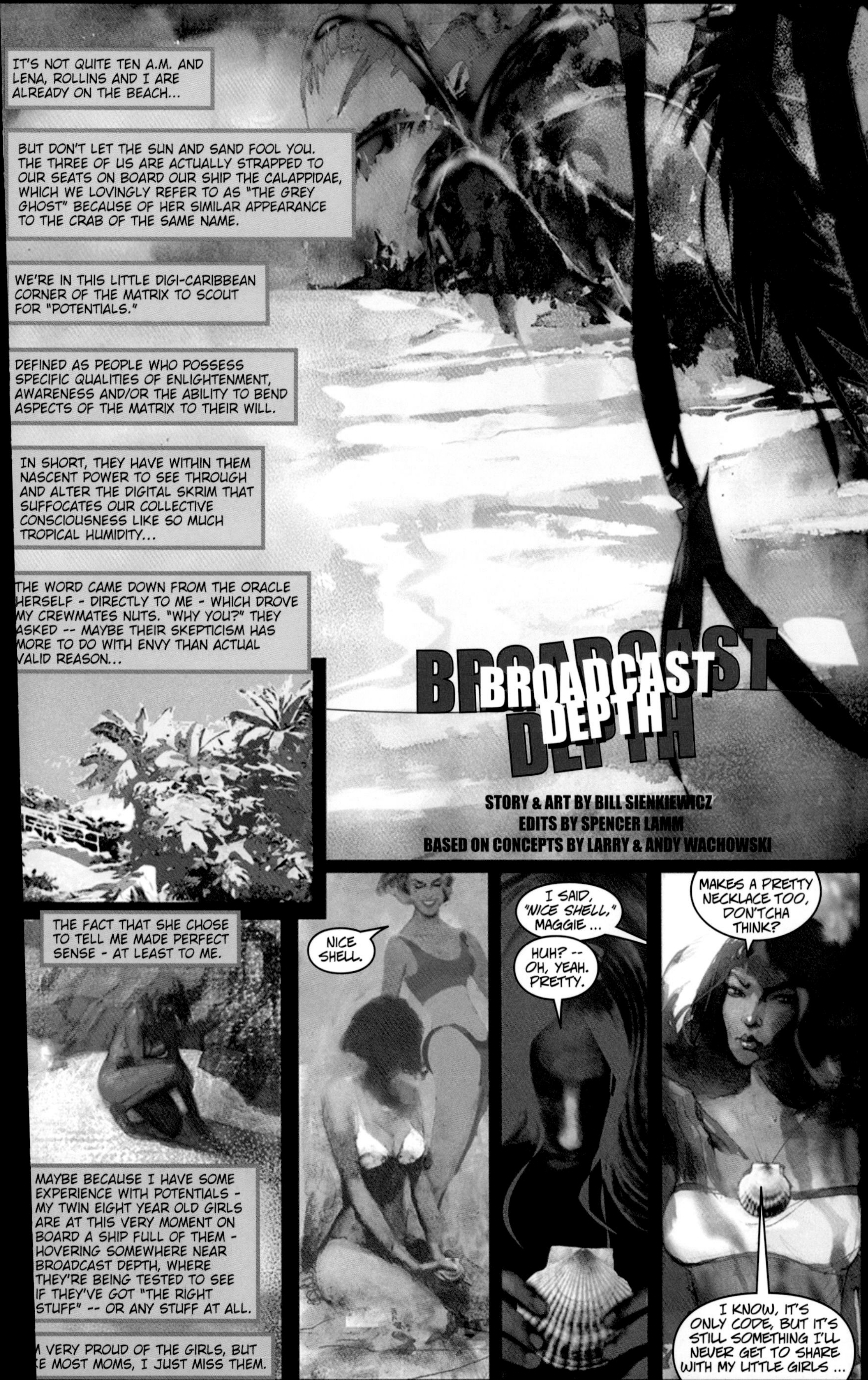
IT'S NOT QUITE TEN A.M. AND LENA, ROLLINS AND I ARE ALREADY ON THE BEACH...
BUT DON'T LET THE SUN AND SAND FOOL YOU. THE THREE OF US ARE ACTUALLY STRAPPED TO OUR SEATS ON BOARD OUR SHIP THE CALAPPIDAE, WHICH WE LOVINGLY REFER TO AS "THE GREY GHOST" BECAUSE OF HER SIMILAR APPEARANCE TO THE CRAB OF THE SAME NAME.
WE'RE IN THIS LITTLE DIGI-CARIBBEAN CORNER OF THE MATRIX TO SCOUT FOR "POTENTIALS."
DEFINED AS PEOPLE WHO POSSESS SPECIFIC QUALITIES OF ENLIGHTENMENT, AWARENESS AND/OR THE ABILITY TO BEND ASPECTS OF THE MATRIX TO THEIR WILL.
IN SHORT, THEY HAVE WITHIN THEM NASCENT POWER TO SEE THROUGH AND ALTER THE DIGITAL SKRIM THAT SUFFOCATES OUR COLLECTIVE CONSCIOUSNESS LIKE SO MUCH TROPICAL HUMIDITY...
THE WORD CAME DOWN FROM THE ORACLE HERSELF - DIRECTLY TO ME - WHICH DROVE MY CREWMATES NUTS. "WHY YOU?" THEY ASKED -- MAYBE THEIR SKEPTICISM HAS MORE TO DO WITH ENVY THAN ACTUAL VALID REASON...
BROADCAST DEPTH
STORY & ART BY BILL SIENKIEWICZ
EDITS BY SPENCER LAMM
BASED ON CONCEPTS BY LARRY & ANDY WACHOWSKI
THE FACT THAT SHE CHOSE TO TELL ME MADE PERFECT SENSE - AT LEAST TO ME.
MAYBE BECAUSE I HAVE SOME EXPERIENCE WITH POTENTIALS - MY TWIN EIGHT YEAR OLD GIRLS ARE AT THIS VERY MOMENT ON BOARD A SHIP FULL OF THEM - HOVERING SOMEWHERE NEAR BROADCAST DEPTH, WHERE THEY'RE BEING TESTED TO SEE IF THEY'VE GOT "THE RIGHT STUFF" -- OR ANY STUFF AT ALL.
M VERY PROUD OF THE GIRLS, BUT E MOST MOMS, I JUST MISS THEM.
NICE SHELL.
I SAID, "NICE SHELL," MAGGIE ...
HUH? -- OH, YEAH. PRETTY.
MAKES A PRETTY NECKLACE TOO, DON'TCHA THINK?
I KNOW, IT'S ONLY CODE, BUT IT'S STILL SOMETHING I'LL NEVER GET TO SHARE WITH MY LITTLE GIRLS ...

LENA LOOKS AT ME FUNNY, SO I DECIDE TO FORGET TO EVEN TRY AND EXPLAIN WHAT I MEAN. SHE DOESN'T HAVE KIDS, AND BESIDES, I'D RATHER TRY TO GET INTO THE ILLUSION OF THIS PLACE -- IF ONLY EVEN FOR A LITTLE WHILE.
I'M GOING FOR A SWIM.
DON'T GO OUT TOO FAR, MAGS -- IN CASE THE ORACLE IS RIGHT, OR IN CASE WE HAVE TO BAIL...
I'LL CHECK IN EVERY FIFTEEN MINUTES...
THE WATER FEELS SO GOOD ON MY SKIN. I'M SWIMMING IN A WOMB. I LAUGH AT THE IRONY OF IT, THINKING OF THE COUNTLESS HUMAN LIVES SPENT IN LIQUID FILLED PODS.
IT'S HARD TO BELIEVE THAT THIS BEAUTIFUL WORLD IS NOTHING BUT LINES OF CODE. WHICH WAS THE WHOLE POINT OF THIS SHELL NECKLACE...

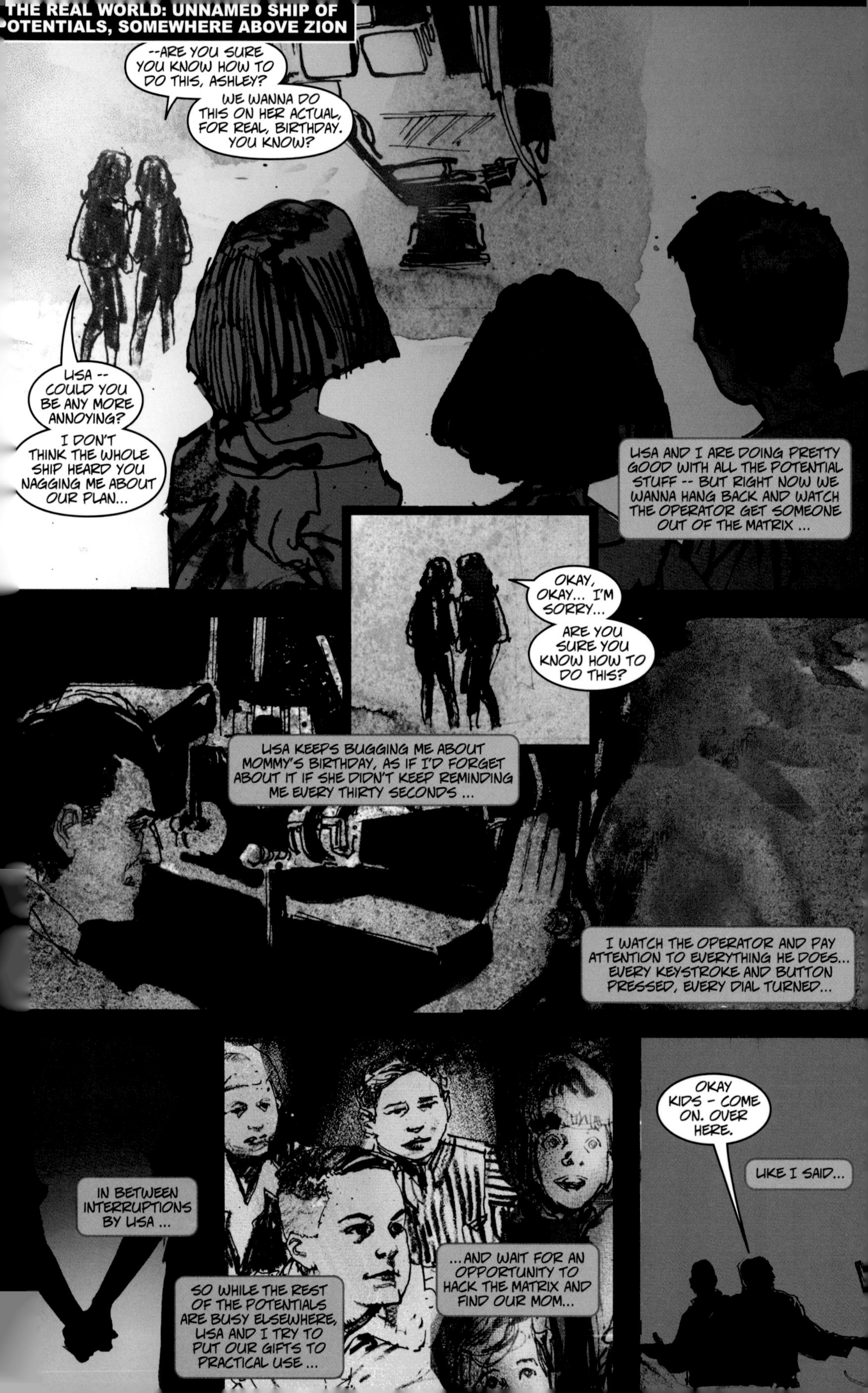
THE REAL WORLD: UNNAMED SHIP OF POTENTIALS, SOMEWHERE ABOVE ZION
--ARE YOU SURE YOU KNOW HOW TO DO THIS, ASHLEY?
WE WANNA DO THIS ON HER ACTUAL, FOR REAL, BIRTHDAY. YOU KNOW?
LISA -- COULD YOU BE ANY MORE ANNOYING?
I DON'T THINK THE WHOLE SHIP HEARD YOU NAGGING ME ABOUT OUR PLAN...
LISA AND I ARE DOING PRETTY GOOD WITH ALL THE POTENTIAL STUFF -- BUT RIGHT NOW WE WANNA HANG BACK AND WATCH THE OPERATOR GET SOMEONE OUT OF THE MATRIX ...
OKAY, OKAY... I'M SORRY...
ARE YOU SURE YOU KNOW HOW TO DO THIS?
LISA KEEPS BUGGING ME ABOUT MOMMY'S BIRTHDAY, AS IF I'D FORGET ABOUT IT IF SHE DIDN'T KEEP REMINDING ME EVERY THIRTY SECONDS ...
I WATCH THE OPERATOR AND PAY ATTENTION TO EVERYTHING HE DOES... EVERY KEYSTROKE AND BUTTON PRESSED, EVERY DIAL TURNED...
IN BETWEEN INTERRUPTIONS BY LISA ...
SO WHILE THE REST OF THE POTENTIALS ARE BUSY ELSEWHERE, LISA AND I TRY TO PUT OUR GIFTS TO PRACTICAL USE ...
...AND WAIT FOR AN OPPORTUNITY TO HACK THE MATRIX AND FIND OUR MOM...
OKAY KIDS - COME ON. OVER HERE.
LIKE I SAID...

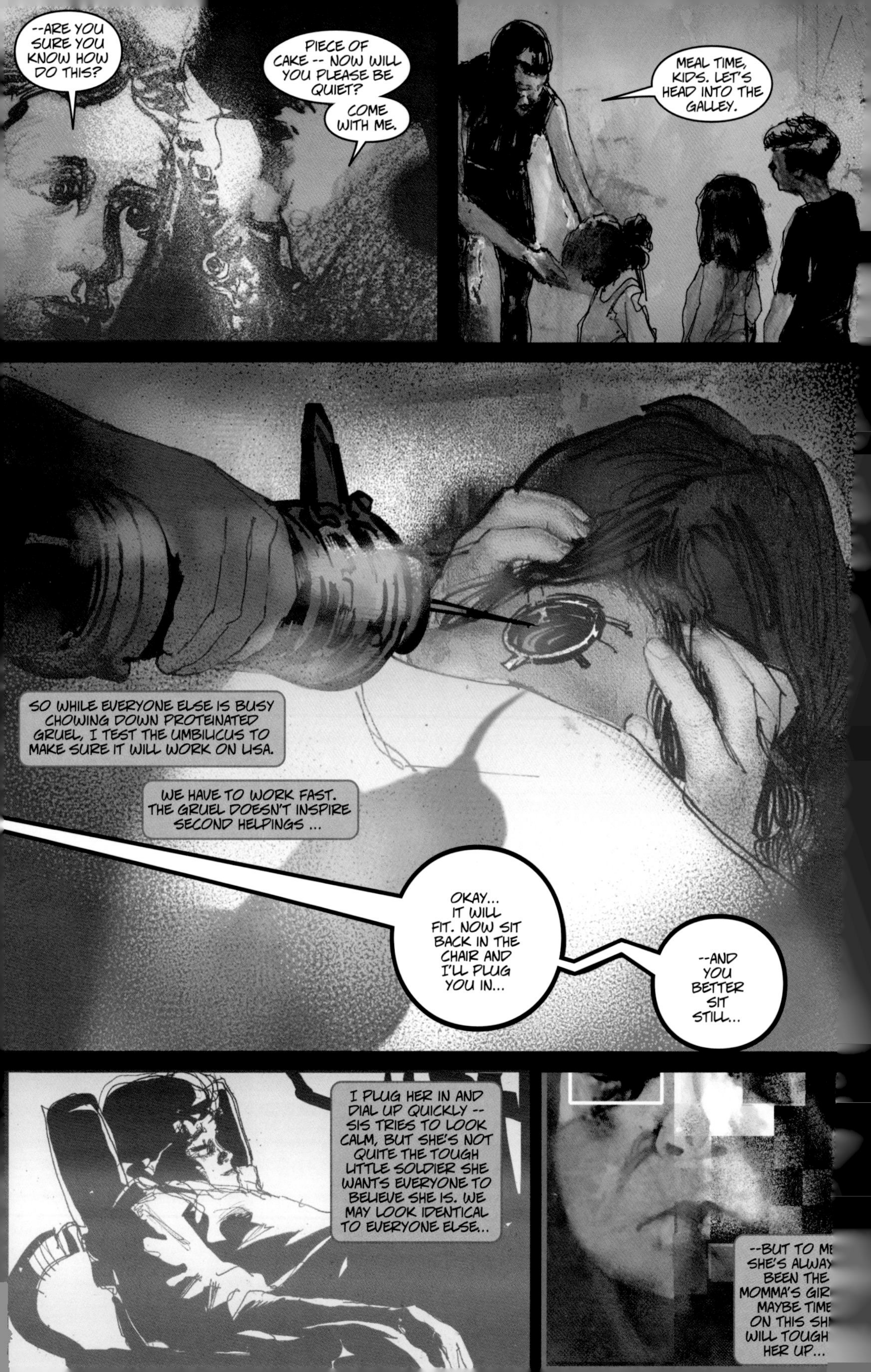
--ARE YOU SURE YOU KNOW HOW DO THIS?
PIECE OF CAKE -- NOW WILL YOU PLEASE BE QUIET?
COME WITH ME.
MEAL TIME, KIDS. LET'S HEAD INTO THE GALLEY.
SO WHILE EVERYONE ELSE IS BUSY CHOWING DOWN PROTEINATED GRUEL, I TEST THE UMBILICUS TO MAKE SURE IT WILL WORK ON LISA.
WE HAVE TO WORK FAST. THE GRUEL DOESN'T INSPIRE SECOND HELPINGS ...
OKAY... IT WILL FIT. NOW SIT BACK IN THE CHAIR AND I'LL PLUG YOU IN...
--AND YOU BETTER SIT STILL...
I PLUG HER IN AND DIAL UP QUICKLY -- SIS TRIES TO LOOK CALM, BUT SHE'S NOT QUITE THE TOUGH LITTLE SOLDIER SHE WANTS EVERYONE TO BELIEVE SHE IS. WE MAY LOOK IDENTICAL TO EVERYONE ELSE...
--BUT TO ME SHE'S ALWAY BEEN THE MOMMA'S GIR MAYBE TIME ON THIS SH WILL TOUGH HER UP...

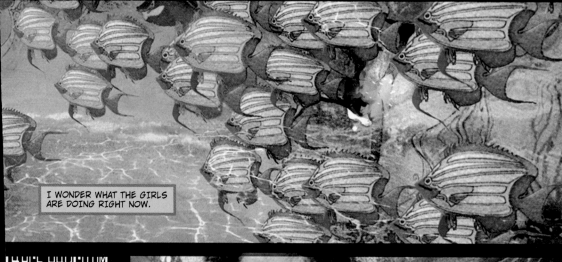

I WONDER WHAT THE GIRLS ARE DOING RIGHT NOW.

TRACE PROGRAM INITIATED.

BOY -- WON'T MOM BE SURPRISED.

I'M THEIR MOTHER, FOR GOD'S SAKE. I'M SUPPOSED TO BE TEACHING THEM HOW TO BE BETTER PEOPLE -- STRONG WOMEN -- SOLDIERS IN THE WAR AGAINST THE MACHINES...

AGAINST THE FATE OF THE MASSES: THE BATTERY FARM.

WONDER HOW I CAN DO THAT I'M STUCK HERE FIGHTING HE "GOOD FIGHT," DAMMIT...

W CAN I TEACH MY GIRLS? W CAN I HELP PREPARE EM FOR THEIR LIVES?

TARGET ACQUIRED.

--ARE WE THERE YET?

EANWHILE, ON HE CALAPPIDAE

RNING RACE LERT

WHOA. HEY. TRACE.

YEAH. DAMN. WHO..?

UNKNOWN... PARR, CAN YOU JAM IT BEFORE WE'RE TARGETED? SENTINELS -- THEY'RE...

I KNOW... I KNOW...

PBEEPBEEPBEEPBEEPBEEPBEEPBEEPBEEPBEEPBEEPBEEPBEEPBEEPBEEPBEEPBEEPBEEPBEEPBEEPBEEPBEEPBEEPBEEPBEEPBEEPBEEP

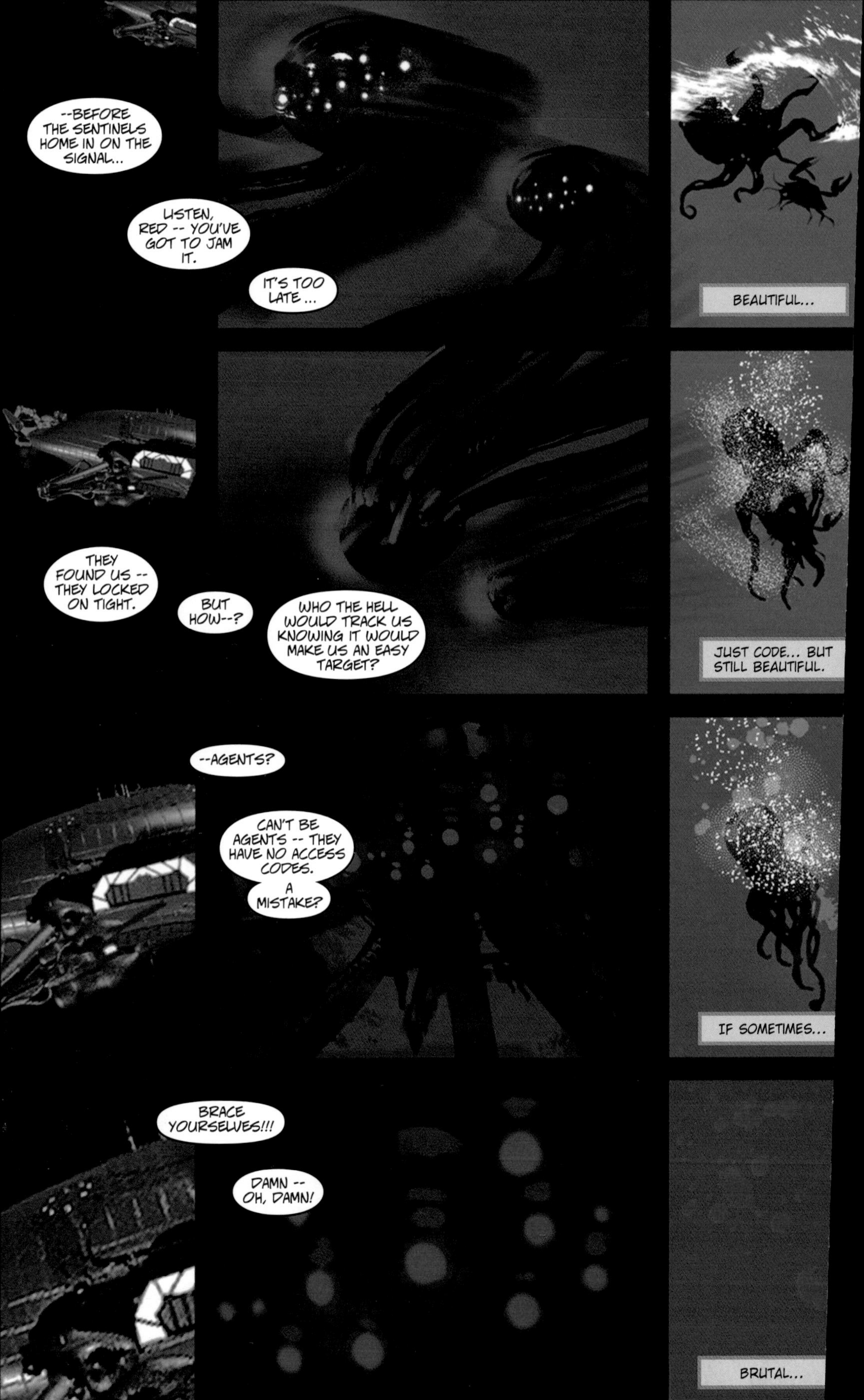
--BEFORE THE SENTINELS HOME IN ON THE SIGNAL...
LISTEN, RED -- YOU'VE GOT TO JAM IT.
IT'S TOO LATE...
BEAUTIFUL...
THEY FOUND US -- THEY LOCKED ON TIGHT.
BUT HOW--?
WHO THE HELL WOULD TRACK US KNOWING IT WOULD MAKE US AN EASY TARGET?
JUST CODE... BUT STILL BEAUTIFUL.
--AGENTS?
CAN'T BE AGENTS -- THEY HAVE NO ACCESS CODES.
A MISTAKE?
IF SOMETIMES...
BRACE YOURSELVES!!!
DAMN -- OH, DAMN!
BRUTAL...

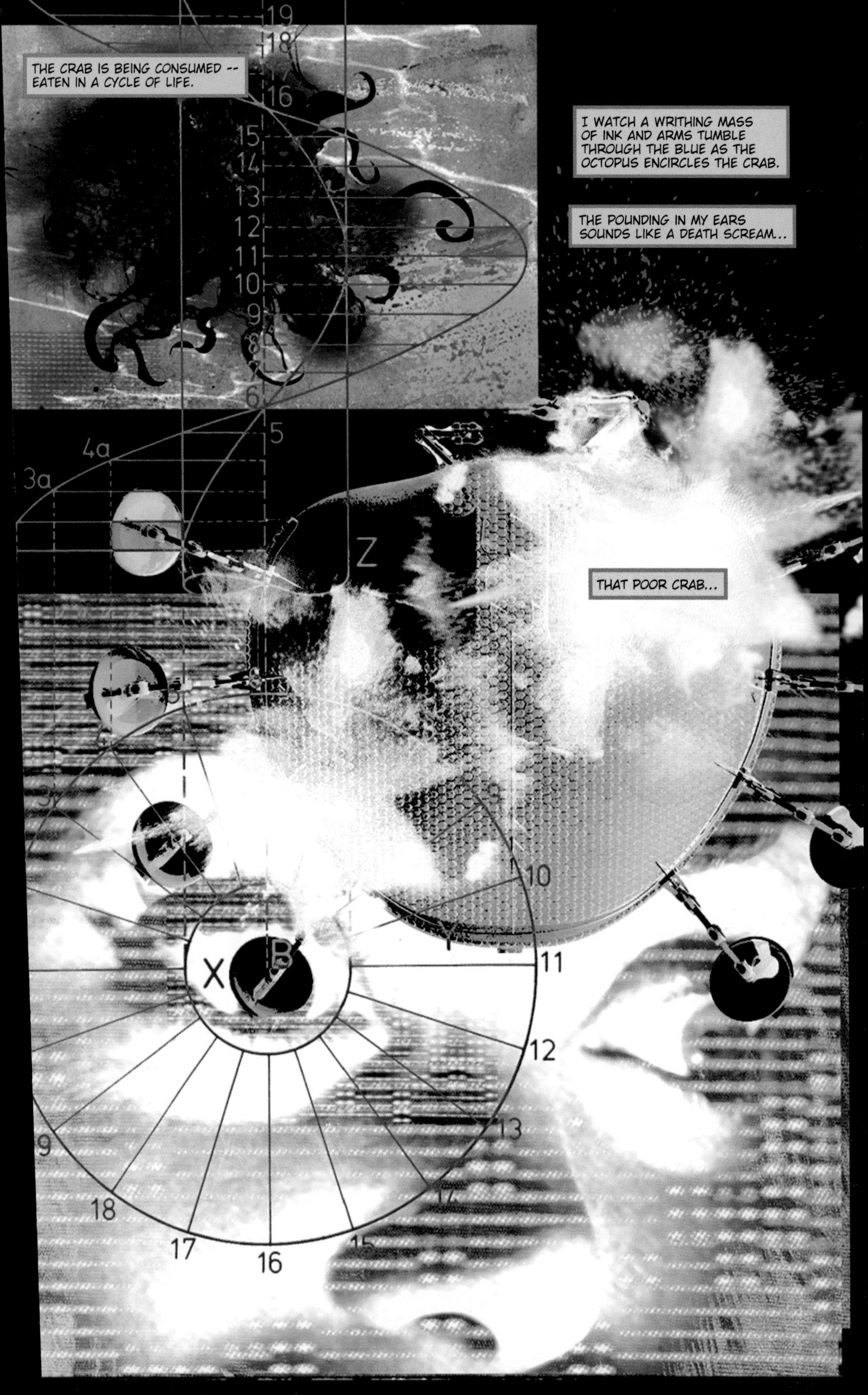
THE CRAB IS BEING CONSUMED -- EATEN IN A CYCLE OF LIFE.
I WATCH A WRITHING MASS OF INK AND ARMS TUMBLE THROUGH THE BLUE AS THE OCTOPUS ENCIRCLES THE CRAB.
THE POUNDING IN MY EARS SOUNDS LIKE A DEATH SCREAM...
THAT POOR CRAB...

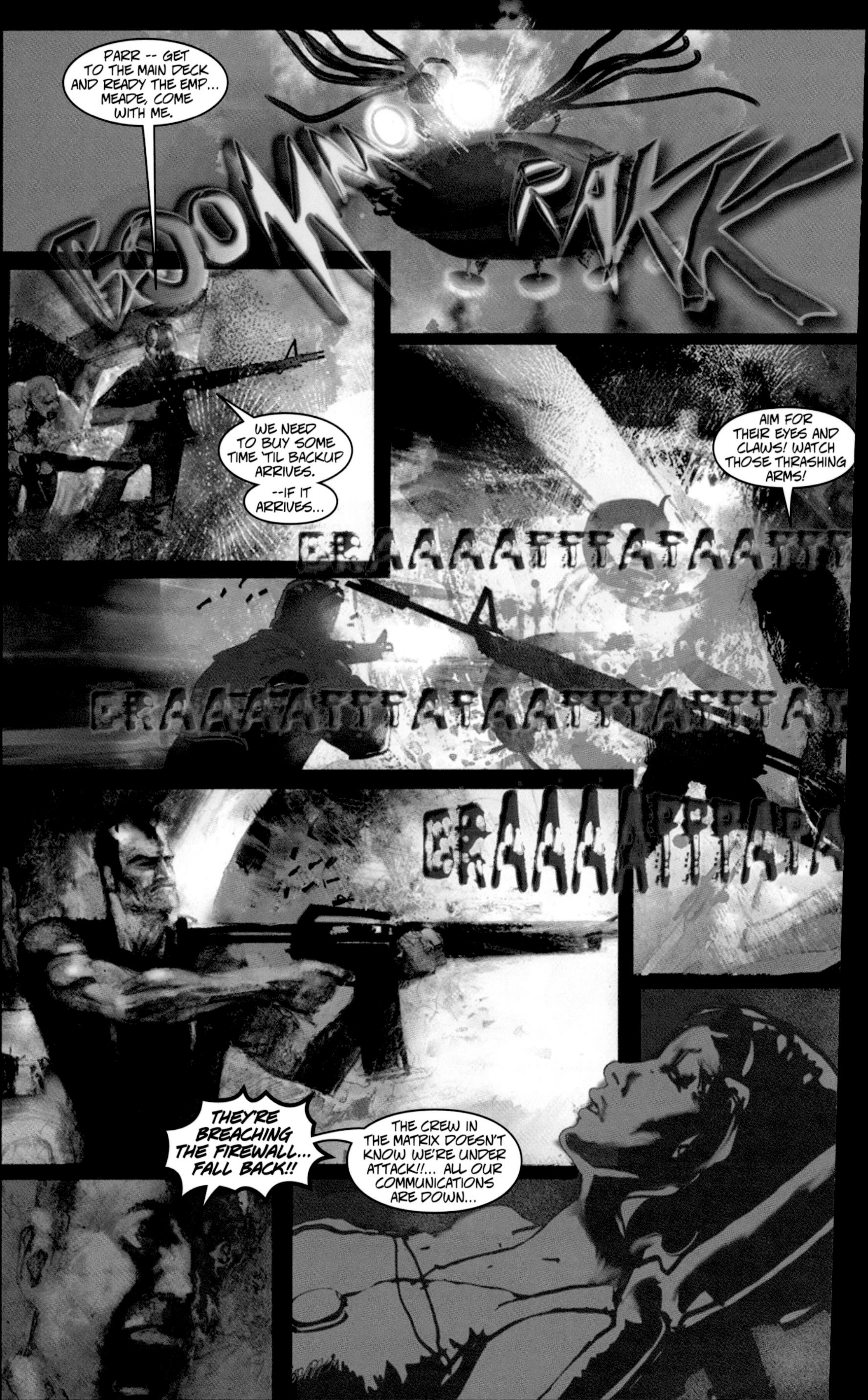
PARR -- GET TO THE MAIN DECK AND READY THE EMP... MEADE, COME WITH ME.
BOOM
RAKK
WE NEED TO BUY SOME TIME 'TIL BACKUP ARRIVES.
--IF IT ARRIVES...
AIM FOR THEIR EYES AND CLAWS! WATCH THOSE THRASHING ARMS!
THEY'RE BREACHING THE FIREWALL... FALL BACK!!
THE CREW IN THE MATRIX DOESN'T KNOW WE'RE UNDER ATTACK!!... ALL OUR COMMUNICATIONS ARE DOWN...

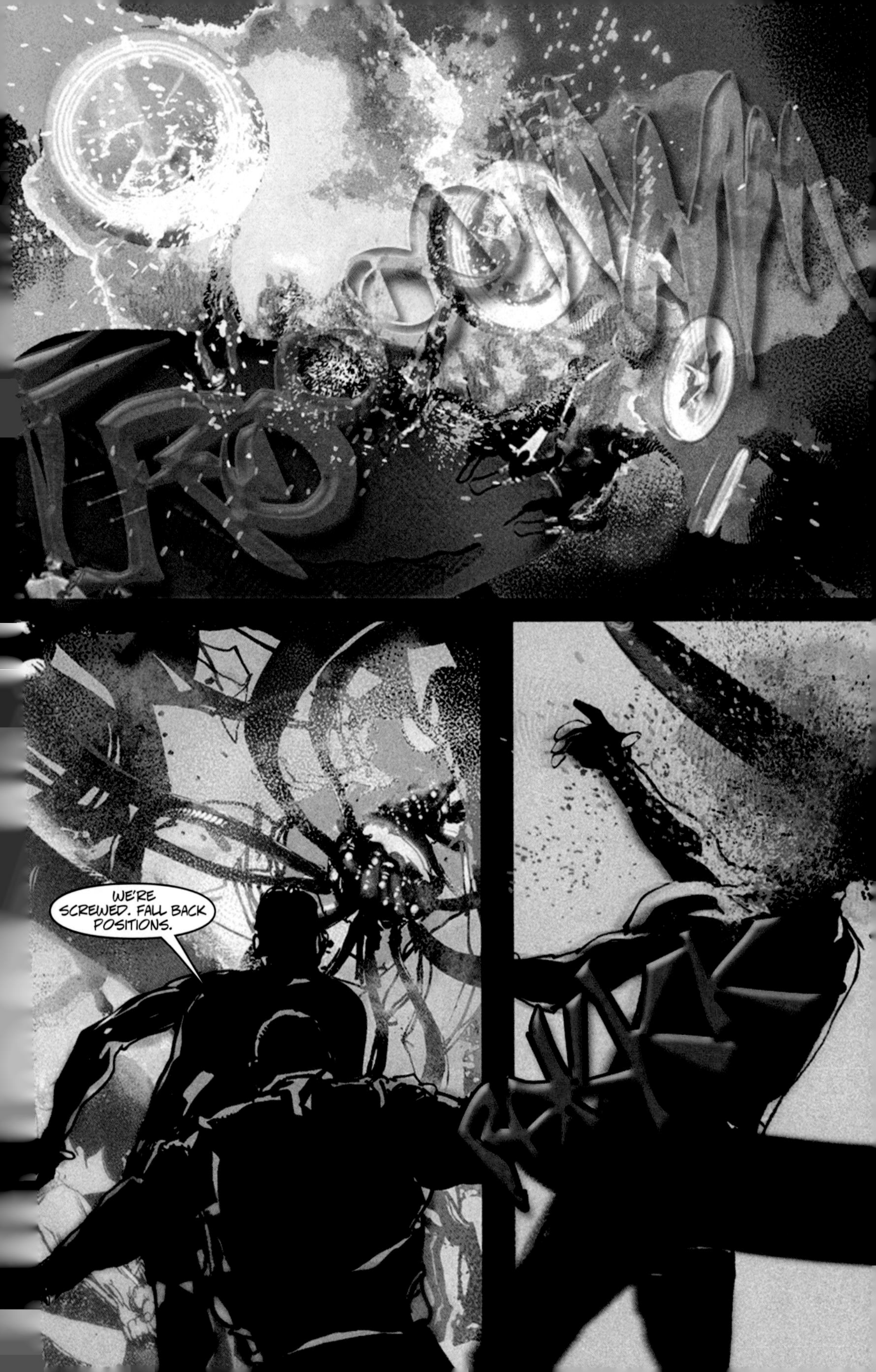
WE'RE SCREWED. FALL BACK POSITIONS.

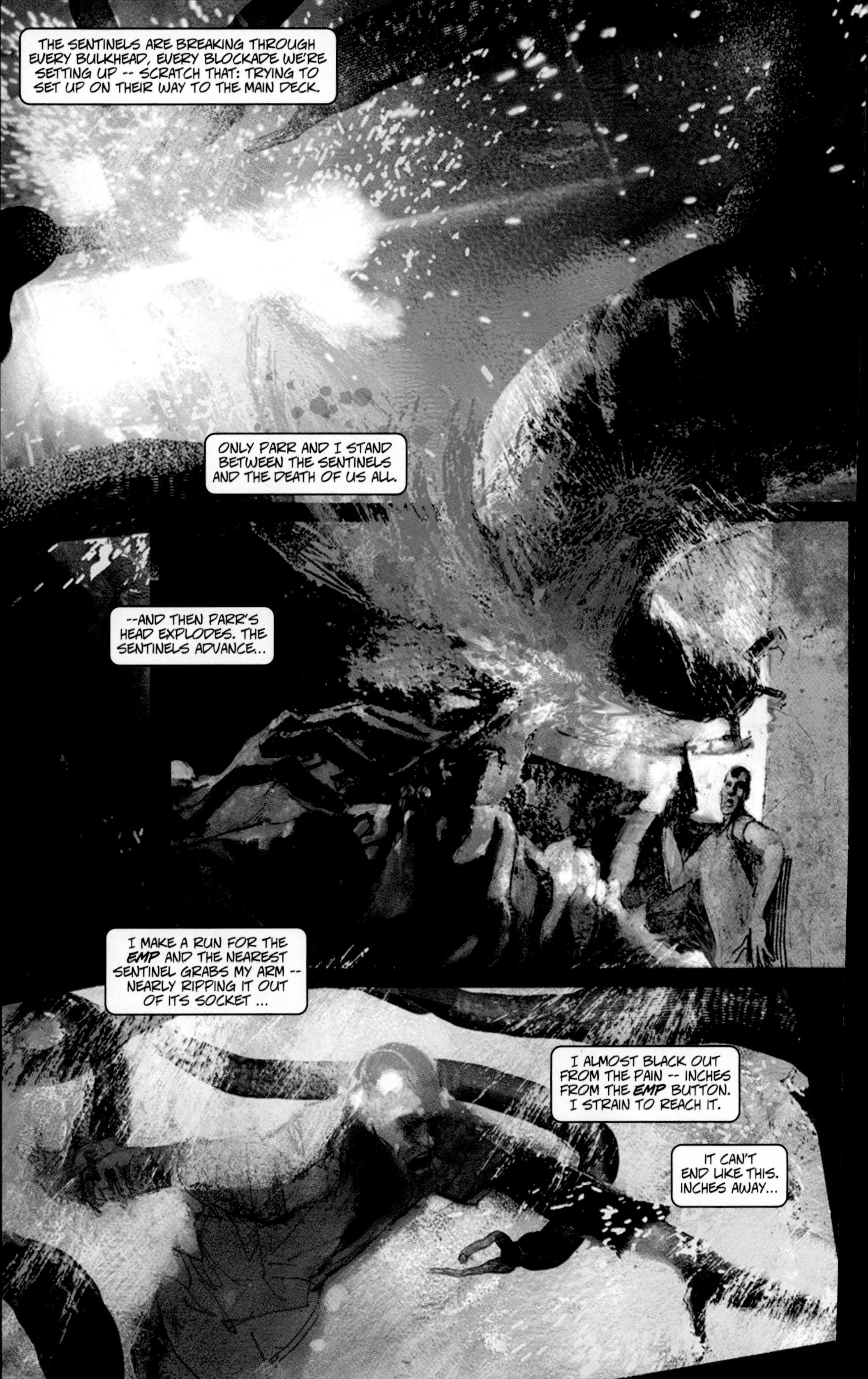
THE SENTINELS ARE BREAKING THROUGH EVERY BULKHEAD, EVERY BLOCKADE WE'RE SETTING UP -- SCRATCH THAT: TRYING TO SET UP ON THEIR WAY TO THE MAIN DECK.
ONLY PARR AND I STAND BETWEEN THE SENTINELS AND THE DEATH OF US ALL.
--AND THEN PARR'S HEAD EXPLODES. THE SENTINELS ADVANCE...
I MAKE A RUN FOR THE EMP AND THE NEAREST SENTINEL GRABS MY ARM -- NEARLY RIPPING IT OUT OF ITS SOCKET ...
I ALMOST BLACK OUT FROM THE PAIN -- INCHES FROM THE EMP BUTTON. I STRAIN TO REACH IT.
IT CAN'T END LIKE THIS. INCHES AWAY...

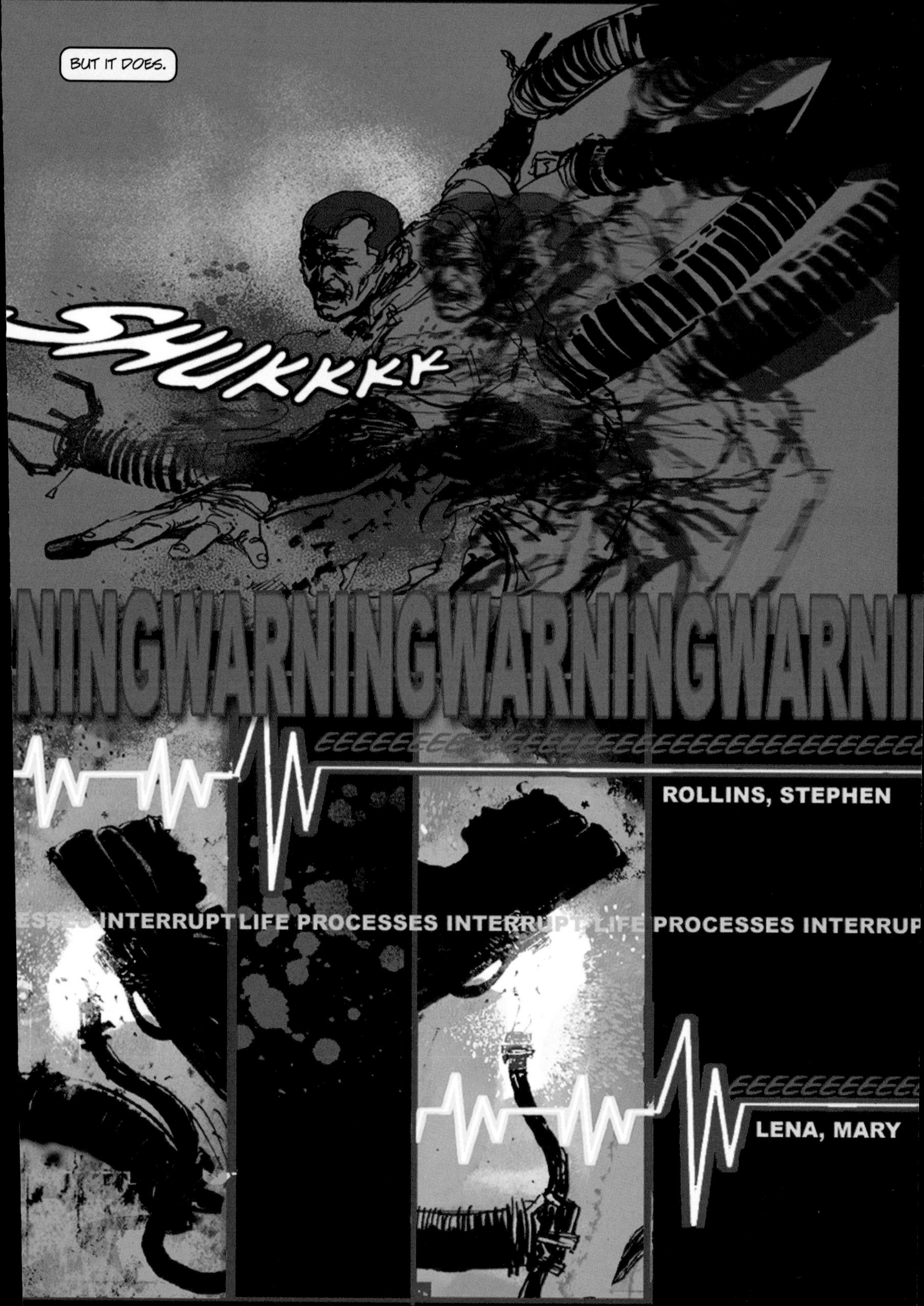
BUT IT DOES.
SHUKKKK
NINGWARNINGWARNINGWARNI
ROLLINS, STEPHEN
INTERRUPT LIFE PROCESSES INTERRUPT LIFE PROCESSES INTERRUP
LENA, MARY

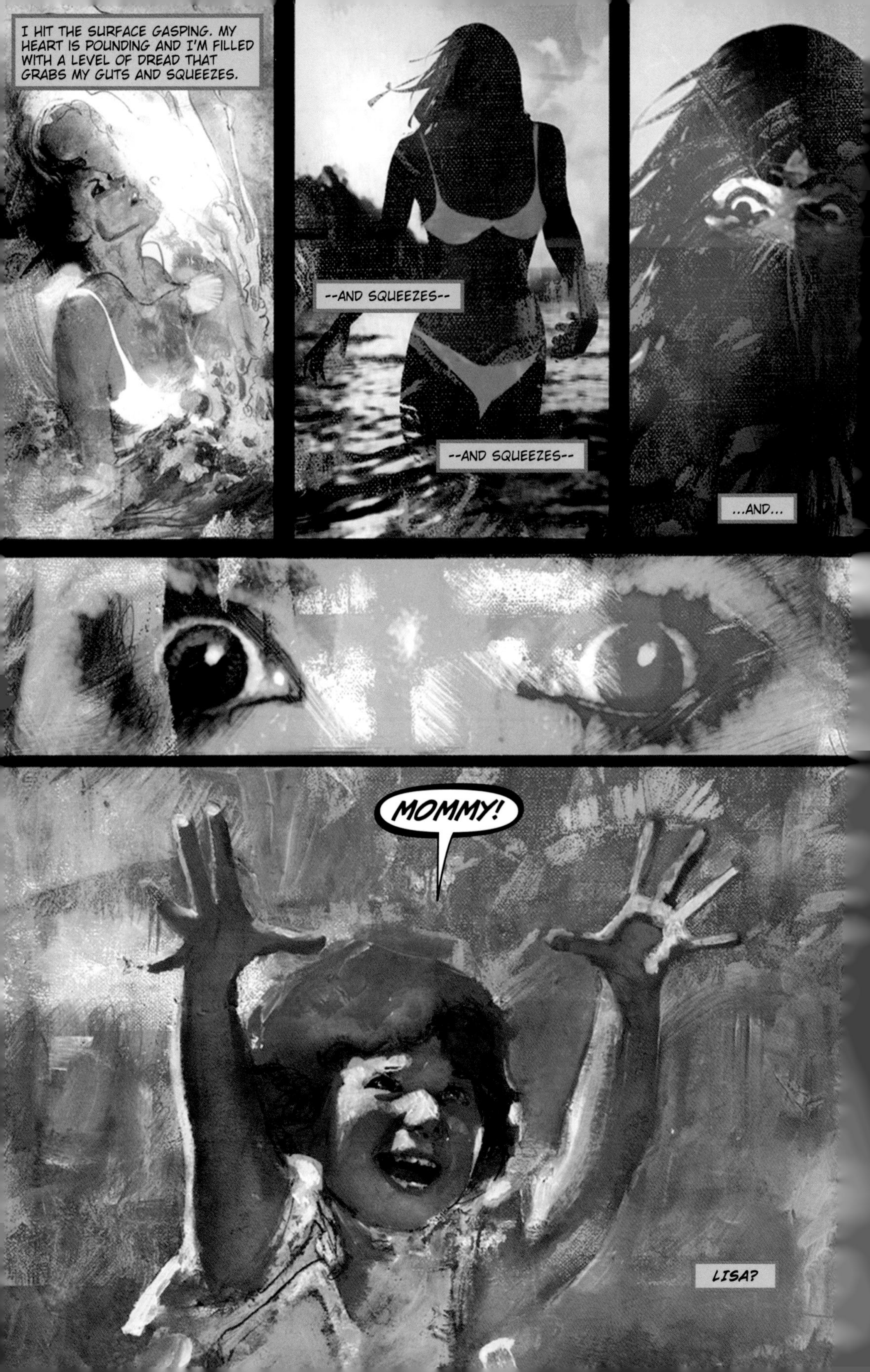
I HIT THE SURFACE GASPING. MY HEART IS POUNDING AND I'M FILLED WITH A LEVEL OF DREAD THAT GRABS MY GUTS AND SQUEEZES.
--AND SQUEEZES--
--AND SQUEEZES--
...AND...
MOMMY!
LISA?

WHERE THE HELL ARE LENA AND ROLLINS? I TRY TO MAKE SENSE AND STAY CALM...

MY HEART JUMPS IN MY THROAT -- LISA -- HERE?!

HONEY... LISA, HONEY, WHAT ARE YOU DOING HERE?

--WHERE'S YOUR SISTER?

ASHLEY'S ON THE SHIP WITH THE OTHER KIDS...

SHE SENT ME HERE.

WE WANTED TO SURPRISE YOU FOR YOUR BIRTHDAY, SO WE HACKED THE MATRIX TO TRACE YOU.

SO NOW IT MAKES SENSE: MY TALENTED, ADORABLE, BRILLIANT LITTLE GIRLS WANTED TO SURPRISE ME ON MY BIRTH...

...DAY...

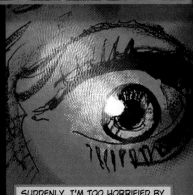

SUDDENLY, I'M TOO HORRIFIED BY WHAT I SEE OUT OF THE CORNER OF MY EYE, TO BE IMPRESSED BY MY SWEET LITTLE POTENTIALS' PRECOCITY...

WHAT'S THE MATTER, MOMMY?

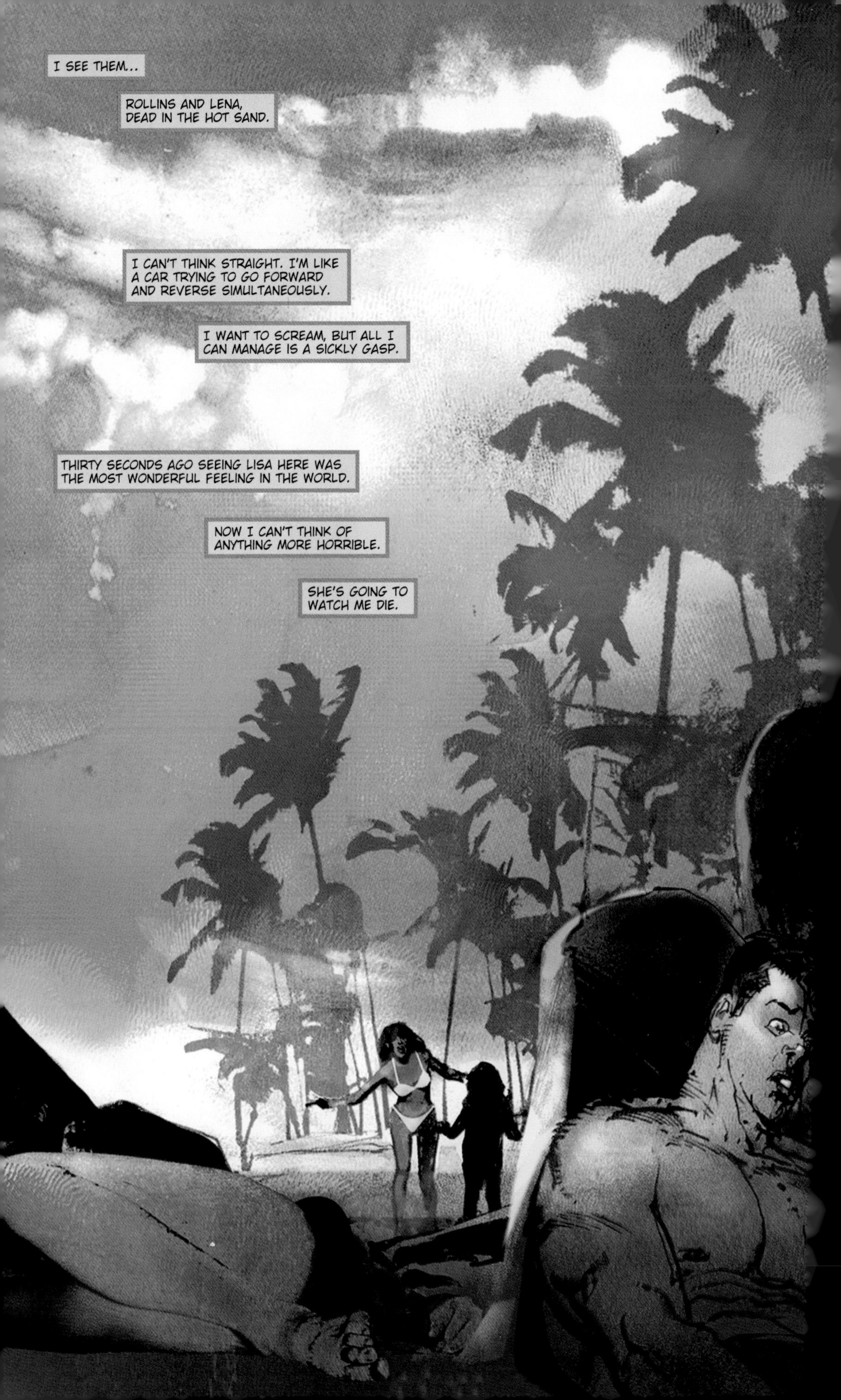
I SEE THEM...
ROLLINS AND LENA, DEAD IN THE HOT SAND.
I CAN'T THINK STRAIGHT. I'M LIKE A CAR TRYING TO GO FORWARD AND REVERSE SIMULTANEOUSLY.
I WANT TO SCREAM, BUT ALL I CAN MANAGE IS A SICKLY GASP.
THIRTY SECONDS AGO SEEING LISA HERE WAS THE MOST WONDERFUL FEELING IN THE WORLD.
NOW I CAN'T THINK OF ANYTHING MORE HORRIBLE.
SHE'S GOING TO WATCH ME DIE.

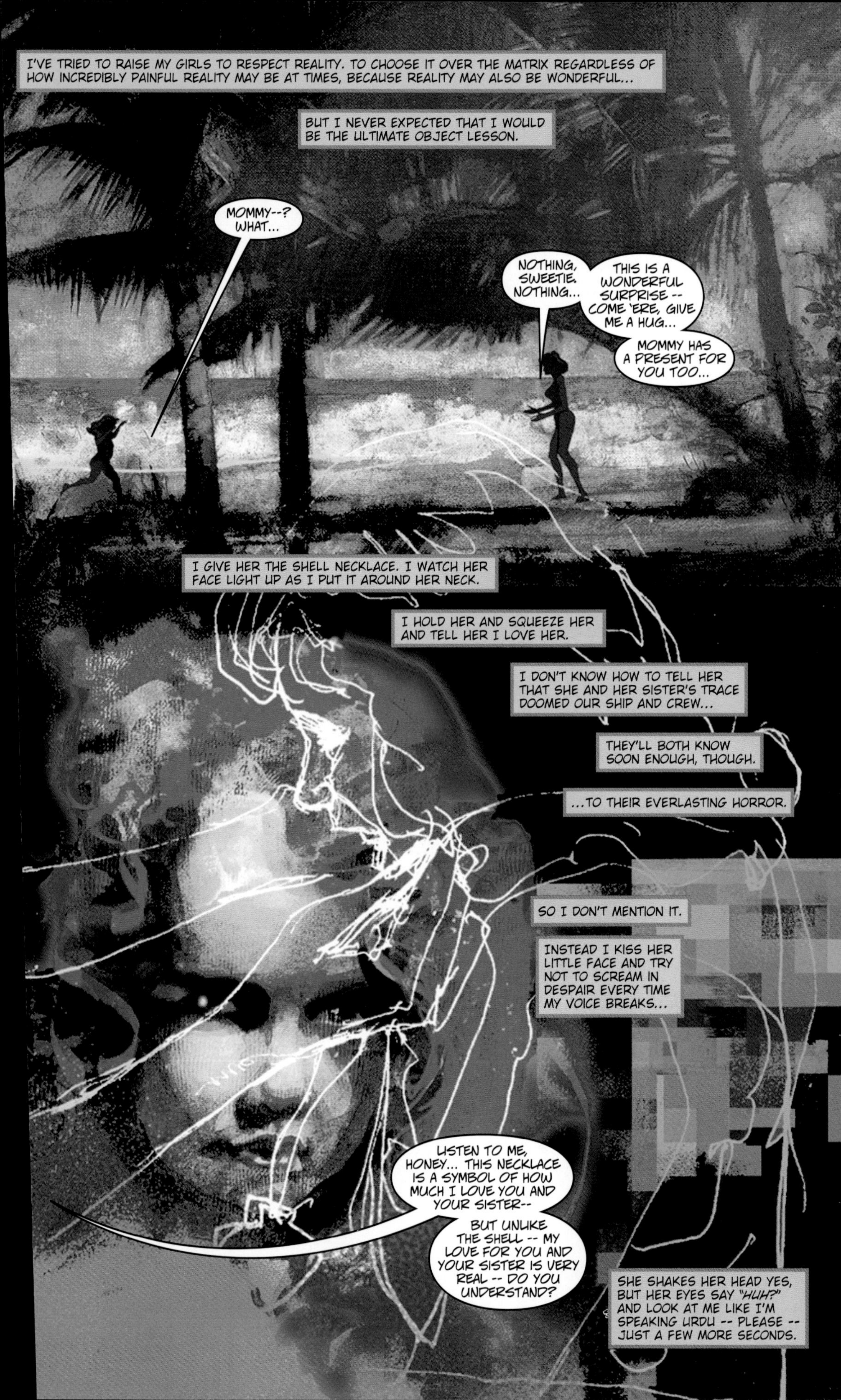

I'VE TRIED TO RAISE MY GIRLS TO RESPECT REALITY. TO CHOOSE IT OVER THE MATRIX REGARDLESS OF HOW INCREDIBLY PAINFUL REALITY MAY BE AT TIMES, BECAUSE REALITY MAY ALSO BE WONDERFUL...
BUT I NEVER EXPECTED THAT I WOULD BE THE ULTIMATE OBJECT LESSON.
MOMMY--? WHAT...
NOTHING, SWEETIE. NOTHING...
THIS IS A WONDERFUL SURPRISE -- COME 'ERE, GIVE ME A HUG...
MOMMY HAS A PRESENT FOR YOU TOO...
I GIVE HER THE SHELL NECKLACE. I WATCH HER FACE LIGHT UP AS I PUT IT AROUND HER NECK.
I HOLD HER AND SQUEEZE HER AND TELL HER I LOVE HER.
I DON'T KNOW HOW TO TELL HER THAT SHE AND HER SISTER'S TRACE DOOMED OUR SHIP AND CREW...
THEY'LL BOTH KNOW SOON ENOUGH, THOUGH.
...TO THEIR EVERLASTING HORROR.
SO I DON'T MENTION IT.
INSTEAD I KISS HER LITTLE FACE AND TRY NOT TO SCREAM IN DESPAIR EVERY TIME MY VOICE BREAKS...
LISTEN TO ME, HONEY... THIS NECKLACE IS A SYMBOL OF HOW MUCH I LOVE YOU AND YOUR SISTER--
BUT UNLIKE THE SHELL -- MY LOVE FOR YOU AND YOUR SISTER IS VERY REAL -- DO YOU UNDERSTAND?
SHE SHAKES HER HEAD YES, BUT HER EYES SAY "HUH?" AND LOOK AT ME LIKE I'M SPEAKING URDU -- PLEASE -- JUST A FEW MORE SECONDS.

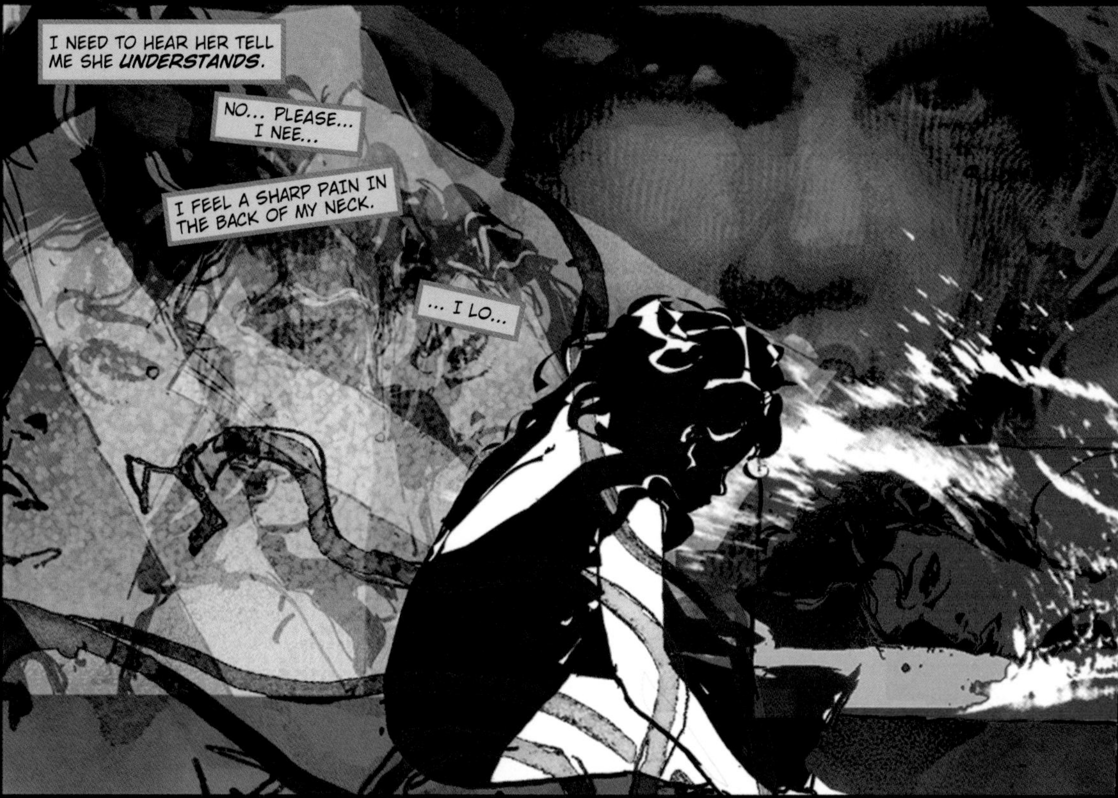
I NEED TO HEAR HER TELL ME SHE UNDERSTANDS.
NO... PLEASE... I NEE...
I FEEL A SHARP PAIN IN THE BACK OF MY NECK.
... I LO...
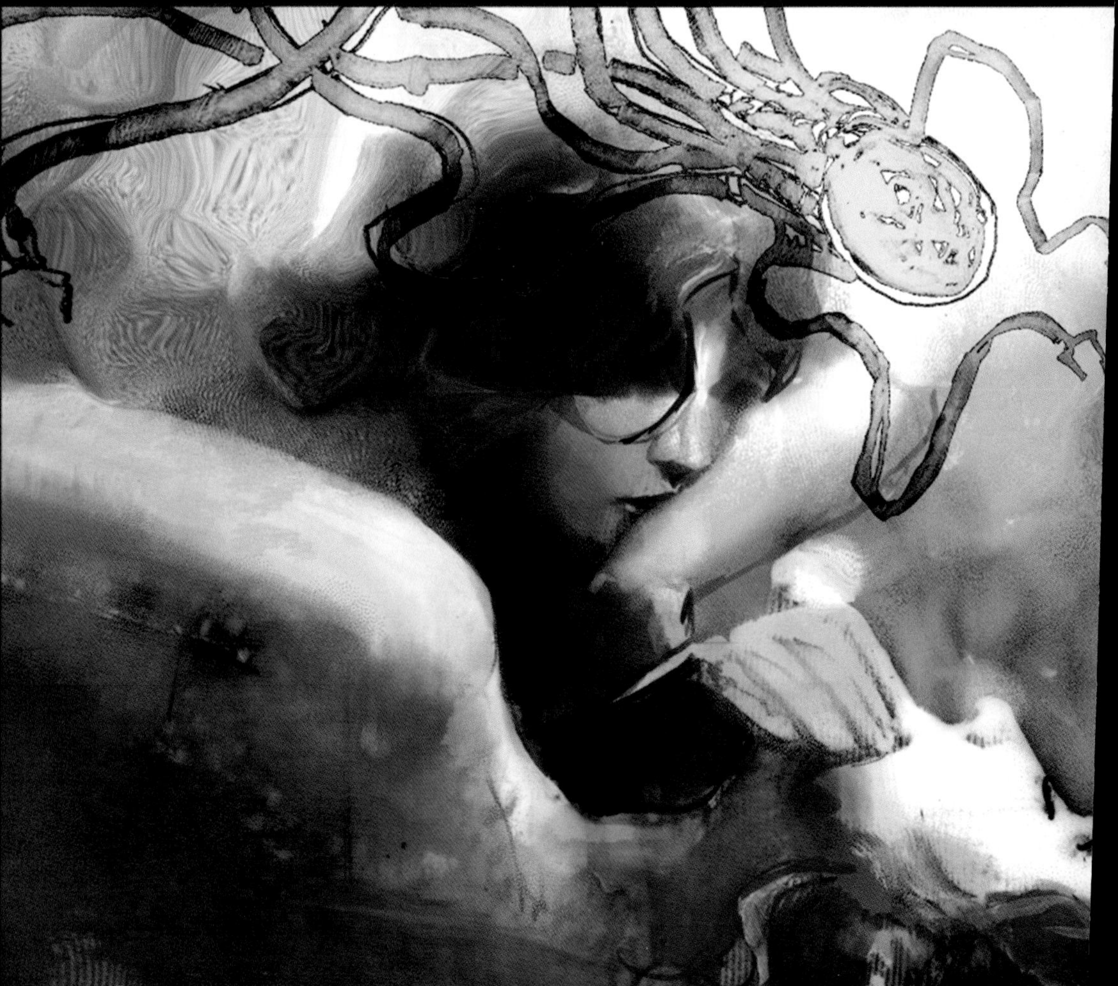

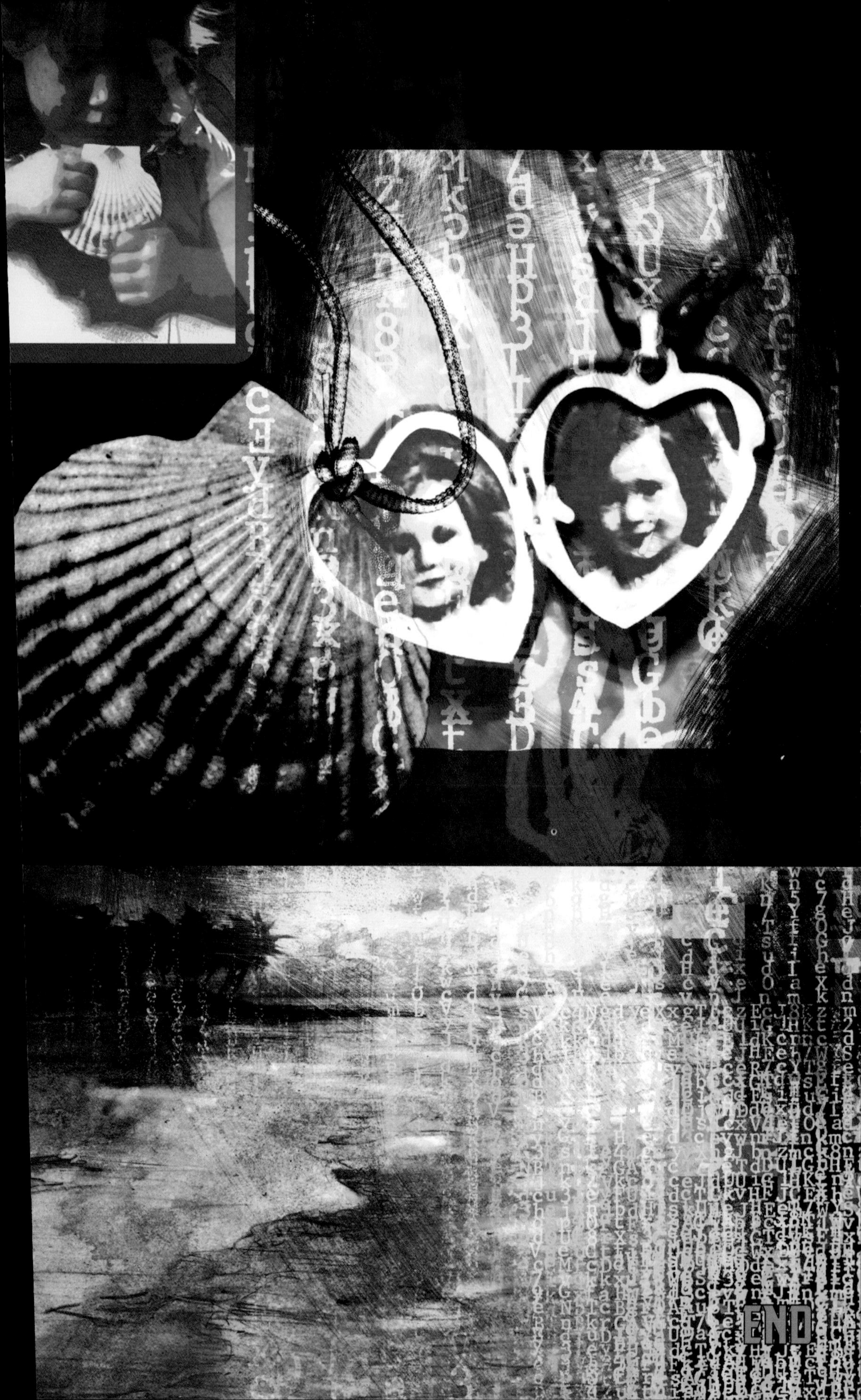
END

**WHO SAYS YOU CAN'T GET
GOOD HELP THESE DAYS?**

STORY & ART BY PETER
BAGGE

Peter Bagge's debut comic strip was seen in The East Village Eye in 1980, and he continued to be published regularly in other periodicals, such as High Times and Screw. In 1985 Peter's first self written and illustrated title came into being: NEAT STUFF. That was followed in 1990 with HATE, a semi-autobiographical comic series set in Seattle, written and illustrated by Peter. A voracious artist, Peter has completed comic strips and other works of art, including DONNA'S DAY: MISSIVE DEVICE, a 16 page color mini comic, and gag panels which appear in KUTIE. Other works can be found in YEAH!, DETAILS, and the one-shot look at Marvel's favorite web-slinger, STARTLING STORIES: THE MEGALOMANIACAL SPIDER-MAN. In addition to more HATE, be sure to check out Peter's monthly comic SWEATSHOP from DC Comics.

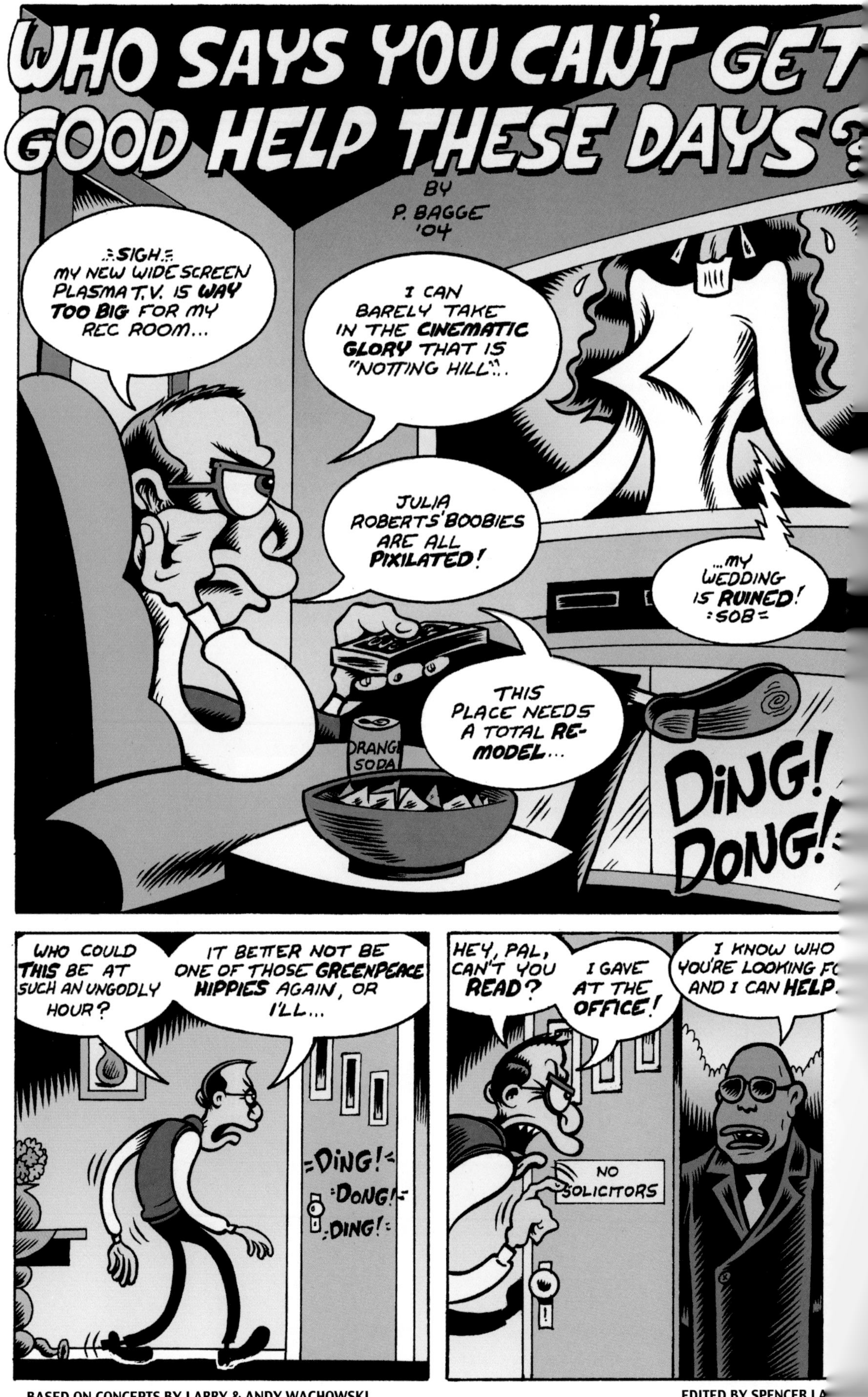
WHO SAYS YOU CAN'T GET GOOD HELP THESE DAYS?
BY P. BAGGE '04
...SIGH... MY NEW WIDE SCREEN PLASMA T.V. IS **WAY TOO BIG** FOR MY REC ROOM...
I CAN BARELY TAKE IN THE **CINEMATIC GLORY** THAT IS "NOTTING HILL"...
JULIA ROBERTS' BOOBIES ARE ALL **PIXILATED**!
...MY WEDDING IS **RUINED**! =SOB=
THIS PLACE NEEDS A TOTAL **RE-MODEL**...
ORANGE SODA
DING! DONG!
WHO COULD **THIS** BE AT SUCH AN UNGODLY HOUR?
IT BETTER NOT BE ONE OF THOSE **GREENPEACE HIPPIES** AGAIN, OR I'LL...
=DING!= =DONG!= =DING!=
HEY, PAL, CAN'T YOU **READ**?
I GAVE AT THE **OFFICE**!
NO SOLICITORS
I KNOW WHO YOU'RE LOOKING F AND I CAN **HELP**.

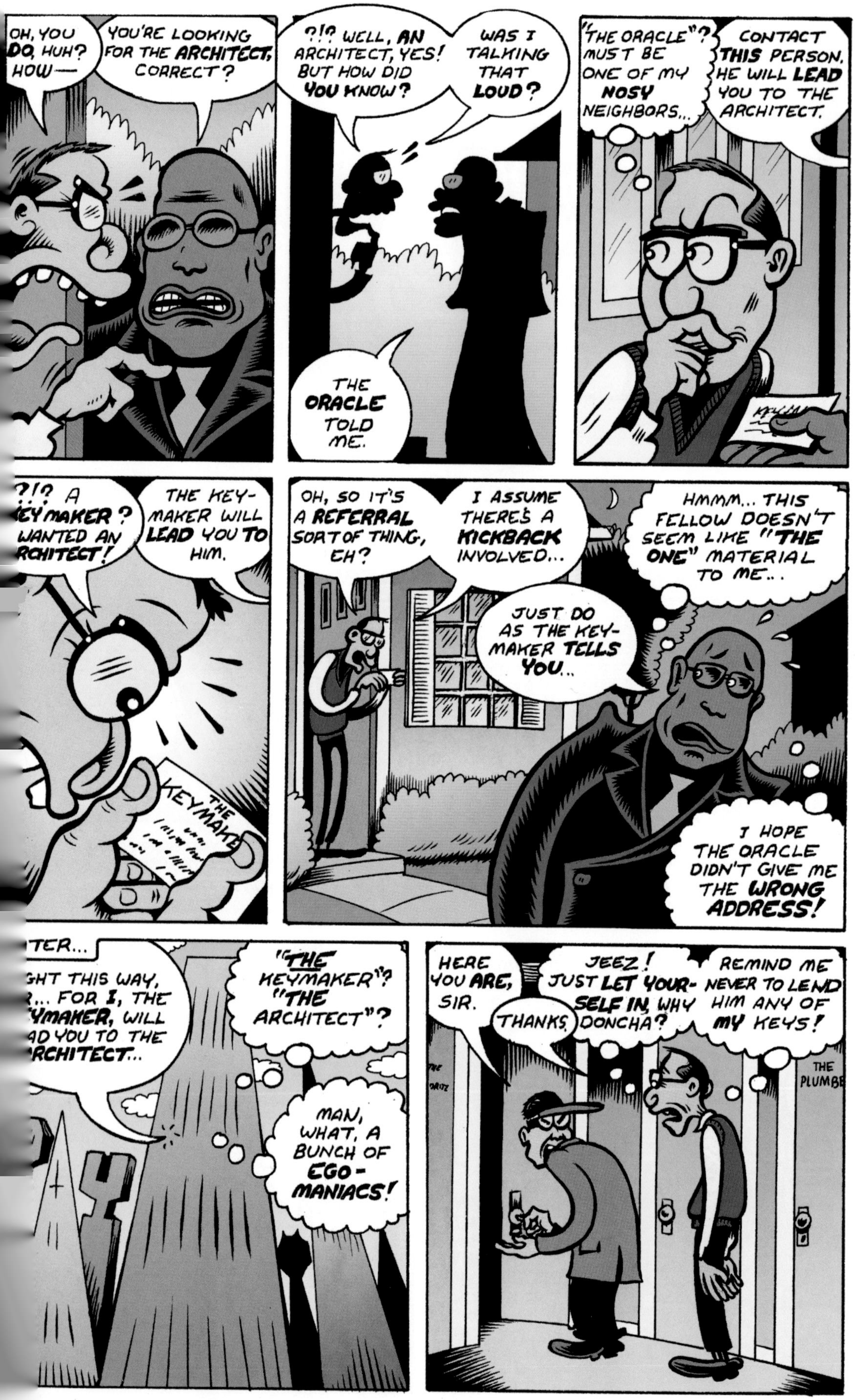
OH, YOU DO, HUH? HOW—
YOU'RE LOOKING FOR THE ARCHITECT, CORRECT?
?!? WELL, AN ARCHITECT, YES! BUT HOW DID YOU KNOW?
WAS I TALKING THAT LOUD?
THE ORACLE TOLD ME.
"THE ORACLE"? MUST BE ONE OF MY NOSY NEIGHBORS...
CONTACT THIS PERSON. HE WILL LEAD YOU TO THE ARCHITECT.
?!? A EYMAKER? WANTED AN RCHITECT!
THE KEY-MAKER WILL LEAD YOU TO HIM.
THE KEYMAKE
OH, SO IT'S A REFERRAL SORT OF THING, EH?
I ASSUME THERE'S A KICKBACK INVOLVED...
HMMM... THIS FELLOW DOESN'T SEEM LIKE "THE ONE" MATERIAL TO ME...
JUST DO AS THE KEY-MAKER TELLS YOU...
I HOPE THE ORACLE DIDN'T GIVE ME THE WRONG ADDRESS!
TER...
GHT THIS WAY, R... FOR I, THE YMAKER, WILL AD YOU TO THE RCHITECT...
"THE KEYMAKER"? "THE ARCHITECT"?
MAN, WHAT A BUNCH OF EGO-MANIACS!
HERE YOU ARE, SIR.
THANKS
JEEZ! JUST LET YOURSELF IN, WHY DONCHA?
REMIND ME NEVER TO LEND HIM ANY OF MY KEYS!
THE PLUMBE

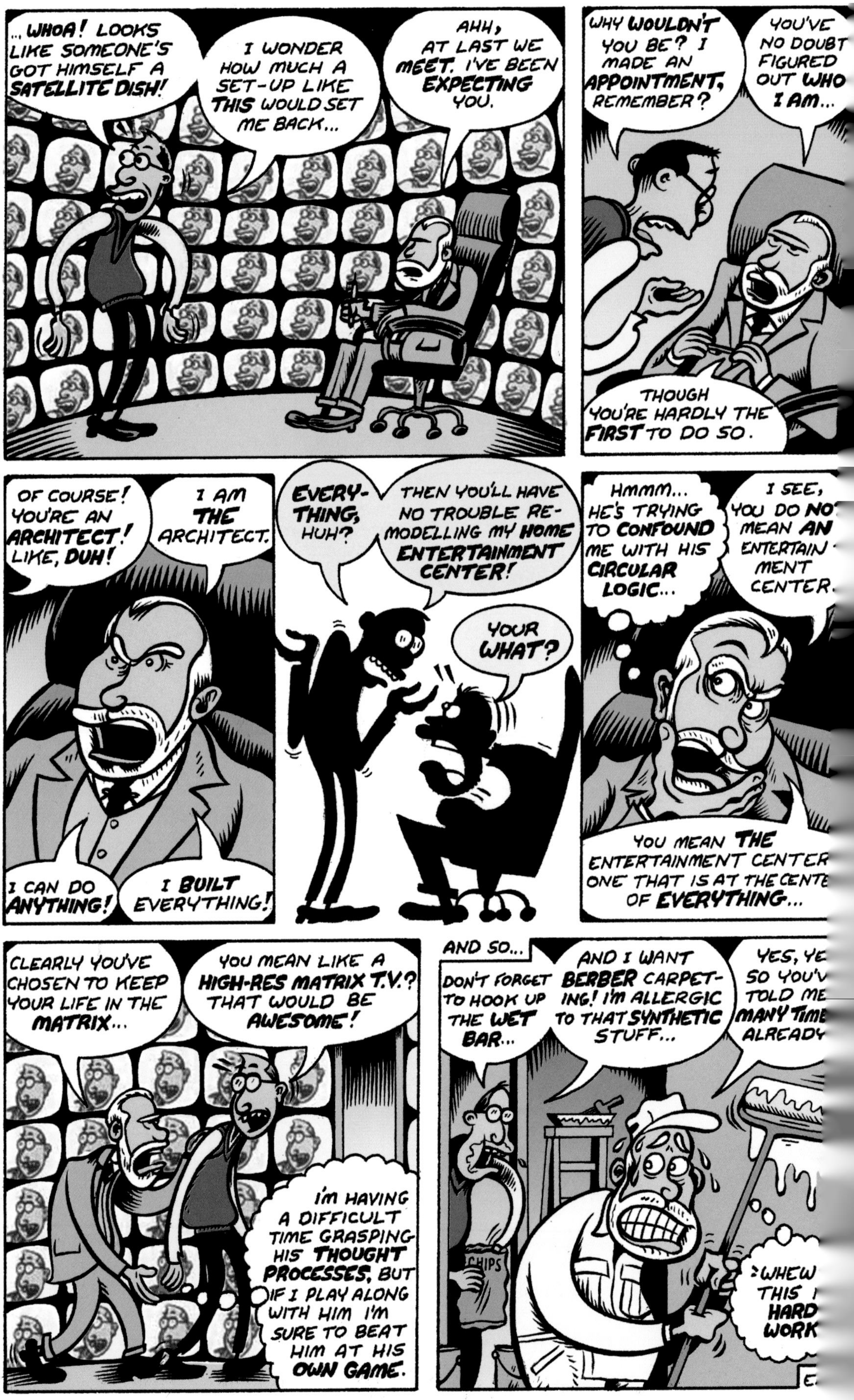
...WHOA! LOOKS LIKE SOMEONE'S GOT HIMSELF A SATELLITE DISH!
I WONDER HOW MUCH A SET-UP LIKE THIS WOULD SET ME BACK...
AHH, AT LAST WE MEET. I'VE BEEN EXPECTING YOU.
WHY WOULDN'T YOU BE? I MADE AN APPOINTMENT, REMEMBER?
YOU'VE NO DOUBT FIGURED OUT WHO I AM...
THOUGH YOU'RE HARDLY THE FIRST TO DO SO.
OF COURSE! YOU'RE AN ARCHITECT! LIKE, DUH!
I AM THE ARCHITECT.
I CAN DO ANYTHING!
I BUILT EVERYTHING!
EVERY-THING, HUH?
THEN YOU'LL HAVE NO TROUBLE RE-MODELLING MY HOME ENTERTAINMENT CENTER!
YOUR WHAT?
HMMM... HE'S TRYING TO CONFOUND ME WITH HIS CIRCULAR LOGIC...
I SEE, YOU DO NOT MEAN AN ENTERTAIN-MENT CENTER.
YOU MEAN THE ENTERTAINMENT CENTER ONE THAT IS AT THE CENTE OF EVERYTHING...
CLEARLY YOU'VE CHOSEN TO KEEP YOUR LIFE IN THE MATRIX...
YOU MEAN LIKE A HIGH-RES MATRIX T.V.? THAT WOULD BE AWESOME!
I'M HAVING A DIFFICULT TIME GRASPING HIS THOUGHT PROCESSES, BUT IF I PLAY ALONG WITH HIM I'M SURE TO BEAT HIM AT HIS OWN GAME.
AND SO...
DON'T FORGET TO HOOK UP THE WET BAR...
AND I WANT BERBER CARPET-ING! I'M ALLERGIC TO THAT SYNTHETIC STUFF...
YES, YE SO YOU'V TOLD ME MANY TIME ALREADY
CHIPS
WHEW THIS HARD WORK

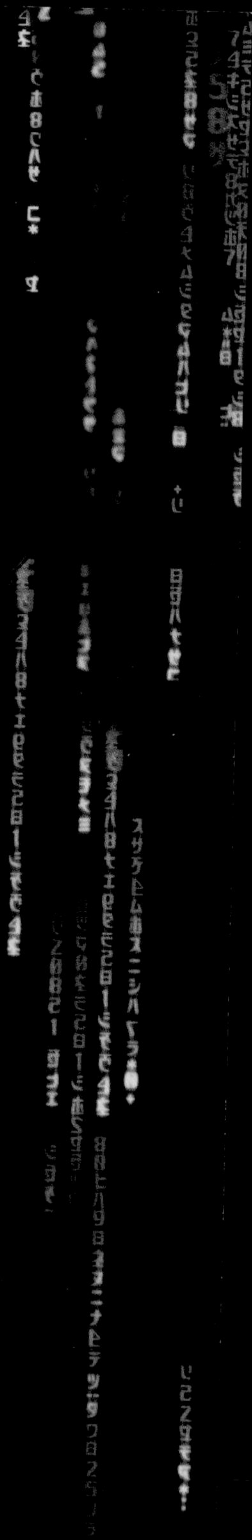

SAVIORS

OF THE MATRIX, THE MATRIX COMICS: VOLUME ONE, and the book you are holding in your hands. He lives in NYC.

ART BY MICHAEL OEMING

Michael Oeming is the co-creator of the Eisner Award-nominated series, POWERS, in collaboration with writer Brian Michael Bendis. His art also appears in the series HAMMER OF THE GODS and BASTARD SAMURAI, among others. His career started early, inking books for Innovation Comics at the age of 14, which prepped him for inking Marvel Comics titles like AVENGERS and DAREDEVIL. Currently, Michael has just finished a run on Marvels' THOR, ending the 40 year old series and has illustrated QUIXOTE, a modern day retelling of the classic novel. Michael now lives in New Jersey with his wife, son and two mice named Mack and Bendis! For more information about Michael, go to www.mike-oeming.com.

COLOR BY JONATHAN LUNA

Jonathan Luna was born in California and launched into a military child life, living in Iceland, Virginia, Sardinia, Sicily, and back in the US. Drawing comics since he was six years old, he attended and earned a Bachelor's Degree of Fine Arts in Sequential Art from the Savannah College of Art and Design in 2001. His experience also reaches into the field of web design. Jonathan currently resides in the Washington, DC metro area again, where he is constantly writing and drawing the Image comic book ULTRA with his brother, Joshua Luna, and eating giant bags of dried mango. You can find more information about Jonathan at

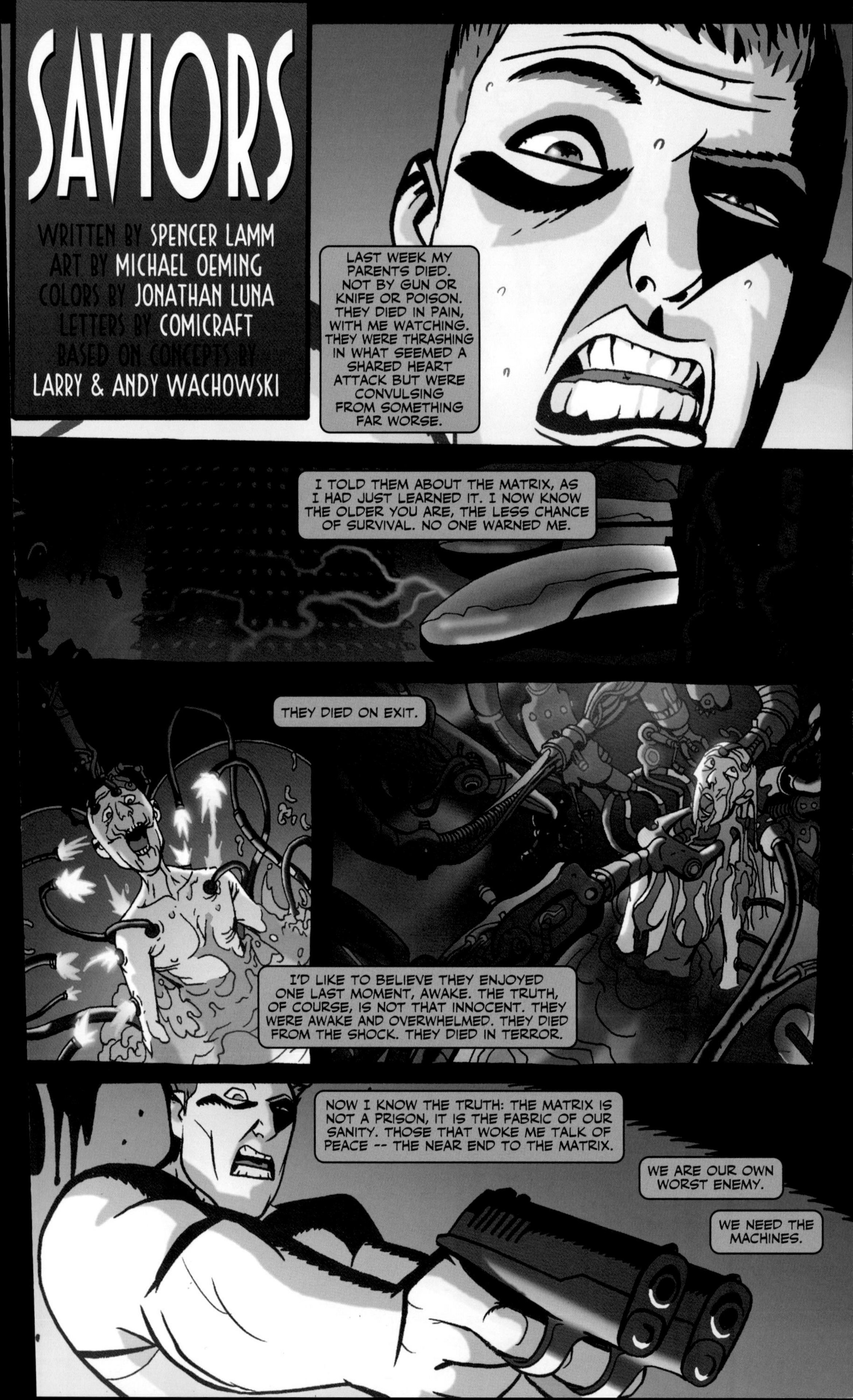
SAVIORS
WRITTEN BY SPENCER LAMM
ART BY MICHAEL OEMING
COLORS BY JONATHAN LUNA
LETTERS BY COMICRAFT
BASED ON CONCEPTS BY
LARRY & ANDY WACHOWSKI
LAST WEEK MY PARENTS DIED. NOT BY GUN OR KNIFE OR POISON. THEY DIED IN PAIN, WITH ME WATCHING. THEY WERE THRASHING IN WHAT SEEMED A SHARED HEART ATTACK BUT WERE CONVULSING FROM SOMETHING FAR WORSE.
I TOLD THEM ABOUT THE MATRIX, AS I HAD JUST LEARNED IT. I NOW KNOW THE OLDER YOU ARE, THE LESS CHANCE OF SURVIVAL. NO ONE WARNED ME.
THEY DIED ON EXIT.
I'D LIKE TO BELIEVE THEY ENJOYED ONE LAST MOMENT, AWAKE. THE TRUTH, OF COURSE, IS NOT THAT INNOCENT. THEY WERE AWAKE AND OVERWHELMED. THEY DIED FROM THE SHOCK. THEY DIED IN TERROR.
NOW I KNOW THE TRUTH: THE MATRIX IS NOT A PRISON, IT IS THE FABRIC OF OUR SANITY. THOSE THAT WOKE ME TALK OF PEACE -- THE NEAR END TO THE MATRIX.
WE ARE OUR OWN WORST ENEMY.
WE NEED THE MACHINES.

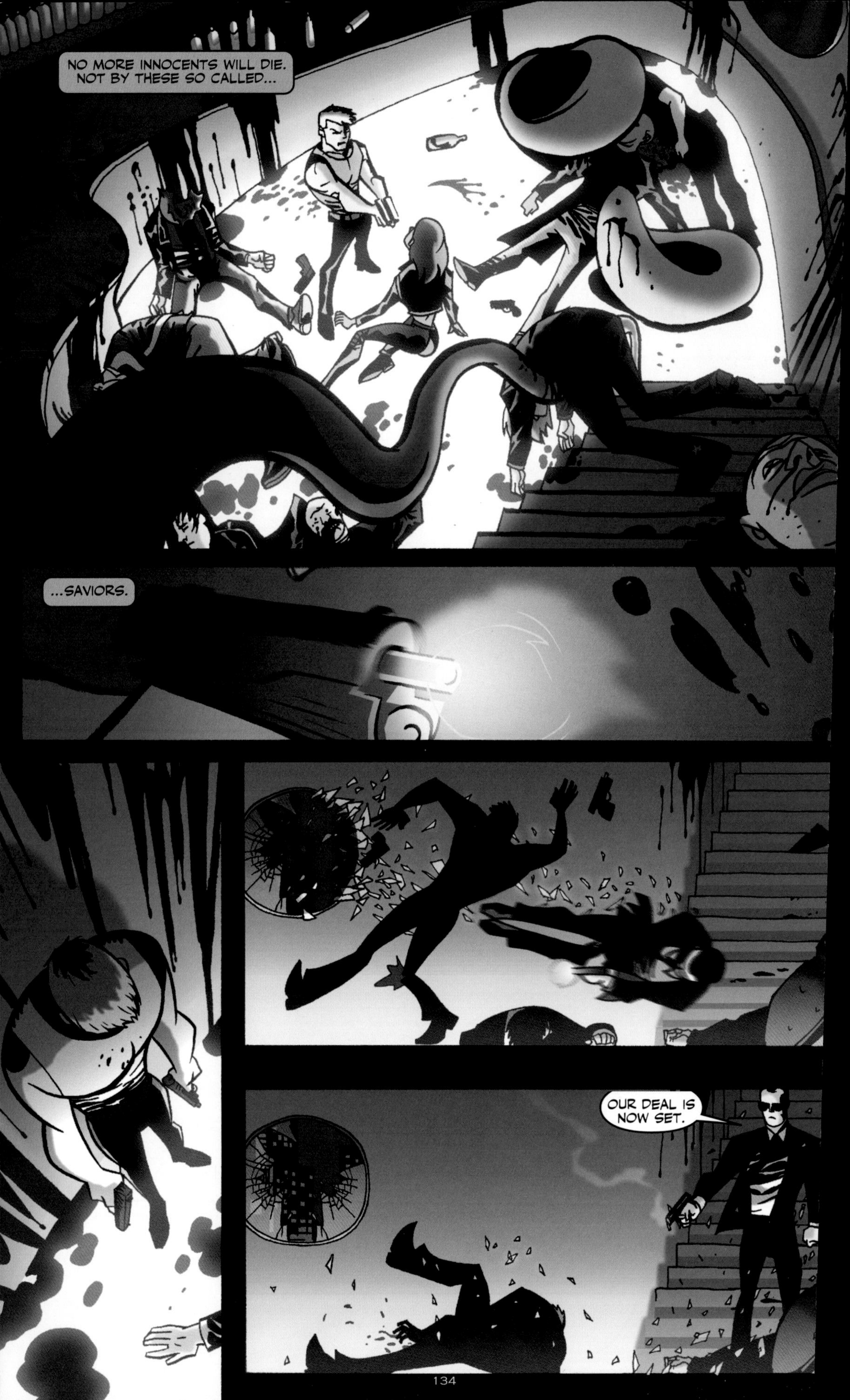
NO MORE INNOCENTS WILL DIE. NOT BY THESE SO CALLED...
...SAVIORS.
OUR DEAL IS NOW SET.

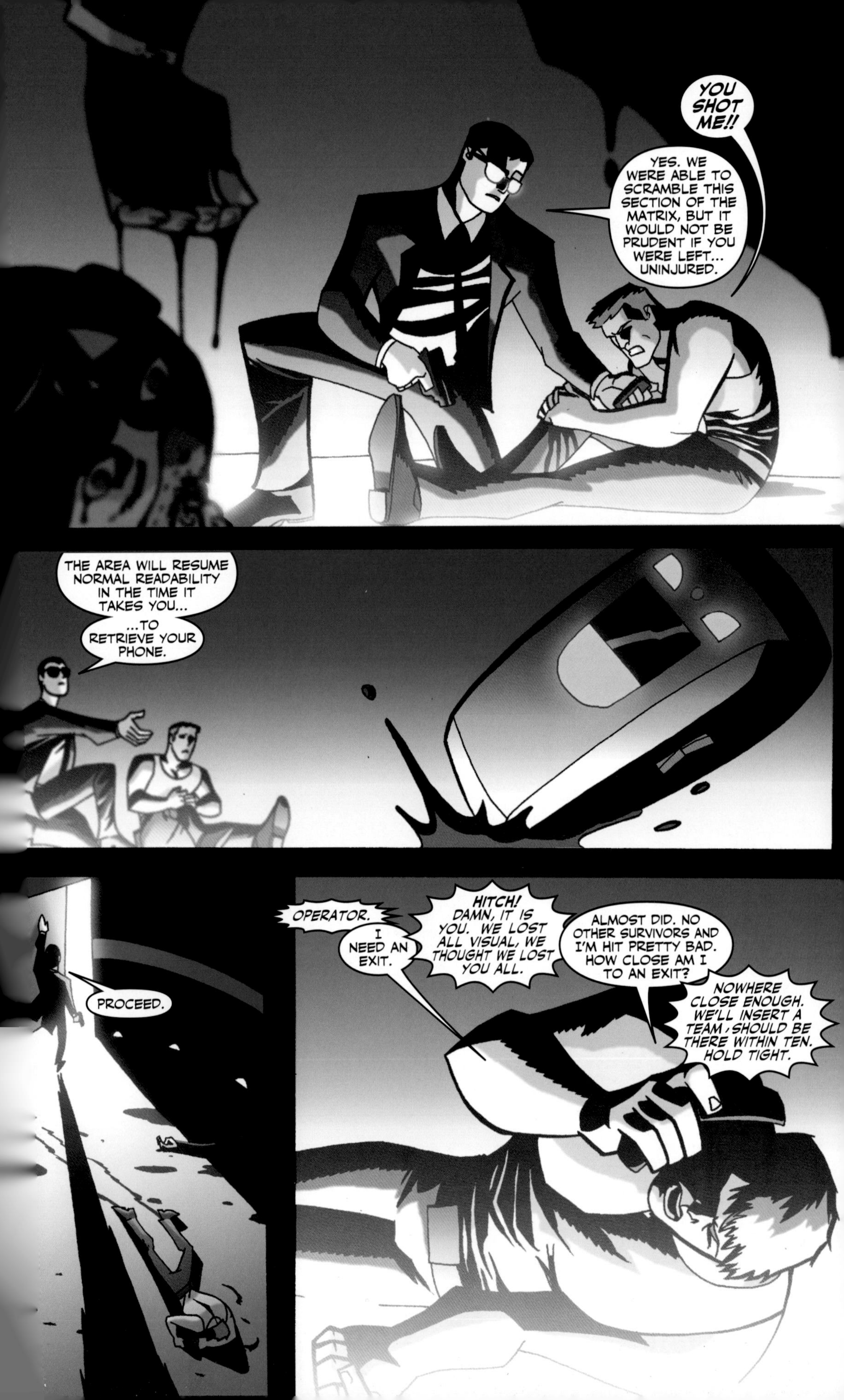
YOU SHOT ME!!
YES. WE WERE ABLE TO SCRAMBLE THIS SECTION OF THE MATRIX, BUT IT WOULD NOT BE PRUDENT IF YOU WERE LEFT... UNINJURED.
THE AREA WILL RESUME NORMAL READABILITY IN THE TIME IT TAKES YOU...
...TO RETRIEVE YOUR PHONE.
PROCEED.
OPERATOR.
I NEED AN EXIT.
HITCH! DAMN, IT IS YOU. WE LOST ALL VISUAL, WE THOUGHT WE LOST YOU ALL.
ALMOST DID. NO OTHER SURVIVORS AND I'M HIT PRETTY BAD. HOW CLOSE AM I TO AN EXIT?
NOWHERE CLOSE ENOUGH. WE'LL INSERT A TEAM, SHOULD BE THERE WITHIN TEN. HOLD TIGHT.

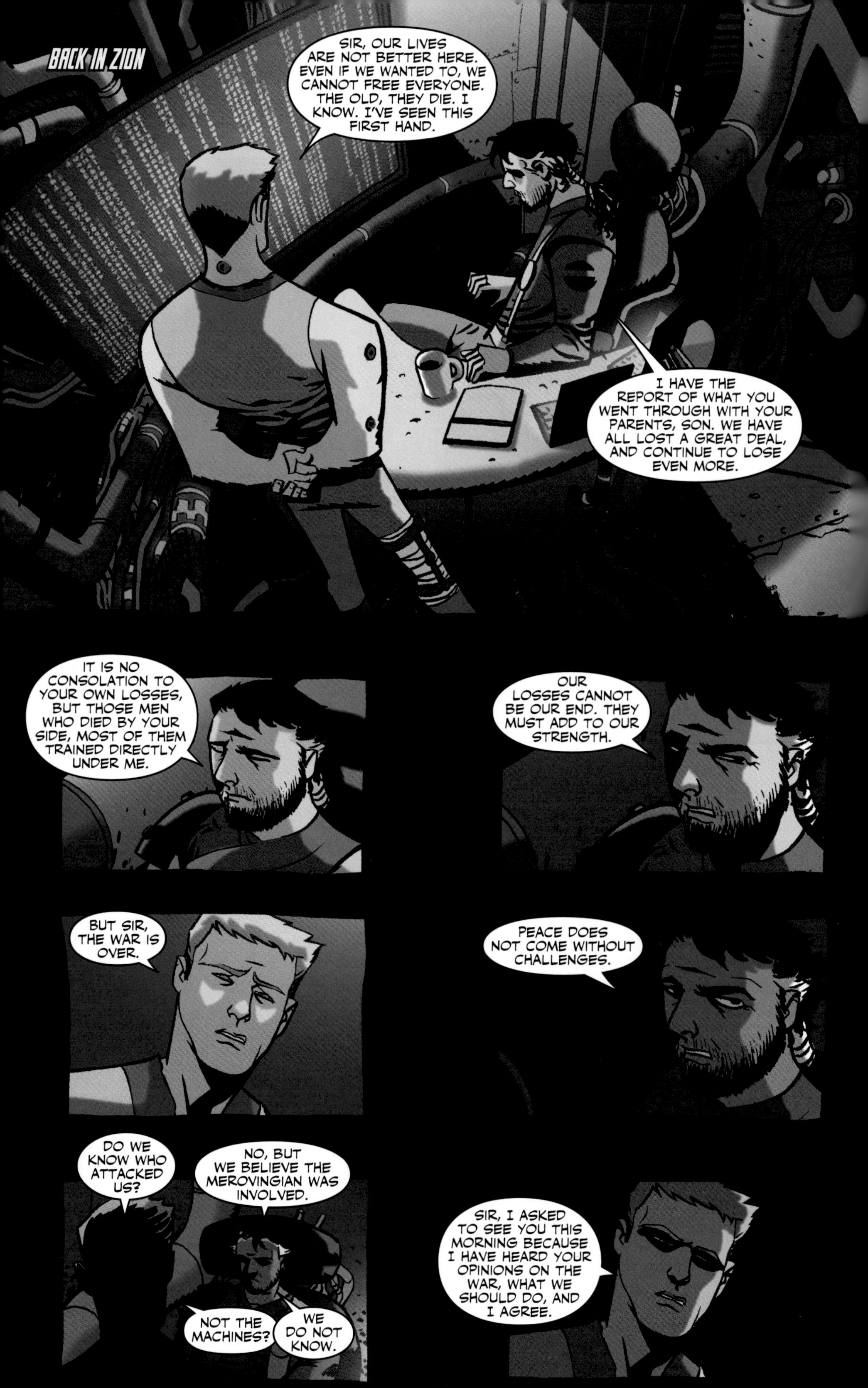
BACK IN ZION
SIR, OUR LIVES ARE NOT BETTER HERE. EVEN IF WE WANTED TO, WE CANNOT FREE EVERYONE. THE OLD, THEY DIE. I KNOW. I'VE SEEN THIS FIRST HAND.
I HAVE THE REPORT OF WHAT YOU WENT THROUGH WITH YOUR PARENTS, SON. WE HAVE ALL LOST A GREAT DEAL, AND CONTINUE TO LOSE EVEN MORE.
IT IS NO CONSOLATION TO YOUR OWN LOSSES, BUT THOSE MEN WHO DIED BY YOUR SIDE, MOST OF THEM TRAINED DIRECTLY UNDER ME.
OUR LOSSES CANNOT BE OUR END. THEY MUST ADD TO OUR STRENGTH.
BUT SIR, THE WAR IS OVER.
PEACE DOES NOT COME WITHOUT CHALLENGES.
DO WE KNOW WHO ATTACKED US?
NO, BUT WE BELIEVE THE MEROVINGIAN WAS INVOLVED.
NOT THE MACHINES?
WE DO NOT KNOW.
SIR, I ASKED TO SEE YOU THIS MORNING BECAUSE I HAVE HEARD YOUR OPINIONS ON THE WAR, WHAT WE SHOULD DO, AND I AGREE.

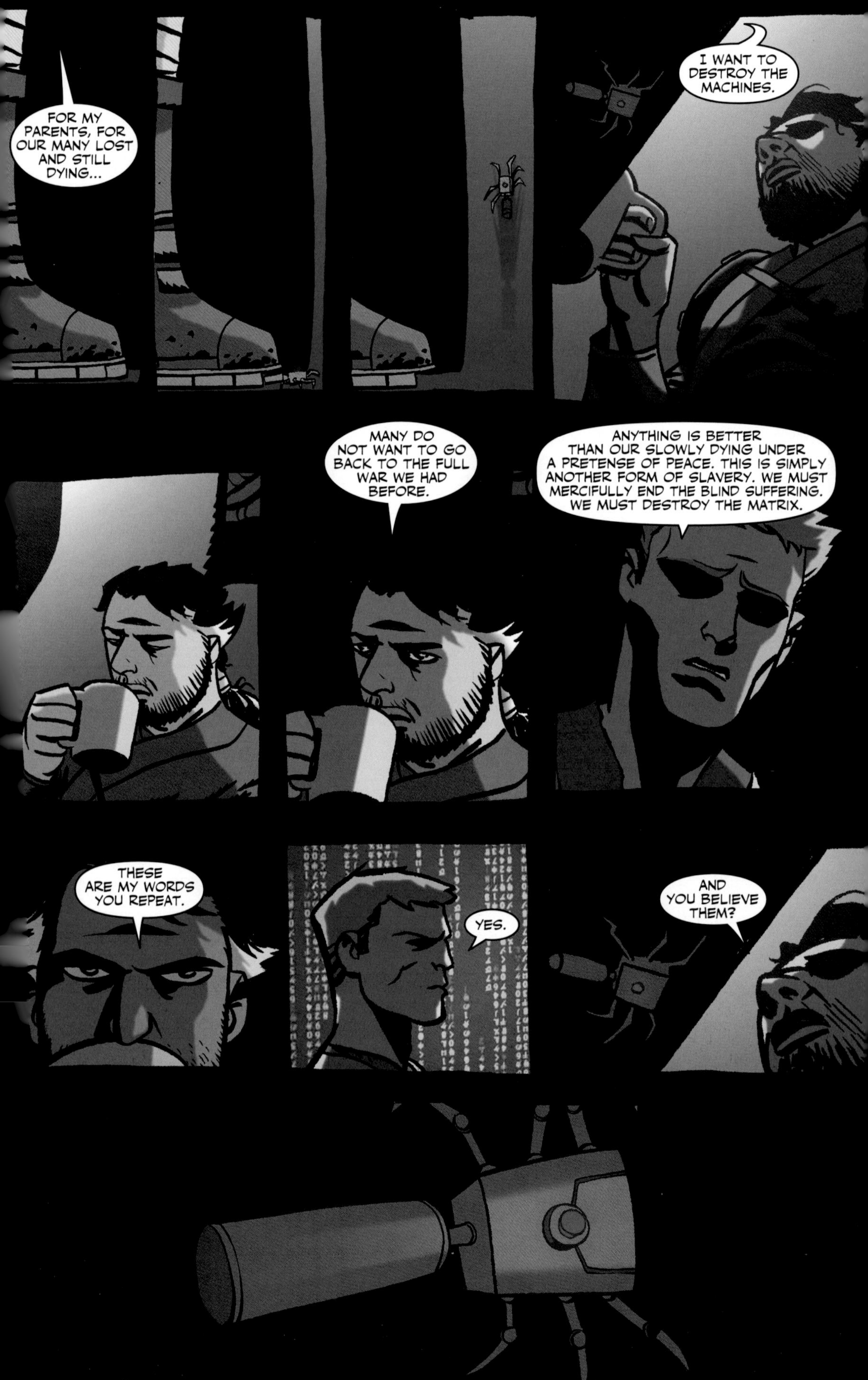
FOR MY PARENTS, FOR OUR MANY LOST AND STILL DYING...
I WANT TO DESTROY THE MACHINES.
MANY DO NOT WANT TO GO BACK TO THE FULL WAR WE HAD BEFORE.
ANYTHING IS BETTER THAN OUR SLOWLY DYING UNDER A PRETENSE OF PEACE. THIS IS SIMPLY ANOTHER FORM OF SLAVERY. WE MUST MERCIFULLY END THE BLIND SUFFERING. WE MUST DESTROY THE MATRIX.
THESE ARE MY WORDS YOU REPEAT.
YES.
AND YOU BELIEVE THEM?

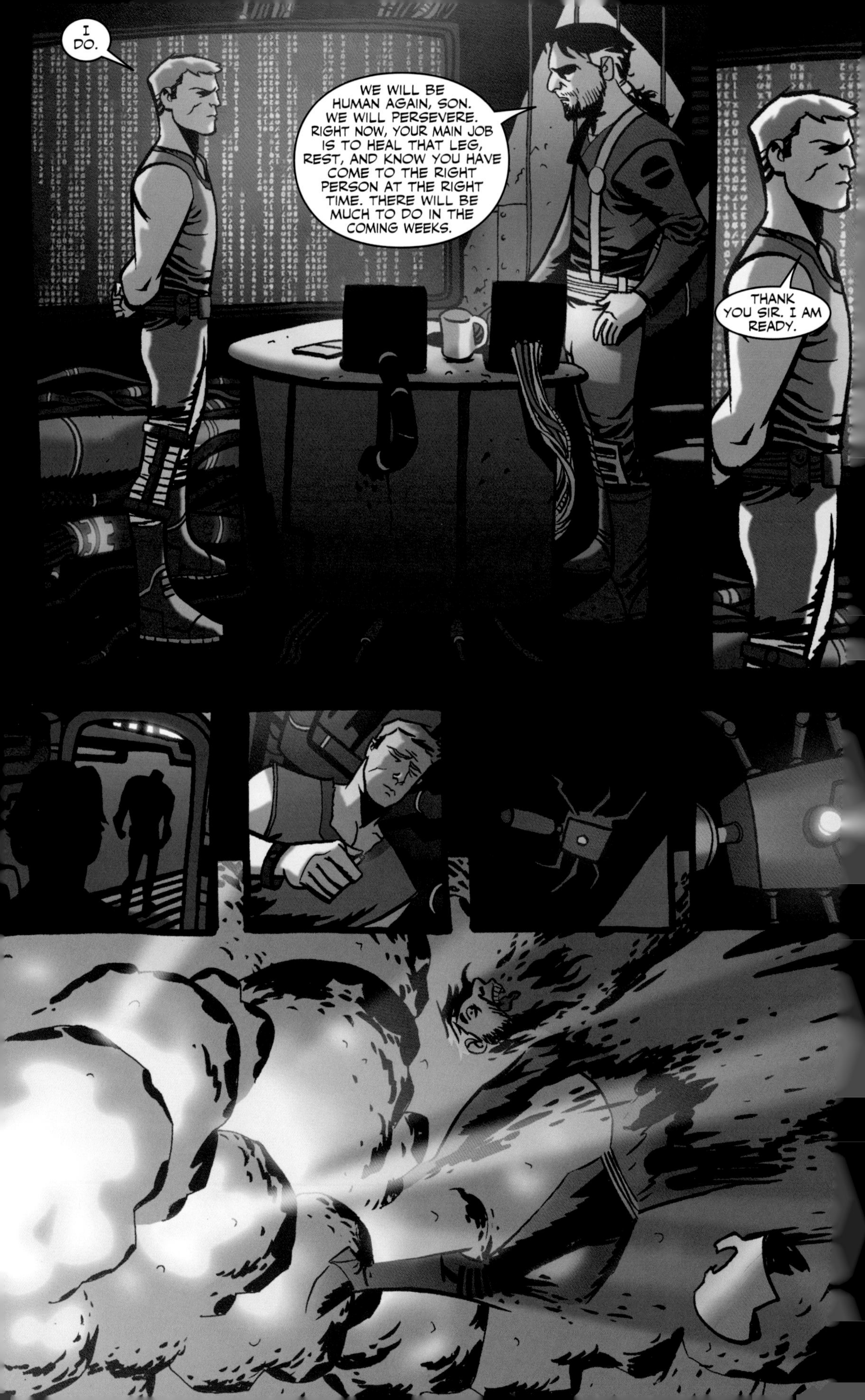
I DO.
WE WILL BE HUMAN AGAIN, SON. WE WILL PERSEVERE. RIGHT NOW, YOUR MAIN JOB IS TO HEAL THAT LEG, REST, AND KNOW YOU HAVE COME TO THE RIGHT PERSON AT THE RIGHT TIME. THERE WILL BE MUCH TO DO IN THE COMING WEEKS.
THANK YOU SIR. I AM READY.

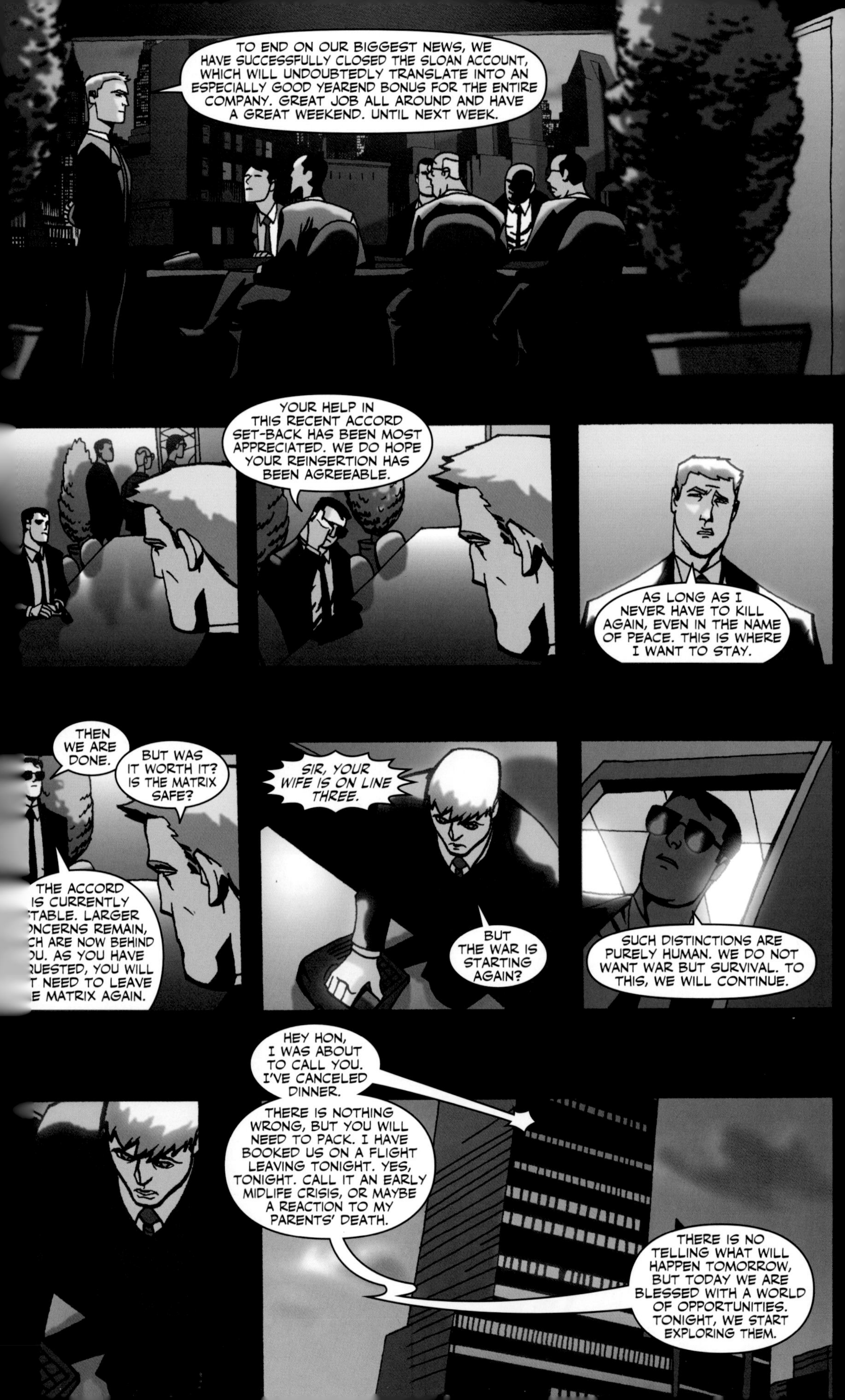
TO END ON OUR BIGGEST NEWS, WE HAVE SUCCESSFULLY CLOSED THE SLOAN ACCOUNT, WHICH WILL UNDOUBTEDLY TRANSLATE INTO AN ESPECIALLY GOOD YEAREND BONUS FOR THE ENTIRE COMPANY. GREAT JOB ALL AROUND AND HAVE A GREAT WEEKEND. UNTIL NEXT WEEK.
YOUR HELP IN THIS RECENT ACCORD SET-BACK HAS BEEN MOST APPRECIATED. WE DO HOPE YOUR REINSERTION HAS BEEN AGREEABLE.
AS LONG AS I NEVER HAVE TO KILL AGAIN, EVEN IN THE NAME OF PEACE. THIS IS WHERE I WANT TO STAY.
THEN WE ARE DONE.
BUT WAS IT WORTH IT? IS THE MATRIX SAFE?
THE ACCORD IS CURRENTLY TABLE. LARGER ONCERNS REMAIN, CH ARE NOW BEHIND OU. AS YOU HAVE QUESTED, YOU WILL T NEED TO LEAVE E MATRIX AGAIN.
SIR, YOUR WIFE IS ON LINE THREE.
BUT THE WAR IS STARTING AGAIN?
SUCH DISTINCTIONS ARE PURELY HUMAN. WE DO NOT WANT WAR BUT SURVIVAL. TO THIS, WE WILL CONTINUE.
HEY HON, I WAS ABOUT TO CALL YOU. I'VE CANCELED DINNER.
THERE IS NOTHING WRONG, BUT YOU WILL NEED TO PACK. I HAVE BOOKED US ON A FLIGHT LEAVING TONIGHT. YES, TONIGHT. CALL IT AN EARLY MIDLIFE CRISIS, OR MAYBE A REACTION TO MY PARENTS' DEATH.
THERE IS NO TELLING WHAT WILL HAPPEN TOMORROW, BUT TODAY WE ARE BLESSED WITH A WORLD OF OPPORTUNITIES. TONIGHT, WE START EXPLORING THEM.

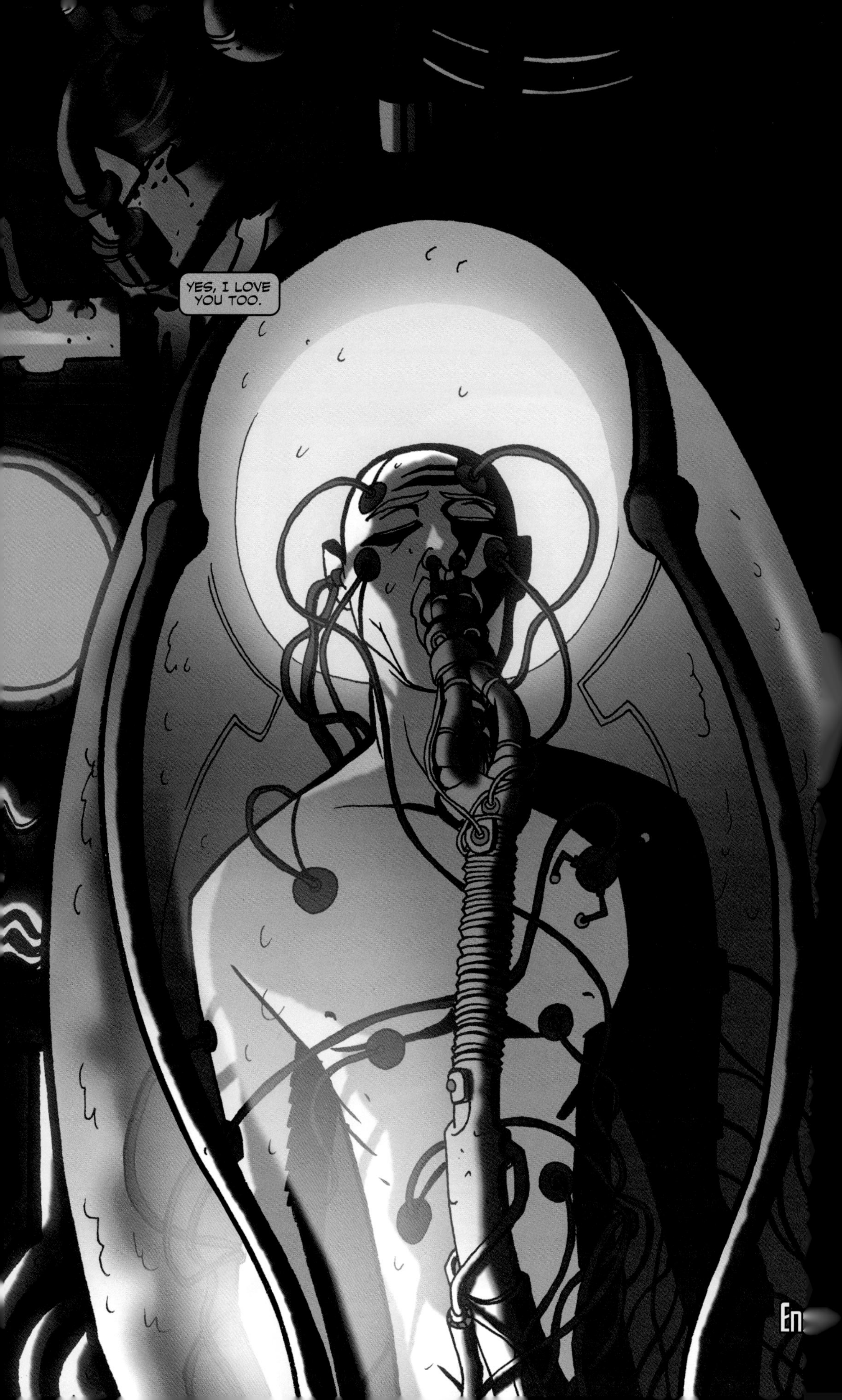
YES, I LOVE YOU TOO.

I KANT

STORY & ART BY KAARE
ANDREWS

A native of Canada, Kaare Andrews has been reading comic books as long as he can remember. Most acclaimed for his digitally painted HULK and SPIDER-MAN covers, he has recently moved into writing and illustrating series for Marvel Comics; titles include issues of TANGLED WEB SPIDER-MAN, X-MEN UNLIMITED and MARVEL MANGAVERSE SPIDER-MAN. Kaare has also directed music videos (Tegan and Sara, Jane Siberry and Mike Clark) and award-winning short films, written a screenplay, and in between comics is working on a feature horror film. His photography has appeared in publications such as SPIN magazine, THE LONDON TIMES and MTV.com. Kaare is currently working on SPIDER-MAN/DOCTOR OCTOPUS: YEAR ONE and is ready to take on the world with his creator owned series HIRO (along with Ron Turner) and a new SPIDER-MAN project that he will be both writing and drawing.

3D MODELING BY RON
TURNER

Ron Turner is an art director and conceptual artist who comes from the world of television animation. Some of the properties he has worked on include BEAST MACHINES, HEAVY GEAR and HOT WHEELS. Currently Ron "The Hammer" Turner is breaking all the rules by introducing 3D modelling into the world of comics, and is ready to battle his way to the World Tag Team Championship with the creator owned comic book series HIRO along with Tag Team partner Kaare "The Mexican Princess" Andrews.

COLOR BY DAVE
McCAIG

Dave McCaig has been working in comics for 12 years, but is perhaps best known for his coloring work on the Dark Horse comics STAR WARS line. With work on SUPERMAN: BIRTHRIGHT for DC and various X-MEN titles for Marvel under his belt, McCaig is also a distinguished illustrator in his own right, having painted covers and pinups for various publishers. Currently Dave is coloring ADAM STRANGE for DC comics, as well as handling lead color design on the Warner Bros. cartoon, THE BATMAN, where he uses his unique palette and style to bring Gotham City to life

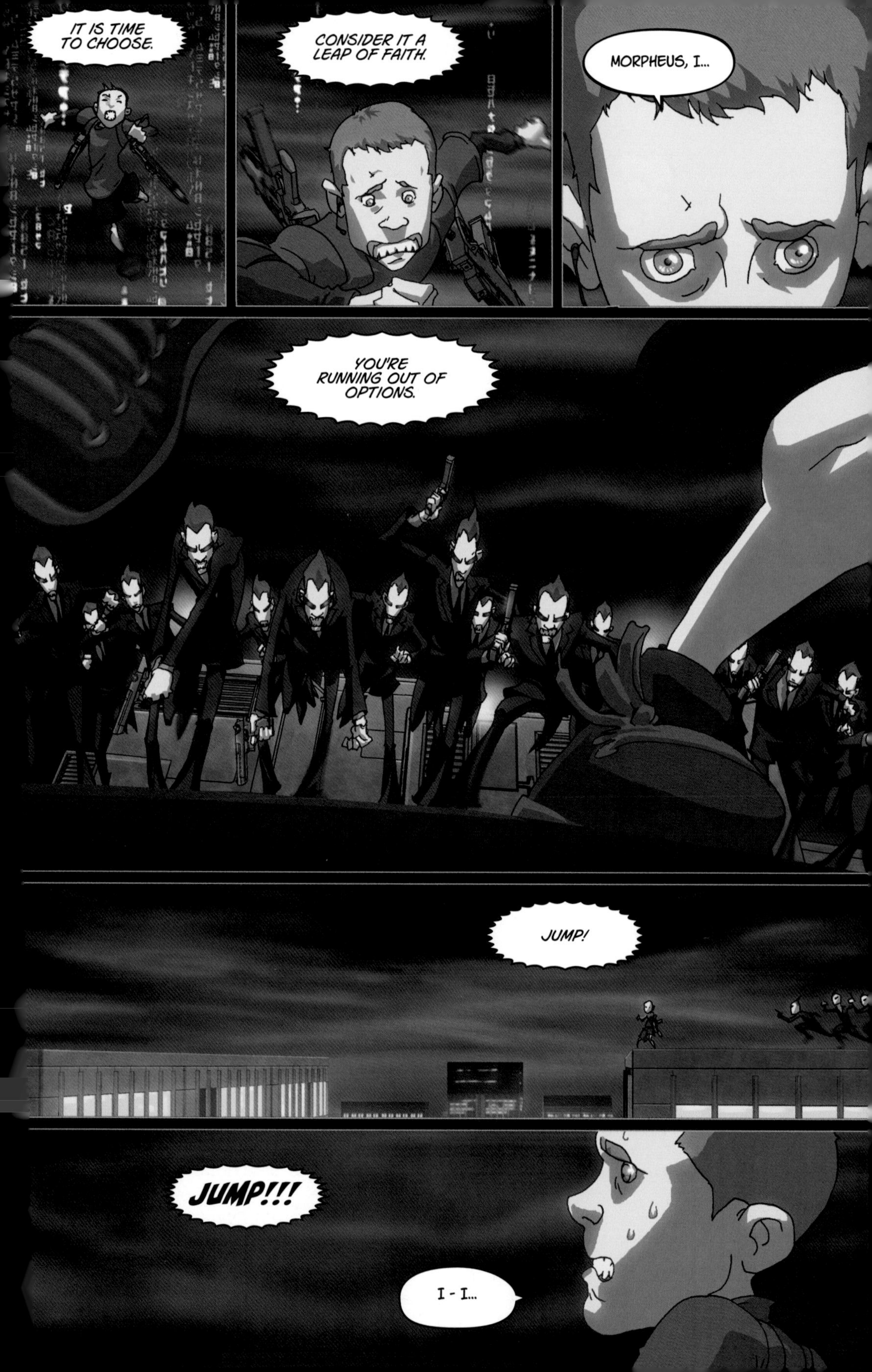
IT IS TIME TO CHOOSE.
CONSIDER IT A LEAP OF FAITH.
MORPHEUS, I...
YOU'RE RUNNING OUT OF OPTIONS.
JUMP!
JUMP!!!
I - I...

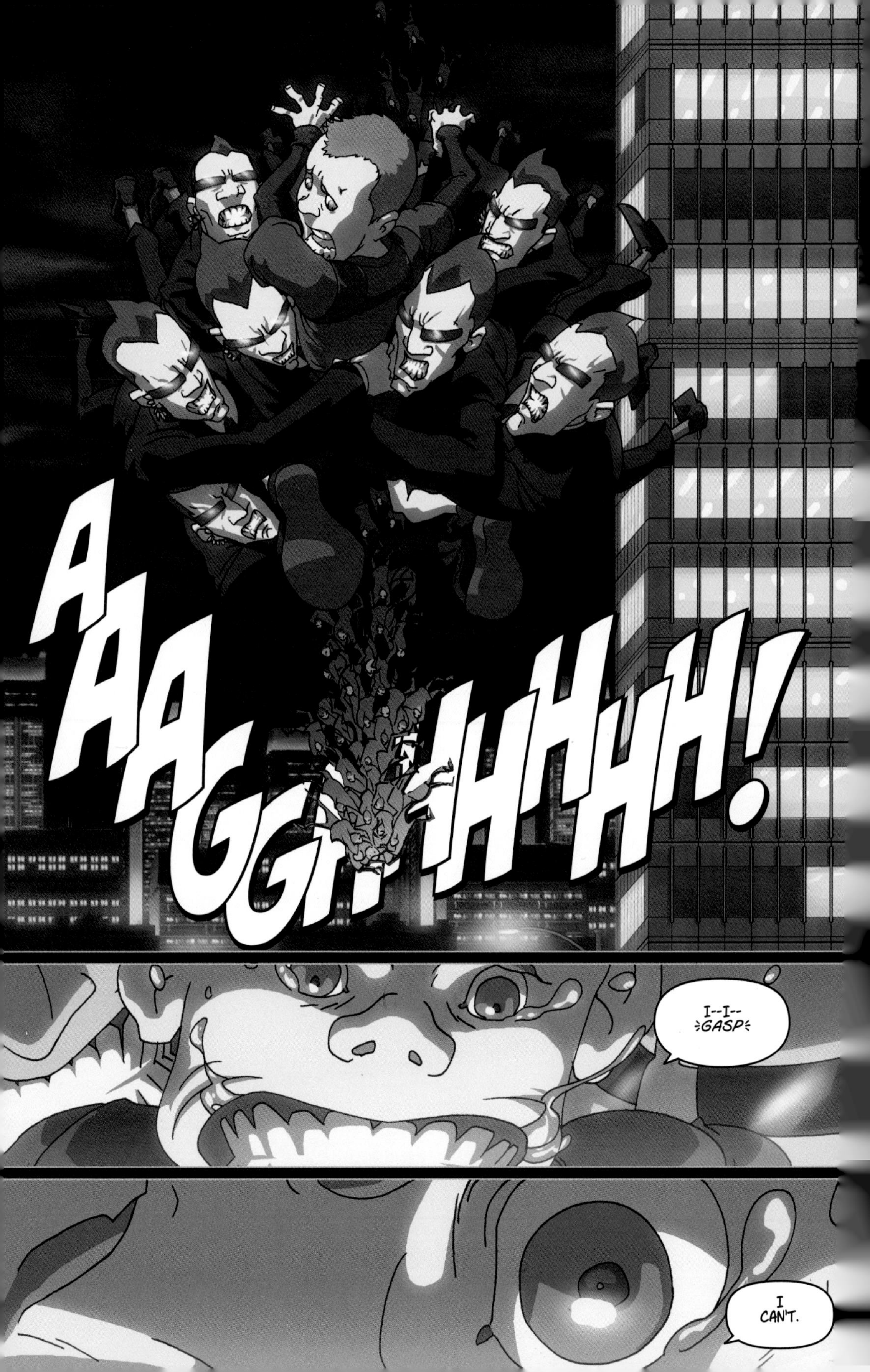
AAAGGHHHHHH!
I--I-- GASP
I CAN'T.

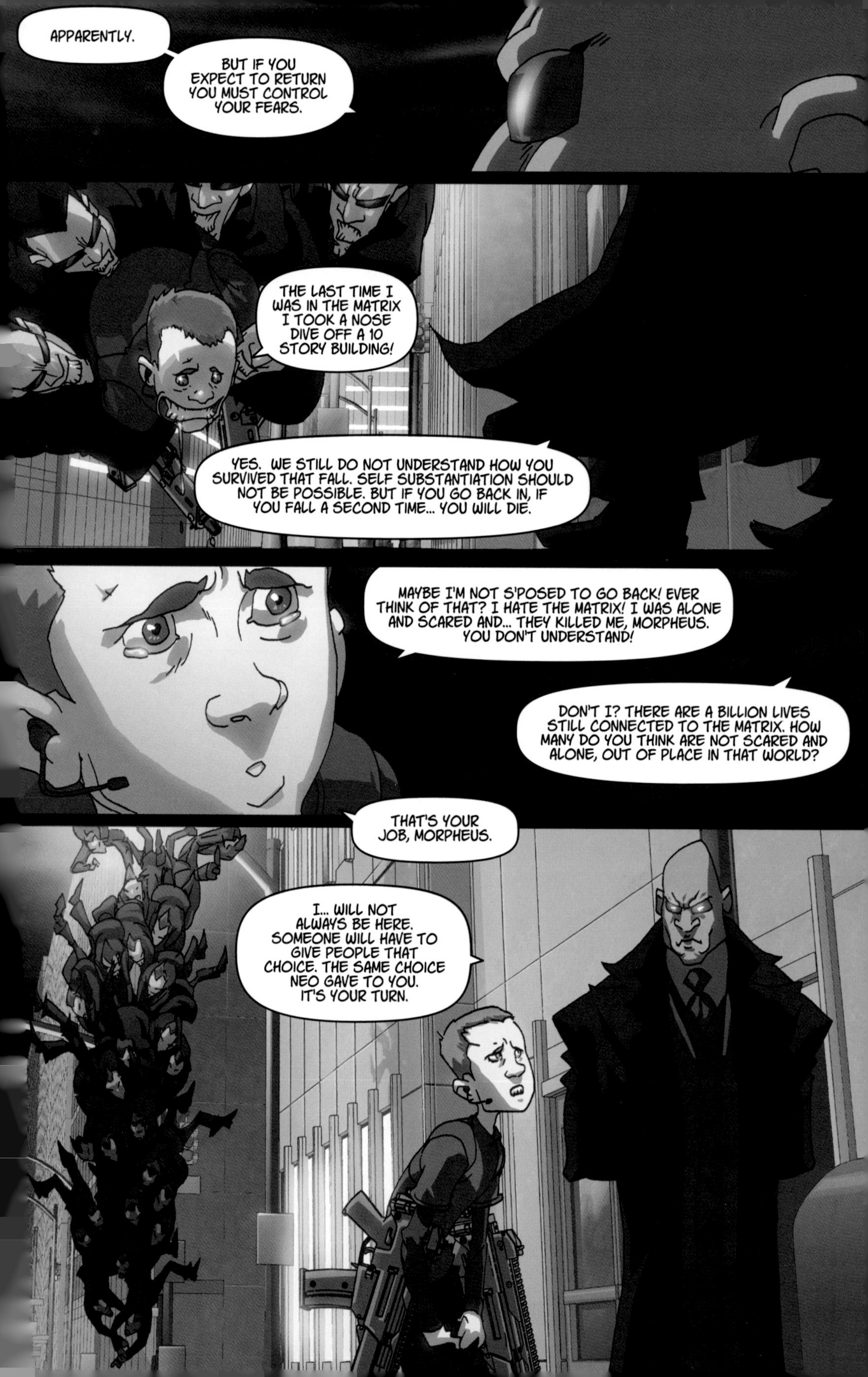
APPARENTLY.
BUT IF YOU EXPECT TO RETURN YOU MUST CONTROL YOUR FEARS.
THE LAST TIME I WAS IN THE MATRIX I TOOK A NOSE DIVE OFF A 10 STORY BUILDING!
YES. WE STILL DO NOT UNDERSTAND HOW YOU SURVIVED THAT FALL. SELF SUBSTANTIATION SHOULD NOT BE POSSIBLE. BUT IF YOU GO BACK IN, IF YOU FALL A SECOND TIME... YOU WILL DIE.
MAYBE I'M NOT S'POSED TO GO BACK! EVER THINK OF THAT? I HATE THE MATRIX! I WAS ALONE AND SCARED AND... THEY KILLED ME, MORPHEUS. YOU DON'T UNDERSTAND!
DON'T I? THERE ARE A BILLION LIVES STILL CONNECTED TO THE MATRIX. HOW MANY DO YOU THINK ARE NOT SCARED AND ALONE, OUT OF PLACE IN THAT WORLD?
THAT'S YOUR JOB, MORPHEUS.
I... WILL NOT ALWAYS BE HERE. SOMEONE WILL HAVE TO GIVE PEOPLE THAT CHOICE. THE SAME CHOICE NEO GAVE TO YOU. IT'S YOUR TURN.

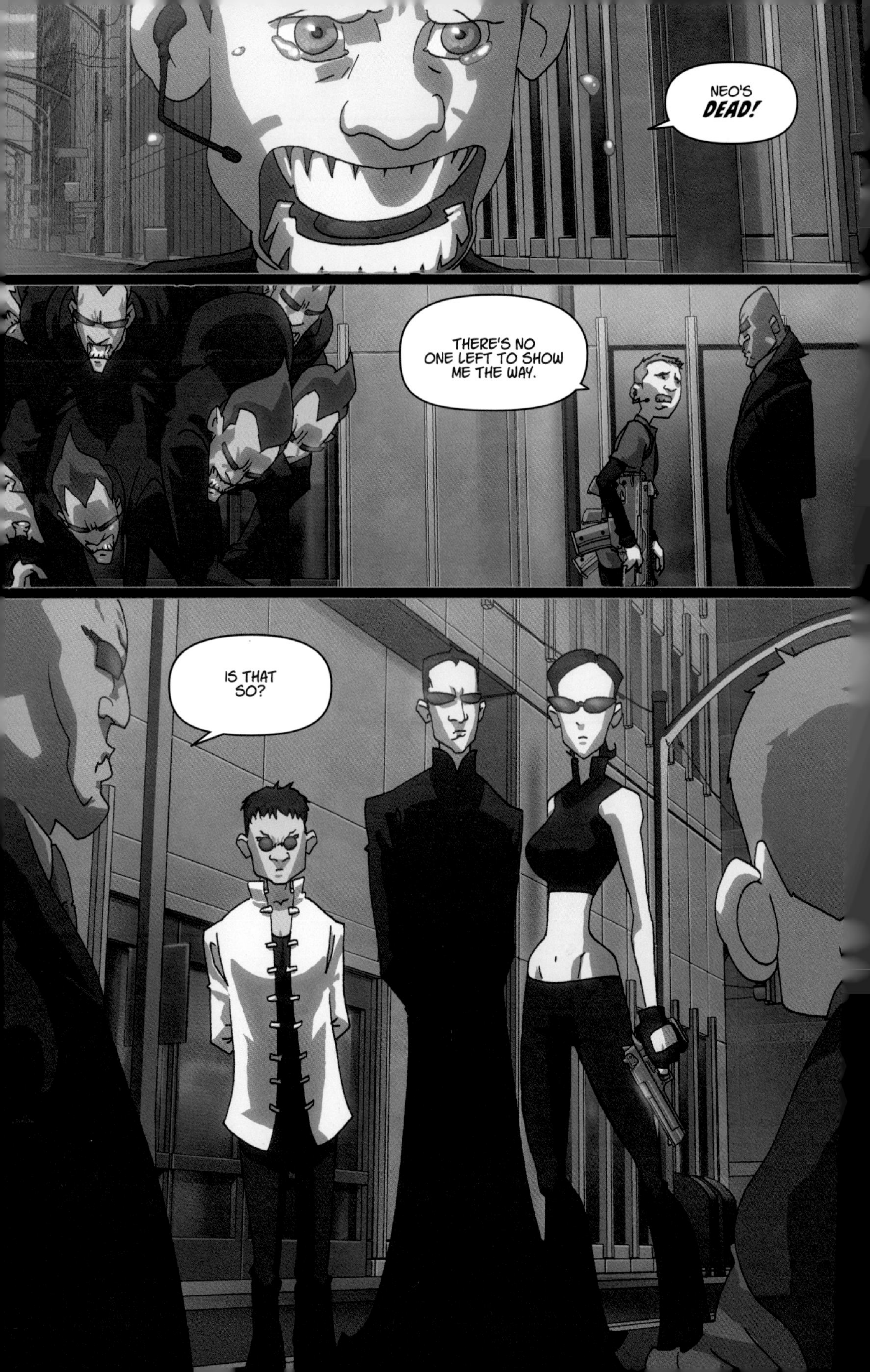
NEO'S DEAD!
THERE'S NO ONE LEFT TO SHOW ME THE WAY.
IS THAT SO?

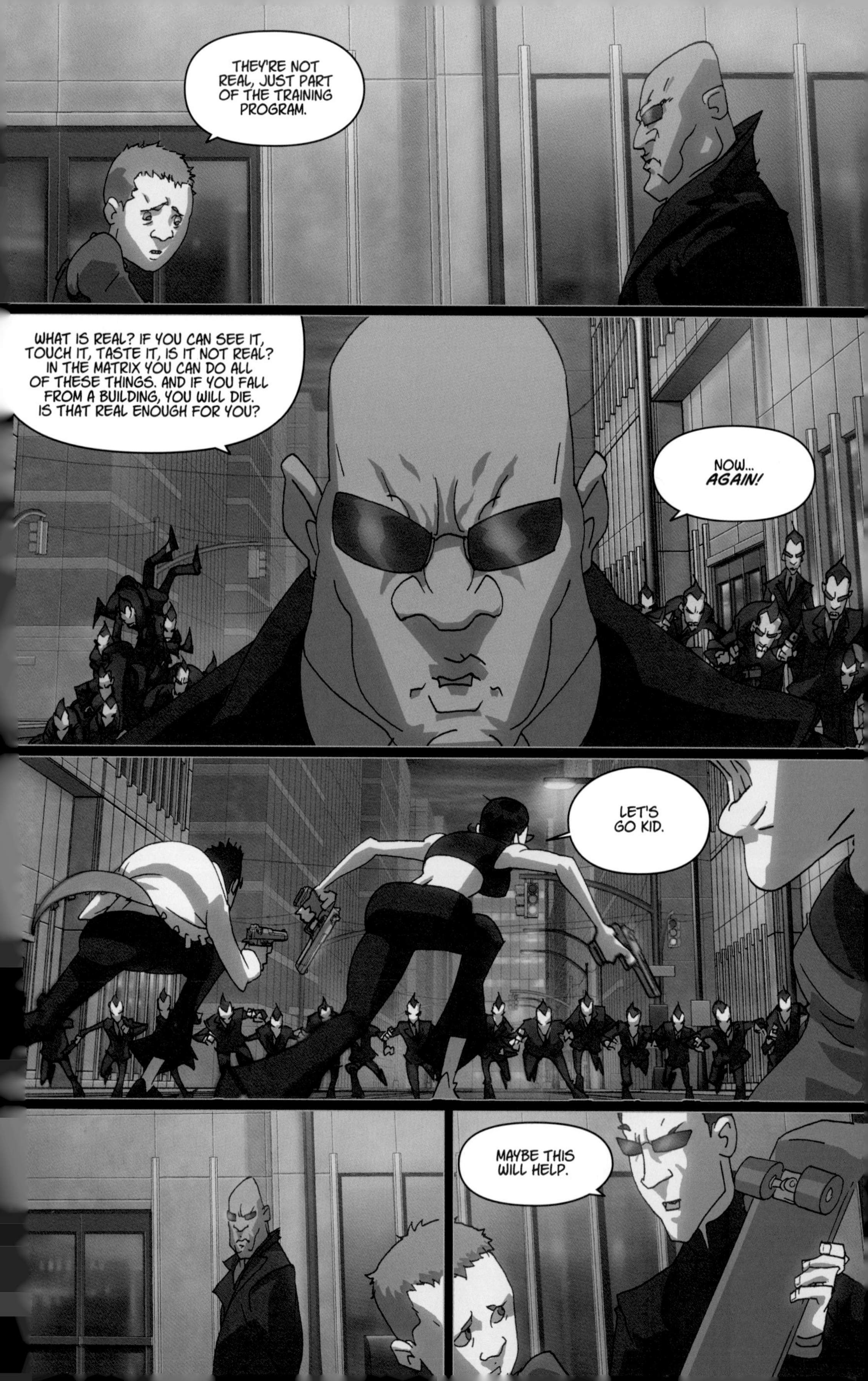
THEY'RE NOT REAL, JUST PART OF THE TRAINING PROGRAM.
WHAT IS REAL? IF YOU CAN SEE IT, TOUCH IT, TASTE IT, IS IT NOT REAL? IN THE MATRIX YOU CAN DO ALL OF THESE THINGS. AND IF YOU FALL FROM A BUILDING, YOU WILL DIE. IS THAT REAL ENOUGH FOR YOU?
NOW... *AGAIN!*
LET'S GO KID.
MAYBE THIS WILL HELP.

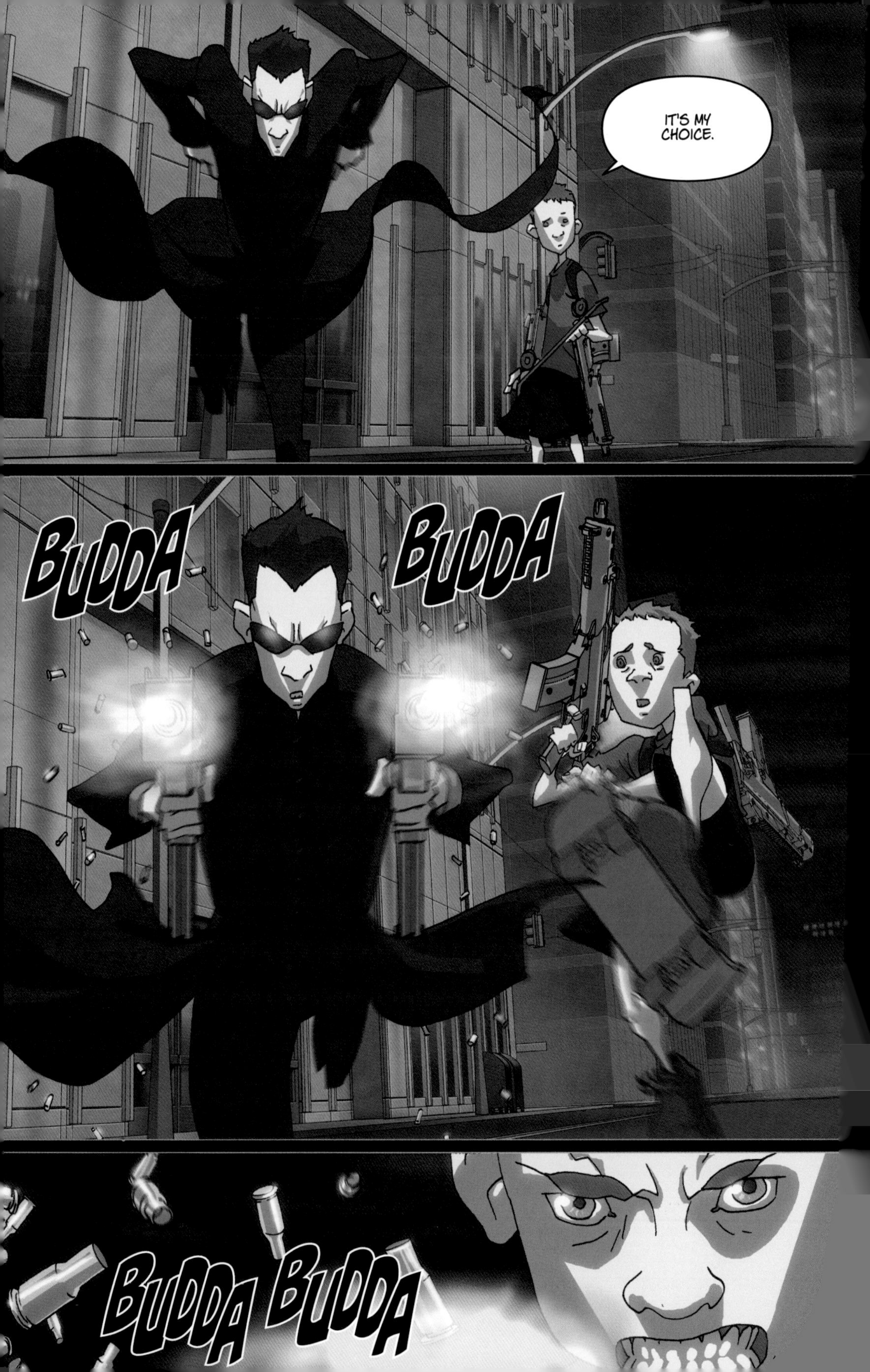
IT'S MY CHOICE.
BUDDA
BUDDA
BUDDA BUDDA

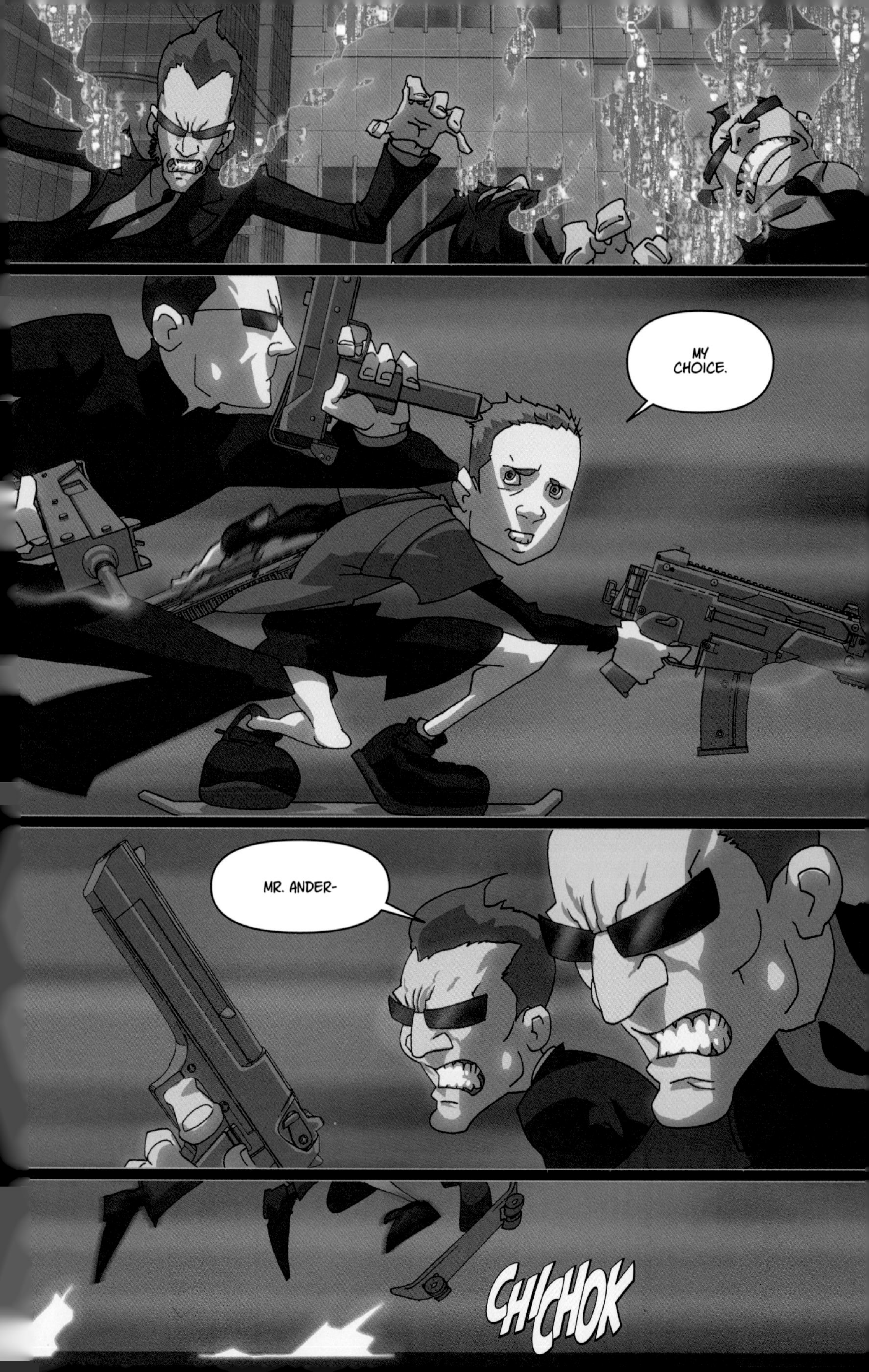
MY CHOICE.
MR. ANDER-
CHICHOK

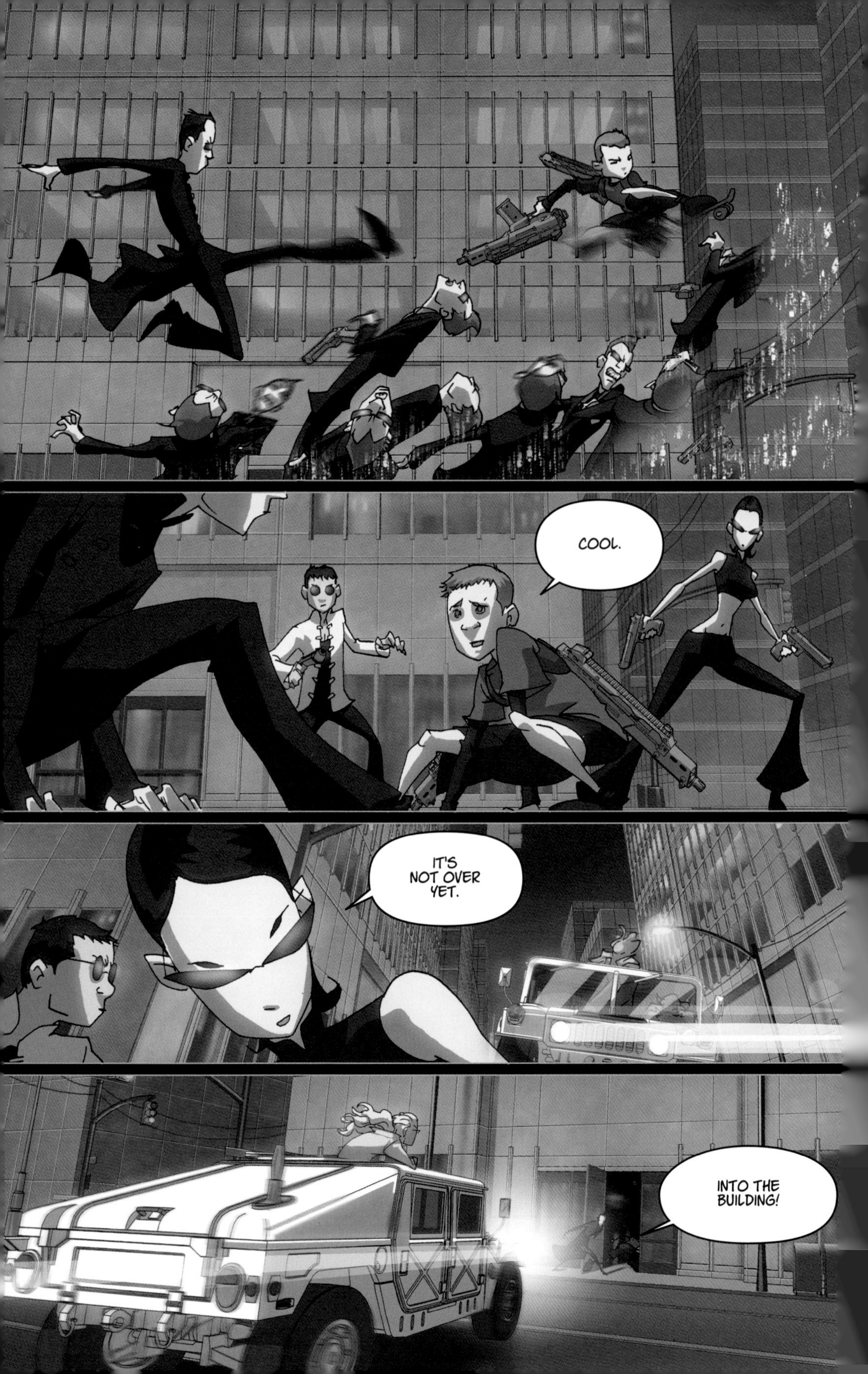
COOL.
IT'S NOT OVER YET.
INTO THE BUILDING!

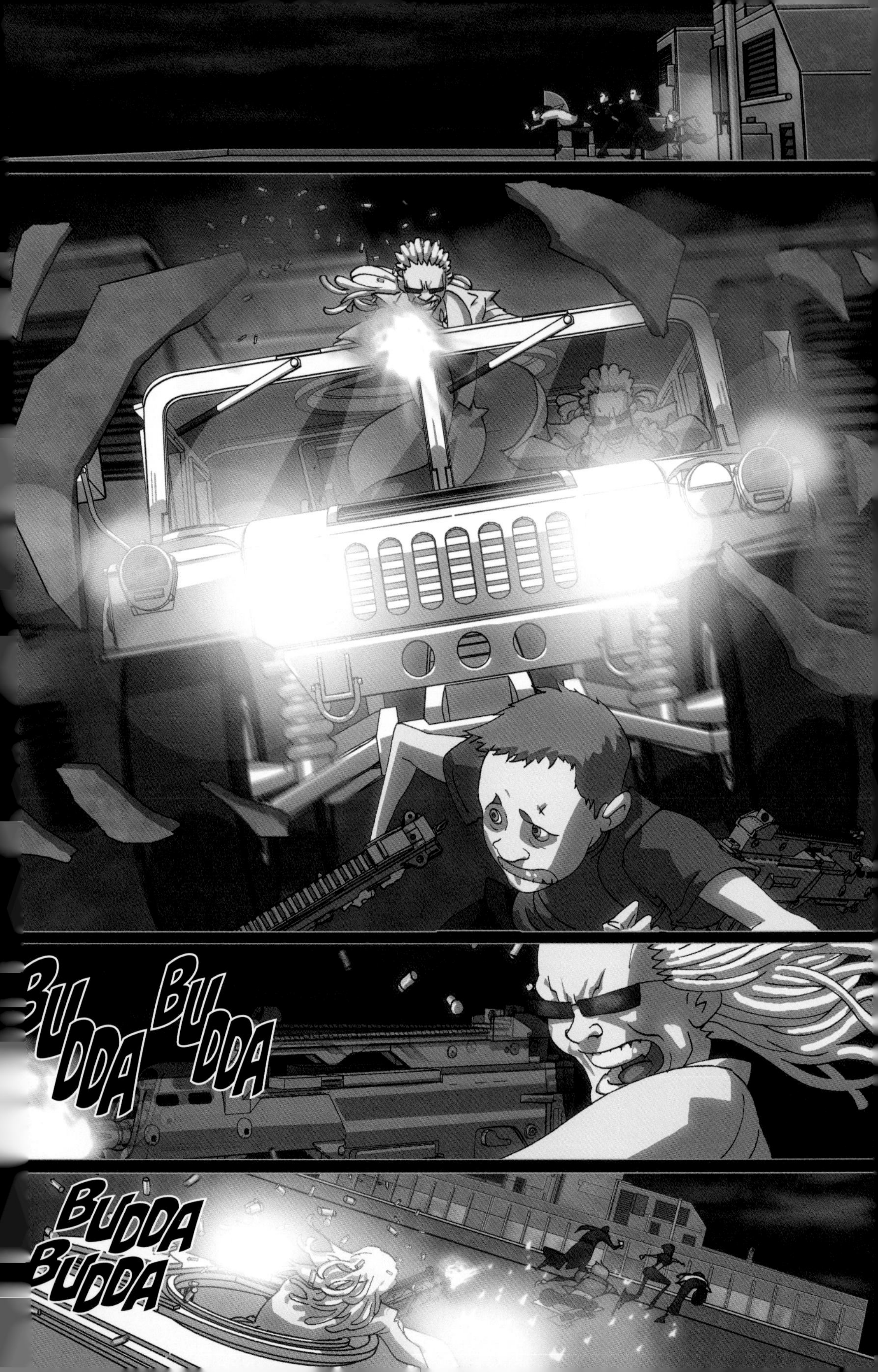
BUDDA BUDDA
BUDDA BUDDA

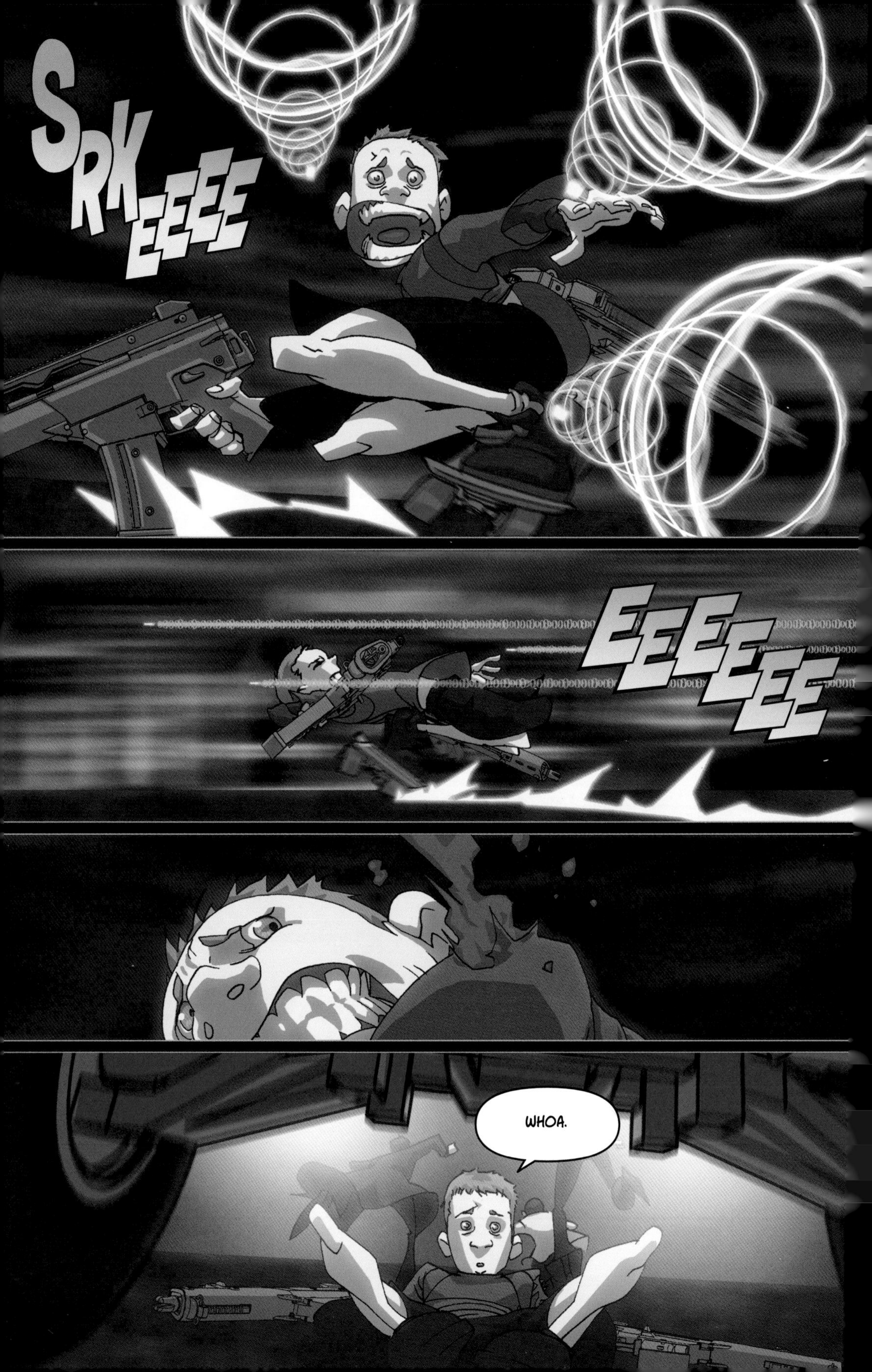
SRKEEEE
EEEEEEE
WHOA.

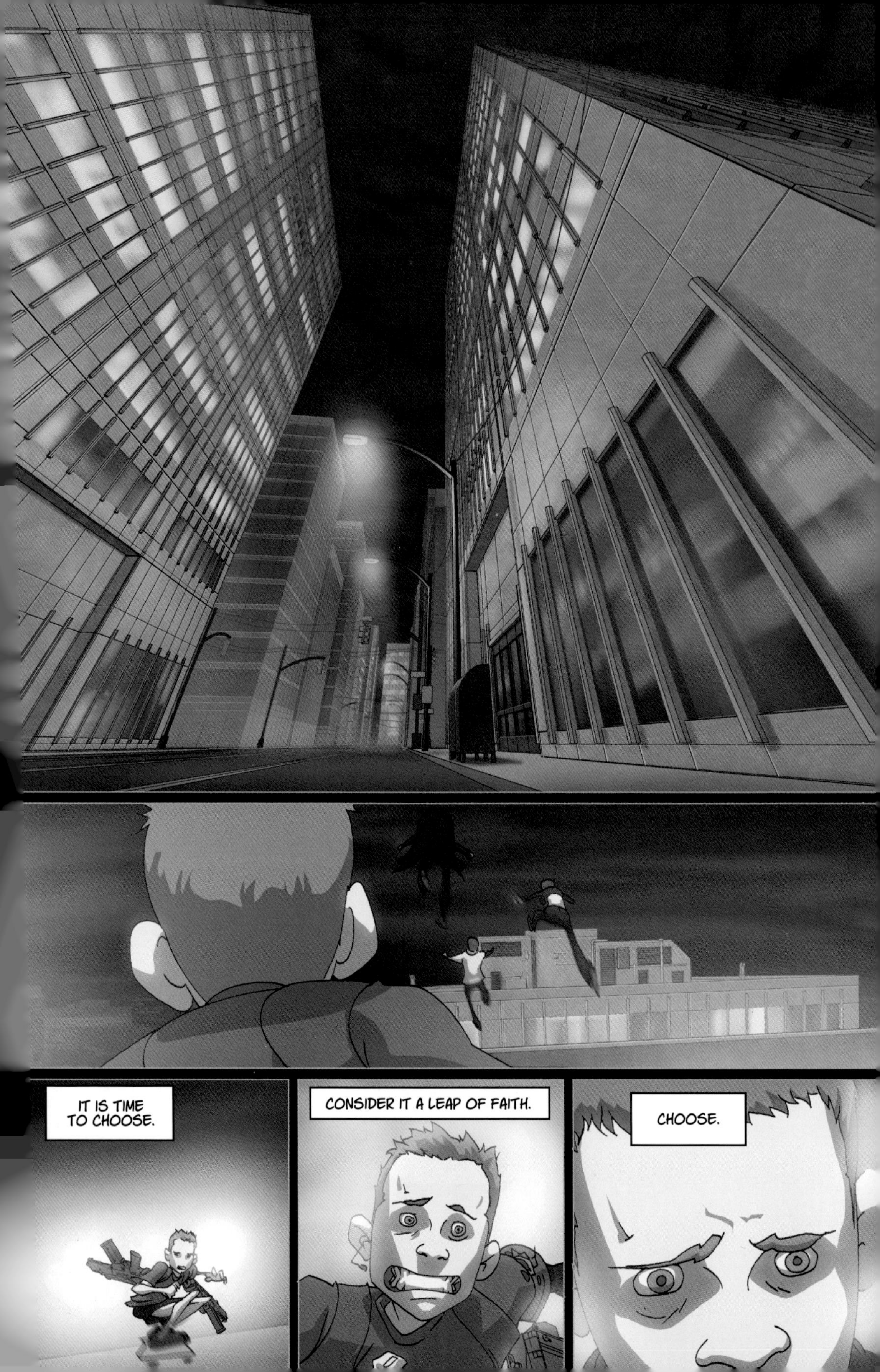
IT IS TIME
TO CHOOSE.
CONSIDER IT A LEAP OF FAITH.
CHOOSE.

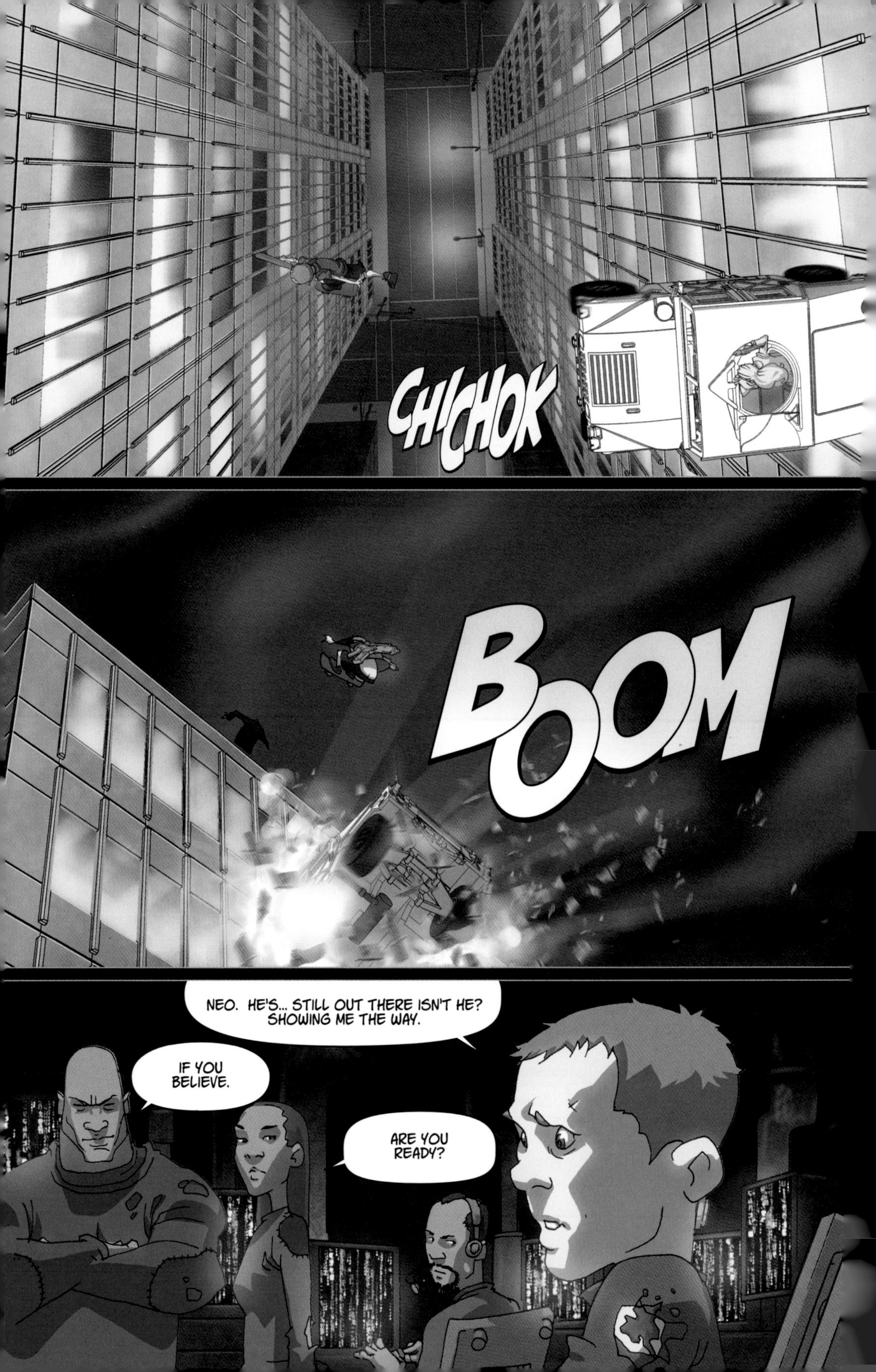
CHICHOK
BOOM
NEO. HE'S... STILL OUT THERE ISN'T HE? SHOWING ME THE WAY.
IF YOU BELIEVE.
ARE YOU READY?

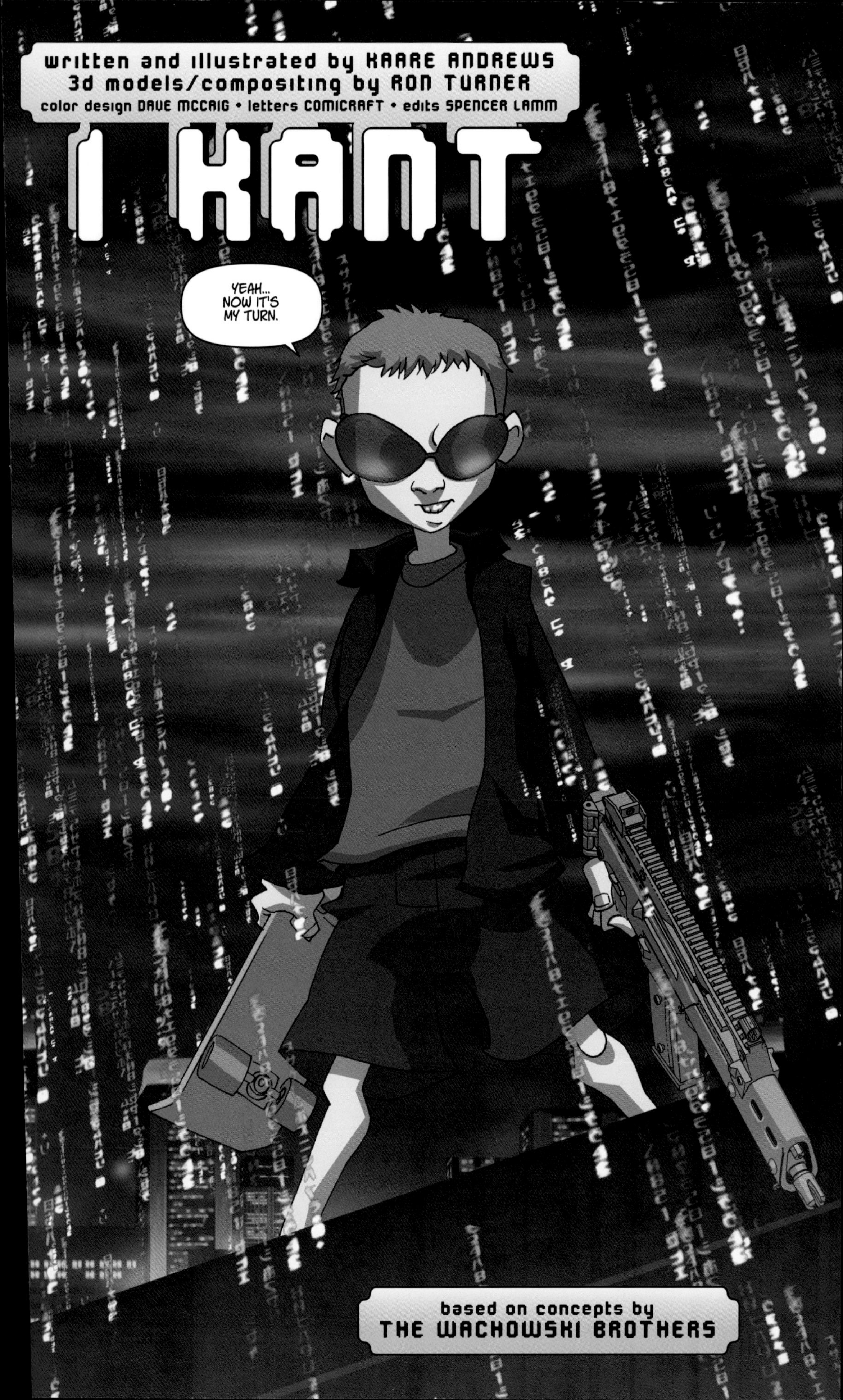
written and illustrated by KAARE ANDREWS
3d models/compositing by RON TURNER
color design DAVE MCCAIG • letters COMICRAFT • edits SPENCER LAMM
I KANT
YEAH... NOW IT'S MY TURN.
based on concepts by THE WACHOWSKI BROTHERS

DOC FRANKENSTEIN
Illlustrated by Steve Skroce

Hi.

Welcome to Burlyman Comics.

Some of you less-than-burly types out there may be wondering what madness could possess us to throw our hat into the cut-throat ring of comic book publishing where there is typically more blood and less rules than in an Ultimate Fighting Championship. The reason is pretty simple; we love comics. Even during the agony of our 48 month labor in which we gave birth to the twins RELOADED and REVOLUTIONS, Friday remained the Day of Succor because DJ, one of our VFX supervisors, would bring us a fresh stack of new releases.

Comics, more than film, gave us an appreciation for the different ways that words and pictures can be used to tell a story. You can say what you want about the industry, but as an art form, the comic book is superior to film in our opinion because of the excessive compromises that must be made every single day on a film set.

Yet there have always been certain comics that have always stood out. While we were growing up, those comics were usually drawn by Jack Kirby. He was our King. Reading one of his comics was like mainlining imagination. He took you places you had never been, showed you action you had never seen. He drew things that could not exist in any other graphic medium. He drew the impossible.

Which is why, for us, so many comics today are disappointments. In a medium where you can draw ANYTHING, how can so many artists be content to simply imitate what's already been done in film and television? The first time we saw HARD BOILED we thought that here was someone who understood the joy of the medium, here was someone who seemed a rightful heir to Kirby's crown. Geof Darrow and Steve Skroce draw the kind of comics we like to read; they take us places we've never been, they show us action we've never seen. They are the reason we started this company. To create a place where people like us could see the stuff that only comics can do, a place where people can still find the Jack stuff, the impossible stuff.

Thanks for buying Burly.

The Wachowski Brothers

THE SHAOLIN COWBOY
Illlustrated by Geof Darrow

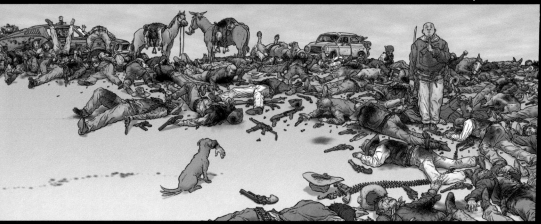

CO-CREATED BY
GEOF DARROW & STEVE SKROCE
WRITTEN BY
THE WACHOWSKI BROTHERS
ILLUSTRATED BY STEVE SKROCE

READ ON FOR PREVIEW

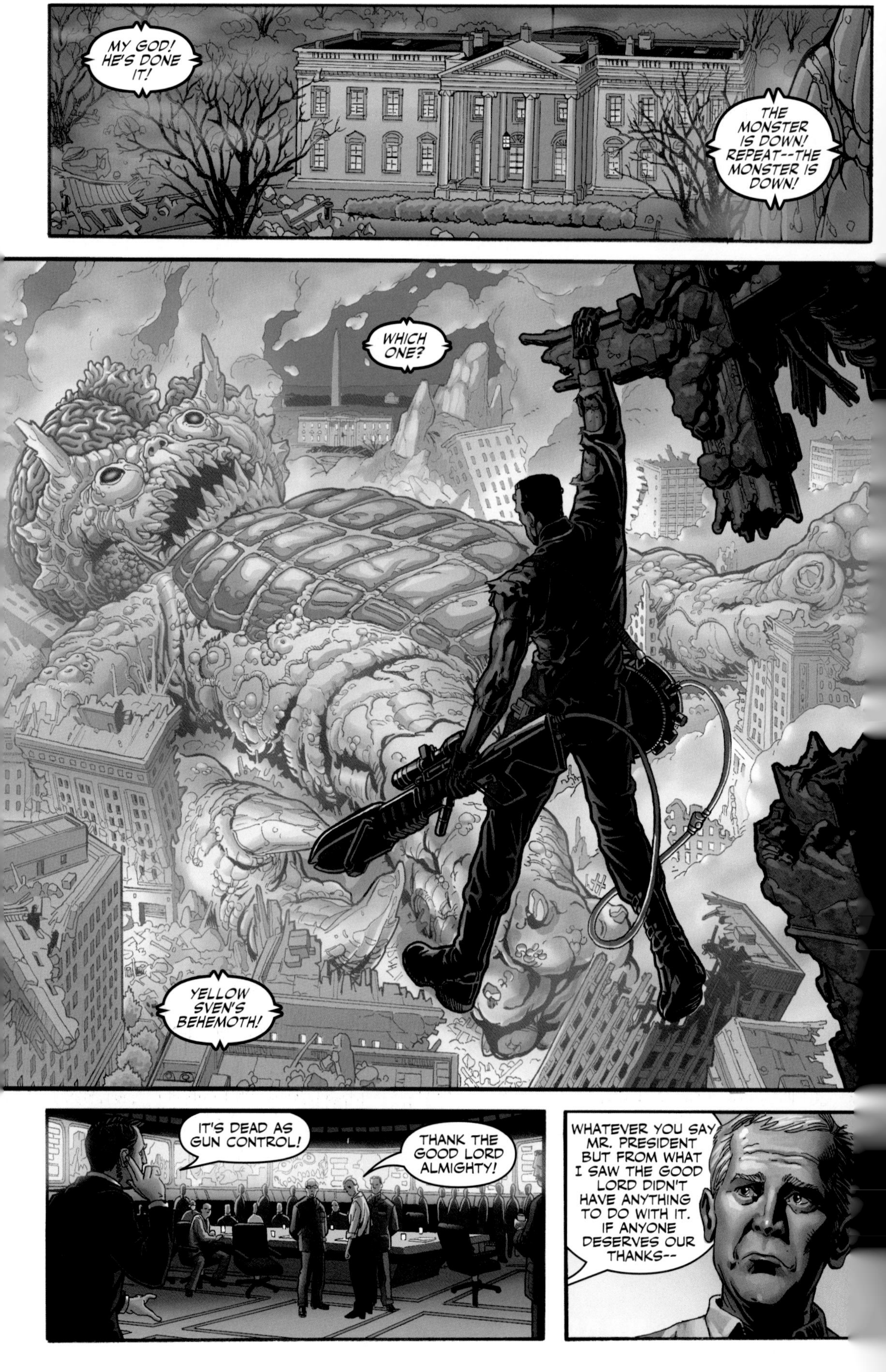
MY GOD! HE'S DONE IT!
THE MONSTER IS DOWN! REPEAT--THE MONSTER IS DOWN!
WHICH ONE?
YELLOW SVEN'S BEHEMOTH!
IT'S DEAD AS GUN CONTROL!
THANK THE GOOD LORD ALMIGHTY!
WHATEVER YOU SAY MR. PRESIDENT BUT FROM WHAT I SAW THE GOOD LORD DIDN'T HAVE ANYTHING TO DO WITH IT. IF ANYONE DESERVES OUR THANKS--

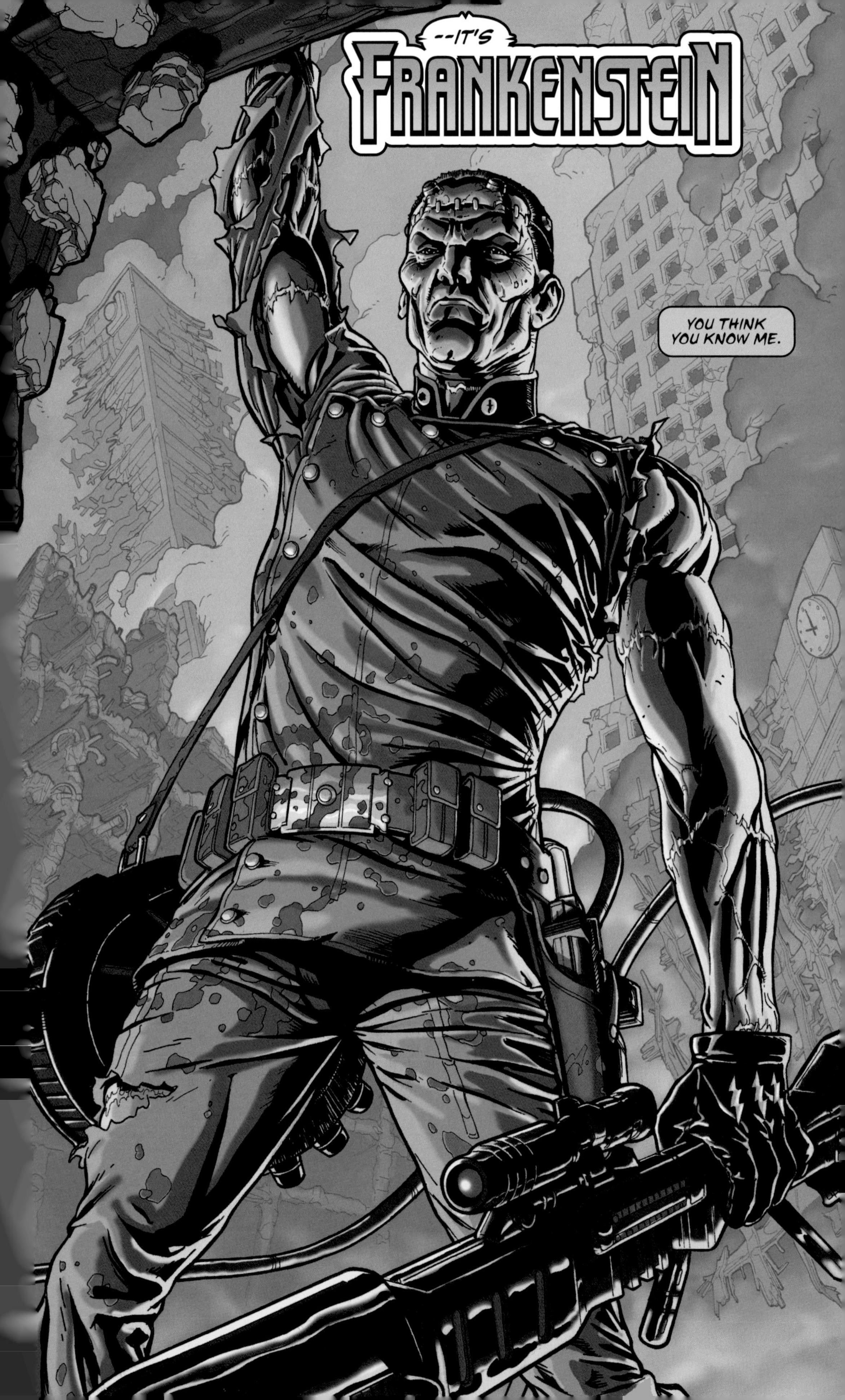
--IT'S
FRANKENSTEIN
YOU THINK YOU KNOW ME.

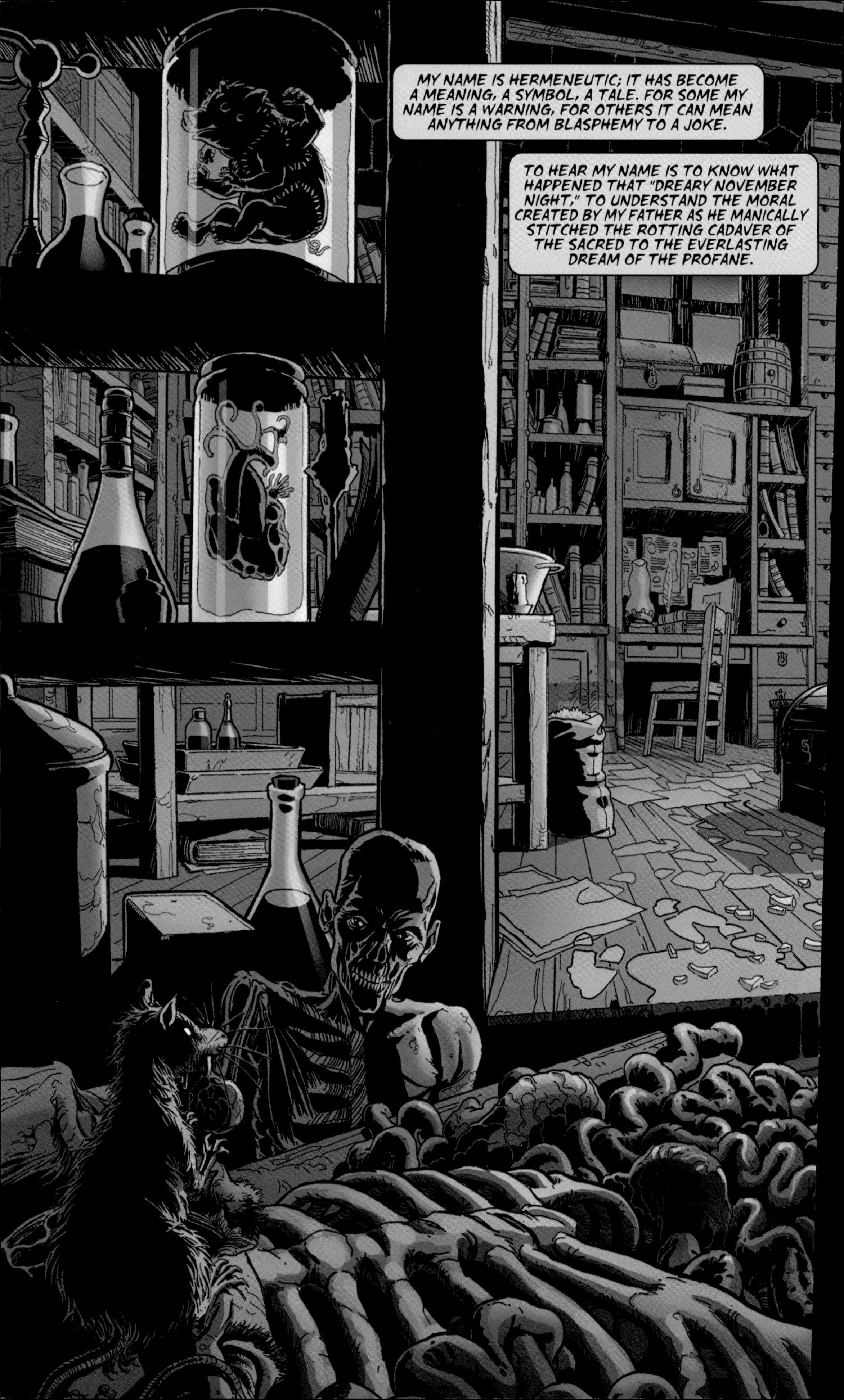
MY NAME IS HERMENEUTIC; IT HAS BECOME A MEANING, A SYMBOL, A TALE. FOR SOME MY NAME IS A WARNING, FOR OTHERS IT CAN MEAN ANYTHING FROM BLASPHEMY TO A JOKE.
TO HEAR MY NAME IS TO KNOW WHAT HAPPENED THAT "DREARY NOVEMBER NIGHT," TO UNDERSTAND THE MORAL CREATED BY MY FATHER AS HE MANICALLY STITCHED THE ROTTING CADAVER OF THE SACRED TO THE EVERLASTING DREAM OF THE PROFANE.

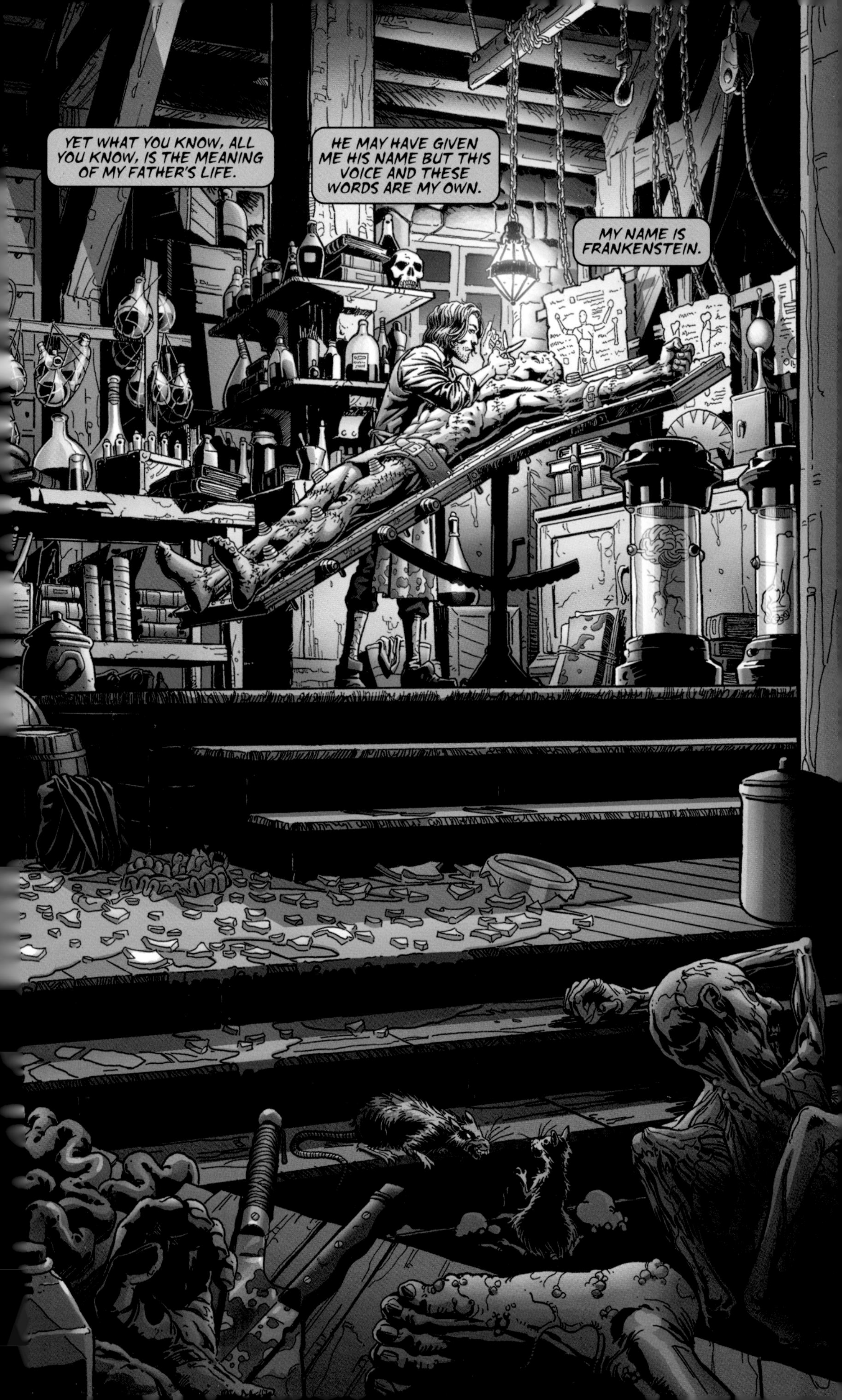
YET WHAT YOU KNOW, ALL YOU KNOW, IS THE MEANING OF MY FATHER'S LIFE.
HE MAY HAVE GIVEN ME HIS NAME BUT THIS VOICE AND THESE WORDS ARE MY OWN.
MY NAME IS FRANKENSTEIN.

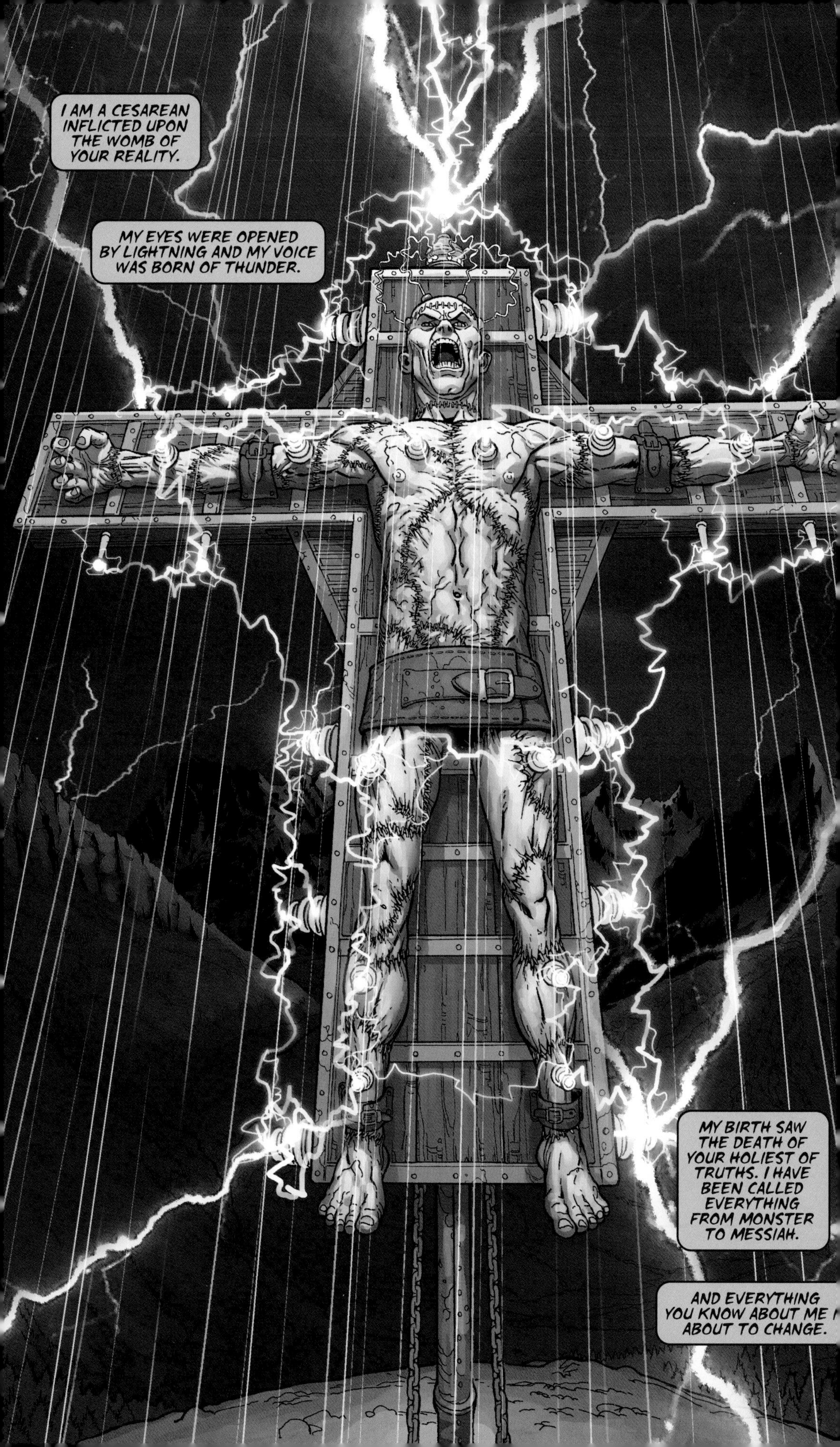
I AM A CESAREAN INFLICTED UPON THE WOMB OF YOUR REALITY.
MY EYES WERE OPENED BY LIGHTNING AND MY VOICE WAS BORN OF THUNDER.
MY BIRTH SAW THE DEATH OF YOUR HOLIEST OF TRUTHS. I HAVE BEEN CALLED EVERYTHING FROM MONSTER TO MESSIAH.
AND EVERYTHING YOU KNOW ABOUT ME I ABOUT TO CHANGE.

--THE ENORMOUS EXPOSED BRAIN WAS THE ACHILLES HEEL AFTER ALL--

THEY ARE CALLING YOU A HERO. HOT-STUFF HERE GOT ALL TEARY WATCHING JENNINGS RABBIT ON ABOUT YOU STANDING BETWEEN THE SYMBOLS OF CIVILIZATION AND THE FORCES OF DESTRUCTION.

WHAT ABOUT O'REILLY?

WHO CARES WHAT THAT A-HOLE SAYS--

I HAVE TOLD YOU TEX, THIS COUNTRY IS CONSERVATIVE BECAUSE THIS COUNTRY IS AFRAID.

AND I TOLD YOU DOC, HOT AIR FROM AN ASSHOLE USUALLY STINKS.

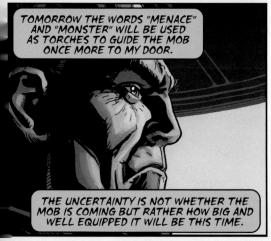

TOMORROW THE WORDS "MENACE" AND "MONSTER" WILL BE USED AS TORCHES TO GUIDE THE MOB ONCE MORE TO MY DOOR.

THE UNCERTAINTY IS NOT WHETHER THE MOB IS COMING BUT RATHER HOW BIG AND WELL EQUIPPED IT WILL BE THIS TIME.

I WONDER IF THERE CAN BE AN END TO THIS CYCLE OR WHETHER THE ONLY PEACE POSSIBLE WILL BE FOUND AT THE BOTTOM OF MY GRAVE.

LONG AGO I ONCE LOOKED FOR THAT PEACE.

FLEEING MY FATHER'S DEATH I SOUGHT THE ONLY HOPE FOR COMFORT I IMAGINED POSSIBLE IN THE BOREAL EMBRACE OF ARCTIC ICE.

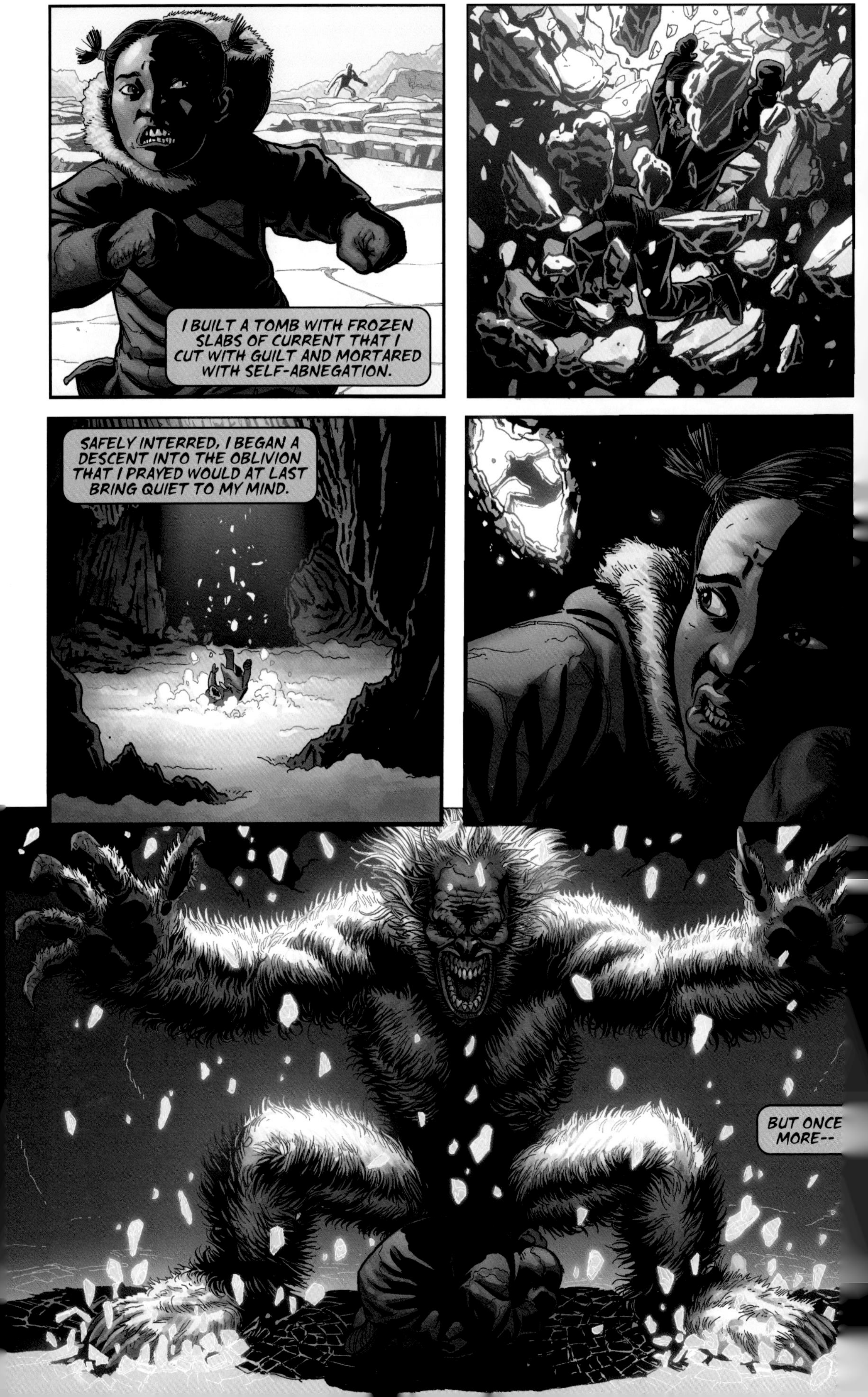
I BUILT A TOMB WITH FROZEN SLABS OF CURRENT THAT I CUT WITH GUILT AND MORTARED WITH SELF-ABNEGATION.
SAFELY INTERRED, I BEGAN A DESCENT INTO THE OBLIVION THAT I PRAYED WOULD AT LAST BRING QUIET TO MY MIND.
BUT ONCE MORE--

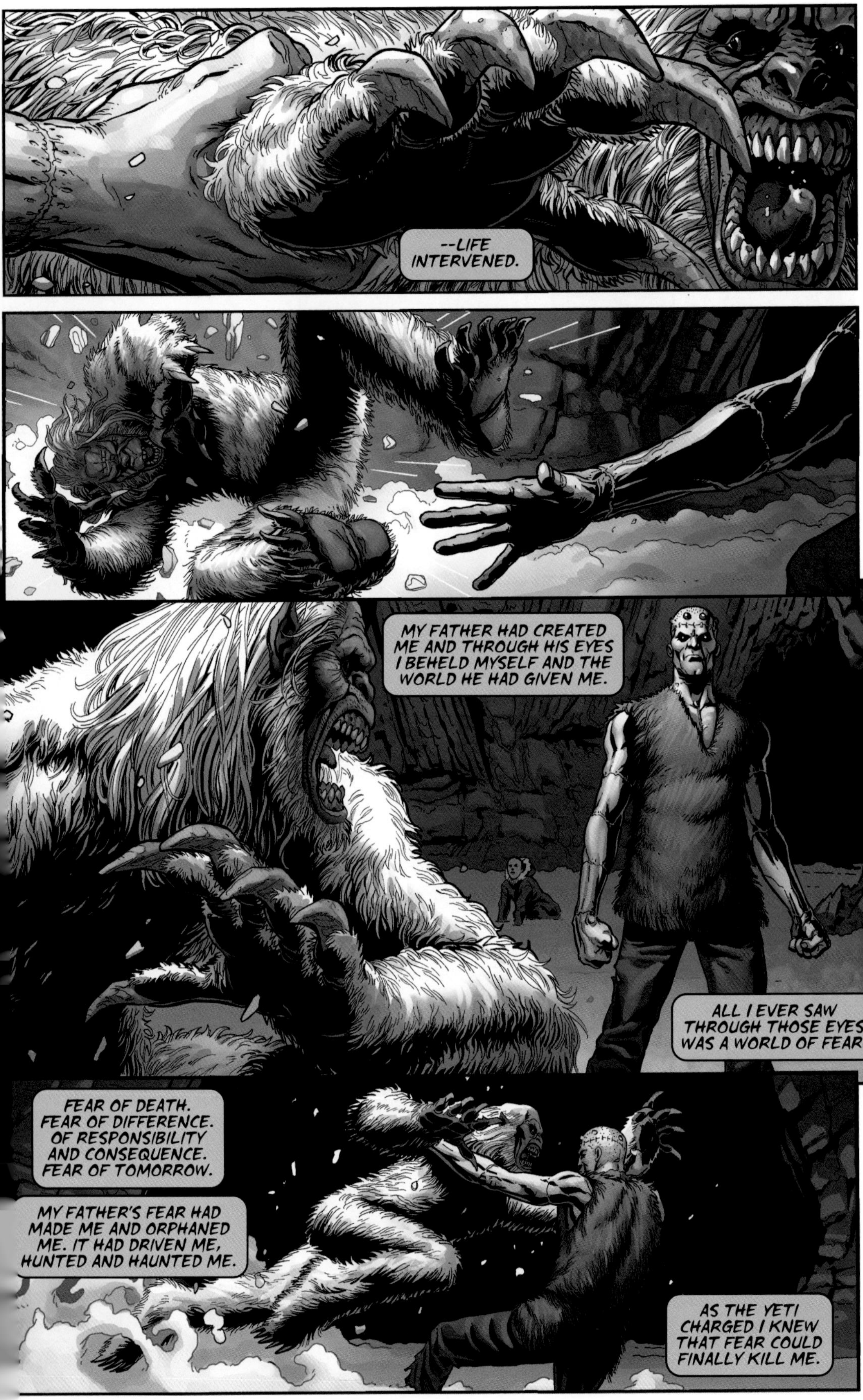
--LIFE INTERVENED.
MY FATHER HAD CREATED ME AND THROUGH HIS EYES I BEHELD MYSELF AND THE WORLD HE HAD GIVEN ME.
ALL I EVER SAW THROUGH THOSE EYES WAS A WORLD OF FEAR.
FEAR OF DEATH. FEAR OF DIFFERENCE. OF RESPONSIBILITY AND CONSEQUENCE. FEAR OF TOMORROW.
MY FATHER'S FEAR HAD MADE ME AND ORPHANED ME. IT HAD DRIVEN ME, HUNTED AND HAUNTED ME.
AS THE YETI CHARGED I KNEW THAT FEAR COULD FINALLY KILL ME.

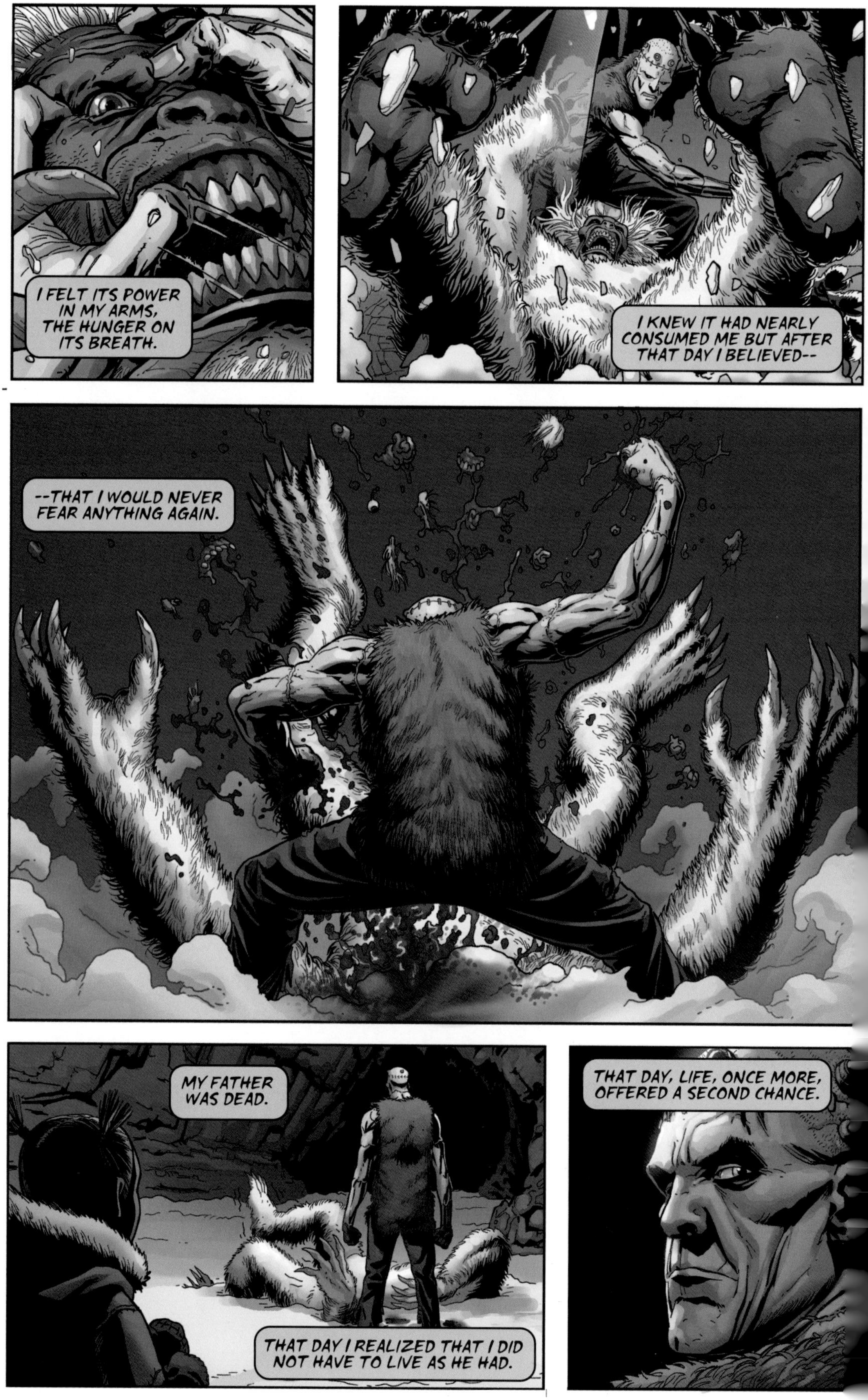
I FELT ITS POWER IN MY ARMS, THE HUNGER ON ITS BREATH.
I KNEW IT HAD NEARLY CONSUMED ME BUT AFTER THAT DAY I BELIEVED--
--THAT I WOULD NEVER FEAR ANYTHING AGAIN.
MY FATHER WAS DEAD.
THAT DAY I REALIZED THAT I DID NOT HAVE TO LIVE AS HE HAD.
THAT DAY, LIFE, ONCE MORE, OFFERED A SECOND CHANCE.

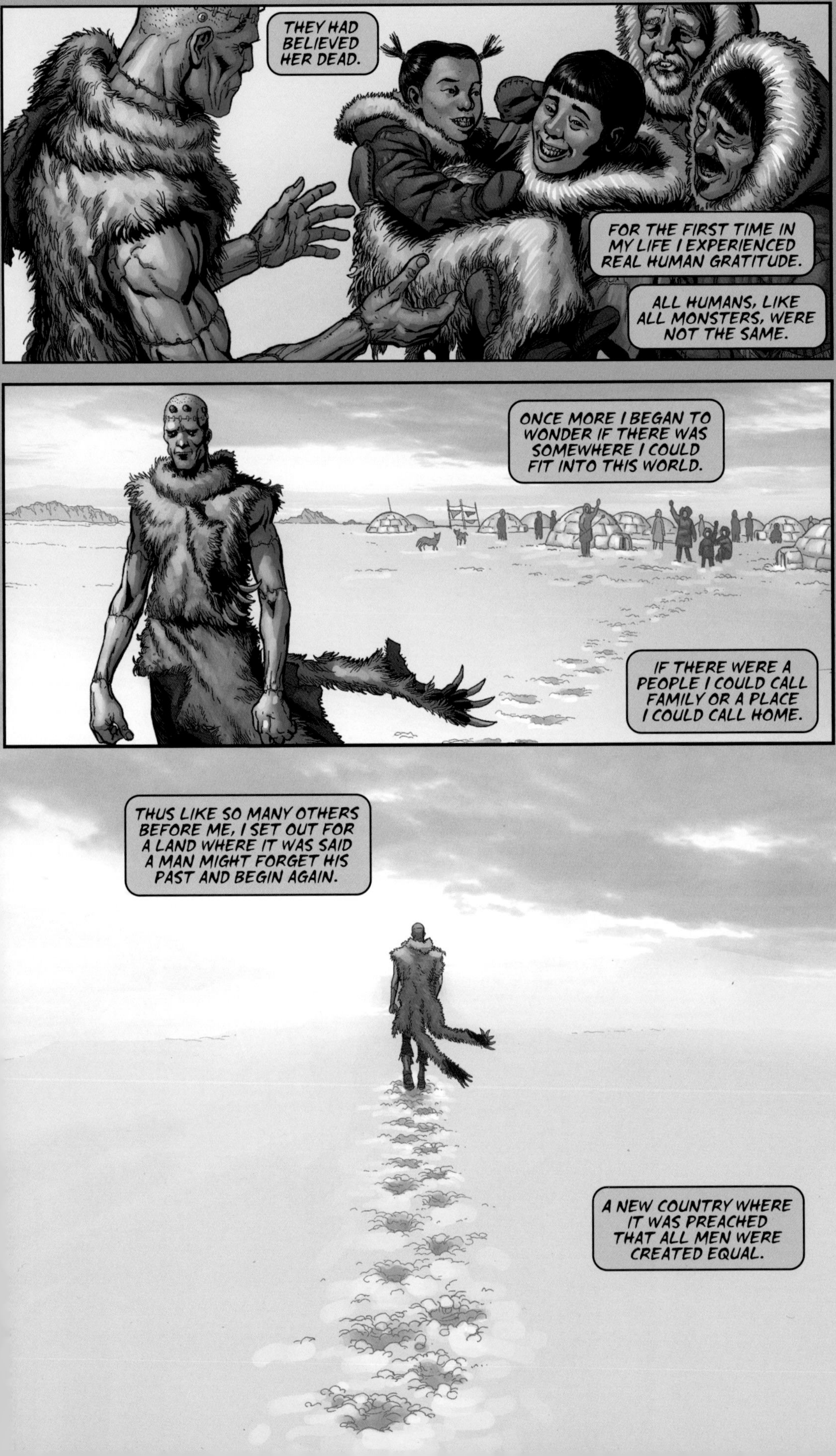
THEY HAD BELIEVED HER DEAD.
FOR THE FIRST TIME IN MY LIFE I EXPERIENCED REAL HUMAN GRATITUDE.
ALL HUMANS, LIKE ALL MONSTERS, WERE NOT THE SAME.
ONCE MORE I BEGAN TO WONDER IF THERE WAS SOMEWHERE I COULD FIT INTO THIS WORLD.
IF THERE WERE A PEOPLE I COULD CALL FAMILY OR A PLACE I COULD CALL HOME.
THUS LIKE SO MANY OTHERS BEFORE ME, I SET OUT FOR A LAND WHERE IT WAS SAID A MAN MIGHT FORGET HIS PAST AND BEGIN AGAIN.
A NEW COUNTRY WHERE IT WAS PREACHED THAT ALL MEN WERE CREATED EQUAL.

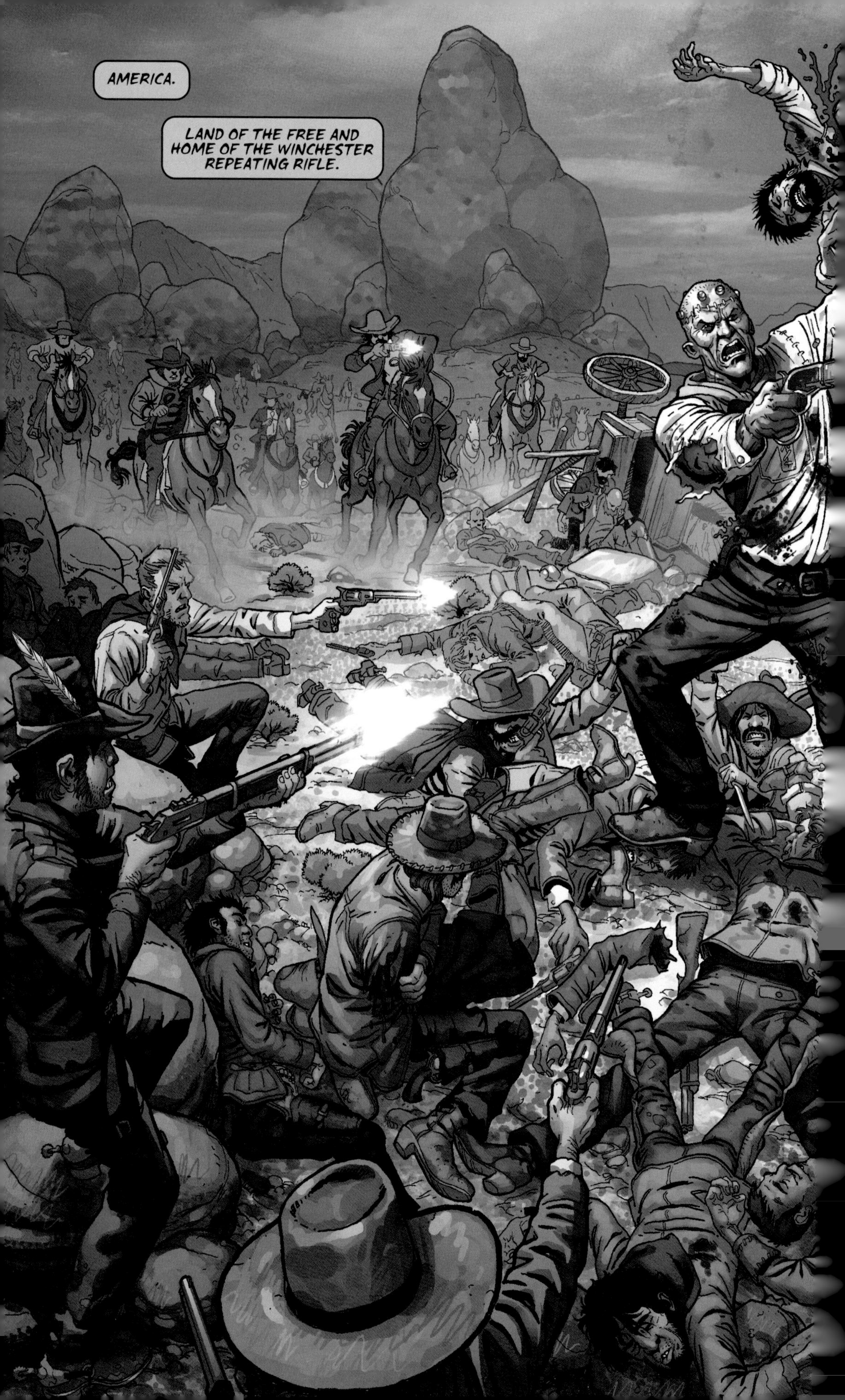
AMERICA.
LAND OF THE FREE AND HOME OF THE WINCHESTER REPEATING RIFLE.

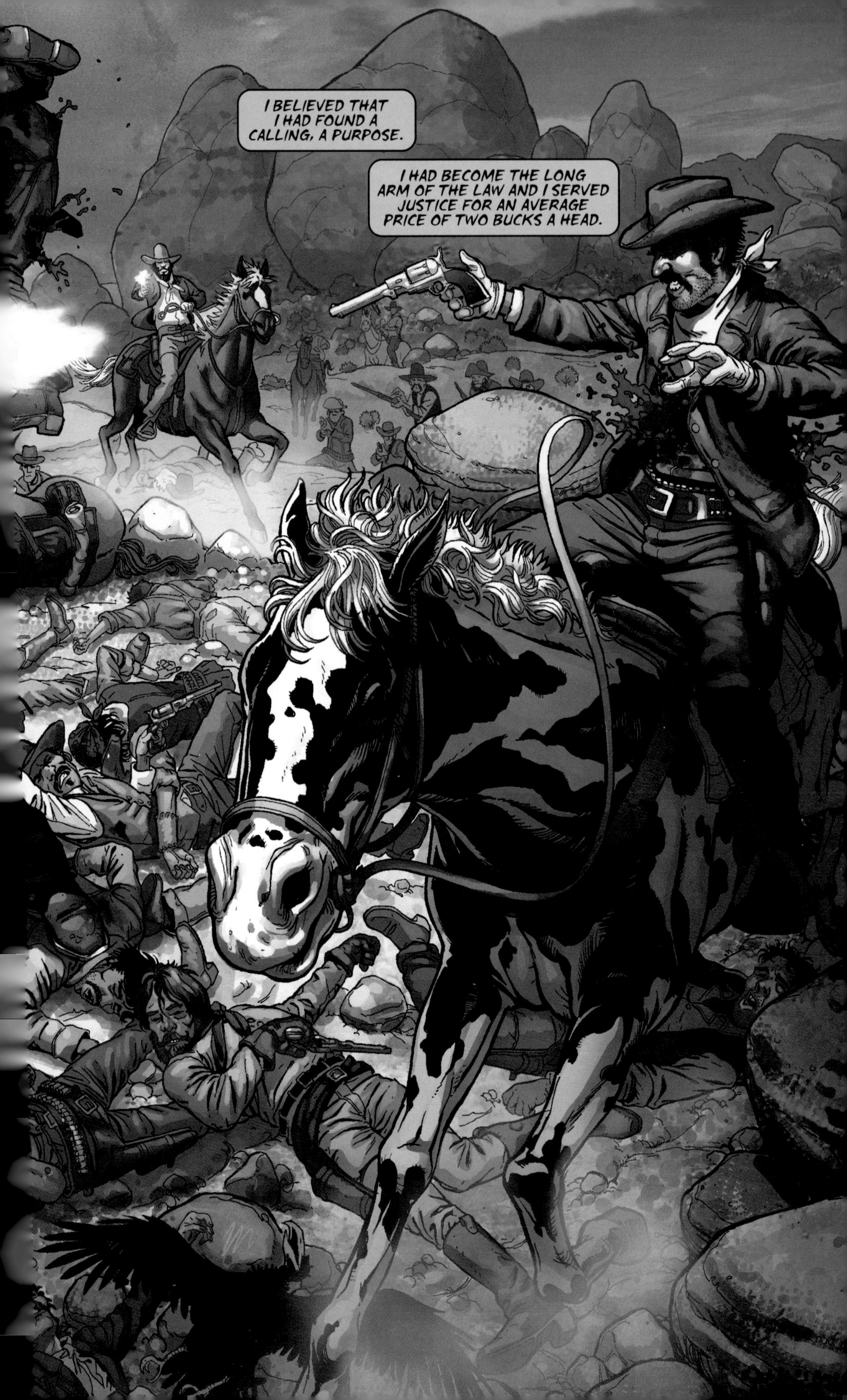
I BELIEVED THAT I HAD FOUND A CALLING, A PURPOSE.
I HAD BECOME THE LONG ARM OF THE LAW AND I SERVED JUSTICE FOR AN AVERAGE PRICE OF TWO BUCKS A HEAD.

THE SHAOLIN COWBOY

CREATED, WRITTEN & ILLUSTRATED BY
GEOF DARROW
FEATURING AN ASS-OLOGUE BY
THE WACHOWSKI BROTHERS

READ ON FOR PREVIEW

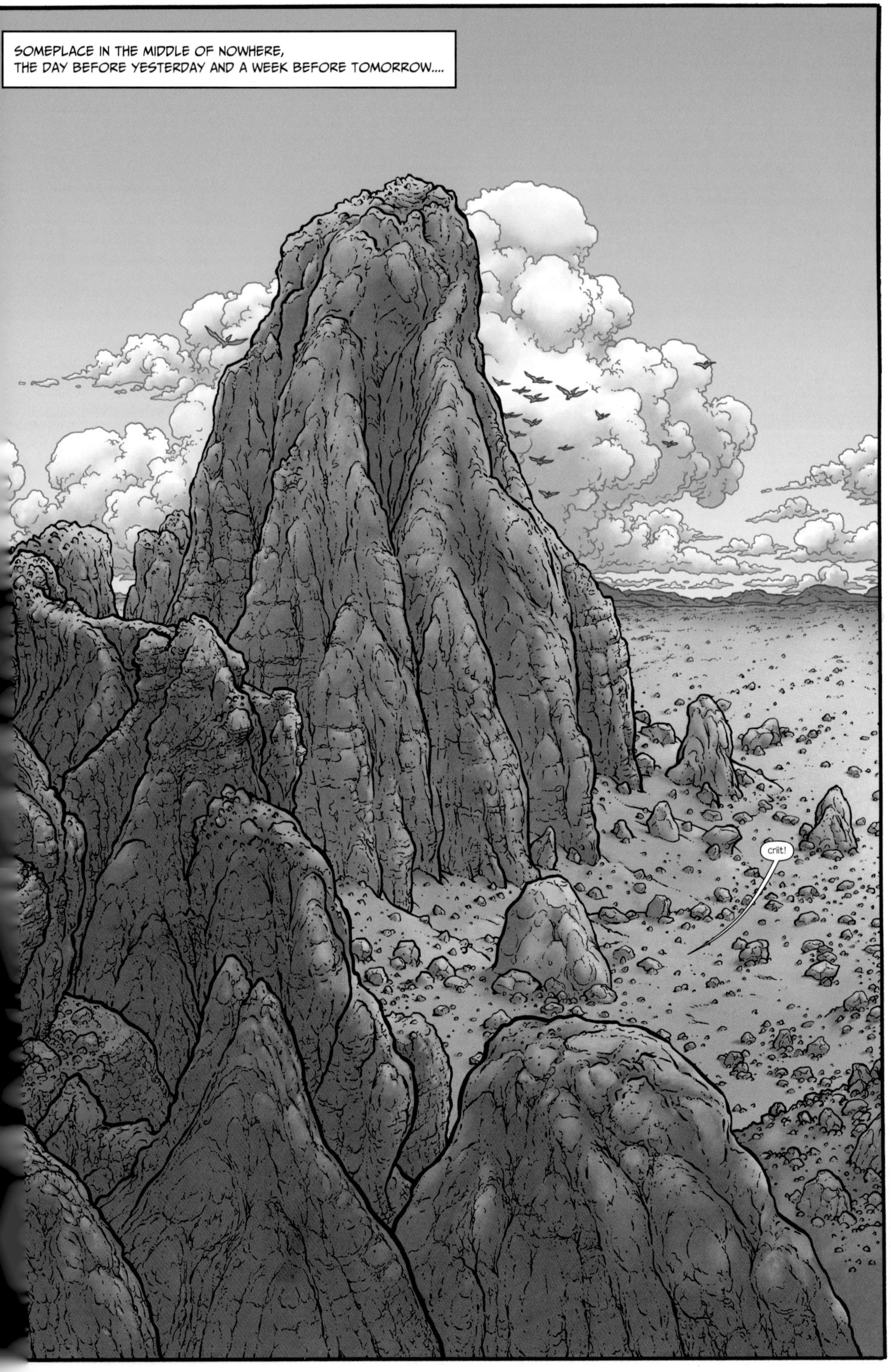
SOMEPLACE IN THE MIDDLE OF NOWHERE,
THE DAY BEFORE YESTERDAY AND A WEEK BEFORE TOMORROW....
criit!

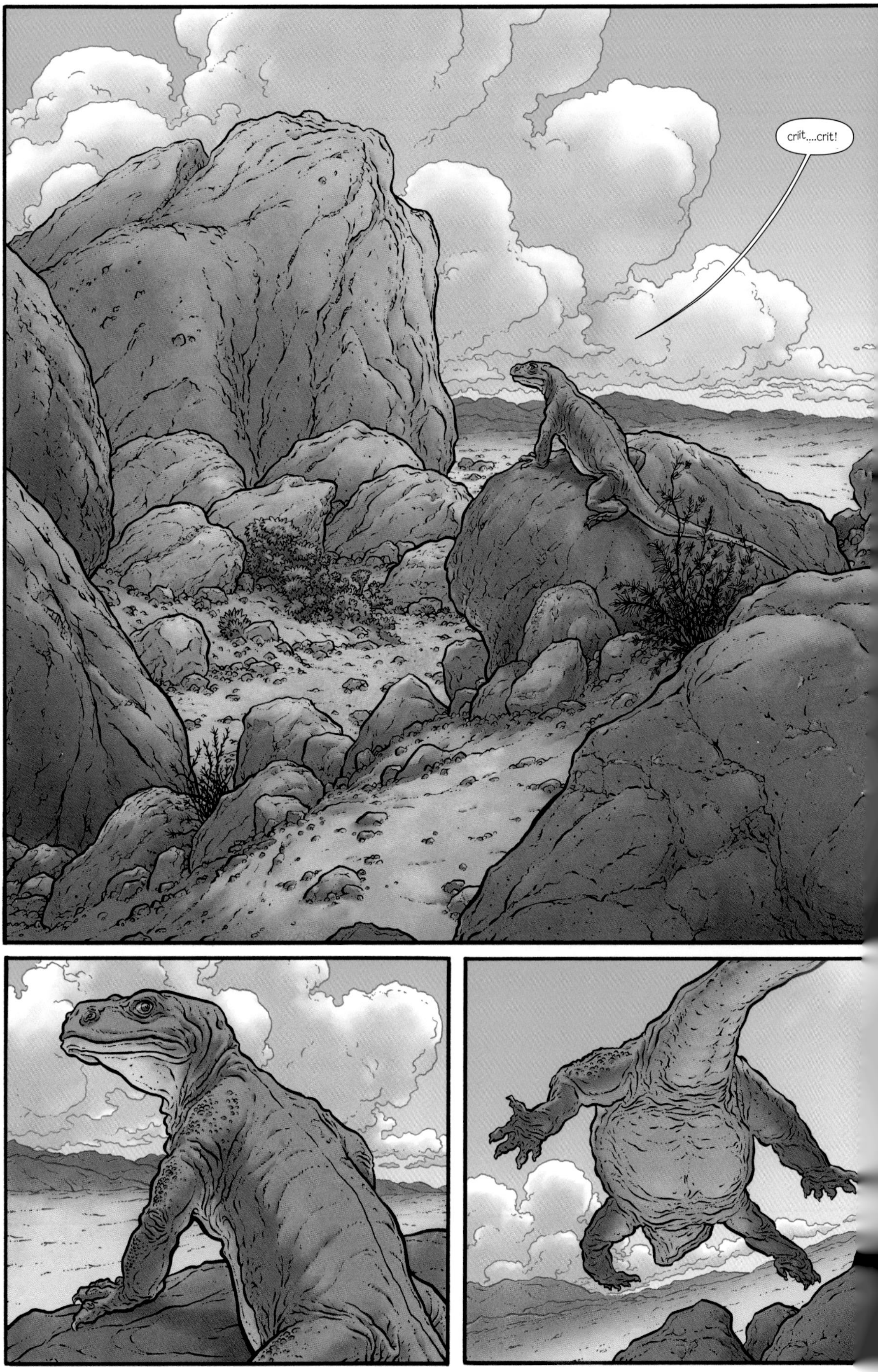
criit....crit!

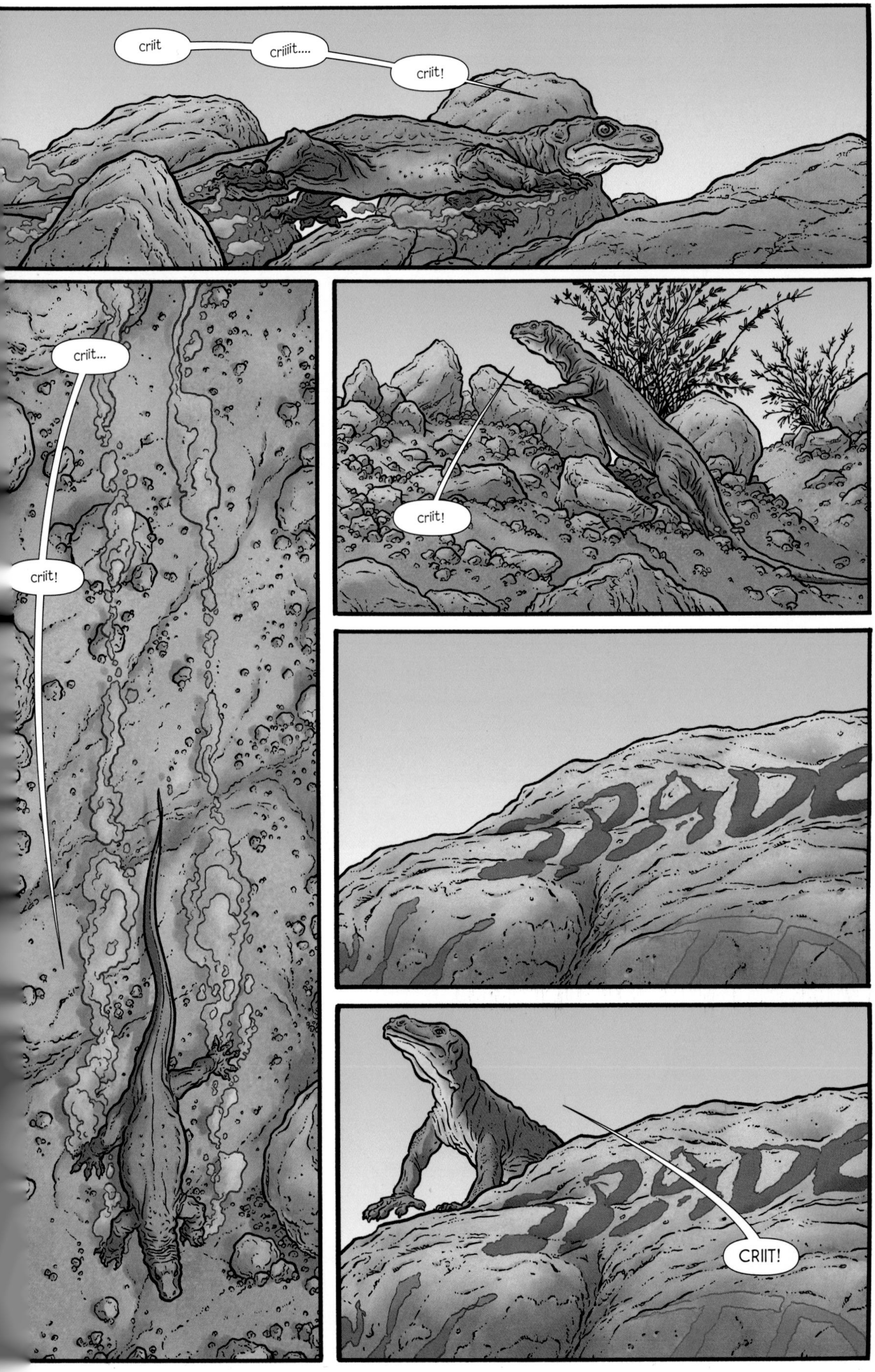
criit
criiiit....
criit!
criit...
criit!
criit!
CRIIT!

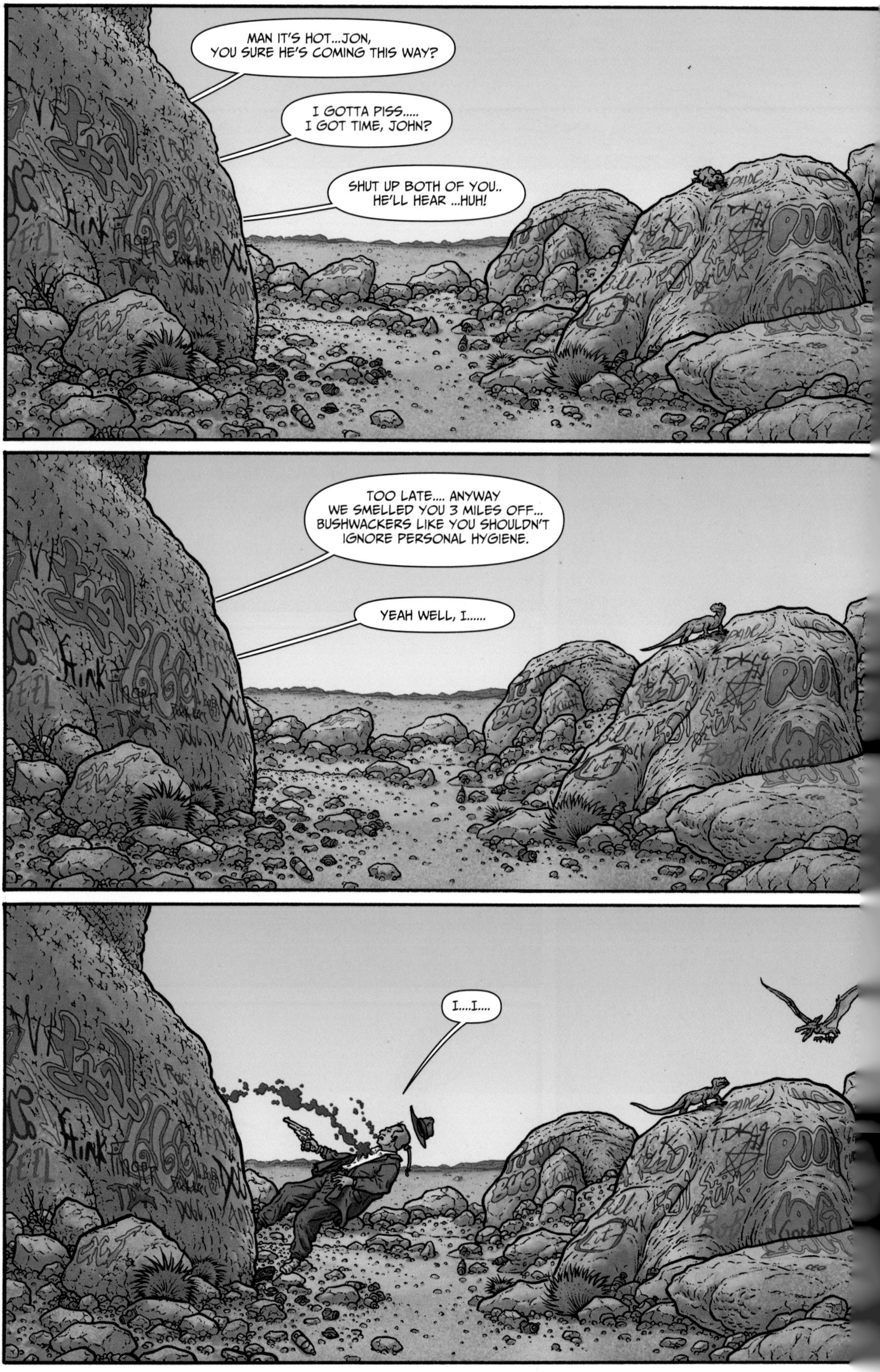
MAN IT'S HOT...JON, YOU SURE HE'S COMING THIS WAY?
I GOTTA PISS..... I GOT TIME, JOHN?
SHUT UP BOTH OF YOU.. HE'LL HEAR ...HUH!
TOO LATE.... ANYWAY WE SMELLED YOU 3 MILES OFF... BUSHWACKERS LIKE YOU SHOULDN'T IGNORE PERSONAL HYGIENE.
YEAH WELL, I......
I....I....

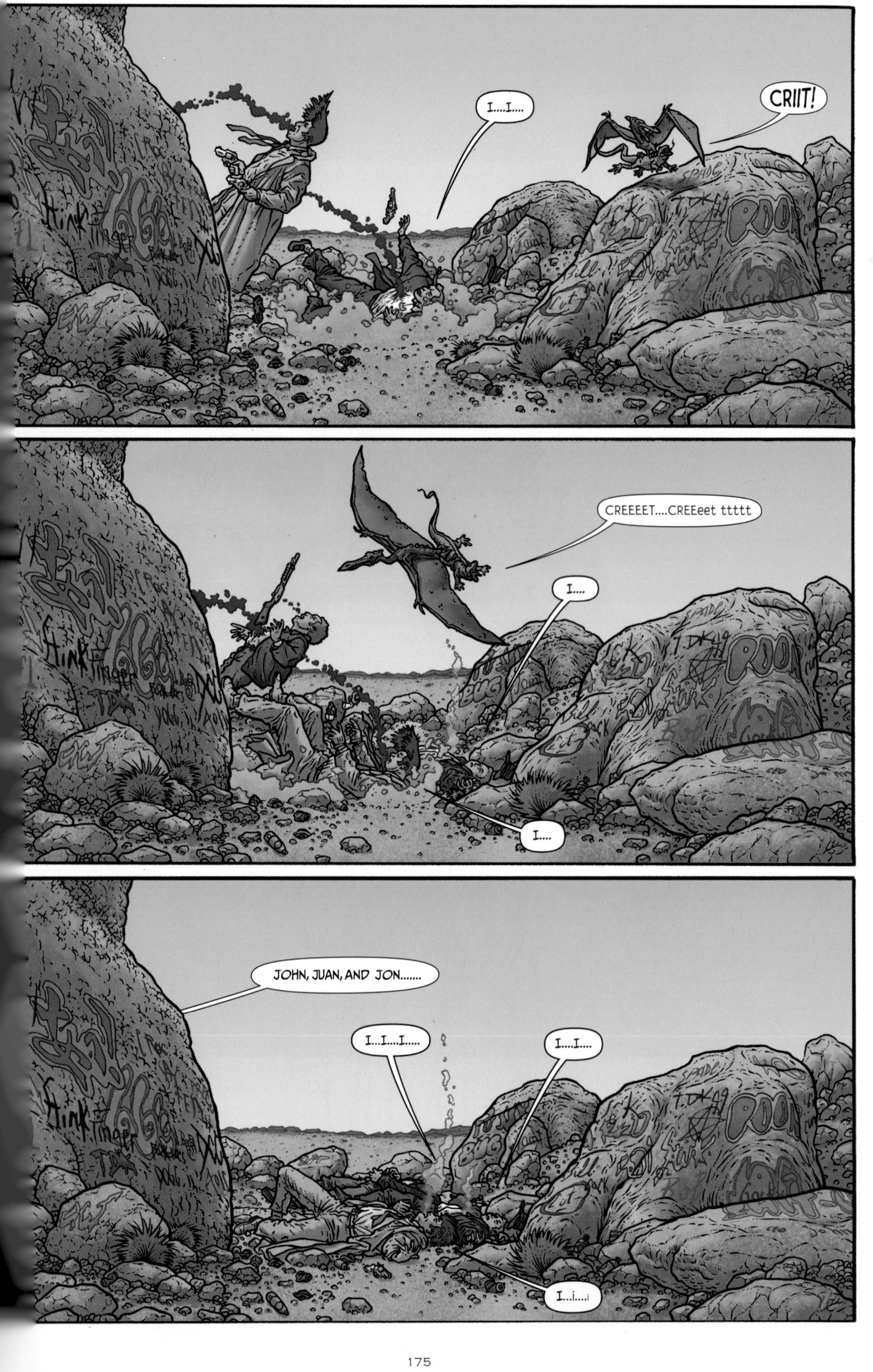
I....I....
CRIIT!
CREEEET....CREEeet ttttt
I....
I....
JOHN, JUAN, AND JON.......
I...I....I.....
I....I....
I...i....i

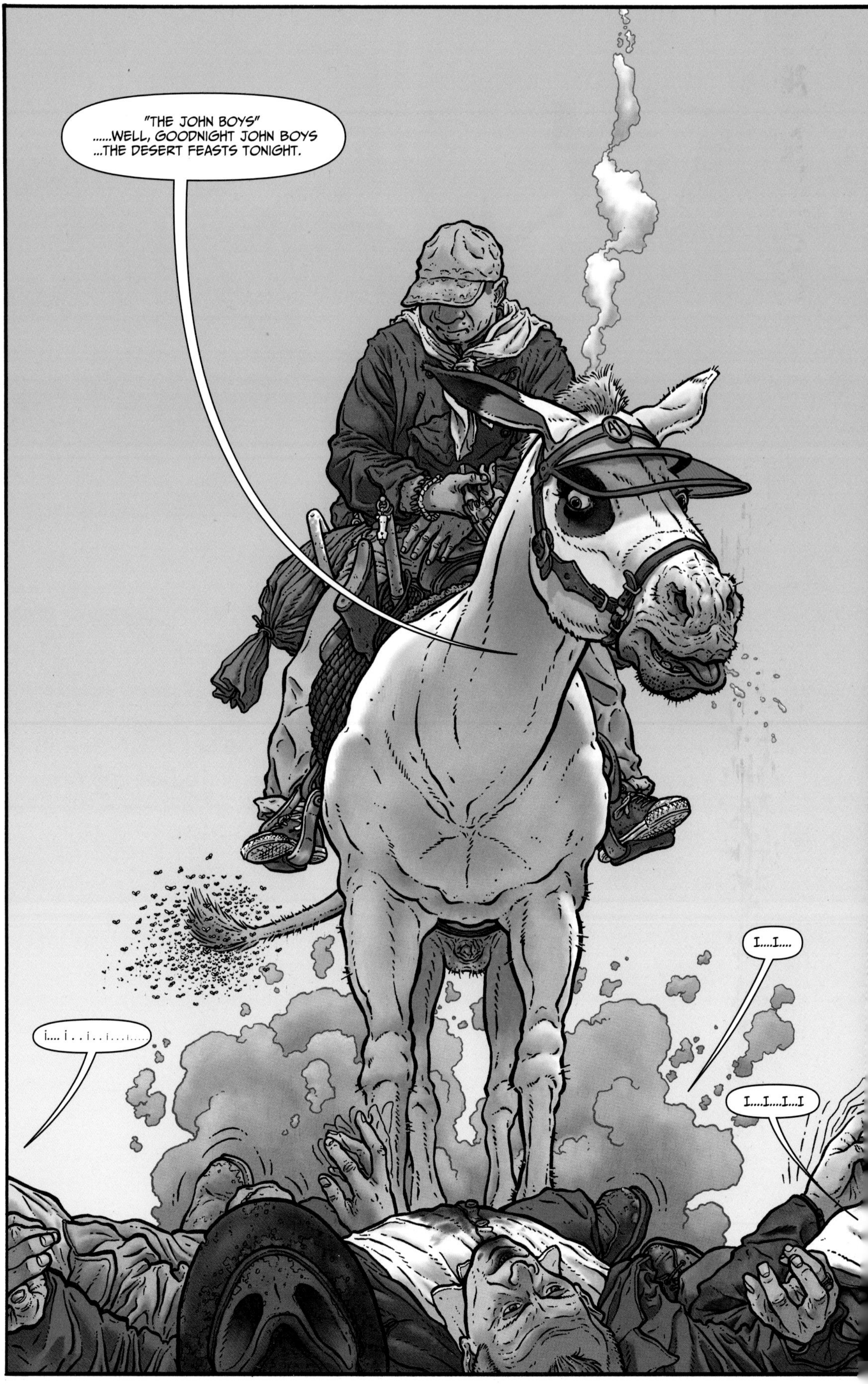
"THE JOHN BOYS" ......WELL, GOODNIGHT JOHN BOYS ...THE DESERT FEASTS TONIGHT.
I....I....
i.... i . . i . . i. . . .i. . . . .
I....I....I...I

ANDY & LARRY WACHOWSKI
EDITORS IN CHIEF

SPENCER LAMM
EDITOR

SHARON BRAY
ASSISTANT EDITOR

COVER &
BACKCOVER ART
KAARE ANDREWS

BURLYMAN
ENTERTAINMENT

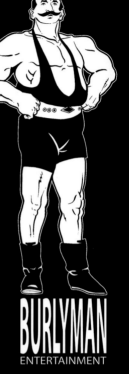

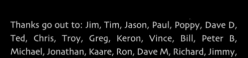

Thanks go out to: Jim, Tim, Jason, Paul, Poppy, Dave D, Ted, Chris, Troy, Greg, Keron, Vince, Bill, Peter B, Michael, Jonathan, Kaare, Ron, Dave M, Richard, Jimmy, Geof, Peter D, and Steve.

Along with: Joel Silver, Steve Richards, Ray Blasingame, Peter Grossman, Kevin (Stickman) Tinsley, Kevin Tsujihara, Jeff Robinov, Laurie Stalter, Lawrence Mattis, Robert Simpson, Jason Williford, Lukasz Lysakowski, Vanessa Carmichael, Bob Perkins, Megan Foord, Eric Showley, Mike Giacomino, Mike Lorusso, John Patzka, Miguel Alcala, Tim Spence, Joel Haverstein, Jeff deLauter, Brian Kruscinski, Skye Herzog, Melanie O'Brien, Steve Fogelson, Paula Allen, Juli Goodwin, Zachary Monge, Irika Slavin, Nick Landau, Vivian Cheung, and David Wilk.

COMPILATION AND DESIGN BY REDPILL PRODUCTIONS

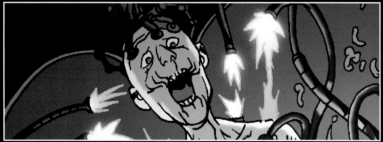

WWW.THEMATRIX.COM WWW.BURLYMANENTERTAINMENT.COM WWW.REDPILL.COM

Inquiries should be addressed to: Permissions Department, PO Box 220426, Brooklyn, NY 11222-0426.
Library of Congress Cataloging-in-Publication data is available upon request.
Printed in the United States of America (Imagine Print Group).

ISBN (softcover): 1-932700-09-9 ISBN (hardcover): 1-932700-14-5

MW00824333

THE

MATRIX

COMICS

VOLUME 2